THE ABERDEEN MEN CAN'T PLAY FOOTBALL

An early history of football in Aberdeen 1881-1903

Fraser Clyne

THE ABERDEEN MEN CAN'T PLAY FOOTBALL

An early history of football in Aberdeen 1881-1903

Fraser Clyne

Published by Fraser Clyne

First published 2012

A catalogue record for this book is available from the British Library

ISBN 978-0-9567561-1-4

Printed by J Thomson Printers, Glasgow

Contents

Foreword

Most people who know a bit about Aberdeen Football Club have it in their knowledge banks that the Club came into being in 1903. This is an indisputable fact, but arguably the history of the club goes back much further. It spreads back through the stories of the three founding clubs to the birth of the original Aberdeen in 1881 when a dozen enthusiasts met to get the round ball game going in the City. Interest grew quickly and many other clubs were founded, including Orion in 1885 and Victoria United in 1889. The three clubs became the dominant triumvirate in the local game, winning virtual every competition available to them and even getting involved in the Scottish Cup competition at the earliest stages, albeit with little success. The ambition to get Aberdeen's football onto the national stage was strong and ultimately these three chose to merge in order to provide a much stronger club to take the City forward. This merger thus ensured that in a sense all three clubs, none of which went out of business as such, live on as an important part of the City of Aberdeen's football heritage.

Needless to say, these three pathfinders could not exist in a local vacuum and many other clubs sprang up in the area, some with rather exotic or romantic names and they all contributed to the development of football in the Northeast. Now Fraser Clyne has grasped the nettle of extensive research and dug into the stories of all of these clubs and the roles of such as Black Diamonds, Carlton, Renton and all of the others. It is a story worthy of the telling, not least because it has never been tackled in any depth before, although others have touched on the pre 1903 period from time to time.

Fraser's efforts have brought to light many characters and controversial moments in that Aberdonian football world of the late Victorian era. He has come closer to the truth of the horrendous drubbing that Bon-Accord suffered at the hands of Bon-Accord. There are stories of riots and floodlights and penalty kicks and of the early football grounds that sprang up around the Silver City. There are plenty of fascinating facts for aficionados of the Dons and Scottish Football to digest and enjoy and many more questions to explore and explain.

Few artefacts from that period are publicly known although there must be souvenirs tucked away around the North East of Scotland, waiting to be unearthed. Visitors can see the Aberdeen FC booklet of 1898 on display at Pittodrie, and it is believed that someone has a copy of a programme published by Orion in the 1890s and there are a couple of menus from special occasions involving Aberdeen but we would all love to hear of anything else and bring more stories into the public domain.

Congratulations must go to Fraser Clyne for his diligence in taking the story of Aberdeen's footballing past to a new stage and providing a springboard for others who might wish to delve even deeper to find out still more about that pioneering era.

Chris Gavin, Aberdeen Football Club Heritage Trust.

About the Author

Fraser Clyne

Fraser Clyne was born and raised in Arbroath. His father played for Arbroath Football Club and Arbroath Victoria Football Club in the early 1950's, but Fraser's sporting career followed a different path as he became involved in athletics. During the 1980's and early 1990's he was one of the country's leading marathon runners. His quickest time of 2hr 11min 50sec was set when finishing second in the US championships at Sacramento in 1984 and he is the fourth fastest Scot of all-time. He represented Great Britain at the World Marathon Cups in Hiroshima (1985), Seoul (1987) and Milan (1989). He also represented Scotland at the 1986 Commonwealth Games in Edinburgh, finishing 10th. Fraser enjoyed overseas success, winning the Oakland marathon, California in 1983 and 1984. He was runner-up at Melbourne (1985) and Casablanca (1988) and was fourth at Twin Cities (Minneapolis-St Paul) in 1988, fifth at San Francisco (1987) and sixth at Berlin (1984). He won five Scottish marathon titles and three Scottish road running grand prix titles. He competed in the world cross country championships five times and once in the world mountain running trophy and represented Scotland and/or Great Britain on the track, road, cross country and mountain running and competed internationally over 3,000m steeplechase, 5,000m, 10,000m, half marathon, marathon and 100Km.

Despite his commitment to athletics, Clyne has remained involved with football and is an Arbroath F.C shareholder. He writes regularly for the club's matchday programme and has been piecing together a comprehensive history of the Red Lichties. Fraser is now a freelance sports writer and running consultant involved in race promotion and management. He also provides advice and motivational talks to runners, either in group sessions or on an individual basis.

Other Books By Fraser Clyne

Arbroath F.C. Miscellany -
Arbroath Trivia, History, Facts & Stats
First published 2010
ISBN 978-0-9567561-0-7

Aberdeen's 10K -
The History of the City's Biggest Road Race.
First published 2011

A Hardy Race -
The Scottish Marathon Championship 1946-2000.
(With Colin Youngson)
First published 2000
ISBN09539602-0-X

Acknowledgements

I am indebted to the many anonymous journalists and commentators who described the early football games in local newspapers and magazines such as Bon Accord, the Aberdeen Journal, Aberdeen Free Press, Evening Express, Dundee Courier, the Arbroath Herald and Arbroath Guide – all of which I trawled through for information. Without their efforts we would have no record of what had gone on. They developed a footballing language, some elements of which have survived, but many of the terms they used have long since been dropped. Visiting teams were described as "strangers", goalkeepers were "custodians" and the goal itself was often referred to as "the citadel" and a player being knocked to the ground by an opponent was described as being "grassed" ....great stuff.

I am also grateful to the staff in the Local Studies section of the Central Library in Aberdeen for fetching roll after roll of microfilm for me as I searched for match reports in the old newspapers.

Graham McKenzie was of immense help throughout this project. Graham is interested in all aspects of life and history in the city and when I told him what I was doing he offered to assist with unbridled enthusiasm. Graham took an interest initially in Victoria United and embarked on a project to record each and every game the Blues played. His meticulous cataloguing and checking of details proved to be of huge benefit to my own work. Graham also undertook to read through and correct various drafts of the book and his input has been invaluable.

Chris Gavin of the Aberdeen Football Club Heritage Trust has also given me encouragement along the way and has shared the information he has gathered on the early history of football in the city. Chris was also able to provide me with copies of some early photos which I have been able to reproduce in this book.

Stevie McRae helped out with locating the old Ordnance Survey maps which show the locations of some of the early football grounds in the city and I am indebted to him for his contribution. Also, thanks must go to the Ordnance Survey for allowing these map extracts to be used.

The majority of photographs used in the book come from the long defunct Bon Accord magazine which so vividly, and often satirically, chronicled all aspects of life in Aberdeen in the late 19th and early 20th Centuries. Other photos have come from private collections.

Keith Fraser must be given a huge vote of thanks for designing the cover of the book and the layout in such an expert fashion. Without his input, this project just would not have come to fruition.

Richard McBrearty at the Scottish Football Museum in Glasgow was another who assisted by giving me access at short notice to some of the wonderful archive material housed at Hampden Park.

I cross-checked many of my Northern League results and tables against the information provided on the Scottish Football Historical website and I have, in some instances, produced slightly different outcomes. This website is a goldmine of material for anyone interested in the roots of our game. The address is www.scottish-football-historical-archive.com

David Ross, author of numerous books on Scottish football and webmaster of another great site, www.scottishleague.net, also chipped in with useful advice.

Fraser Clyne, October 2012

Introduction

"The Aberdeen men...can't play football."

These damning words were penned by an anonymous reporter in the aftermath of Arbroath's crushing 36-0 demolition of Aberdeen's Bon Accord in a Scottish Cup tie at Gayfield Park on a rain-lashed Saturday afternoon in September 1885. On the same day, another Aberdeen club, Rovers, travelled to East Dock Street Park in Dundee and lost 35-0 to the green-shirted local Irish side, Harp, also in the Scottish Cup. The Rovers performance was rather conservatively described as *"mediocre"* and not surprisingly their goalkeeper was portrayed as having given *"a particularly weak-kneed exhibition."* The previous weekend, the original Aberdeen F.C. lost 7-0 to another Arbroath side, Strathmore, in the same round of the national tournament at the Angus club's Damley Park.

In the space of one week, therefore, three Aberdeen sides had conceded 78 goals and scored none in reply in three matches. Such scorelines were remarkably common in the mid-1880's as Aberdeen's footballing pioneers tested their emerging, but rudimentary and often naive skills, against clubs from other parts of the country. Arbroath seemed to take particular pleasure in handing out severe lessons to teams from the Granite City. In 1886 the Red Lichties clobbered Aberdeen's Orion 20-0 in a Scottish Cup tie, and twelve months later, again in the national competition, the Gayfield side thrashed the same opponents 18-0. Rovers suffered another hammering in Dundee in the 1887 Scottish Cup, going under by 10-0 to the local Wanderers. But it wasn't all doom, gloom and humiliation. These results were excessive, but heavy hammerings were interspersed with the occasional encouraging performance. As early as 1882 the fledgling Aberdeen F.C. eked out a 2-2 draw with the vastly more experienced Arbroath in the Scottish Cup, albeit losing the replay 7-0. There was a genuine willingness amongst the Aberdeen footballing fraternity to learn more about the game and progress was made, albeit in often staccato fashion.

This book tells the story of Aberdeen's earliest clubs, from the founding of the original Aberdeen FC in 1881. It charts some of the key moments during the rapid explosion in the popularity of football in the 1880's and 1890's when teams were established in most neighbourhoods of the city. Aberdeen was growing rapidly at this time, the population of the Parliamentary burgh having risen from just over 68,000 in 1871 to 105,000 by 1881 and then to 144,000 by 1901. Of the dozens of clubs formed in this period, Aberdeen and Orion emerged as the best of the bunch in the late-1880's and Torry's Victoria United, formed in 1889, became a significant force in the 1890's. But there were many other clubs who appeared fleetingly during the Victorian era. They included teams bearing such long forgotten names as Caledonian, Britannia, Carlton, Gladstone, Reform, Alpine, Our Boys, Emerald, Playfair, Rosebery, and the exotically named Prairie Flower F.C. – although the last named, as with many others, didn't last very long at all. Then there was Bon Accord, City Rangers, Black Diamond, Aberdeen Athletics … ….and so the list went on. The clubs would eventually split into senior and junior grades with the big three, Aberdeen, Orion and Victoria United, ultimately becoming the only senior outfits in the city. Professionalism also became a factor in the game, with Orion and Victoria United embracing the idea before Aberdeen took it on.

There have been a number of excellent books chronicling the history of the current Aberdeen Football Club. These include 'The Dons', written by Jack Webster in 1978 to celebrate the club's 75th anniversary, and subsequently updated. There's also Jim Rickaby's statistical bible, 'Aberdeen – A Complete Record 1903-1987' and Alastair Guthrie's 1988 publication, 'A Pictorial History of the Dons.' More recently Kevin Stirling wrote 'Aberdeen – A Centenary History 1903-2003'. These have all briefly summarised the early history of football in the city, focussing primarily on the lead up to the merger of the original Aberdeen, Orion and Victoria United to form the club we know now. But I wanted to know more about those pioneering days. Having been born and raised in Arbroath before moving to Aberdeen in 1973, but remaining a fan of the Red Lichties, I had always been familiar with my club's famous 36-0 pasting of Bon Accord in 1885. My interest in the early history of football in Aberdeen stemmed from this game as I wanted to explore the background to it, to try to establish whether there was any truth in the often quoted story that Bon Accord wasn't really a football club. Some sources suggest that the Aberdeen men were actually cricketers who had, by chance, been invited to take part in the Scottish Cup. I was sceptical of this line of argument and wanted to determine the facts, so set about my research. In looking at what was going on in the world of football in Aberdeen in the 1880's I soon became fascinated by some of the details I came across and took the view that I shouldn't restrict myself to just looking at the Bon Accord story. There were so many more fascinating stories to be explored and recounted. I unearthed details I had previously not known about local football in the 19th century. I had read in other publications that a Scottish international select played in Aberdeen in the late 1880's, but it was still a great thrill to discover the full story behind these matches, two of which were played at the Chanonry in Old Aberdeen. It was also exciting to find out about the lauded English Champions, Sheffield United, complete with giant goalkeeper 'Fatty' Foulke, being humbled by Victoria United in Torry. The Yorkshire side wasn't the first English club to play in the city, however, that honour going to the famous Notts County who faced Aberdeen at the Chanonry in January 1893. Then there's the story of Glasgow Rangers' first visit to the city, in 1894, to play Aberdeen. Celtic was, however, the first Old Firm side to appear in Aberdeen, crushing Victoria United 10-0 in the Torry side's first game, played on a Friday evening at the Victoria Bridge Grounds in August 1889. English champions Sunderland visited the Chanonry at the height of their powers while Liverpool were among the many distinguished visitors to Torry. This was an era, however, when clubs such as Queen's Park, East Stirlingshire and Stenhousemuir were considered 'big' names capable of attracting sizeable crowds to the various Aberdeen grounds for challenge matches. There was a genuine fascination amongst local followers of the game in seeing teams from other parts of the country.

The game being played at this time was barely recognisable to what we see nowadays. The pitches were marked out differently and the rules of the game were also different. In the early years, a goalkeeper for instance, was allowed to handle the ball anywhere in his own half of the pitch so long as he was trying to defend his goal. He could not, however, carry the ball in his hands.

Goals were often scored following a 'scrimmage' during which a mob of attacking players would force the ball over the line, often bundling an equally large squad of defenders out of the way in the process. Initially there was no such thing as a penalty kick and, as a consequence, fouls and deliberate handballs to prevent goals often went unpunished. The kick and rush style of play was common while some players tried to dribble with the ball as long as possible without a thought of passing. The more scientific 'combination' and passing game was only just beginning to emerge.

I was surprised to learn that the first floodlit match in the city took place in 1892, at Central Park, in a benefit match for a young Culter footballer who had died as a result of an injury sustained in a match. Despite the charitable aspect of the game, many fans avoided paying the entry money by climbing over the boundary walls under the cover of darkness. Another night time game was played at the Wellington Bridge Grounds, near what is now Old Ford Road, some eighteen months later, in a benefit match to raise funds to support striking joiners.

I've discovered some colourful characters along the way. John Forsyth, for instance, was known to be a popular but troublesome player who came close to death after being knifed during a drunken brawl in a city centre street. He was one of the first players to ply his trade as a professional before deciding to seek a bigger fortune in the gold mines of South Africa. Then there was Joe Davidson, the Aberdeen player who ended up in jail after assaulting a water bailiff. Arbroath native Willie Stewart gained notoriety by becoming the first man to be dismissed in a major Aberdeen game when he was sent off when playing for Victoria United in the 1892-1893 Charity Cup Final, an incident which sparked a riot. There are also the stories of Wilfred Toman and Sandy Caie, the first local players to earn big money transfers to England. Other talented players, such as Orion's Donald Currie, enjoyed success by choosing to stay in the city.

Numerous tales of fisticuffs on the field of play, and anti-social behaviour off it, came to light in the course of my work. Police were on occasion called upon to break up fights and sometimes escort players to safety. Residents in the Clifton Road area at one point petitioned Aberdeen Town Council asking for Orion's lease of the Cattofield grounds to be relinquished because of trouble caused by fans. Throughout the period, concerns were expressed on a regular basis about the foul and abusive language used by spectators. A Dundee Wanderers player once had to be smuggled out of Torry and taken by ferry across the Dee to avoid an angry mob of Victoria United supporters.

But is has been frustrating not to have discovered more about the ordinary lives of the men who pioneered the sport in the city. There is so much more to be uncovered about the personalities in the 19th Century game in Aberdeen. Some key individuals were involved from the early days and remained in important roles well beyond 1903. Jimmy Philip, for instance, the first manager of the 1903 Aberdeen F.C., had been an official with various local clubs in the latter part of the 19th Century and remained in charge at Pittodrie until 1926. Peter Simpson, the Aberdeen trainer from 1903 until 1922, played for Victoria United in their first match in 1889 and remained involved with the club in one capacity or another until 1903. These and others, were hugely significant characters in the development of football in Aberdeen.

Wouldn't it be wonderful if there was some motion film of an early game? The first record of any filming of a local match can be traced to the Victoria United – Aberdeen Northern League game on 12th March 1898 when *"Messrs Walker and Co's cinematograph"* was used. Unfortunately it is highly unlikely that this footage will have survived. If it has, it hasn't come to light so far.

There has long been speculation about the origins of Aberdeen's playing colours and I have picked up some detail about this along the way. In the early days of the merger talks, during the 1902-1903 season, one correspondent suggested that the new club should wear red tartan jerseys and white shorts. He also recommended that a new 30,000 capacity ground should be built and that it should be named Balmoral Park.

Scottish League membership was for many years the holy grail for local clubs. Victoria United applied for membership in 1895 but this bold idea came to nothing. Even Bon Accord F.C. was alleged to have applied for membership at one stage. And in 1896 a mysterious syndicate tried, but failed, to take over Orion with a view to forming a single all-powerful club in the city capable of achieving First Division status. In 1902 there were rumours that Aberdeen might secure a First Division presence through the relocation of Hibernian from Edinburgh. As the years passed it became obvious, however, that the city's best hope of achieving its ambition of hosting a league side would come about only if the main clubs pulled their resources together and merged. Serious discussions around this were first hinted at in the late 1890's but it never came to pass until 1903.

This book is by no means a complete piece of work, nor can I guarantee that everything recorded here is entirely accurate despite painstaking efforts to do so. As ever with projects of this nature, once you start to scratch the surface, all sorts of additional areas of possible enquiry open up. But hopefully it will provide a decent base from which further research can be undertaken. I may not have tracked down the result of every game played by the main clubs, although I have tried my best. Trawling through thousands of microfilmed pages of old newspaper files is a slow process and it's quite possible to miss some details. Sometimes, in the local press, there wasn't even agreement about the results of some games. Results were, in the early days, submitted to the newspapers by club secretaries, and occasionally the secretaries from rival clubs would submit different accounts of the same game! I may also have missed some key moments in the development of the game. And I certainly have not been able to unearth as much detail as I would have liked about the men who played for these and other local clubs, nor their backers, trainers and managers. Ideally I would also like to have included team line-ups for as many games as possible, but time simply defeated me on this one. I have, however, throughout the book, summarised many of the key games played and the line-ups from these matches are included. I hope that this will prove to be a useful starting point for those who wish to take the subject further. Hopefully some people may recognise the names of players and officials and this might prompt folk to have a look in their lofts and attics in search of long forgotten footballing memorabilia which might help historians fill in the many gaps in our knowledge of the sport at local level. I have been surprised at just how little documentation survives from this era. Much more has to be uncovered and many more fascinating stories have undoubtedly still to surface. There is also a lack of action photos from games during this period. The few which I have found are of a rather poor quality but are reproduced here.

1881-1882
Formation of the Aberdeen Maroons

In 2009 a former Millwall player, Barry Rowan, presented Aberdeen Football Club with an important historical document. It was a small pamphlet, published on 26th February 1898, and it outlined, very briefly, the origins of the first Aberdeen club which had been founded in 1881. The booklet contains a wonderful photograph of the 1881 team and another of the Aberdeenshire Cup winning side of 1889-1890. It had been given to Rowan many years earlier by a neighbour of his in London, an Aberdonian. I subsequently discovered that a rather fragile copy of this pamphlet is also held in Aberdeen's Central Library. As far as I am aware, this is the oldest surviving Aberdeen footballing document in existence which is publicly available. It contains 32 pages, 15 of which are advertisements and most of these are for pubs and hotels. These adverts include one for The New Bar at 96 High Street, Old Aberdeen which is described as *"The Favourite Resort of Footballers,"* on account of its proximity to Aberdeen's home ground at The Chanonry, while the Butcher's Arms and the Northern Bar, both in George Street, boasted of having *"Football scores every Saturday night."*

Surprisingly few documents are known to have survived from Aberdeen's Victorian footballing past despite the large number of clubs that formed and the hundreds of games that took place. The Orion club produced a regular publication called the 'Orion Observer' which was the 19th Century equivalent of a match day programme or magazine. It was first published in August 1895 for a friendly against Port Glasgow at Cattofield. The programme comprised six pages and cost *"the modest sum of one half penny."* When its editor, Mr James Russell, died in

Front cover of the 1898 souvenir pamphlet

August 1899, a local newspaper reported that the success of the Observer had been due to its *"racy writing"*. A framed copy of the front page of the Observer, from October 1898, adorns a corridor inside Pittodrie Stadium. It was published for a match against Raith Rovers and I believe a complete copy of that Orion programme exists in a private collection. Many other publications came out at this time but none seem to have survived, or at least their whereabouts are unknown.

John McHardy – driving force behind the formation of Aberdeen Football Club in 1881.McHardy also filled many important roles on the club committee and he was an important player in the early years of the club

The People's Journal in the 1890's published 'The Football Handbook' and the 'Northern League Football Annual and League Companion'. Both of these would surely have contained useful information about the game in Aberdeen, but I have not been able to unearth any copies. Aberdeen Library holds a couple of copies of The Northern Cricket and Football Annual (1889-1890 and 1891-1892), a booklet which was published by the Greyfriars Press, 14 Gallowgate, Aberdeen - and these contains some useful information on the local footballing scene.

The 1898 Aberdeen FC Souvenir booklet describes the setting up of the city's first club 17 years earlier. There is, however, reference in the Aberdeen Journal to an 'Aberdeen Football Club' being founded in the early 1870's, but this was actually a rugby club. Cricket, golf and rugby were the big sports of this period and rugby was more commonly known as football. Football, as we now know it, was distinguished from rugby football by being described as being played under 'association rules' rather than 'rugby' rules and it wasn't until 1881 that the 'association' game first emerged in the city. A meeting of those interested in forming a club to play

William Stewart – a founder member of Aberdeen Football Club in 1881

Charles Glennie – a founder member of Aberdeen Football Club in 1881

exclusively by association rules was held in Mr James Stuart's Albert Hotel, 9 ½ Correction Wynd, on Saturday 8th October 1881. The meeting had been arranged by Mr J. A. McHardy, a teacher at Woodside Public School and two of his Woodside colleagues, Charles E. Glennie and William Stewart.

Twelve people turned up: five other teachers, two bookbinders, a medical student and a tailor. The meeting decided that the name of the club should be the Aberdeen Association Football Club and the colours to be worn by the members should be *"maroon jerseys and blue knickerbockers with stripe."*

Mr Stewart, 275 George Street, was appointed Secretary and he was instructed to secure a dozen jerseys (maroon), two balls and one inflator.

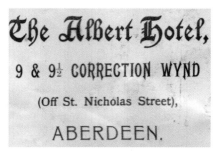

Advert for the Albert Hotel where Aberdeen Football Club was founded. It advertised itself as "Aberdeen's oldest hotel."

Earliest photograph of Aberdeen FC – 1881.
Back - J. Bennie, Thomson, J.A. McHardy, C. E. Glennie, Steel
Middle - W. Stewart, J. Haise, A.V. Lothian, Farrell
Front - Ross, Hyslop, D.B. Lothian
Notes: McHardy was the man who organised the meeting at which the football club
was formed. Haise, the captain, is the only player with AFC sewn onto his jersey

The lack of such goods in Aberdeen meant that they had to be purchased from Messrs H. & P. McNeil in Glasgow. In addition to Mr Stewart, the following other office bearers were appointed: Mr J. A. McHardy, Vice - President; Mr J. H. Haise, captain; Mr Charles E. Glennie, vice captain; and Mr A. M.Duncan, treasurer. A President wasn't appointed at this time. Five others were elected to the committee, namely Messrs A.V. and D. B. Lothian, A. Steel, James D. Hendry and John Burns. In optimistic fashion, an advert was placed in a Glasgow newspaper announcing the creation of the new club and stating that, *"The Secretary will be happy to hear of any club wishing to pay a visit to the Granite City, this being the first attempt to start the dribbling game in Aberdeen."* There was to be no rush of clubs taking up this invitation.

Following the inaugural meeting, the members decided that a practice game should be arranged immediately, to be played at the Links, although a sub-committee was formed *"to procure a suitable field"* for matches. On 4th November 1881 Mr A. V. Lothian was appointed to the vacant President's post and the following day the club played another practice match at Hayton, Woodside on a field owned by a Mr. Arthur Angus. At a further meeting, again held in the Albert Hotel, on 15th December 1881, interest in the new club was reflected in the admission of nine new members. A decision was also taken to secure a part of the Holburn cricket ground for the use of the club. The Holburn ground, occupied by Aberdeenshire cricket club at that time, comprised an expanse of land which has long since been developed. It was located in the area now bounded by Irvine Place, Pitstruan Place, Broomhill Road and Allan Street. Despite the fact that no competitive games had yet been played or were even scheduled, the committee decided to select a first choice team which was named in the 2-2-6 formation of the day. Unfortunately, records show the names of only 10 of these players, namely: Goal, Rose; Backs, A.V. Lothian and Hyslop; half-backs , McHardy and Ross; Forwards, Steele, Burns, Stewart, Lothian and Glennie. It was noted that nine of the eleven players were teachers. The club captain, J. H. Haise, wasn't selected because he *"seemed to feel uncomfortable in his position on the field."* The committee invited him to resign his position *"both for the benefit of himself and the club."*

The club applied for admission to the Scottish Football Association on Valentine's Day 1882 and the long wait for a competitive game finally ended on 11th March 1882 when the Aberdeen players paid their own train fares to get to Coupar Angus to play the Perthshire side at Larghan Park. The visitors put in a brave performance but eventually lost 4-0. The Aberdeen Journal put an optimistic front on the outcome, however, stating: *"A very evenly contested game thus resulted rather unfortunately for the Aberdeen players in a win for the home players of four goals to love. The Aberdeen club, in this their first match, showed that with a little practice together and a few more matches, they will, by another season, be in good form and formidable opponents."*

A friendship was struck between the clubs and Coupar Angus were invited to play a return game in Aberdeen on 15th April 1882, the day after the club's first annual Supper which was to be held in the Queen's Restaurant. The match was played at the

GRAND FOOTBALL MATCH.
COUPAR ANGUS F.C. V. ABERDEEN F.C.

THE above MATCH (the first played in Aberdeen under Association Rules) will be Played on the HOLBURN CRICKET GROUNDS on SATURDAY First, the 15th April. Kick off at 2·30 P.M. Admission to the Grounds 6d. Ladies Free.

Holburn ground with a 2-30pm kick-off. Admission was 6d (2.5p) but ladies were allowed in free of charge for what was billed as the first association football match played in Aberdeen.

Unfortunately, a strong north easterly wind blasted flurries of snow across the ground, keeping the attendance well below expectations. After some end to end play the visitors took the lead following a scrimmage during which a mass of players forced the ball over the line. The windy weather made good play difficult and there was no more scoring before the interval. The wind dropped in the second period and Aberdeen came more into the game but it was Coupar who scored again. The Perthshire men then made it 3-0 although this goal was disputed on account of a foul on an Aberdeen player before the ball crossed the line. Just before the final whistle Aberdeen scored through a scrimmage, with the name of the man who got the last touch not being recorded. Unfortunately, therefore, we don't know who had the honour of scoring the first goal in the club's history. It's interesting to note that J. H. Haise, who earlier had been forced to resign the captaincy, was brought back into the side. In the evening both teams met in the Waverley Hotel where they had tea together, and *"spent a few hours enjoyably."* The Coupar Angus team returned home on the Sunday, catching the 12.30 train.

So, the first season ended with Aberdeen having played just two games, both against Coupar Angus. The seeds of interest had been sewn, however, and at the first annual meeting it was reported that there were 22 members. The club had also joined the Scottish Football Association, which meant that entry would be given to the following season's Scottish Cup.

23

Notable Games

Coupar Angus 4, Aberdeen 0
Larghan Park, Coupar Angus, 11th March 1882

This was Aberdeen's first competitive match played on the same day that Scotland thrashed England 5-1 at Hampden. The game started at 3-30pm in front of *"a large concourse of spectators"*. Aberdeen won the toss and chose to defend the southern goal. This gave them the advantage of a strong wind, but despite almost constant pressure, the visitors couldn't crack the home defence and the interval was reached with the game goalless. It's not clear whether Aberdeen captain A.V. Lothian sustained a first half injury, but he spent the second half in goal where, apparently, he showed no lack of skill. Despite his efforts, however, Coupar dominated and rattled home four goals without reply. After the game the visitors were taken for tea to the Royal Hotel where *"a couple of hours were very pleasantly spent."*

Aberdeen – A. Millar; A. V. Lothian (captain) and R. Hyslop; J. A. McHardy, J. Burns, J.C Ross; A. Steele, W. Thomson, W. Stewart, D.B. Lothian and C.E. Glennie. Umpire J. Bennie, Referee J. Brown.

Aberdeen 1, Coupar Angus 3 (one disputed)
Holburn Cricket Grounds, 15th April 1882

This was the first competitive association football match played in Aberdeen and it came the day after the club held its first supper in the Queen's Restaurant. The Aberdeen Journal gave a detailed account of the match and this is reproduced in full as it gives a wonderful flavour of the occasion:-

"The game for the first few minutes was played in a violent storm of wind and snow, but the atmosphere speedily cleared, and the remainder of the match was played in good weather, the only drawback being the somewhat slippery state of the ground consequent on the melting of the snow. The Aberdeen captain won the toss, and elected to play from the east, with a strong wind in his favour. The ball was started by the strangers, who, after some desultory play on both sides, gradually worked their way into the home team's territory, but were forced to retire by the backs. Some bungling by the latter again allowed the Coupar Angus to get near their opponents' goal, but the custodian prevented them from scoring. The local forwards, by a good passing run, transferred the scene of action to the other

end, where they obtained the first corner of the game: but the kick was badly managed, and the ball went behind. After this the strangers pressed their opponents for a time, and were swarming round their goal on several occasions, but the goalkeeper, assisted by the backs, frustrated all their efforts to score. The Aberdeen thereafter gradually took the ball into their opponents' ground, but they shot too soon, and the goalkeeper had no difficulty in stopping the ball. Coupar Angus held the advantage for some time after this, their combined action and passing telling severely on the home team who played too close together, while several of them failed to keep their places, and hampered their fellow players, whose efforts to score were thus rendered abortive. The Coupar Angus were more than once on the point of scoring, but the good play of the local goalkeeper, who several times saved his charge when all the backs had been passed, rendered their attempts fruitless. The Aberdeen had a run to the other end, but their chance of scoring was again neutralised by one of the forwards kicking the ball into touch on the goal line. The throw in was of no use, and the strangers, after being forced to retreat more than once, by wide passing and good headwork, invaded the opponents ground, and in spite of the stubborn defence, scored their first goal out of a scrimmage. After the kick off from the centre, the visitors still retained the supremacy and pinned their opponents in their own quarters. Shot after shot was made at the goal, but the ball either went behind or was thrown out by the goalkeeper. The Aberdeen ultimately succeeded in breaking away and took the ball well up the field, but the fault already noticed - a shooting for goal when too far from it - was again repeated, and the goalkeeper returned the ball at his leisure. The Aberdeen goal had a narrow escape immediately thereafter, the ball almost touching one of the posts, and two corner kicks fell to the strangers, but they were both mismanaged, and the home team retaliated by paying a visit to the other end, where they sent the ball behind. Shortly afterwards they again had a chance of lowering their opponents' colours, but the ball was kicked too hard, and being unable to follow it up in time, the opportunity was lost. During the remainder of the half the ball was almost constantly in local territory, but the backs, one or two of whom had been making a poor show prior to this, were now playing better, and with their assistance, and an occasional inroad by the forwards into their opponents quarters, the goalkeeper was enabled to preserve his charge intact until the call of time.

It was expected from the splendid display the strangers made against the strong wind in the first half, that they would have things pretty much their own way in the second period, but these surmises were not borne out. The wind had by this time fallen away very much, and as the Aberdeen had greatly improved in their play, the game was contested on more equal terms. For some time after the kick off the home team held the advantage, and put the ball over their opponents lines, a compliment the latter returned by repeating the same performance at the other end. The Coupar Angus again returned to the charge and this time there appeared no hope of the home citadel being saved, but the custodian caught the leather in his hands, and overturning one of his opponents who attempted to charge him through the posts, threw the ball out. After some desultory play in midfield, the right wing of the strangers got hold of the leather and by a fine passing run, the ball was worked well up, and being judiciously centred, one of the forwards was enabled to lower the colours of the home team for a second time. Hardly had the ball been kicked off before it was again run up and shot through, but as some doubt existed as to whether the leather was fouled previous to being put between the posts, it was agreed to let it stand as a disputed goal. The game continued with varying fortune for sometime afterwards, both goals being in turn menaced, but the local club generally kicked too strong when in front of the posts, by which they lost more than one opportunity of scoring, whilst their opponents always kept the ball near their feet, and were therefore extremely dangerous when nearing the goal. For the last ten minutes the Aberdeen, by playing more freely and adopting their opponents' passing tactics, had decidedly the best of the game, and as time was on the point of being called, they were rewarded by scoring their first and only goal out of a scrimmage. The game thus resulted in favour of the strangers by three goals (one disputed) to one. The visitors without exception played an excellent game. The home team numbers several very speedy players and good 'kicks', but their want of combination told sadly against them on Saturday. As already stated, one or two of the backs in the first half made a poor exhibition, as did a few of the forwards, who, had they kept their places instead of muddling the ball and hampering their fellow players, would have distressed themselves less, and been of more service in their proper sphere. However, they improved very much during the second period, and gave the visitors more trouble. The goalkeeper played magnificently, and saved his charge many times."

Aberdeen – A. V. Lothian: R. Hysop and W Farrel; J. C. Ross, J. Brown; A. Steel, C. E. Glennie, W. Stewart, J. H. Haise, D. B. Lothian, G. F. Hall.
Coupar Angus – A. McIntosh; W Davidson, W Barnett; D Adam, J Mitchell; Anderson, J Doig, A Blair, D Stewart, J Forbes, J Davidson.

Aberdeen F.C. - 1881-1882

Competition	Date		Opposition	F	A	Venue
Friendly	11/03/1882	Aberdeen	Coupar Angus	0	4	Larghan Park,Coupar Angus
Friendly	15/04/1882	Aberdeen	Coupar Angus	1	3	Holburn

1882-1883
Montrose thrashed in historic first win

Aberdeen's first foray into the Scottish Cup saw them drawn against Dundee's Harp, a side made up almost exclusively from the Tayside city's immigrant Irish community. Harp had been formed in 1879 and enjoyed a colourful history before going out of business in the mid 1890's. They won the Forfarshire Cup three seasons in a row between 1884-1885 and 1886-1887 to earn the nickname of "The Invincibles," and they would, as we shall see later, clock up a rather emphatic Scottish Cup victory over another Aberdeen club. The 1882-1883 national tournament, the 10th in the history of the competition, attracted more than 100 entrants, including many clubs which enjoyed only a fleeting existence. Names such as Plains Bluebell, Apsley, Addiewell, Perseverance, Pilgrims, Alcutha and Mavisbank all featured in the draw for the First Round which was made on a regional basis. Aberdeen had time for just one game before the visit of Harp, and again it was old friends Coupar Angus who provided the opposition at Larghan Park. The Perthshire side maintained its unbeaten record against the maroons, but this time just one goal separated the sides at the end of a five-goal encounter. Aberdeen led 1-0 at the interval, but Coupar Angus equalised before D. Smith put the visitors ahead. The home team grabbed two late goals, both disputed, to win the match. Unfortunately the scorers are not known as newspaper accounts are rather sketchy. Aberdeen's Scottish Cup tie, a week later, on 5th October 1882, was played at the Grammar School grounds and the pitch was considered to be *"in splendid condition."* There was no shortage of controversy as Harp had an early goal disallowed before taking the lead shortly before the halfway point. Aberdeen thundered back into contention in the second period with D.B. Lothian grabbing the equaliser and

in doing so he claimed his place in history as the first Aberdeen player to score in the Scottish Cup. The Dundee men regained the lead with another disputed goal before making sure of victory by scoring again near the end.

D. B. Lothian –
First Aberdeen player to score a Scottish Cup goal

It was a decent performance against a more established team and must have given the Aberdeen players some encouragement for the future. Harp's Cup run didn't last much longer, however, as they went out in the next round, thumped 5-0 by Dunblane. Dumbarton won the trophy that season, defeating Vale of Leven 2-1 in a replay at Hampden Park following a 2-2 draw.

In November Aberdeen made their first visit to Dundee to play Strathmore at Rollo's Pier. The game, played on a pitch described as being in *"bad condition"* attracted a *"large crowd."* Aberdeen surprised the light blue-shirted Dundonians by taking the lead through W. Thompson, but the home men fought back and eventually ran out 2-1 winners. The game was played in two periods of 30 minutes because of the poor light. After the match both teams sat down to tea in Lamb's Hotel, where *"the friendship made during the game was further developed."* Aberdeen had now played five competitive games since the club's formation, and although never being totally outclassed, had still to enjoy a first win. That historic moment finally came on the windswept Links at Montrose on 2nd December 1882. And it could hardly have been more emphatic as the visitors raced into a five goal lead before a late strike gave Montrose some consolation. Victory signified the toppling of another barrier to progress.

Coupar Angus returned to Aberdeen in January 1883 and won a thrilling encounter 4-3. The Perthshire men took a 4-0 lead in the first half but the home side fought back to reduce the winning margin to one goal at the close of play. Then, in February, a Montrose team visited the Holburn grounds where Aberdeen handed out a 6-2 beating, William Stewart and Ross (2) being amongst the scorers. Curiously, the Dundee Courier reported that another Montrose X1 defeated Brechin 4-0 at Montrose on the same day.

And a fortnight after that, Aberdeen made their first visit to Arbroath's Gayfield Park for a game which attracted an estimated 2,000 spectators. The home side played with a gale force wind at their backs in the opening 40 minute period while the visitors also had a low sun in their faces. It was little surprise that the Red Lichties went in at the interval with a 5-0 lead and had another two goals disallowed. Aberdeen's A. C. Black fractured his collarbone after colliding with one of his team-mates and had to leave the field. A doctor was called, and after providing some assistance, he instructed that Black should endure *"one month's total abstinence from physical exercises."* Despite facing the elements in the second half Arbroath added another goal to their tally to run out 6-0 winners. So, the second season ended with seven games played and two victories recorded.

Notable Games

Aberdeen 1, Harp, Dundee 3
Scottish Cup, Aberdeen Grammar School, 5th October 1882

This was Aberdeen's first Scottish Cup tie. Within the opening minute the green-shirted Harp thought they had taken the lead but, according to the Aberdeen Journal, the umpires disallowed it for some unknown reason. The Dundee Courier's account of the match, however, states that the goal was a legitimate one and was allowed to stand. The game was evenly balanced throughout the remainder of the opening period but Harp made the breakthrough shortly before the interval. Only *"the coolness"* of the Aberdeen goalkeeper, Jamieson, prevented further scoring at times. Aberdeen pressed hard after the restart, however, and it was little surprise when D. B. Lothian equalised, much to the delight of the home spectators. Harp retaliated and with 20 minutes to go, claimed a second goal, only for it to be chalked off for an infringement. After a *"squabble"* the umpires decided to restart the game with a drop ball a few yards from the Aberdeen goal. Harp quickly gained possession and scored, much to the anger of the home side. The goal seemed to deflate Aberdeen and shortly before the end Harp added a third (or fourth, if The Courier is to be believed).
Aberdeen - J. Jamieson, A. V. Lothian, H. Hyslop, C. E. Glennie, J. A. McHardy, C. Wilson, A. Steele, D. M. Smith, W. Stewart, A.T Ross, D. B. Lothian.
Harp - Hugh McTaggart, J. Clarke, M. Dorsey, C. Cluskey, B. Holmes, G. Shields, F. M. Riley, A. McMahon, P. Rock, J. Costro, R. Scutten

Montrose 1, Aberdeen 5
Montrose Links, 2nd December 1882

Another significant moment: Aberdeen's first win. Despite the cold and windy weather, a large crowd gathered to watch the match which the visitors dominated. D.B. Lothian grabbed the opener for Aberdeen with a stinging shot which goalkeeper Reid got his hands to but couldn't prevent crossing the line. Shortly afterwards Ross made it 2-0 with a shot which went in via a post. A third was scored, then R. Hyslop made it 4-0 before half-time. Lothian added a fifth early in the second half before E. Savage grabbed a consolation for the home side. Montrose pressed for more goals as they tried to take advantage of the strong wind at their backs but Jamieson repelled all their efforts.

Aberdeen – J. Jamieson, W. C. Farrel, A.V. Lothian (Captain), W. Thompson, C. E. Glennie, W. Stewart, R. Hyslop, J. A. McHardy, R. Black, A. T. Ross, D. B. Lothian. Umpire – J. Reid

Montrose – W. Reid, E. Lindsay, D. Clarke, J. Hector, J. Hampton, E. Wallace, J. Low, E. Savage, J. Hunter (Captain), A. Morrison, R. Baird. Umpire – W. Davie. Referee – J. Brown

Aberdeen F.C. - 1882-1883

Competition	Date		Opposition	F	A	Venue
Friendly	30/09/1882	Aberdeen	Coupar Angus	2	3	Larghan Park,Coupar Angus
Scottish Cup 2R	05/10/1882	Aberdeen	Harp,Dundee	1	3	Grammar School
Friendly	20/11/1882	Aberdeen	Strathmore, Dundee	1	2	Rollo's Pier
Friendly	02/12/1882	Aberdeen	Montrose	5	1	Links,Montrose
Friendly	20/01/1883	Aberdeen	Coupar Angus	3	4	Holburn
Friendly	10/02/1883	Aberdeen	Montrose	6	2	Holburn
Friendly	24/02/1883	Aberdeen	Arbroath	0	6	Gayfield Park,Arbroath

1883-1884
Almost a Scottish Cup shock, but progress remains slow

The 1883-1884 season got underway with a Scottish Cup tie against Arbroath. The Red Lichties were carving out a reputation as one of the country's top provincial sides at this time, so Aberdeen travelled to Gayfield more in hope than expectation, especially as they had lost 6-0 on their last visit at the tail end of the previous season. The home side might have expected to enjoy a comfortable victory but the Red Lichties soon had any complacency firmly knocked out of their system as Aberdeen battled back from 3-1 down at the interval to earn an impressive 3-3 draw.

The replay was again played at Gayfield one week later, and *"a large turnout of spectators lined the ropes."* Arbroath seemed determined to make amends for what was widely believed to be a poor performance the previous Saturday and within three minutes had opened the scoring. There was to be no way back for the visitors as the home side totally dominated play and ran out comfortable 7-0 winners.

It was even worse a few months later when the Lichties travelled to the Holburn Grounds for a friendly which ended with Aberdeen being on the wrong end of a 9-1 hammering despite the match being restricted to two halves of 35 minutes. D. Smith got Aberdeen's consolation goal. Aberdeen managed to fit in just three more fixtures before the end of the season, losing 6-1 to Harp at Viewforth Park in Dundee, and 4-1 to Montrose United in Angus before finishing up with a 3-3 draw against Montrose United at the Grammar School grounds. I found reference to Aberdeen having arranged a late season match against Sunnyside Asylum near Montrose but I was unable to find the outcome of this one. So, the campaign ended with two draws and four defeats. Only two matches were played in Aberdeen, a fact which did little to promote the sport in the north east. Part of the problem was the lack of any other local sides to play against. In January 1884 a match was arranged between Aberdeen and Marischal College but this had to be abandoned due the *"Marischal players failing to turn up in sufficient numbers."* A contemporary review of the season concluded that such a low level of activity *"cannot but damp the enthusiasm of the members."* The author of the review wondered why the city's many factories and workshops hadn't produced teams in the same way as the shipyards of Dumbarton which had generated some of the country's best players of *"the dribbling game."* It is interesting to note that the Aberdeen club at this time was dominated by teachers and other players from middle class or mainly 'professional' backgrounds with very little interest until then coming from what would have been known as the traditional working classes. That would change in the years ahead. In the meantime, although the season had come to an end, the club decided that practise sessions would continue one night a week throughout the summer.

Notable Games

Arbroath 3, Aberdeen 3
Scottish Cup, Gayfield Park, 8th September 1883

This was expected to be a comfortable win for Arbroath but after 15 minutes D. Smith shocked the Lichties by putting the visitors ahead. Jim Robertson soon equalised with a *"judicious kick"* and Tackett then fired Arbroath into the lead *"with a swift screw shot,"* before Fyffe made it 3-1 for the Gayfield men at half-time. Arbroath, playing into a low sun, conceded a second goal midway through the second period before having a goal disallowed because of a foul during the build-up. Aberdeen shocked their hosts by grabbing an equaliser to ensure a replay would be necessary.

Arbroath – Milne, Grant, Milne; Guild, Bruce, Rennie; Robertson, Tackett, Fleming, Stirling, Fyffe.

Aberdeen - Jamieson, Farrel, A. V. Lothian (captain); McHardy, Glennie; Hyslop, Stewart, Smith, Clark, Hunter, D. B. Lothian.

Ref: A. M. Anderson, Edinburgh University

Arbroath 7, Aberdeen 0
Scottish Cup Replay, Gayfield Park, 15th September 1883

The Red Lichties ensured there would be no second chance for Aberdeen. William Mann put Arbroath ahead inside the opening three minutes and from there on it was all one way traffic as the home side coasted to victory.

Arbroath – Milne, Christie, Grant; Guild, Milne, Bruce, Robertson, Fyffe, Stirling, Mann, Fleming.

Aberdeen – Jamieson, A. V. Lothian, Hunter, McHardy, Glennie, Stewart, Hyslop, D. B. Lothian, Smith, W. Clark, J. Clark.

Ref: Mr Ness, Glasgow

Aberdeen F.C. - All Games 1883-1884

Competition	Date		Opposition	F	A	Venue
Scottish Cup 1R	08/09/1883	Aberdeen	Arbroath	3	3	Gayfield
Scottish Cup 1R	15/09/1883	Aberdeen	Arbroath	0	7	Gayfield
Friendly	01/12/1883	Aberdeen	Arbroath	1	9	Holburn
Friendly	01/03/1884	Aberdeen	Harp	1	6	Viewforth Park,Dundee
Friendly	15/03/1884	Aberdeen	Montrose United	1	4	Links,Montrose
Friendly	12/04/1884	Aberdeen	Montrose United	3	3	Grammar School

1884-1885
The emergence of Rovers and Bon Accord

T he 1884-1885 season got underway with a 4-1 Scottish Cup win over Lindertis at Kirriemuir. The Angus side opened the scoring but founder member John McHardy equalised before the break and second half goals from R.S. Black, D.B. Lothian and D. Smith gave Aberdeen victory, their first in the national tournament. This earned the north east men a second round tie against old foes Arbroath. There was considerable interest in the Arbroath match which was played at the Recreation Grounds, Inches, with a 3pm kick-off. A healthy turnout of spectators paid the 3d admission money to see the match. Aberdeen's progress in the competition was, however, brought to a shuddering end as the Red Lichties ran out 7-1 winners. So, it was back to friendly games for the rest of the season. There was, nonetheless, a most significant development in the early months of 1885 when a couple of new clubs appeared on the local scene. Aberdeen Rovers and Bon Accord were formed to play the association game and they met for the first time on 7th February 1885 at the Recreation Grounds. Rovers' colours were blue jerseys and white knickers while Bon Accord played in black and white striped jerseys and white knickers. Bon Accord won 5-3. According to Scottish Football Association records, both clubs were formed in 1884 so this may have been the first competitive game either side played. If it was, it certainly didn't attract any significant attention. The following month Rovers played Peterhead at Duthie Park, losing 1-0, while the return game at Peterhead saw the new Aberdeen side lose narrowly again, by 2-1. Peterhead had also been formed in late 1884 when their new committee decreed that the club *"costume"* would be *"blue and white jerseys, blue and white stockings and blue necktie."* Aberdeen visited Peterhead to play the new boys in March 1885, winning 4-0 on a snow covered pitch. Although only a handful of games were again played during the season, the emergence of Bon Accord, Rovers and Peterhead meant that Aberdeen at least now had some local opposition to test themselves against. At the Aberdeen annual meeting held in the Shiprow café at the end of the season, it was announced that the Recreation grounds, Inches had again been secured for the following year and that practice sessions would be held on Tuesday evenings, beginning 26th May. J. Rose was elected President for the following season with

J.A. McHardy stepping down to Vice President. A.V. Lothian was appointed captain and R. Hyslop vice captain. D.V. Lothian would be treasurer and William Stewart, Tanfield Walk, took on the role of secretary. The committee comprised J. Bennie, W.C. Farrell, J. Edgar, J. Reid and D. Williamson.

Notable Games

Lindertis 1, Aberdeen 4

Scottish Cup, Kirriemuir, 13th September 1884

This was Aberdeen's first victory in a Scottish Cup tie. Lindertis took an early lead but a *"raking shot"* from McHardy levelled the scores before halftime. In the second period Aberdeen's R. Smith and R. Black put the visitors ahead by *"a splendid rush (which) carried ball and goalkeeper through."* Lothian *"whose dodging elicited frequent applause from the spectators",* made it 3-1 before M. D. Smith added a fourth.

Aberdeen – Jamieson, Farrel, Hyslop (Captain), McHardy, Williamson, Glennie, Black, R. Smith, M.D. Smith, Stewart, Lothian. Umpire – J. Bennie

Lindertis – Neil, Brown, Haggarty, Watson, McGregor, Milne, James, George, Lindsay (Captain), Strachan, Black. Umpire – J. Black

Referee – Mr J. Robertson (Perseverance, Dundee)

Aberdeen 1, Arbroath 7

Scottish Cup, Recreation Grounds, Inches, 4th October 1884

Aberdeen kicked off but immediately lost possession and for the opening half hour Arbroath had the home side penned in their own half of the field.The Lichties scored three times during this spell and could have doubled that had it not been for some fine defensive play. Aberdeen performed better in the opening stages of the second half but Arbroath extended their lead before the home fans were able to cheer a goal from their side, albeit from a miskick by Arbroath right back Gray, but three quickfire strikes from the visiting forwards soon had the Lichties well ahead again.

Aberdeen – A.V. Lothian, R. Hyslop, W. Farrel, C. Glennie, J. McHardy, J. Crow, R.S. Black, R. Smith, W. Stewart, D. Smith, D.B. Lothian.

Arbroath – Milne, Gray, Rennie, Christie, Milne, Bruce, Marshall, Stirling, Mann, Crawford, Tackett.

Games Played by Aberdeen Clubs – 1884-1885

Competition	Date		Opposition	F	A	Venue
Scottish Cup 1R	13/09/1884	Aberdeen	Lindertis	4	1	Kirriemuir
Scottish Cup 2R	04/10/1884	Aberdeen	Arbroath	1	7	Recreation Grounds,Inches
Friendly	07/02/1885	Rovers	Bon Accord	3	5	Recreation Grounds,Inches
Friendly	07/03/1885	Rovers	Peterhead	0	1	Duthie Park
Friendly	21/03/1885	Aberdeen	Peterhead	4	0	Peterhead
Friendly	08/04/1885	Rovers	Peterhead	1	2	Links,Peterhead

1885-1886
The mystery of Bon Accord and the formation of Orion

There was an explosion of interest in football at the beginning of the 1885-1886 season with clubs sprouting up all over the city. It's not clear what the catalyst was for this remarkable upsurge in enthusiasm, but before the year was out Aberdeen, Rovers and Bon Accord had been joined by new clubs such as Orion, Carlton, Gladstone and Reform. Aberdeen, Rovers and Bon Accord were all members of the Scottish Football Association, having paid the five shillings (25p) annual subscription, and therefore they all entered the Scottish Cup. No-one could have imagined, however, that the Scottish Cup campaign of September 1885 would still be talked about almost 130 years later. But then no-one could have anticipated what was about to happen. On 29th August Aberdeen and Bon Accord opened their season with a match aimed at preparing themselves for the forthcoming Scottish Cup ties. Aberdeen dominated the game, winning 4-0 courtesy of goals from D.B. Lothian (2), D. Smith and William Stewart. The following week Bon Accord defeated Rovers 1-0 at the Recreation Grounds, Inches, while Aberdeen travelled to Arbroath to face Strathmore in the Scottish Cup at Damley Park and suffered a 7-0 beating. The following Saturday, 12th September, was to turn out exceptionally stormy, both climatically and in a footballing sense, for followers of the game in Aberdeen.

Ferocious waves crashed against Arbroath's harbour walls as a brewing storm exerted its malicious force across the grey North Sea. Later that day a German barque would be wrecked on the notorious Bell Rock, 12 miles off the Angus coast, the crew fortuitously taking refuge in Robert Stevenson's lighthouse built 75 years earlier in a bid to prevent vessels from straying onto the lethal reef. Onshore, teenager John Petrie made his way along the rain-soaked streets to Gayfield Park, the home ground of Arbroath Football Club. The pitch sat within spitting distance of the shore and was fully exposed to the elements. Arbroath F.C., formed in 1878, had previously played on the links at Elliot a couple of miles along the coast, but relocated to Gayfield which was considered *"more sheltered,"* a description which is hard to believe. Petrie had established himself as a regular in the Red Lichties side. He sometimes played in the centre, other times on the wing. Now, aged 17, he and his team-mates would unwittingly secure a place in Scottish footballing folklore by participating in one of the most remarkable games in the history of the sport. Football was mushrooming in popularity. Clubs were sprouting up in cities, towns and villages across the land. No fewer than 128 sides featured in the draw for the First Round of that season's Scottish Cup, Long forgotten clubs such as Broxburn Shamrock, Lugar Boswell, Rock, Edina and Union all appeared on the list of entrants. Arbroath, considered one of the strongest provincial clubs of that era, found themselves paired with Aberdeen's recently formed Bon Accord club. Bon Accord had been drawn out of the hat first and would have been given the choice of whether to play the tie at home or away if they had an enclosed ground of their own. However, as the Aberdonians only had the use of a public park at the Inches, the tie was switched to Gayfield. And the outcome was to be an unashamed massacre of innocents. The Lichties showed no mercy by romping to a remarkable 36-0 win. Seven further 'goals' were disallowed for one reason or another. This remains the biggest victory recorded in a senior football match anywhere in the world. Teenager Petrie scored 13 of the 36 while the other scorers were Munro (7), Robertson (6), David Crawford (6), Jim Marshall (2) and Johnny Tackett (2).

Petrie's tally remains a record for the number of goals scored in a single match in British football history. But if that wasn't bad enough, on the same afternoon, 18 miles along the Angus coast, another Aberdeen outfit, Rovers, captained by George Anderson, lost 35-0 to Dundee's Harp at East Dock Street Park, also in the Scottish Cup. Rovers didn't help their cause by turning up with just ten men, but it is doubtful if that made much difference.

The Aberdeen press, not surprisingly, gave little mention of these two matches. Only a couple of sentences appeared in the Aberdeen Journal which simply stated: *"Bon-Accord v Arbroath. These clubs played their cup-tie match at Gayfield Park, Arbroath. The Aberdeen men received a merciless beating, the*

Arbroath's John Petrie – 13 goals

register at the close showing the unprecedented tale of 36 goals to nil against them." The paper also included a rather understated account of Rovers' 35-0 loss at Dundee Harp, stating quite simply and concisely that: *"The strangers (visitors) were seldom or never in the game."*

The Dundee Courier, not surprisingly, gives more detail. It described the Arbroath-Bon Accord match as an *"extraordinary farce,"* and pointed out that the game was so one sided that *"Milne, the goalkeeper of the Arbroath, neither touched the ball with hand or foot during the match but remained under the friendly shelter of an umbrella the whole time."* The Scottish Athletic Journal stated: *"The leather was landed between the posts 41 times, but five of the times were disallowed. Here and there, enthusiasts would be seen scoring sheet and pencil in hand, taking note of the goals as one would score runs at a cricket match."*

So, in the space of one week, three Aberdeen clubs lost Scottish Cup ties, two in Arbroath and one in Dundee, conceding a total of 78 goals and scoring none. It prompted one commentator in the Scottish Athletic Journal to advocate that the Aberdeen teams should consider amalgamating if the city was to salvage any hope of producing a team capable of competing at national level. A pulling together of the resources of Aberdeen, Bon Accord and Rovers would, however, have been unlikely to have been of any great benefit as even the best players from all three would still have struggled.

The Arbroath-Bon Accord result, being the biggest score, has since attracted the most attention. In some quarters, it has been claimed that Bon Accord wasn't a football club at all. One source of this version of events can be traced to an article which appeared in the Sunday Standard newspaper in 1983, written by William Lawson, in which he refers to a story told some years earlier by a Miss Isobel Mitchell of Laurencekirk. According to Lawson's article, Miss Mitchell had discovered an old football programme which belonged to her father and contained a tribute to him. The article apparently mentioned that Mr. Mitchell had been a member of the Aberdeen Orion Cricket Club which had been surprisingly invited by the Scottish Football Association to take part in the Scottish Cup. Flattered by the invitation, the cricketers, some of whom also played football, accepted the invitation, but they decided to play under the name Bon Accord as it supposedly sounded more suitable for football than Orion. Why this would be so, I have no idea. Afterwards, according to Lawson's story, the SFA sent them a letter of apology and explained the invitation had been intended for the Aberdeen Orion Football Club. So, is this true or not? Well, it's an interesting story, but not one to which I give very much credence. Firstly, as seen earlier in this Chapter, it is clear that Bon Accord Football Club did exist for some time before the Scottish Cup tie. Two weeks before the debacle at Gayfield, the Aberdeen Journal carried a report on a match between Aberdeen and Bon Accord which referred to the fact that the sides were preparing for their respective forthcoming Scottish Cup ties. There was no speculation in the Aberdeen press that either side was anything other than a football club. Aberdeen won that game 4-0. There is also evidence, as shown earlier in this book, that Bon Accord Football Club was plying its trade at least as early as February 1885 when there is a record of them playing Rovers. We also know that Bon Accord was affiliated to the Scottish Football Association that season. The SFA Annual for the 1885-1886 refers to Bon Accord as having been formed in 1884. They had 26 registered members and played at the Recreation Grounds, Inches and the club secretary was Mr. William McLean, 57 Huntly Street, Aberdeen. The rules for competing in the Scottish Cup at that time required all players to be registered with the SFA at least one month in advance of any game, so it would have been impossible for any unknown people to have taken part. Bon Accord played regularly against other Aberdeen clubs throughout the remainder of the 1885-1886 season. A month after the Arbroath match a Bon Accord and Rovers select lost 4-0 to Aberdeen at the Recreation Grounds. Orion wasn't formed until October 1885, after the Scottish Cup ties had been played and they weren't at that time members of the SFA which means they could not possibly have been invited to take part in the Scottish Cup and could not, therefore, have received a letter about this matter as Lawson suggests. In early November 1885 Bon Accord defeated Orion 2-0, again at the Recreation Grounds, and in a return match at Duthie Park a few weeks later, these sides drew 1-1. I have also been able to establish that the Bon Accord team at this time included two players called Mitchell, one of whom may have been Miss Mitchell's father. G. A. Mitchell was a goalkeeper and A. Mitchell was an outside left. It is quite possible, of course, that the footballers of Bon Accord were also cricketers in the summer months. This was quite common. Many cricketers played football in the winter.

There is, however, some degree of mystery as to who actually played for Bon Accord that fateful day. Wikipedia, which of course doesn't reveal its sources or authors, lists the Bon Accord team that played Arbroath as being:- Andrew Lornie, David Donoghue, James Connell, Brendan Keeley, Ian Whelan, Keith Lowry, Eammon Sutty, Richard Doherty, Larry Behan, Conor Conorson, Joe McManus. The goalkeeper, Lornie, has long been associated with the match. A Perthshire-born man, he was a tinsmith and gas fitter by trade. However, I have not been able to find either his name, or any of the other Wikipedia names, in any other Bon Accord or any other Aberdeen club line-ups during that season. Nor have I found any of these names associated with any Aberdeen cricket side during this period. Also, the Wikipedia line-up doesn't tie up with the Sunday Standard story as there is no Mitchell in the team. In scanning through local newspapers for Bon Accord team player names from this period I came across just a couple of line-ups, both from games a few months after the 36-0 result. In January 1886 Bon Accord defeated Carlton 5-1 at the Links and the team was as follows: G. A. Mitchell, J. Mellis, J. Robertson, D. Main, A. Kelly, S. Kelly (captain), J. Gordon, T. McElroy, H. Clarkson, J. Hutcheon, A. Mitchell. And in February 1886 the Bon Accord team for a match against Gladstone was: A. Smith; J. Robertson, J. McFarland, J. Robertson, A. Kelly, S. Kelly (captain), F G Jones, J. Garden, J. Meller, J. Hutcheon, A. Mitchell. None of the Wikipedia names are listed but the name of Mitchell does appear. Whatever the truth of the matter, I am certain that the Bon Accord which faced Arbroath in the Scottish Cup was a bona fide football outfit. Not a very good one, it must be said. But high scores were far from rare in this era, as can be seen from the 35-0 thumping endured by Rovers on that same day. Arbroath would also thrash Orion 20-0 and 18-0 in Scottish Cup ties in 1886 and 1887 respectively. Indeed, the Aberdeen Journal report on Orion's 20-0 defeat the following season made reference to Bon Accord's 36-0 defeat twelve months earlier, and didn't cast any doubt on whether or not the Aberdeen side was a football club. Football in Aberdeen at this time was still in its relative infancy as an organised sport and understanding of the game was probably a few years behind that of clubs even in the Angus area.

Meanwhile, Bon Accord continued to play in the aftermath of their Arbroath humiliation and, in 1886, the MP Mr James Bryce, became a patron of the club. Just a few weeks after he aligned himself to this position, however, the team was involved in a bizarre incident. During a match with Aberdeen, in February 1886, the Bon Accord players walked off the pitch following a disputed offside decision. On a snow-covered pitch at the Recreation Grounds, Aberdeen had raced into a 3-0 lead through Tom Ketchen (2) and Clark. The Bon Accord men objected to Clark's strike but the referee stood by his decision, so the Bons walked off. It's not clear what happened immediately after that, but a few weeks later there was a curious announcement in the local press saying that the club had been taken over by members of the Good Templar Festival Choir. Interestingly, many of the office bearers of the new club were involved with the previous outfit, including the Mitchells. A team bearing the Bon Accord name continued to play in Aberdeen football circles for a number of years and in 1887 they got a dose of their own medicine. A feisty match against a local club called St. Mirren ended abruptly when the Saints left the field after disputing a goal. By late 1887, however, Bon Accord had two teams playing in local matches which suggests the club was still in a reasonable state of health.

Orion Football Club wasn't formed until autumn 1885, a month or so after Arbroath's 36-0 win over Bon Accord. The Aberdeen Journal, on Monday 5th October, announced that the Orion Cricket Club had decided to form a football club and the following office bearers were appointed: Captain - J. D. Crow; Vice captain, J. M. Beveridge; Secretary and Treasurer, James Dunn 87 Causewayend; Committee - Messrs John Benton, Wm. Jaffray, John Dunn and Robert Davidson.
Orion's first game seems to have been against Aberdeen at the Recreation Grounds on 30th October 1885, when the teams played out a 2-2 draw. Aberdeen played with ten men. Orion then played Bon Accord twice, the first at the Recreation Grounds which Bon Accord won 2-0. A press report complimented the Orion by stating: *"The play of the Orion was very good for a new club."* The return match, at Duthie Park, ended in a 1-1 draw after Orion had taken a first half lead. The first Orion team line-up I have been able to find is for their game against Rovers in January 1886. It was as follows:- John Dunn, J. Mackay, J.M. Beveridge, J.B. Crow (Captain), W. Anderson, A.G. Allan, J. Benton, R. Davidson, James Dunn, W.M. Jaffray, G. Pollock.

It is interesting to note that right back John Mackay and inside left William Jaffray would, 17 years later, both find themselves on the first Board of Directors of the new Aberdeen Football Club.

Meanwhile, Aberdeen F.C's season, aside from the Scottish Cup, was reasonably successful. The club played 12 games, losing just two – to Arbroath's Strathmore and to one of Scotland's top sides of this era, Dumbarton. The biggest win of the season was a 13-1 thrashing of Gladstone, the scorers being Allan (4), Clark (3), Preston (2), Hyslop, Shand, Munro and the other goal coming from a scrimmage. The visit of Dumbarton to Aberdeen in January 1886 marked another important landmark in the development of football in the city. This was the first time a club from the Central Belt had been encountered and the Sons of the Rock at this time were one of the country's leading sides. Five years later they would be joint champions with Rangers in the first Scottish League competition. In 1886 Dumbarton included a number of Scottish internationals in their squad, so there was widespread interest in their appearance at the Recreation Grounds to play an Aberdeen side which also included Kelly of the Bon Accord.

Aberdeen F.C. 1885-1886. It is presumed that the hooped jerseys were black and gold in colour.

The curtain came down on the season with a charity match played at the Recreation Grounds between Aberdeen and a 'Clubs of the Town' select in aid of the Royal Infirmary. The select side comprised players from Orion, Rovers, Bon Accord and Gladstone. Despite the poor weather *"there was a good turnout of spectators"*. The select took an early lead but Aberdeen soon equalised before Clark edged them into a 2-1 lead. A third was scored before half-time. The slippery underfoot conditions made good play impossible but Aberdeen grabbed a fourth while another effort was disallowed because of an infringement.

Notable Games

Strathmore, Arbroath 7, Aberdeen 0

Scottish Cup, Damley Park, Arbroath, 5th September 1885

The Arbroath Guide's reporter at the match was impressed with his first viewing of the visitors. He wrote: *"The Aberdonians, whose physique and calibre were greatly admired, were the first to enter the arena."* However, it the home side which went on to dominate, Steele opening the scoring after 25 minutes, Lowe adding a second and Stewart soon making it 3-0. The maroon-shirted Aberdeen side struggled to stem the tide and further goals followed from Steele and McDonald with another two unknown scorers giving Strathmore victory by 7-0.

Aberdeen - Bennie, Farrel, A. Lothian (captain), Williamson, McHardy, Glennie, Stewart, Hislop, Smith, Edgar, D. Lothian.

Arbroath Strathmore - Johnston, Airth, Dorward, Buick, McDonald, Mathers, Steele, Findlay, Stewart, Lowe, Renny.

James Bennie – Aberdeen's goalkeeper in the 7-0 defeat by Arbroath Strathmore.

This is believed to be the only game he played for the club. Bennie died suddenly in 1896. A schoolteacher, firstly at Causewayend, then Frederick Street, he was one of the founding members of the club. He was also actively involved with the Educational Institute of Scotland. A foot injury sustained when he was a youngster meant he could only play in goal. But his opportunities were limited. He was club secretary for a number of years and he enjoyed many other sports. He also fulfilled duties as an umpire at many games including Aberdeen's first match, against Coupar Angus.

Arbroath 36, Bon Accord 0
Scottish Cup, Gayfield Park, Arbroath, 12th September 1885

The Bon Accord men were shown no mercy as the Arbroath Guide's report on the match described in some detail. It is best read in full, so here goes:

"Arbroath v Bon Accord (Aberdeen) – The meeting of these teams in the first round of the Scottish Cup ties was expected to end in an easy win for the Arbroath, but few anticipated the farce enacted at Gayfield last Saturday. The Bon Accord had the good grace to save a journey to the Arbroath men by electing to play off the tie at Arbroath and punctually to time both teams appeared on the field. It would have been difficult to choose a stronger team out of the club than that representing the Arbroath. Winning the toss, Milne, the Arbroath captain, chose to defend the east goal, and then began the most amusing football match ever seen in Arbroath. There could scarcely be said to have been any play shown on the part of the Bon Accord, and from the beginning of the game the goals began to accumulate at an alarming rate, Petrie opening the account with two in succession, and Marshall immediately adding another couple. After Munro had put on the fifth goal a slight rest in the reckoning occurred, the Aberdeen men somehow managing to keep the ball for a short time near midfield. Then the Arbroath forwards seemed to get thoroughly into the fun of the game and before the call of half-time had scored other ten goals. After the thirteenth goal had been got, the Aberdeen forwards had a momentary encounter with the backs near the Arbroath goal, but this was the only time they got away from their own territory. The second half was simply a repetition of the first, five goals being registered within the first fifteen minutes, and sixteen during the other thirty minutes. In the course of this half, however, the Bon Accord were within an ace of scoring, the only shot they had at the Arbroath goal going apparently beyond Milne's reach, when it was intercepted by Collie. When the whistle blew, intimating the close of the game, the score stood – Arbroath 36 goals; Bon Accord 0. The Aberdeen men never seemed to be dismayed by the turn of events

FOOTBALL.

SCOTTISH CUP TIE—FIRST ROUND.

BON-ACCORD, ABERDEEN, v. ARBROATH,
GAYFIELD PARK —TO-DAY.

Kick-off at 3.30 P.M.

Admission, 3d ; Ladies Free. Grand Stand, 3d extra.

throughout the match, and to the close did what little they could to keep off their opponents. They cannot play football, but Saturday's lesson will have shown them how it is done. Petrie was the most successful of the Arbroath forwards at goal, he being credited with thirteen. An opportunity of having the recent improvements effected upon the ground thoroughly tested occurred last Saturday, and notwithstanding the heavy rain which fell from early morning the park was free from surface water, and otherwise in good condition."

Harp, Dundee 35, Rovers, Aberdeen 0
Scottish Cup, East Dock Street, Dundee, 12th September 1885

Had it not been for events 18 miles along the coast in Arbroath this same afternoon, this would have been the best known match in football history. Harp led 16-0 at halftime. Harp's captain, D'Arcy, scored 10 while the other goals came from McGirl six, Murphy five, Murray four, Rock three, Lees three, Neill three and D'Arcy senior, one. Captain D'Arcy's tally included five in a row in the second half. The Courier described events in the following manner: *"This match took place on the ground of the latter at East Dock Street. Considering the state of the elements, the ground was in fair condition and there was a large attendance. The Rovers were the first to step over the ropes and were well received, the Harp making their appearance shortly afterwards. The strangers won the toss and elected to play towards the north goal. Play commenced at 3.25 by Murphy collaring the ball and scoring the first goal for his side in less time than it takes to write it. Rock scored goal No.2 with ease, getting on the ball at the kick-off, walking up with it and coolly putting it through. It is needless to give the play in detail, as it was from start to finish, all on one side. Suffice it to say that the Harp scored ten goals in as many minutes, and during the remainder of this period other six fell to their lot. The second period was a repetition of the first, the Harp putting on goals at the average of one in a little over two minutes. The Rovers team is a young organisation, having previously only taken part in one match, that with the Bon Accord, Aberdeen, and it joined the Association for the first time this year. Their play, with the exception of Anderson on the left, who at times, though perfectly unsupported, made an occasional brilliant run, was of a mediocre type. Their custodian especially gave a perfectly weak-kneed exhibition of goalkeeping. The Harp had the game all their own way, as from start to finish it was only a question*

THE ABERDEEN MEN CAN'T PLAY FOOTBALL

of walking up to their opponents' goal and putting through the leather. The strangers played a man short, but this fact could not have discounted the result to any appreciable extent." I understand that the Rovers goalkeeper, William Wilson, was the grandfather of an Aberdeen woman called Olive Lornie, who, incredibly, was married to Sidney Lornie – the grandson of Andrew Lornie who, apparently, was the Bon Accord goalkeeper in the 36-0 defeat by Arbroath.

Aberdeen 4, Combined Team of Rovers and Bon Accord 0
Benefit Game for the Sutherland Memorial Fund, Recreation Grounds, 24th October 1885
There was a good attendance for this match which Aberdeen dominated. They took a 2-0 lead before the interval and added another two in the second period. The scorers were Munro (2), Smith and Clark.
Aberdeen – Wood, Hyslop, A.V. Lothian (captain), McHardy Glennie, Stewart, Preston, Clark, Smith, Munro, D.B. Lothian.
Combined Team – D. Wilson (Rovers), Mellis (Bon Accord), Kelly (Bon Accord), Auld (Rovers), Main (Bon Accord), H. Wilson (Rovers), Anderson (Rovers), Mitchell (Bon Accord), Carson (Rovers), Jones (Bon Accord), Gordon (Bon Accord).

Aberdeen 0, Dumbarton 7
Friendly, Recreation Grounds , 5th January 1886,
This was the first visit to Aberdeen of a team from the Central Belt. The pitch was covered in several inches of snow and the cold weather *"had a prejudicial effect upon the attendance of spectators."* Despite the treacherous conditions Dumbarton soon settled and their Scotland international goalkeeper James McAulay, interestingly playing as a forward, opened the scoring after five minutes. McAulay was capped nine times by Scotland, making his debut as a forward then playing the other eight games as goalkeeper. Remarkably, he was never in a losing Scotland team. Aberdeen settled after the early setback and defended well for a while but McAulay was again on the mark to make it 2-0 and a third goal followed before the half-time interval. The home side crumbled after the break with the visitors scoring four more times in the opening 15 minutes. After that the clubs agreed to play the remaining half-hour by dividing the teams, and playing the Dumbarton forwards with the Aberdeen half-backs, backs, and goal-keeper,

against the Aberdeen forwards and Dumbarton half-backs, backs and goal-keeper. The result of the last half-hour's play was that two goals went to the Dumbarton backs and one goal to the Dumbarton forwards. The Aberdeen Journal's account of the game gave credit to the home side: *"Aberdeen played a plucky defensive game, their back play being very strong. All the forwards played a good game although they were overpowered by the heavy mettle of their opponents."*

Aberdeen - D. Wood, A.V. Lothian (Captain), R. Hyslop; McHardy, Kelly (Bon Accord); Stewart, Munro, Preston, Clark, D. Lothian, Allan.

Dumbarton - A. McK. Kennedy; Millar, McMillan; Liddle, A. Kennedy, Keir, J. Kennedy; Hartley, Wilson, Aitken, McAulay.

Aberdeen F.C. - 1885-1886

Competition	Date		Opposition	F	A	Venue
Friendly	29/08/1885	Aberdeen	Bon Accord	4	0	
Scottish Cup	05/09/1885	Aberdeen	Strathmore, Arbroath	0	7	Damley Park,Arbroath
Friendly	24/10/1885	Aberdeen	Rovers & Bon Accord Select	4	0	Recreation Grounds
Friendly	31/10/1885	Aberdeen	Orion	2	2	Recreation Grounds
Friendly	28/11/1885	Aberdeen	Carlton			Recreation Grounds
Friendly	19/12/1885	Aberdeen	Orion	6	2	Recreation Grounds
Friendly	26/12/1885	Aberdeen	Gladstone	13	1	Recreation Grounds
Friendly	05/01/1886	Aberdeen	Dumbarton	0	7	Recreation Grounds
Friendly	20/02/1886	Aberdeen	Bon Accord	3	0	Recreation Grounds
Friendly	27/02/1886	Aberdeen	Montrose	1	1	Montrose
Friendly	27/03/1886	Aberdeen	Clubs of Town	4	1	Recreation Grounds
Friendly	10/04/1886	Aberdeen	St Laurence	1	1	Laurencekirk

Note: Aberdeen v Carlton 28th November. No score given but Aberdeen won the match.

Orion F.C. - 1885-1886

Competition	1885-1886		Opposition	F	A	Venue
Friendly	31/10/1885	Orion	Aberdeen	2	2	Recreation Grounds
Friendly	07/11/1885	Orion	Bon Accord	0	2	Recreation Grounds

Competition	1885-1886		Opposition	F	A	Venue
Friendly	28/11/1885	Orion	Bon Accord	1	1	Duthie Park
Friendly	05/12/1885	Orion	Rovers	2	3	Links
Friendly	19/12/1885	Orion	Aberdeen	2	6	Recreation Grounds
Friendly	26/12/1885	Orion	Carlton	5	0	Links
Friendly	02/01/1886	Orion	Gladstone	8	0	Inches
Friendly	09/01/1886	Orion	Grammar School	1	1	Grammar School
Friendly	16/01/1886	Orion	Rovers	1	3	Links
Friendly	30/01/1886	Orion	Carlton	4	0	Links
Friendly	13/02/1886	Orion	Alliance	2	2	Links
Friendly	13/03/1886	Orion	Rovers	5	3	Links
Friendly	20/03/1886	Orion	Gladstone	2	1	Links

Bon Accord F.C - 1885-1886

Competition	Date		Opposition	F	A	Venue
Friendly	29/08/1885	Bon Accord	Aberdeen	0	4	Not Known
Friendly	05/09/1885	Bon Accord	Rovers	1	0	Recreation Grounds
Friendly	12/09/1885	Bon Accord	Arbroath	0	36	Gayfield, Arbroath
Friendly	24/10/1885	Rovers & Bon Accord Select	Aberdeen	0	4	Recreation Ground
Friendly	07/11/1885	Bon Accord	Orion	2	0	Recreation Grounds
Friendly	28/11/1885	Bon Accord	Orion	1	1	Duthie Park
Friendly	05/12/1885	Bon Accord	Carlton	5	1	Links
Friendly	12/12/1885	Bon Accord	Gladstone	4	0	Links
Friendly	23/01/1886	Bon Accord	Carlton	5	1	Links
Friendly	20/02/1886	Bon Accord	Aberdeen	0	3	Recreation Grounds

Rovers F.C. - 1885-1886

Competition	Date		Opposition	F	A	Venue
Friendly	05/09/1885	Rovers	Bon Accord	0	1	Recreation Grounds
Scottish Cup 1R	12/09/1885	Rovers	Harp,Dundee	0	35	East Dock Street

Competition	Date		Opposition	F	A	Venue
Friendly	24/10/1885	Rovers & Bon Accord Select	Aberdeen	0	4	Recreation Grounds
Friendly	31/10/1885	Rovers	Hall Russell's	0	1	Links
Friendly	05/12/1885	Rovers	Orion	3	2	Links
Friendly	02/01/1886	Rovers	Laurencekirk	0	4	Recreation Grounds
Friendly	16/01/1886	Rovers	Orion	3	1	Links
Friendly	23/01/1886	Rovers	Reform	4	0	Links
Friendly	06/02/1886	Rovers	Gladstone	7	3	Links
Friendly	20/02/1886	Rovers	Carlton	7	0	Links
Friendly	13/03/1886	Rovers	Orion	3	5	Links
Friendly	10/04/1886	Rovers	Reform	0	1	

1886-1887
Football's surge in popularity

T he surge in interest in playing and watching association football in 1885-1886 became a frenzy over the next twelve months as the game continued to flourish. I found results from more than 160 games played by more than 30 different clubs in the city and surrounding area, during the 1886-1887 season. In addition to these, many clubs had second elevens which also played on a regular basis. Most games were played at the Links, which were becoming increasingly congested, although Aberdeen's home matches were held at the Holburn Grounds. Other venues commonly used included the Recreation Grounds, Inches and Aulton Links. The Grammar School playing fields and Hammerfield were also used on occasion. This was also the season that school football appears to have started in Aberdeen, with games featuring King Street, Skene Street, Commerce Street and Causewayend schools. The first recorded school game seems to have been on 5th March 1887, King Street defeating Causewayend 2-1.

The clubs which featured during that season were:

Aberdeen	Playfair
Aberdeen Athletic	Rangers, Aberdeen (formerly called Carlton)
Albert	Rosebery
Balmoral	Rovers
Black Diamond	Shamrock
Bon Accord	St Laurence
Britannia	St Mirren, Aberdeen
Caledonian	St Ronald's
Emerald	Stonehaven
Faithlie,Fraserburgh	Swifts
Gladstone	Unicorn
Grammar School	University
Granite City	Reform
Herald	Victoria
Orion	Woodside
Our Boys	

Orion's debut appearance in the Scottish Cup was almost as disasterous as that of Bon Accord the previous season. Again, Arbroath's Gayfield Park was the setting for another humiliating defeat, the Angus side blasting 20 goals past the Aberdeen men who could not respond. Reports suggest it could have been much worse as the maroons throttled back in the second period. Aside from this result, however, Orion enjoyed a decent season by getting the upperhand over all the city clubs other than Aberdeen. Perhaps surprisingly, however, out of town sides Stonehaven and St Laurence proved harder nuts to crack. Aberdeen remained the dominant club on the local scene at this time although there remains a degree of mystery over their failure to compete in the Scottish Cup. They were drawn against Dundee's East End, but the tie was never played and the Dundee side progressed to the next round of the competition. According to the Dundee Courier, Aberdeen *"telegraphed to Dundee early on Saturday forenoon to the effect that they had scratched."* Perhaps they were wary of taking part given the record of north east clubs in the national competition the previous year. Aberdeen's season subsequently started with an 8-3 defeat at Damley Park, Arbroath in a friendly rematch with the Strathmore side that had dumped them out of the Scottish Cup the previous year.

On the home front, however, Aberdeen proved almost unbeatable. Grammar School managed to hold the Holburn side to a 3-3 draw but that aside, the city's oldest club won all their matches. The main game of the season was the charity fixture, in aid of the Royal Infirmary, between Aberdeen and a select side 'Clubs of the Town'. This match was scheduled to take place at the Recreation Grounds one week before Christmas. The pitch was, however, covered by four inches of snow and the bitterly cold conditions deterred many people from coming along to watch. It was decided to play a practice game, which Clubs of the Town won 2-1, but the official fixture was rescheduled to the following March when Aberdeen won 4-2. Snow again fell during the rearranged match, but not enough to cause a postponement. Clubs of the Town and Aberdeen met again a few weeks later in a benefit game for a *"Gladstone player who had suffered a serious accident"*. Aberdeen won 2-0.

Aberdeen's heaviest defeat was a 10-1 drubbing at Montrose. The Links Park side led by six before Clark grabbed Aberdeen's solitary goal. Montrose had two efforts chalked off but still got into double figures by the end of what the Aberdeen Journal oddly described as *"a very enjoyable game."*

One of the most forward-thinking of the new clubs formed at the start of the season was Caledonian F.C who would demonstrate their ambitions by joining the Scottish Football Association. The Caledonian, who turned out in blue and black vertically striped jerseys, played 14 games, winning seven, drawing three and losing four. The new club's first match was against an Aberdeen X1 and was played at Holburn on 23rd October 1886. According to reports *"on both sides there were players who had not previously taken part in an association match, so that, as was expected, the combination was very poor, but some of the players showed qualities which, when developed by practice, should make them worthy exponents of the game."* The Aberdeen team won 3-2. The Caledonian side was described as containing *"some speedy men, and they are on the whole, fairly heavy."* That same day the Aberdeen first team travelled to Laurencekirk to play the local side, St Laurence, on the glebe of the Ecclesiastical Manse, surely one of the most unusual settings that an Aberdeen team has played in. A Tom Ketchen hat-trick and goals from Stewart and Younnie contributed towards a 6-0 win even though the city team played with just ten men.

The rudimentary nature of the local football at this time is reflected in some of the bizarre incidents which often disrupted proceedings. Aberdeen's game against Aberdeen Rangers in December 1886 was, for instance, restricted to two halves of 30 minutes because so many players were late in showing up and the kick-off was delayed. Even at that, the match finished in darkness, with Aberdeen winning 6-0, the best being an overhead kick from Tom Ketchen. An Aberdeen club going by the name of St Mirren was often involved in curtailed matches. The Saints seemed to have a number of somewhat temperamental characters in their ranks, as twice during the season, in games against Bon Accord and Our Boys, they walked off the pitch when decisions went against them, leaving their opponents to claim victory. The Caledonian team also left the pitch after scoring against Rangers. The goal was disputed and an argument followed, but no agreement could be reached about whether it should stand or not, so the scorers packed up and went home. Caledonian were involved in another abandoned game when, after building up a 5-0 lead over Britannia at the Links, two balls burst in quick succession, leaving the teams with nothing to play with. And when Orion entertained Granite City, the start of the game was delayed by 30 minutes to allow the hosts to get their photograph taken. Sometimes there wasn't even agreement on the final score of a game. The Aberdeen Journal on more than one occasion carried two different results for the same match. Often it depended on who sent in the result – and sometimes club secretaries had different opinions about the outcomes as there were frequently debates over disputed goals!

At the end of the season the Aberdeen Journal carried an announcement that a new club was to be formed in the city and it would be called Aberdeen Wanderers. The promoter of the club was said to be an Edinburgh player who had recently moved to the north east and he was keen to sign most of the best local players. According to the report: *"The forwards will be a fast and speedy lot, for none are to be chosen to play unless they can cover the 120 yards in a stated time."* Although a City Wanderers club was formed, they don't appear to have made much of an impact.

Notable Games

Arbroath 20, Orion 0

Scottish Cup First Round, Gayfield Park, Arbroath, 11th September 1886

Rain had fallen non stop for five hours before the game got underway, leaving the pitch in a *"deplorable state"*. A crowd of 500 turned up to watch Orion kicking off with the advantage of a strong wind at their backs but Arbroath's superiority was such that they cruised to a 5-0 halftime lead. Despite this thrashing, the Aberdeen Journal remained optimistic by stating: *"The Orion is composed of men of fine physique, possessing considerable speed and a fair knowledge of the Association code, and with practice should develop into a good team."*

Aberdeen 4, Caledonian 1

Friendly, Holburn Grounds, 12th February 1887

This was the first match between these two clubs. Caledonian had aspirations to become the top side in the city but they were well beaten by their more experienced opponents. Tom Ketchen opened the scoring for Aberdeen and Clark made it 2-0 at before halftime. J. Bannochie reduced the leeway early in the

A. Clark, Aberdeen F.C.

second period but Aberdeen extended their lead through further goals from Munro and Ketchen.

Aberdeen - D. Wood, J.F. Vass, A.V. Lothian (captain), J.A. McHardy, C.E. Glennie, J. S. Preston, J. Cunningham, H.T. Hinton, T. Ketchen, W.J. Munro, A. Clark.

Caledonian - A. Brown, A. Craig, J. Clark, J.N. Melville, C. Mackenzie, W.G. Bannochie, W. Ross, J. Bannochie, G.H. Anderson, J. Bonar, B. Brown

Aberdeen 4, Club of the Towns 2
Royal Infirmary Benefit, Recreation
Grounds, Inches, 12th March 1887

Aberdeen turned out in amber and black shirts while the select side played in white. This appears to have been Aberdeen's regular colours over the course of the season. Despite the game starting in a snowstorm there was a good turnout of spectators. Fyfe put the Select ahead in the first half. John MacKay missed a chance to make it 2-0 before Munro grabbed an equaliser for Aberdeen. Mitchell then missed an open goal as the Select tried to regain the lead but the Orion man made amends soon after but shooting home *"a splendid goal."* Soon after the second half got under way Clark got Aberdeen back on level terms for the second time. Clark thought he had scored again but the goal was chalked off because of offside. The Aberdeen forward was having a great game, however, and he soon gave his side the lead. Shortly before the end a scrimmage gave Aberdeen a decisive fourth goal.

Aberdeen - D. Wood, A.V. Lothian, W. A. Key; H.T. Hinten, C. E. Glennie, I. Preston; W.J.T. Munro, J. Cunningham, T. Ketchen, A. Clark, C. Hazlewood.

Clubs of Town - J. McPherson (Rangers), G. Fettis (Orion), A. Aitchison (Rangers); W. Tawse (Rovers), J. Campbell (Gladstone),F. Reid (Gladstone); W. Fyfe (Orion), J. Mackay (Orion, captain), C. Christie (Orion), W. Lawson (Rovers), A. Mitchell (Orion)

Aberdeen F.C - 1886-1887

Competition	Date		Opposition	F	A	Venue
Scottish Cup		Aberdeen	East End, Dundee			
Friendly	04/09/1886	Aberdeen	Strathmore, Arbroath	3	8	Damley Park,Arbroath
Friendly	02/10/1886	Aberdeen	Grammar School	3	3	Grammar School
Friendly	09/10/1886	Aberdeen	Montrose	2	0	Holburn Grounds
Friendly	16/10/1886	Aberdeen	Reform	6	2	Holburn Grounds
Friendly	23/10/1886	Aberdeen	St Laurence	6	0	Episcopal Manse Glebe,Laurencekirk
Friendly	13/11/1886	Aberdeen	Gladstone	2	1	Holburn Grounds
Friendly	27/11/1886	Aberdeen	Ellon Gordon	11	0	
Friendly	11/12/1886	Aberdeen	Rangers, Aberdeen	6	0	Holburn
Friendly	18/12/1886	Aberdeen	Clubs of Town	1	2	Recreation Grounds
Friendly	08/01/1887	Aberdeen	University	8	0	Holburn
Friendly	15/01/1887	Aberdeen	Orion	5	1	Holburn
Friendly	22/01/1887	Aberdeen	Montrose	1	10	Links Park, Montrose
Friendly	12/02/1887	Aberdeen	Caledonian	4	1	Holburn
Friendly	26/02/1887	Aberdeen	Granite City	6	0	Holburn
Friendly	05/03/1887	Aberdeen	Laurencekirk	4	1	Holburn
Friendly	12/03/1887	Aberdeen	Clubs of Town	4	2	Recreation Grounds
Friendly	19/03/1887	Aberdeen	Orion	4	2	Recreation Grounds
Friendly	02/04/1887	Aberdeen	Clubs of Town	2	0	Recreation Grounds

Note: Aberdeen failed to turn up for the Scottish Cup tie with East End

Orion F.C. - 1886-1887

Competition	1886-1887		Opposition	F	A	Venue
Scottish Cup 1R	11/09/1886	Orion	Arbroath	0	20	Gayfield Park, Arbroath
Friendly	25/09/1886	Orion	Rangers, Aberdeen	5	2	Links
Friendly	02/10/1886	Orion	Gladstone	1	0	Links
Friendly	09/10/1886	Orion	Rovers	2	0	Recreation Grounds

Competition	1886-1887		Opposition	F	A	Venue
Friendly	16/10/1886	Orion	Gladstone	3	0	Recreation Grounds
Friendly	23/10/1886	Orion	Rangers, Aberdeen	1	0	Recreation Grounds
Friendly	30/10/1886	Orion	St Laurence	1	5	Laurencekirk
Friendly	27/11/1886	Orion	Caledonian	4	4	
Friendly	04/12/1886	Orion	St Laurence	2	4	Links
Friendly	11/12/1886	Orion	Rovers			Recreation Grounds
Friendly	08/01/1887	Orion	Rangers, Aberdeen	3	0	Recreation Grounds
Friendly	15/01/1887	Orion	Aberdeen	1	5	Holburn
Friendly	29/01/1887	Orion	Gladstone	5	3	Recreation Grounds
Friendly	12/02/1887	Orion	Granite City	5	2	Recreation Grounds
Friendly	26/02/1887	Orion	Gladstone	2	1	
Friendly	05/03/1887	Orion	Caledonian	4	2	Recreation Grounds
Friendly	19/03/1887	Orion	Aberdeen	2	4	Recreation Grounds
Friendly	26/03/1887	Orion	Granite City	2	1	Recreation Grounds
Friendly	09/04/1887	Orion	Arbroath	3	9	Recreation Grounds
Friendly	23/04/1887	Orion	Strathmore (Arbroath)	1	3	Recreation Grounds
Friendly	30/04/1887	Orion	Stonehaven	5	0	Urie

Note: The Orion – Rovers game on 11th December 1887 was drawn, but the score isn't known.

Some of the many games played by city clubs - 1886-1887

Competition	Date			F	A	Venue
Friendly	04/09/1886	Strathmore, Arbroath	Aberdeen	8	3	Damley Park
Scottish Cup	11/09/1886	Aberdeen	East End, Dundee			Dundee
Scottish Cup 1R	11/09/1886	Arbroath	Orion	20	0	Gayfield
Friendly	11/09/1886	Rovers	Bon Accord			Links
Friendly	11/09/1886	Rangers, Aberdeen	Gladstone	1	0	
Friendly	18/09/1886	Gladstone	Rovers	2	0	Links
Friendly	25/09/1886	Orion	Aberdeen Rangers	5	2	Links

Competition	Date		Opposition	F	A	Venue
Friendly	02/10/1886	Orion	Gladstone	1	0	Links
Friendly	02/10/1886	2nd Rovers	Bon Accord	8	0	Links
Friendly	02/10/1886	Rovers	Reform	4	0	Recreation Grounds
Friendly	02/10/1886	Aberdeen	Grammar School	3	3	Grammar School
Friendly	09/10/1886	Aberdeen	Montrose	2	0	Holburn Grounds
Friendly	09/10/1886	Rovers	Orion	0	2	Recreation Grounds
Friendly	09/10/1886	Rangers, Aberdeen	Grammar School	5	0	Grammar School
Friendly	16/10/1886	Aberdeen	Reform	6	2	Holburn Grounds
Friendly	16/10/1886	Orion	Gladstone	3	0	Recreation Grounds
Friendly	16/10/1886	Granite City	2nd City Rangers	0	0	Aulton Links
Friendly	16/10/1886	Woodside	St Ronald's	0	14	Woodside
Friendly	23/10/1886	St Laurence	Aberdeen	0	6	Ecclesiastical Glebe, Laurencekirk
Friendly	23/10/1886	Caledonian	2nd Aberdeen	2	3	Holburn Grounds
Friendly	23/10/1886	Orion	Rangers, Aberdeen	1	0	Recreation Grounds
Friendly	23/10/1886	2nd Rangers	Albert	2	1	Links
Friendly	23/10/1886	Gladstone	Reform	2	0	Links
Friendly	23/10/1886	Granite City	2nd Rovers	2	2	Links
Friendly	23/10/1886	2nd Orion	Gladstone	2	1	Links
Friendly	30/10/1886	Granite City	Our Boys	3	0	Links
Friendly	30/10/1886	St Laurence	Orion	5	1	Laurencekirk
Friendly	13/11/1886	Our Boys	Emerald	4	0	
Friendly	13/11/1886	Aberdeen	Gladstone	2	1	Holburn
Friendly	13/11/1886	Caledonian	Britannia	5	0	Links
Friendly	13/11/1886	Granite City	Bon Accord	1	1	Links
Friendly	20/11/1886	Rovers	Rangers, Aberdeen	3	2	
Friendly	20/11/1886	Caledonian	Granite City	4	0	Links
Friendly	20/11/1886	Stonehaven	2nd Gladstone	1	2	Urie

Competition	Date			F	A	Venue
Friendly	20/11/1886	Gladstone	Bon Accord	3	1	Links
Friendly	27/11/1886	Aberdeen	Ellon Gordon	11	0	
Friendly	27/11/1886	Aberdeen 2nd	Granite City	2	0	Hammerfield
Friendly	27/11/1886	Albert	2nd Orion	3	2	Links
Friendly	27/11/1886	Our Boys	Rosebery	2	1	Links
Friendly	27/11/1886	Bon Accord	Emerald	4	0	Links
Friendly	27/11/1886	Rangers, Aberdeen	Gladstone	1	0	Links
Friendly	27/11/1886	Orion	Caledonian	4	4	
Friendly	04/12/1886	Orion	St Laurence	2	4	Links
Friendly	04/12/1886	Albert	Rosebery	2	1	Links
Friendly	04/12/1886	Rangers, Aberdeen	Granite City	0	0	Links
Friendly	04/12/1886	Caledonian	Rovers	2	2	Links
Friendly	11/12/1886	Aberdeen	Rangers (Aberdeen)	6	0	Holburn
Friendly	11/12/1886	Rovers	Orion			Recreation Grounds
Friendly	18/12/1886	Aberdeen	Clubs of Town	1	2	Recreation Grounds
Friendly	18/12/1886	Caledonian	2nd Aberdeen	4	2	
Friendly	25/12/1886	St Mirren, Aberdeen	Emerald	0	0	Links
Friendly	25/12/1886	Our Boys	Rosebery	1	1	Links
Friendly	01/01/1887	Gladstone	St Laurence	3	2	Recreation Grounds
Friendly	08/01/1887	Caledonian	Balmoral	7	0	Links
Friendly	08/01/1887	Orion	Rangers, Aberdeen	3	0	Recreation Grounds
Friendly	08/01/1887	University	Aberdeen	0	8	Holburn
Friendly	08/01/1887	Aberdeen Athletic	Our Boys	2	1	Links
Friendly	15/01/1887	Orion	Aberdeen	1	5	Holburn
Friendly	15/01/1887	Caledonian	Gladstone	0	0	Links
Friendly	15/01/1887	Britannia	Rovers	2	2	Aulton Links
Friendly	15/01/1887	Our Boys	Emerald	4	1	Links

Competition	Date		Opposition	F	A	Venue
Friendly	15/01/1887	Granite City	Albert	2	0	Links
Friendly	15/01/1887	St Mirren, Aberdeen	2nd Caledonian	1	0	Links
Friendly	15/01/1887	Rangers, Aberdeen	Rosebery	7	0	Links
Friendly	15/01/1887	Balmoral	Aberdeen Athletics			Links
Friendly	29/01/1887	Orion	Gladstone	5	3	Recreation Grounds
Friendly	29/01/1887	Our Boys	St Mirren, Aberdeen	4	1	Links
Friendly	29/01/1887	2nd Orion	Britannia	0	0	Aulton Links
Friendly	29/01/1887	Granite City	Aberdeen Athletics	3	1	Links
Friendly	29/01/1887	Rosebery	Albert	2	1	Links
Friendly	29/01/1887	Caledonian	Rangers, Aberdeen	1	0	Links
Friendly	05/02/1887	Swifts	Britannia	2	0	Aulton Links
Friendly	05/02/1887	2nd Orion	Albert	0	0	Recreation Grounds
Friendly	05/02/1887	Stonehaven	Grammar School	2	2	Urie
Friendly	05/02/1887	Caledonian	Rovers	1	0	Links
Friendly	05/02/1887	Our Boys	Bon Accord	3	0	Links
Friendly	05/02/1887	Emerald	2nd Rosebery	1	0	Links
Friendly	05/02/1887	Rangers, Aberdeen	Granite City	2	1	Links
Friendly	05/02/1887	Faithlie, Fraserburgh	Gladstone	1	0	Fraserburgh
Friendly	12/02/1887	Aberdeen	Caledonian	4	1	Holburn
Friendly	12/02/1887	Orion	Granite City	5	2	Recreation Grounds
Friendly	12/02/1887	Our Boys	2nd Rovers	1	0	Links
Friendly	12/02/1887	Albert	Emerald	4	0	Links
Friendly	12/02/1887	Gladstone	Britannia			Aulton Links
Friendly	12/02/1887	2nd Gladstone	Swifts	2	1	Links
Friendly	19/02/1887	Caledonian	Gladstone	8	2	Recreation Grounds

Competition	Date		Opposition	F	A	Venue
Friendly	19/02/1887	Rangers, Aberdeen	Rovers	4	0	Links
Friendly	19/02/1887	Bon Accord	St Mirren, Aberdeen	2	0	Links
Friendly	19/02/1887	Albert	Balmoral	8	0	Links
Friendly	19/02/1887	Emerald	Herald			Links
Friendly	26/02/1887	Orion	Gladstone	2	1	
Friendly	26/02/1887	Aberdeen	Granite City	6	0	Holburn
Friendly	26/02/1887	Albert	Caledonian	5	2	Links
Friendly	26/02/1887	Rosebery	Emerald	2	0	Links
Friendly	26/02/1887	Our Boys	Aberdeen Athletics	2	0	Links
Friendly	05/03/1887	Aberdeen	Laurencekirk	4	1	Holburn
Friendly	05/03/1887	Orion	Caledonian	4	2	Recreation Grounds
Friendly	05/03/1887	Rosebery	St Mirren	2	0	
Friendly	05/03/1887	Rangers, Aberdeen	Albert	6	0	
Friendly	05/03/1887	Gladstone	Aberdeen Athletics	4	1	Links
Friendly	05/03/1887	Britannia	2nd Rovers	2	0	Aulton Links
Friendly	12/03/1887	Aberdeen	Clubs of Town	4	2	Aberdeen
Friendly	19/03/1887	Aberdeen	Orion	4	2	Recreation Grounds
Friendly	19/03/1887	Rosebery	Aberdeen Athletics	2	2	
Friendly	19/03/1887	Our Boys	St Mirren, Aberdeen	3	0	
Friendly	19/03/1887	Granite City	Britannia	3	0	
Friendly	26/03/1887	Our Boys	Rosebery	2	1	
Friendly	26/03/1887	Emerald	Herald	1	0	
Friendly	26/03/1887	Gladstone	Britannia	3	0	Aulton Links
Friendly	26/03/1887	Albert	Bon Accord	5	0	Links
Friendly	26/03/1887	Orion	Granite City	2	1	Recreation Grounds
Friendly	02/04/1887	Aberdeen	Clubs of Town	2	0	Recreation Grounds

Competition	Date	Opposition		F	A	Venue
Friendly	02/04/1887	2nd Rosebery	Bon Accord	3	1	
Friendly	09/04/1887	Orion	Arbroath	3	9	Recreation Grounds
Friendly	16/04/1887	Granite City	Rosebery	3	2	Links
Friendly	16/04/1887	St Mirren, Aberdeen	Bon Accord	2	0	Links
Friendly	23/04/1887	Orion	Strathmore, Arbroath	1	3	Recreation Grounds
Friendly	23/04/1887	Aberdeen Athletics	Roseberry	2	2	Links
Friendly	23/04/1887	Albert	St Mirren, Aberdeen	3	0	Links
Friendly	23/04/1887	Bon Accord	Playfair	1	1	Links
Friendly	23/04/1887	Granite City	Rovers	2	1	Links
Friendly	30/04/1887	Stonehaven	Orion	0	5	Urie
Friendly	30/04/1887	Granite City	Hibernians			
Friendly	30/04/1887	St Mirren, Aberdeen	Playfair	6	0	Links
Friendly	30/04/1887	2nd St Mirren, Aberdeen	Balmoral	1	0	Links
Friendly	14/05/1887	St Mirren, Aberdeen	Bon Accord	1	0	Links
Friendly	14/05/1887	Playfair	Strathmore	3	0	Links

Notes: 11/9/1886 Rovers v Bon Accord. Rovers won but the score is not known.
11/9/1886 Aberdeen failed to turn up for the Scottish Cup tie with East End.
15/1/1887 Balmoral v Aberdeen Athletics was a draw (score not known)
12/2/1887 Gladstone beat Britannia (score not known)
19/2/1887 Emerald v Herald was a draw (score not known)
30/4/1887 Granite City beat Hibernians (score not known)`

1887-1888
Scotland at the Chanonry

The Orion and Aberdeen clubs both secured the use of new grounds during the season and a new competition, the Aberdeenshire Cup, was introduced as the sport continued to develop. The lack of any structure to the football season in previous years led to the leading clubs forming the Aberdeenshire Football Association which initially had 15 members. John McHardy, who had been instrumental in forming Aberdeen F.C. in 1881, was again at the forefront of the new organisation and he was elected as President. The full list of office bearers was as follows:- President: Mr J. McHardy (Aberdeen); Vice President: Mr G. Fettes (Orion); Secretary: William Jaffray, 20 Jasmine Terrace (Caledonian); Treasurer: Mr. R. Gillies (Aberdeen Athletics); Committee: Messrs Paterson, Styles, Collie, Bain, Fairweather, Aitken.

The member clubs were (with club secretaries, where known) are shown in the accompanying table.

Aberdeenshire Football Association Member Clubs and Secretaries 1887-1888

CLUB	SECRETARY
Aberdeen	C. Glennie, 11 Richmond Terrace
Orion	James Dunn, 69 Causewayend
Caledonian	William Jaffrey, 20 Jasmine Terrace
Aberdeen Athletics	James Gillies, 4 Lemon Street
Rovers	James Collie, 11 Rosebank Place
Black Diamond	Alexander Paterson, 41 Regent Quay
Our Boys	P. MacKenzie, 20 Jack's Brae
Albert	William Guyan, 36 St Clement's Street
Rosebery	Robert Aitken, 56 Skene Square
Britannia	James Phillips, 47 Canal Road
Granite City	Charles Styles, 111 Gallowgate
City Wanderers	George Potter, 31 Mealmarket Street
Bon Accord	George Hughes,3 Cottage Brae,Nellfield Place
Balmoral	Not known
Rangers	Not known

The Association was soon able to announce that its Honorary President, Dr. F. Maitland-Moir, had presented a Cup to be played for by member clubs. This was a major step forward as the Aberdeenshire Cup would provide a real focus for local clubs and would stimulate greater interest in the game. The first round of the new competition was not, however, scheduled until December 1887 leaving the early months of the season open for Scottish Cup ties and friendlies.

Aberdeen, Orion and Rovers were the only local clubs to join the S.F.A. that year and so all three again took part in the Scottish Cup - and all three fell at the first hurdle. Aberdeen entertained Dundee's Our Boys, and before the match, the Courier warned that *"the West Craigie lads intend to treat the Aberdonians to a hot hour and a half's leather hunting."* And so it proved. The occasion marked the opening of Orion's new ground at Kittybrewster – Central Park - which Aberdeen had leased for the occasion. Aberdeen blasted home four goals but it was to no avail as the visitors hit nine to send the home side out of the competition.

Orion's Scottish Cup adventure ended with another heavy double-digit defeat. They travelled to Gayfield for the second year in a row hoping to improve on the 20-0 humiliation of their previous visit. Unfortunately their improvement was only marginal, the Red Lichties restricting themselves to an 18-0 victory on this occasion. One newspaper report claimed, nevertheless, that the Orion goalkeeper was one of their best players and he was *"repeatedly cheered for clever saving."* Goodness knows what might have happened had he not done so well! Rovers nervously ventured to Dundee to face Wanderers and received a 10-0 beating which would certainly have been significantly worse had the home side not decided to have a bit of fun with their visitors rather than try to run up a massive score. It was better, however, than the 35-0 loss suffered at the hands of Harp two years earlier. The Courier's report of the game made entertaining reading: *"The Rovers are evidently new to the game, and it was somewhat amusing to see the awkward shapes they made in attempting to tackle and kick. The Wanderers played to the west goal in the first period, and piled on seven goals in a leisurely manner, and in the second half they had a little fun in running the ball up to the Rovers' charge and shooting wild; indeed the Wanderers' fronts were sometimes seen vigorously defending the Rovers' fortress, and but for this there would have been a host of goals against the strangers. The Wanderers were content with three other goals, which were unavoidable, and the most complete farce that was ever performed in Morgan Park closed in favour of the Wanderers by 10 goals to 0. The Rovers were a very quiet set of fellows on the field, and seemed anxious to learn the 'fly tips' of the game."* Obviously, the Aberdeen clubs still had a lot to learn.

Orion moved into their new ground the week after Aberdeen christened it by losing to Our Boys in the Scottish Cup. The Orionites at least had the satisfaction of getting off to a winning start on their new patch, comfortably defeating the local Rangers 3-1. That was followed by a 5-1 win over Granite City and a 5-0 humbling of Black Diamond before Orion, playing in amber jerseys, suffered their first Kittybrewster defeat, going under by 4-2 to Arbroath Nomads.

The inaugural Aberdeenshire Cup got under way on 3rd December 1887 and it didn't lack incident or drama. The First Round match between Caledonian and Black Diamond at the Links ended in a 4-4 draw, but the Diamonds were awarded the tie when their opponents failed to show up for the replay a week later. The Diamonds were involved in another controversial incident in the Second Round against Rovers when, with 11 minutes remaining, the referee left the field after an argument with the Rovers umpire and the game was abandoned. Rovers were leading 4-0 at the time but the game had to be replayed and on this occasion they narrowly defeated the Diamonds 3-2. Aberdeen's win over Our Boys in the semi final was the first game played at the Chanonry grounds in Old Aberdeen. Aberdeen would, in 1888, reach agreement to lease these grounds as their permanent home. Rangers thrashed Rovers 4-1 in the other semi final. The first Final was also played at the Chanonry and an estimated crowd of 1,000 turned up, despite persistent heavy rain, to see Aberdeen race to a crushing 7-1 victory with Tom Ketchen grabbing four of the goals. The following week the cup winners returned to the Chanonry to face a select side drawn from the other member clubs of the Aberdeenshire F.A in a charity match in aid of the Royal Infirmary. Three members of the defeated Rangers side were included in the select team which won 5-3 in front of a crowd considered as being much larger than for the Cup Final.

The season finished with a match which captured the imagination of the local public when an Aberdeen select took on a Scotland select at the Chanonry. The

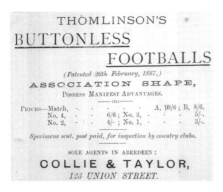

THÓMLINSON'S

BUTTONLESS
FOOTBALLS

(Patented 26th February, 1887,)

ASSOCIATION SHAPE,

POSSESS MANIFEST ADVANTAGES.

——:o:——

PRICES—Match, · · · · A, 10/6 ; B, 8/6.
No. 4, · · 6/6 ; No. 3, · · 5/-.
No. 2, · · 4/- ; No. 1, · · 3/-.

Specimens sent, post paid, for inspection by country clubs.

SOLE AGENTS IN ABERDEEN :

COLLIE & TAYLOR,
123 UNION STREET.

idea for such a game had been hatched during Dumbarton's New Year visit to the Granite City. Dumbarton, Scottish Cup finalists the previous season, crushed Aberdeen's finest by 12-3 and at a meeting held at the Cafe in Shiprow on the evening after the game, the visiting club's official, Alex Kennedy, who also happened to be President of the Scottish Football Association, promised local representatives that he would do everything in his power to bring the national side to the city to play an exhibition match before the end of the season. Plans were subsequently put in place, a financial deal was thrashed out, and the game was confirmed. Trials were held to select the best eleven men from the city's clubs and when the local side was named it included seven representatives from Aberdeen F.C, two from Orion, and one each from Black Diamond and Rangers. A decision was taken to play the game at the new Chanonry field where Aberdeen had taken out a lease to play their home matches.

On the big day Old Aberdeen became the focus of interest for everyone in the city as thousands flocked to the novel event. The Bon Accord newspaper described the bustling scene: *"The peaceful streets presented an unusually animated appearance... the incessant rattle of numerous cabs and 'busses, and the steady and continuous tramp of the foot passengers, which aroused the inhabitants from their accustomed lethargy, evidently portended the occurrence of something extraordinary."*

A crowd estimated as being anywhere between 3,000 and 4,000 crushed into the confines of the Chanonry ground where a wooden fence had been built around the pitch. The Scotland team, although not at full strength, totally outclassed the home side. The style of play of the experienced internationals caused great excitement among the watching fans. One of the top men in the Scotland side, Walter Arnott of Queen's Park, who was also an outstanding bowler, tennis player and yachtsman, impressed the Aberdeen Journal's scribe at the match, who wrote: *"Arnott's kicks, especially his screws, were of a fine description."* The Bon

Accord newspaper reporter was equally enthused by the quality of the visiting side. He wrote: *"'The visitors gave a beautiful exposition of scientific football… ..nothing finer has been seen in Aberdeen than the graceful dribbling of Berry and Higgins, the short and accurate passing of the whole line of forwards and the good all-round display of half and back play."* Despite the gulf in class and experience between the two sides, the Aberdeen select battled gamely, and at the close of play the hosts had been beaten by what was deemed to be a reasonably respectable scoreline of 6-1.Tom Ketchen, who was making a name for himself as a prolific scorer, had the honour of grabbing Aberdeen's goal in the first half to reduce the leeway to 2-1. He was probably the top local player of the season, having also scored four of his club's seven goals in the previous month's Aberdeenshire Cup Final victory. Afterwards, the players and officials of both sides were treated to dinner in the Queen's Restaurant and a promise was made to bring the international side back for a future exhibition game.

In May the Aberdeenshire F.A. organised a five-a-side tournament at the Chanonry, in aid of the Sick Children's Hospital. This was the first time such a competition had been held in the city and it attracted *"a large turnout of spectators."* Orion defeated Black Diamond in the final. That was followed a few weeks later by the Aberdeen F.C. sports day, also at the Chanonry, in which players from local sides tested themselves in a series of track events. There was also another five-a-side football competition, which Aberdeen won by defeating Orion in the final. The Aberdeenshire F.A. held its first annual meeting at which a profit of £22 14s 11d was announced. The following office bearers were elected for the next season: President: Mr J. McHardy (Aberdeen); Vice President: Mr John Mackay; Secretary: William Jaffray, 20 Jasmine Terrace (Caledonian); Treasurer: Mr. James Phillips.

At the end of 1887-1888 it was reported in the Aberdeen Journal that Aberdeen FC had played 25 games, the only defeats being to 'foreign' clubs, i.e. Dumbarton (12-3), Our Boys, Dundee (9-4), Montrose (6-0) and Nairn (4-1) although in the last mentioned game only four first team regulars were available. They also lost 5-3 to a combined city select. It was also reported that Aberdeen were negotiating for the Chanonry to become their permanent home ground.

Aberdeen's captain from 1882-1888, A.V. Lothian, announced his retirement from the game although he would subsequently make occasional appearances to help the club out when players were injured. Lothian, a schoolteacher, was a founder member of the club after moving to the north east from his native Wishaw. He played in the club's opening game against Coupar Angus and although he was a regular full-back he occasionally took over the goalkeeping duties in an emergency. In 1891 Lothian moved back to the Central Belt to take up a post as Lecturer on Mathematics and Physics at the Glasgow Church of Scotland Training College.

A.V. Lothian, Aberdeen F.C.

Notable Games

Aberdeen 4, Our Boys, Dundee 9
Scottish Cup, Central Park, 3rd September 1887

This was the first game played at Orion's Central Park which Aberdeen hired for the occasion. Clark gave the home side a perfect start by netting inside the opening two minutes while Tom Ketchen made it 2-0 shortly afterwards. But the Dundee side stormed back into the game and rapidly turned things around with four goals in the final 15 minutes of the first half. Aberdeen pulled one back shortly after the interval. Our Boys then responded with another three goals before the home side scored again. The scoring was completed with two more for the visitors who ended up winning 9-4. The style of reporting of this game was very different from what we are familiar with today, one of the goals being described as follows: *"The seventh goal for Dundee, which was disputed and settled by an appeal to the referee, was scored at five minutes past four."*

Aberdeen - D. Wood; A. V. Lothian (captain), W. A. Key; C.E. Glennie, J. A. McHardy, J. Preston; A. Kelly, A.D. McYonnie, T. Ketchen, J. Ferry, A. Clark.

Our Boys – Douglas, Leighton, Saunders, Gillan, McIntosh, Findlay, Chalmers, Kidd, Hall, Pearson, Moore

Orion 3, Rangers, Aberdeen 1
Friendly, Kittybrewster Park, 10th September 1887

This was Orion's first game at their new home and they ran out comfortable winners. Dunn opened the scoring for the home side and a second followed from a header following a scrimmage in the home goal area. Orion claimed a third immediately after when the goalkeeper caught the ball but was standing behind the line, to give the hosts a 3-0 half-time advantage. Dunn and Mitchell gave the visiting defence a hard time but couldn't make any further breakthrough. Indeed it was Rangers who got the only goal of the second period but they never looked like clawing their way back into the game.

Orion - J. Diack; George Fettes (Captain), J.J. Jarvis; A. Milne, J. Gordon, W. Anderson; W. Fyfe, G. Christie, A. Morrison, J. Dunn, A. Mitchell.

Rangers, Aberdeen - J. L. McPherson; A. Aitchison (Captain), A. Paterson; F. Ross, A. Kelly, J. Fairweather; G. Anderson, A. Bowman, W. Downie, T. Irvine, C. Sutherland

Aberdeen 3, Dumbarton 12
Chanonry, 4th January 1888

Dumbarton, beaten finalists in the previous season's Scottish Cup, fielded two Scotland internationals, Leitch Keir and Ralph Aitken. Bell and Aiken scored twice for the visitors inside the opening 20 minutes and a third followed soon afterwards. An own goal gave Aberdeen some hope but full-back Barr made it 4-1 before halftime. Dumbarton quickly raced into a 7-1 lead before Lumsden got Aberdeen's second and Clark grabbed a third much to the delight of the home fans.The Sons of the Rock responded by adding another five to secure a comprehensive victory.

Aberdeen – D. Wood, Thomson, Key, Emslie, Preston, Hinton, Clark, Ferry, T.Ritchie, A. Lumsden, W. Mackenzie

Dumbarton – Taylor, Stewart, Barr, Keir, George Dewar, Tom McMillan, Lapsley, Low, Bell, R. Aitken, Liddel

Aberdeen 10, Our Boys, Aberdeen 2
Aberdeenshire Cup Semi Final, Chanonry, 25th February 1888

This was the first game played by Aberdeen at the Chanonry Grounds and conditions were poor with about two inches of snow covering the ground. Tom Ketchen opened the scoring for Aberdeen, the first goal scored on the new pitch, and Haslewood soon made it 2-0. Ketchen then added a third. The striped shirted Our Boys fought back, however, and grabbed a goal before Haslewood restored Aberdeen's three goal advantage. T. Wood got a second for the Boys before the interval, his shot striking the bar before crossing the line to make it 4-2 for the Whites at the interval. An own goal by Still three minutes after the break made it 5-2 and from then on Aberdeen dominated, adding a further five goals before the end. Despite the heavy defeat, MacDonald in the Our Boys goal,was praised for making some *"clever saves."*

Aberdeen 7, Rangers, Aberdeen 1
Aberdeenshire Cup Final, Chanonry, 24th March 1888

This was the first Aberdeenshire Cup Final. Rangers entered the field *"gracing the occasion by a fine display of new jerseys"* (black and gold in colour) and the match duly kicked off at 3-30pm. Aberdeen made a fine start and Tom Ketchen opened the scoring after just five minutes. The Whites' superiority was underlined when Ketchen soon made it 2-0. Rangers fought back and the spectators became increasingly animated as one report described: *"The contest was carried on amidst the alternate shouts, hootings and jeerings of the crowd, the Rangers evidently having a large number of sympathisers among the more youthful of the spectators."* Aberdeen weathered a brief Rangers storm before Ketchen almost grabbed a third, his shot rebounding from the crossbar. The goal was delayed only for a few moments, however, as Aberdeen's Thomson, going by the splendid nickname of 'Dodger' scored a fine solo effort. Ketchen then completed his hat-trick to give the Whites a 4-0 interval lead. Ketchen added to his tally early in the second half then Dodger added a sixth before Sutherland pulled one back for the Rangers, a goal *"greeted with quite an excess of enthusiasm."* Lumsden then completed the scoring to give Aberdeen an emphatic 7-1 victory. Afterwards Rangers lodged a protest on the grounds that the goal posts were six inches too high and that this in some way affected the outcome. Their appeal was subsequently dismissed.

Aberdeen: Wood, Key, Lothian, Hinton, Thomson, Glennie, Haslewood, Lumsden, Ketchen, Ferry, Clark.
Rangers: MacPherson, Aitchison, Sievewright, Fairweather, Sutherland, Ross, Anderson, Downie, Bowman, McKay, Irvine.
Referee: Mr Fettes (Orion).
Umpires: Messrs Melville and Collie

Aberdeen 3, Combined Team 5
Charity Match, Chanonry, 31st March 1888

Irvine opened the scoring for the Select after 30 minutes and this was followed by another two from MacKay and Cannon before Ketchen pulled one back five minutes before half-time. Aberdeen applied pressure at the start of the second period and Ketchen scored again on the hour mark. The Whites went all out for an equaliser but the Select hit the net twice more before Haslewood's late consolation for Aberdeen.

Aberdeen: Wood, Key, Lothian, Milne (Orion), Thomson, Glennie, Haslewood, Lumsden, Ketchen, Ferry, Clark.
Combined Team: Diack (Orion), Campbell (Granite City), Jarvis (Orion), Fairweather (Rangers), Campbell (Rovers), Gordon (Orion),Fyfe (Orion), Christie (Orion), Cannon (Black Diamond), Mackay (Rangers), Irvine (Rangers)

Aberdeen Select 1, Scotland X1 6
Chanonry, 21st April 1888

Football in Aberdeen was given a huge boost by the visit of an international select and the game attracted *"the largest crowd which had ever been seen at any similar sporting event in the city."* Estimates of the attendance ranged from 3,000 to 4,000. Although the homesters were outclassed they were by no means disgraced and forward Tom Ketchen showed he could compete well against some of the country's top players. Kilmarnock's John McPherson, later to become a director of Glasgow Rangers, scored two of the Scotland goals, the others coming from Robertson 2, Higgins and Berry.

Aberdeen Select – Diack (Orion), Key (Aberdeen), Lothian (Aberdeen), Milne (Orion), Thomson (Aberdeen), Glennie (Aberdeen), Haslewood (Aberdeen) Cannon (Black Diamond), Ketchen (Aberdeen), Irvine (Rangers), Clark (Aberdeen).

Scotland – Lindsay (Renton), Arnott (Queen's Park), Smellie (Queen's Park), Stewart (Queen's Park), Dewar (Dumbarton), Robertson (Cowlairs), Hamilton (Queen's Park), Berry (Queen's Park) Higgins (Kilmarnock), McPherson (Kilmarnock), Munroe (Abercorn)

Aberdeen F.C - 1887-1888

Competition	Date		Opposition	F	A	Venue
Scottish Cup 1R	03/09/1887	Aberdeen	Our Boys, Dundee	4	9	Central Park
	17/09/1887	Aberdeen	Stonehaven	9	0	Urie Park, Stonehaven
	01/10/1887	Aberdeen	Grammar School	5	1	Holburn
	05/10/1887	Aberdeen	Nairn	1	4	Nairn Links
	08/10/1887	Aberdeen	Aberdeen Athletics	9	1	Holburn
	15/10/1887	Aberdeen	Black Diamond	3	1	Holburn
	22/10/1887	Aberdeen	Rovers	6	3	Holburn
	29/10/1887	Aberdeen	Britannia	10	0	Holburn
	05/11/1887	Aberdeen	Rangers, Aberdeen	5	1	Holburn
	19/11/1887	Aberdeen	Orion	3	3	Central Park
	26/11/1887	Aberdeen	Granite City	5	0	Holburn
Aberdeenshire Cup 1R	03/12/1887	Aberdeen	Albert	11	0	Holburn
	10/12/1887	Aberdeen	Our Boys,Aberdeen	5	0	Holburn
	02/01/1888	Aberdeen	Nairn County	4	1	Holburn
	04/01/1888	Aberdeen	Dumbarton	3	12	Holburn
	07/01/1888	Aberdeen	Orion	2	1	Holburn
	14/01/1888	Aberdeen	Caledonian	5	1	Holburn
	21/01/1888	Aberdeen	Rovers	5	0	Holburn
Aberdeenshire Cup 2R	28/01/1888	Aberdeen	Orion	6	1	Holburn
	11/02/1888	Aberdeen	Rangers,Aberdeen	2	1	Holburn
Aberdeenshire Cup Semi Final	25/02/1888	Aberdeen	Our Boys, Aberdeen	10	2	Chanonry
	03/03/1888	Aberdeen	Montrose	0	6	Links Park, Montrose
Aberdeenshire Cup Final	24/03/1888	Aberdeen	Rangers, Aberdeen	7	1	Chanonry

Competition	Date		Opposition	F	A	Venue
Charity Match	31/03/1888	Aberdeen	Combined Team	3	5	Chanonry
	28/04/1888	Aberdeen	Rangers,Aberdeen	4	1	Chanonry

Orion F.C - 1887-1888

Competition	Date		Opposition	F	A	Venue
Scottish Cup 1R	03/09/1887	Orion	Arbroath	0	18	Gayfield, Arbroath
	10/09/1887	Orion	Rangers,Aberdeen	3	1	Central Park
	17/09/1887	Orion	Granite City	5	1	Central Park
	24/09/1887	Orion	Black Diamond	5	0	Central Park
	01/10/1887	Orion	Arbroath Nomads	1	4	Central Park
	08/10/1887	Orion	Black Diamond	6	1	Central Park
	15/10/1887	Orion	Caledonian	16	1	Central Park
	29/10/1887	Orion	Our Boys, Aberdeen	3	3	Central Park
	12/11/1887	Orion	Britannia	14	0	Central Park
	19/11/1887	Orion	Aberdeen	3	3	Central Park
	02/01/1888	Orion	Glasgow Thistle	1	3	Central Park
	07/01/1888	Orion	Aberdeen	1	2	Holburn
Aberdeenshire Cup 2R	28.01.1888	Orion	Aberdeen	1	6	Holburn
	04/02/1888	Orion	Our Boys,Aberdeen	7	0	Central Park
Competition	**Date**		**Opposition**	**F**	**A**	**Venue**
	11/02/1888	Orion	Caledonian	9	0	Central Park
	25/02/1888	Orion	Albert	10	2	Central Park
Benefit for Orion	07/04/1888	Orion	Rangers, Aberdeen	3	2	Central Park
	28/04/1898	Orion	Thistle,Stonehaven	3	1	Urie
	12/05/1888	Orion	Port Elphinstone	6	0	Pt Elphinstone

Aberdeenshire Cup 1887-1888

Competition	Date		Opposition	F	A	Venue
First round	03/12/1887	Aberdeen	Albert	11	0	Holburn
First round	03/12/1887	Balmoral	Our Boys	0	9	Duthie Park
First round	03/12/1887	Granite City	Rangers, Aberdeen	2	3	Central Park
First round	03/12/1887	Caledonian	Black Diamond	4	4	Links

Competition	Date		Opposition	F	A	Venue
First round	03/12/1887	Port Elphinstone	Rovers	1	10	Port Elphinstone
First round	10/12/1887	Black Diamond	Caledonian	w	o	
Second round	28/01/1888	Aberdeen	Orion	6	1	Holburn
Second round	28/01/1888	Rovers	Black Diamond	4	1	Links
Second round	28/01/1888	Rangers, Aberdeen	Britannia	3	0	Central Park
Second round	04/02/1888	Rovers	Black Diamond	3	2	Links
Semi Final	25/02/1888	Aberdeen	Our Boys	10	2	Chanonry
Semi Final	03/03/1888	Rovers	Rangers, Aberdeen	1	4	Holburn
Final	24/03/1888	Aberdeen	Rangers, Aberdeen	7	1	Chanonry

1888-1889
Football thrives despite heavy defeats, modest quenching and rough play

Football was thriving and the Aberdeenshire Football Association continued to grow with 21 clubs joining for the 1888-1889 season. The member clubs were: Aberdeen, Albert, Ashley, Black Diamond, Britannia, Caledonian, Crescent, Ellon, Froghall, Granite City, Orion, Playfair, Port Elphinstone, Rangers, Rosebery, Rovers, St. Crispin, St George, Union, Vale of Dee and Victoria. In December 1888 Rangers merged with Granite City to form City Rangers. A Charity Cup knockout competition was introduced alongside the Aberdeenshire Cup and a series of inter-county representative matches were added to the fixture list. The season would be capped once again with a high profile game between an Aberdeen select and a Scotland XI at the Chanonry.

Charity Cup

Aberdeen, Orion and Rovers all retained their membership of the S.F.A. and took part in the Scottish Cup, but, as was becoming common, none survived the first hurdle. Rovers were drawn to face Dundee Wanderers in the First Round but decided to withdraw, no doubt recalling the previous year's visit to the Tayside club which ended in a 'could have been much worse' 10-0 defeat. Aberdeen put in a battling performance against Arbroath but lost 4-3 at the Chanonry, while Orion went under by 3-2 to Lochee in a thrilling match at Central Park. Lochee led 3-0 at half-time but second half goals from Gloag and Mackay gave Orion hope of salvaging the game. The visitors managed to hold out while the home side was left to rue a series of missed chances.

Aberdeen and Orion established themselves as the leading clubs in the city. Aberdeen won the Aberdeenshire Cup for the second year in a row, defeating Orion 4-3 in the final while Orion took revenge in the inaugural Aberdeen Charity Cup, defeating the Whites 4-1 in the first round before crushing City Rangers 8-1 in the Final. Aberdeen played 33 games, winning 20, losing 10 and drawing three, scoring 189 goals and conceding 90. Seven of the defeats were inflicted by clubs from outside the area and two came within a few hours of each other at the Chanonry on an exhausting New Year's Day. The Whites, despite taking an early lead through Morrison, lost 8-1 to Stirling's King's Park in the morning game which kicked off at 11-30am, then went under by 6-1 to a Queen's Park second eleven in the afternoon. In the aftermath of these performances, one local journalist posed the following questions of the Aberdeen players: *"It would be interesting to know how many took part in the small hours of the morning in the ancient custom of first footing, how many 'modest quenchers' represented their contribution to the general celebrations of the birth of 1889, what hour they got to bed, and, how they felt when called upon to turn out to fulfil their Chanonry engagement."*

Aberdeen's biggest defeat had, however, come on the opening day of the season when Third Lanark handed out a 10-2 thrashing. Thirds would go on to win the Scottish Cup that season, defeating Celtic 2-1 in the Final. Rovers scored a surprise 3-1 win over Aberdeen at the Chanonry in November 1888 but that can be explained by most of the home side's best players being away on Inter-County duty that same day, helping Aberdeenshire defeat Inverness-shire 2-1 at Central Park. The only other defeats inflicted on Aberdeen by local clubs were both at the hands of Orion.

On the plus side, Aberdeen hit double figures in six games, sweeping aside Rosebery 23-0 in the Aberdeenshire Cup Second Round and also trouncing Rovers 14-2, Stonehaven Thistle 12-2, Aberdeen St Mirren 11-0, Black Diamond 10-0 and Elgin Rangers 11-1, all in friendly challenge matches. In the Rosebery game Tom Ketchen scored the first four goals and notched nine in total, J.Key got seven, C. Christie four, Allan two and J. Smith one. This would remain the biggest victory in the history of the club.

Orion won 13, lost nine and drew five of their 27 matches during the season. They played Aberdeen six times and the outcomes show how evenly matched the sides were, each winning twice, losing twice and drawing twice. No other local side got the better of the Central Park club. Orion only ventured away from Aberdeen on two occasions, losing 13-0 to Montrose at Links Park and 4-0 to Fair City Athletic in Perth. Clubs visiting Kittybrewster from outside the local area also tended to inflict defeats on the home team. East Stirlingshire won 6-1 on New Year's Day and Cowlairs won 7-4 twenty four hours later. It appears that the Cowlairs players enjoyed a good night out before returning home, with reports of them wandering the streets beating a drum and playing penny whistles, prompting locals to ask *"what lunatic asylum had been let loose."*

Orion had opened the season with a demoralising 11-2 home defeat by Forfar Athletic but a couple of months later they recorded their biggest win, a 17-0 thumping of Victoria in the Aberdeenshire Cup. (Victoria were in no way associated with the Victoria United club which was formed the following year). Three Inter-County matches were played with the Aberdeenshire Select losing 7-3 to Perthshire at the Chanonry, defeating Inverness 2-1 at Central Park and drawing 2-2 with the Inverness men in the Highland capital. A 7-2 friendly victory was also recorded over an Elgin select side. Selection for these games was considered to be a great honour and players would often wear their county badges or caps on their club shirts throughout the season. The trip to Inverness certainly seemed to be enjoyed by the players, who indulged in a night of high jinks at the Glenalbyn Hotel where the *"edibles and drinkables were good"*. The social formalities, on the eve of the match, ended at 1am, but the Aberdeen men were in no mood to stop partying and continued to *"socialise"* until the early hours. A morning trip to Culloden Moor preceded the game and no doubt allowed heads to be cleared. On returning to Inverness the visitors were within minutes of being involved in a serious accident. They had just left the carriage taking them to the game when two of the horses pulling the vehicle broke free and a passing man was seriously injured. The carriage crashed into a bank building, narrowly missing many passers-by.

The Aberdeenshire officials, in December 1888, decided that the select team would play in scarlet jerseys as their first choice colour, so it is possible to trace the current Dons colours back to this period. The select also played a Scotland XI for the second year in a row at the Chanonry and on this occasion the international side ran out 10-0 winners.

Rough play and disputes of one form or another continued to prevail. After the February 1889 Orion v Aberdeen Charity Cup match 'a Glasgow footballer' wrote to the Aberdeen Journal to express his concerns about the violent nature of the game. He said: *"Being a visitor to Aberdeen on Saturday and hearing that two of the best local clubs were to play in the first round of the Charity Cup, I went over to Chanonry, and I am sorry to say was a witness to one of the roughest played matches that ever I saw. To think that one of the Orion men should get so easy off for striking one of the Aberdeen team is a shame. Why, had it been in Glasgow he would immediately have been put off the field, besides being suspended for the season. Indeed I saw nothing in the Orion's play but rough work all the time."*

There had been some ill-feeling before the match, however, because of a dispute over where it should be played. Aberdeen had been drawn at home but the Aberdeenshire F.A. decided to move the fixture to Orion's Central Park. This was because Aberdeen wanted to charge one guinea for the use of Chanonry and for their members to be allowed free entry, whereas Orion offered Central Park at a slightly cheaper rate of 20 shillings with no free entry for club members. Aberdeen threatened to withdraw from the competition and that was enough to persuade the A.F.A to reverse their decision.

As for the game itself, Milne gave Orion the lead after eight minutes but J. Key equalised for the home side. Morrison then made it 2-1 for the visitors before Orion's Irvine and Aberdeen's McCann got involved in a fight. The home fans screamed for Irvine to be sent off, but the referee took no action. Orion added two more goals in the second half to ease through to the semi final although Aberdeen considered protesting on the grounds of the alleged rough play of their opponents. Nothing came of this protest.

The behaviour of spectators also caused concerns, prompting numerous letters to be sent to the local press expressing disgust at the behaviour of some fans, who were making derogatory comments players.

Efforts by some clubs to raise money also caused friction on occasion. Only Aberdeen and Orion enjoyed the benefit of enclosed grounds, the others having to make do with public playing fields, such as the Links which became known as *"The People's Park."* It was impossible for these clubs to charge an entrance fee so they often tried to bolster funds by taking a collection at matches. The Black Diamonds' Aberdeenshire Cup second round match against Albert at the Inches was a case in point. The tie attracted a big crowd and, despite there having been a prior announcement that a collection would be taken to boost the Diamonds funds, it was difficult to extract any cash from those watching the game. There was another problem for the Diamonds as the Albert protested afterwards on the grounds that the pitch hadn't been roped off, another difficulty groundless clubs endured. The protest was nevertheless dismissed. Aberdeen's Chanonry ground was often shared with other clubs but this sometimes presented difficulties. For instance, the Aberdeen v Dunfermline game on 6th October didn't start until after 4-30pm because of the late finish to the Caledonian v Britannia Aberdeenshire Cup tie played on the same park earlier in the afternoon.

Football was still booming although not everyone was pleased by the upsurge in interest which led to youngsters practising their skills on the streets. An anonymous letter to the Editor of the Aberdeen Journal in April 1889, advocated stern action should be taken against street football on Sundays. The letter said:
"Evidently Sunday is a favourite day for young Aberdeen working off the Saturday football exhilaration, if one is to judge by the number of boys and young men engaged in kicking anything handy enough to represent the leather.
In a thoroughfare in the northern district of the city might have been witnessed half a dozen young men at the exciting pastime of kicking a large potato along the road. Then in a centrical street there were a number of boys kicking about a small ball; in another street, about the centre of the city, more boys were playing at this game; while on the vacant ground at the Shorelands a further group were doing their best to imitate this pastime. Who is to blame for this perpetual annoyance on Sundays? Don't you think it is high time that the birch rod was brought to bear upon the backs of these recalcitrant youths, and thus ensure

safety to pedestrians." No doubt the writer would have loved the "No Ball Games" signs which proliferate on so many small pieces of open ground nowadays.

Notable Games 1888-1889

Aberdeen 2, Third Lanark 10
Chanonry, 25th August 1888

A crowd of 1,000 turned up on a warm afternoon at the Chanonry for the opening match of the season. Aberdeen opened the scoring after 15 minutes through A. Clark, but Thirds soon got into their stride and roared into a 6-1 lead by the interval. Shortly after the break it was 7-1, but Ferry pulled one back for the home side. Three further goals

David Wood – the Aberdeen and Aberdeenshire goalkeeper

completed the scoring for the visitors who fielded eight of the men who would later in the season play in their Scottish Cup Final win over Celtic.

Aberdeen - D. Wood, W. Still, W.R. Key, C. E. Glennie, J. Thomson, B. McCann, A. Clark, R. M. Ferry, T. Ketchen, C. Christie, J. Smith.

Third Lanark - R. Downie, A. Thomson, J. Rae, J. Meikle, J. Auld, A. Ferguson, W. Marshall, Thomson, J. Oswald, Hannah, W. Johnstone.

Aberdeen 3, Arbroath 4
Scottish Cup, Chanonry, 1st September 1888

Aberdeen raced into a 2-0 lead before half-time, Christie beating Arbroath's Scottish international goalkeeper Ned Doig to claim both goals. The Red Lichties fought back after the interval and soon levelled through Smith and Collie. But Aberdeen responded and Clark put them ahead again before Smith again equalised with 15 minutes remaining. Arbroath's Fleming was criticised for some rough play as Arbroath upped the tempo. Willocks then headed the Lichties ahead for the first time, although the home side claimed he had handled the ball. Despite some late pressure from Aberdeen, the visitors held on to progress to the next round. The Lichties side included the famous Jocky Petrie, scorer of 13 goals

81

against Bon Accord three years earlier.

Aberdeen – Wood, Key, Still, McCann, Thomson, Glennie, Smith, Christie, Ketchen, Ferry, Clark.

Arbroath – Doig, Collie, Fleming, McDonald, Milne, Mowatt, Mackie, Petrie, Smith, Willocks, Buick.

Orion 2, Lochee 3
Scottish Cup, Central Park, 8th September 1888

Lochee played downhill with the wind behind in the first half and Millar soon gave them the lead. Shortly before the break Burke and Johnstone added to the Dundee side's total so they turned around with a 3-0 lead.

Orion came out battling in the second half and Willie Gloag quickly opened the Aberdeen men's account. (This was the first goal Orion scored in the Scottish Cup since the club made it's first appearance in the competition in 1885). Orion continued to press and a shot grazed the bar. Then, with five minutes remaining, Mackay made it 3-2 with a great shot.The home side could not, however, get an equaliser. The game, which started at 2pm, attracted a crowd of 500.

Orion - Diack, Fettes, Jarvis, Milne, Mackay, Ewan, Fyffe, Gloag, Banks, Dunn, Whitehead.

Lochee - Steadman, Steene, Craig, Shepherd, Tosh, Millar, McLaren, Doick, Macready, Johnstone, Burke.

Aberdeenshire 3, Perthshire 7
Inter County game , Chanonry, 27th October 1888

The first Inter County game attracted a 1,500 crowd to Chanonry. County caps were highly prized, being rated second only to international caps by players of this era. The visitors took a two goal early lead before Ketchen reduced the leeway. Perth quickly restored their two goal advantage, Ketchen again pulled one back but the visitors struck again to lead 5-2 at the interval. It was 7-2 soon after the restart, but Smith grabbed a third for the homesters before the end. Immediately after the inter-county game Aberdeen reserves played Old Aberdeen, winning 6-2 despite the second half being played in darkness.

Aberdeenshire - D. Wood (Aberdeen), W.A. Key (Aberdeen), Campbell (Granite City), G. Robertson (Rovers), J. Thomson (Aberdeen), C.E. Glennie (Aberdeen), J.

Smith (Aberdeen), C. Christie (Aberdeen), T. Ketchen (Aberdeen), T. Mackay (Rangers), T. Irvine (Orion).

Perthshire - Thomson (St Johnstone), Robertson (St Johnstone), McMahon (Erin Rovers), Cameron (Dunblane), Mackenzie (Dunblane), Reekie (Fair City), Duncan (Coupar Angus), Mead (Erin Rovers), Eadie (St Johnstone), Lawson (Coupar Angus), Weir (Dunblane)

Aberdeenshire 2, Inverness-shire 1
Inter County game, Central Park, Kittybrewster, 10th November 1888

This was the first time a North of Scotland select side had ventured to Aberdeen but the visitors quickly showed they would not be overawed by the occasion. The Inverness men enjoyed some good early pressure and came close to scoring on a number of occasions. Aberdeenshire had their chances too, but by half-time neither side had scored in a game which was surprisingly entertaining despite the windy conditions. Inverness shocked the hosts early in the second half, however, when W. Fraser fired them in front. This setback spurred the home side into action and straight from the restart Irvine blasted home an equaliser *"while Gloag attended to the goalkeeper."* Both sides had further chances before Gloag headed what proved to be the winner.

Aberdeenshire - Diack (Orion), J.M. Jarvis (Orion), W.A. Key (Aberdeen), J. Campbell (Rovers), J. Thomson (Aberdeen), B. McCann (Aberdeen), T. Irvine (Orion), Brown (Black Diamonds), W. Watson (Black Diamonds), Gloag (Orion), Smith (Aberdeen).

North of Scotland F.A. (Inverness-shire) - J. Fraser (Caledonian), MacPhee (Union), Walker (Northern Counties), Davidson (Clachnacuddin), Munroe (Caledonian), Macgregor (Caledonian), D. Mathieson (Union), A. Wells (Union), MacDougall (Caledonian), C. Smith (Thistle), W. Fraser (Crown).

Aberdeen 4, Orion 3
Aberdeenshire Cup Final, Chanonry, 16th February 1889

Despite the poor weather and the fact that admission charges had been raised 50% from 6d to 9d, a large crowd *"perhaps a larger number than has ever assembled at Old Aberdeen on any previous occasion"* turned up. The players struggled to cope with the very wet and muddy conditions with many losing their footing at vital moments. Both sides missed good chances before J. Key fired Aberdeen in front and straight from the kick-off the Cup holders charged forward again and Smith scored a second goal. Orion fought back and just before half-time their pressure paid off when Wood knocked the ball into his own goal to reduce the leeway. Aberdeen went two ahead again early in the second half, then grabbed another to make it 4-1. Orion again battled back and scored two goals in quick succession to set up an exciting finish. They pressed hard and in one attack an Orion forward barged into Aberdeen keeper Davie Wood who was badly injured. Play was held up for a long time while he was treated and time ran out. The trophy wasn't presented until more than two months later at a smoking concert in the Queen's Rooms, Aberdeen on Saturday 20th April 1889. It was stated in the Aberdeen Journal report of the occasion that Aberdeen F.C, *"having gained it (the cup) twice in succession, retain it as their own property."* Dr Maitland Moir presented the trophy.

Aberdeen - Wood, Key, J. Wood, McCann, Thomson, Glennie, Smith, Mitchell, Ketchen, J. M. Key, Brown.

Orion - Diack, Fettes, Jarvis, Milne, McKay, Ewan, Fyfe, Gloag, A. Whitehead, F. Whitehead, Irvine.

Ref: Mr Strachan, Montrose

Umpires – Mr. Jaffrey (Hon Secretary A.F.A.), Mr Lornie (Vale of Dee).

Orion 8, City Rangers 1
Aberdeen Charity Cup Final, Chanonry, 11th May 1889

On a pleasant day in front of a large crowd, Orion opened up a 2-0 first half lead through goals from Whitehead and Fyfe.The floodgates opened after the interval with Borthwick making it 3-0 before Gloag completed his hat-trick with goals four and five. Borthwick added a sixth with a long range effort then Whitehead became the second Orion hat-trick hero with the seventh and eighth goals. Rangers grabbed a last minute consolation following a scrimmage.

Orion - Diack, Fettes, Jarvis, Milne, McKay, Ewan, Fyfe, Gloag, Borthwick, F. Whitehead, Irvine.

City Rangers – The goalkeeper was McPherson – other names not found.

Aberdeen Select 0 v Scotland XI 10
Chanonry, 1st June 1889

The internationalists had been in action the previous evening when they thrashed a Perthshire Select 14-2, but this obviously hadn't taken too much out of them. The Scots caught an early train up to Aberdeen the following morning, checked into the Palace Hotel for lunch, then enjoyed a sight-seeing tour of the city in open carriages before being taken by bus to Old Aberdeen for the match. Included in the Scottish line-up was Glasgow-based Peterhead man William Sellar, who scored two of the Scotland goals. The Queen's Park player won nine Scotland caps between 1885 and 1893 and was considered one of the greatest forwards of that era. He helped his club win the Scottish Cup twice and was in the side which lost to Blackburn Rovers in the 1885 F.A. Cup Final. He later became President of the Scottish Amateur Athletic Association. The Bon Accord newspaper report of the 1889 game spared the home side no mercy. Its scribe stated: *"The spectators were very much disappointed with the poor play of several of the home team….. Wood at goal has played some wonderfully good games this season, but on Saturday he was clean off colour…….Brown on the left wing was of no use whatsoever."* Ketchen, the goalscorer in 1888, was however praised after playing as a full-back on this occasion: *"He was here, there and everywhere, working like the proverbial horse and occasionally enlivening the proceedings by some smart tackling – more than once sending his opponents on their beam ends."* The paper did concede, however, that the local men were facing some quality opponents: *"The play of the internationalists from the kick-off to the call of time was, we are safe to say, the most finished exhibition of football ever witnessed in Aberdeen."* Although no accurate crowd figure was given there were reports of *"an exceptionally large number of spectators, including a goodly sprinkling of ladies"* and the match was a financial success with takings amounting to just under £60, a princely sum in those days.

Aberdeen Select – Wood (Aberdeen), Key (Aberdeen), Ketchen (Aberdeen), Baird (Black Diamond), Thomson (Aberdeen), Ewan (Orion), Smith (Aberdeen), Gloag (Orion), Borthwick (Orion), Brown (Black Diamond), Irvine (Orion).

Scotland – J. Wilson (Vale of Leven), W. Arnott (Queen's Park), R. Smellie (Queen's Park), , Robertson (Queen's Park), J. Kelly (Celtic), J. McLaren (Celtic), W. Sellar (Queen's Park), W. Berry (Queen's Park), J. Oswald (Third Lanark), J. MacPherson (Cowlairs), Colman (Celtic).

Aberdeen F.C. - 1888-1889

Competition	Date		Opposition	F	A	Venue
	25/08/1888	Aberdeen	Third Lanark RV	2	10	Chanonry
Scottish Cup 1R	01/09/1888	Aberdeen	Arbroath	3	4	Chanonry
	15/09/1888	Aberdeen	Montrose	1	5	Chanonry
	22/09/1888	Aberdeen	St Mirren, Aberdeen	11	0	Chanonry
	29/09/1888	Aberdeen	Black Diamonds	10	0	Chanonry
	06/10/1888	Aberdeen	Dunfermline Athletic	2	2	Chanonry
	13/10/1888	Aberdeen	Caledonian	9	0	Chanonry
	03/11/1888	Aberdeen	Orion	2	2	Chanonry
	10/11/1888	Aberdeen	Rovers	1	3	Chanonry
Aberdeenshire Cup 2R	17/11/1888	Aberdeen	Rosebery	23	0	Chanonry
	24/11/1888	Aberdeen	2nd Aberdeen	6	2	Chanonry
Aberdeenshire Cup 3R	08/12/1888	Aberdeen	Ashley	6	1	Chanonry
	15/12/1888	Aberdeen	Crown Inverness	5	0	Inverness
	22/12/1888	Aberdeen	Rovers	6	1	Chanonry
	29/12/1888	Aberdeen	Montrose	0	4	Links Park, Montrose
	01/01/1889	Aberdeen	Kings Park	1	8	Chanonry
	01/01/1889	Aberdeen	Queen's Park	1	6	Chanonry
	05/01/1889	Aberdeen	Britannia	8	0	Chanonry
	12/01/1889	Aberdeen	Orion	3	5	Central Park
Aberdeenshire Cup Semi Final	19/01/1889	Aberdeen	Britannia	6	1	Chanonry
	02/02/1889	Aberdeen	Black Diamond	4	1	Chanonry
	09/02/1889	Aberdeen	Playfair	9	2	Chanonry
Aberdeenshire Cup Final	16/02/1889	Aberdeen	Orion	4	3	Chanonry
Charity Cup 1R	23/02/1889	Aberdeen	Orion	1	4	Chanonry
	02/03/1889	Aberdeen	Rovers	14	2	Chanonry
	09/03/1889	Aberdeen	City Rangers	6	3	Chanonry

Competition	Date		Opposition	F	A	Venue
	16/03/1889	Aberdeen	Orion	4	4	Central Park
	30/03/1889	Aberdeen	Stonehaven Thistle	12	2	Stonehaven
	13/04/1889	Aberdeen	Orion	3	1	Chanonry
	20/04/1889	Aberdeen	Crown,Inverness	6	2	Chanonry
	27/04/1889	Aberdeen	Dundee Strathmore	2	8	Dundee
	04/05/1889	Aberdeen	Montrose	7	3	Chanonry
	06/05/1889	Aberdeen	Elgin Rangers	11	1	Elgin

Orion F.C. - 1888-1889

Competition	Date		Opposition	F	A	Venue
	18/08/1888	Orion	Forfar Athletic	2	11	Central Park
Scottish Cup 1R	08/09/1888	Orion	Lochee	2	3	Central Park
	15/09/1888	Orion	Ashley			Central Park
	22/09/1888	Orion	Britannia	6	2	Central Park
Aberdeenshire Cup 1R	06/10/1888	Orion	Victoria	17	0	Central Park
	03/11/1888	Orion	Aberdeen	2	2	Chanonry
	24/11/1888	Orion	Rangers, Aberdeen	10	1	
	01/12/1888	Orion	Black Diamond	3	1	Central Park
Aberdeenshire Cup 3R	08/12/1888	Orion	Rovers	4	0	Central Park
	15/12/1888	Orion	Rovers	2	2	Central Park
	29/12/1888	Orion	Albert	2	2	Central Park
	01/01/1889	Orion	East Stirlingshire	1	6	Central Park
	02/01/1889	Orion	Cowlairs	4	7	Central Park
	12/01/1889	Orion	Aberdeen	5	3	Central Park
Aberdeenshire Cup Semi Final	19/01/1889	Orion	Playfair	6	2	Central Park
	02/02/1889	Orion	Rovers	3	0	Central Park
Aberdeenshire Cup Final	16/02/1889	Orion	Aberdeen	3	4	Chanonry
Charity Cup 1R	23/02/1889	Orion	Aberdeen	4	1	Chanonry
	09/03/1889	Orion	Ashley	2	2	Central Park

Competition	Date		Opposition	F	A	Venue
	16/03/1889	Orion	Aberdeen	4	4	Central Park
	23/03/1889	Orion	Fair City Athletic	5	3	Central Park
	30/03/1889	Orion	Montrose	0	13	Links Park, Montrose
	06/04/1889	Orion	Dundee Wanderers	4	9	Central Park
	13/04/1889	Orion	Aberdeen	1	3	Chanonry
	20/04/1889	Orion	Fair City Athletic	0	4	Perth
Charity Cup Semi Final	27/04/1889	Orion	Rovers	4	1	Chanonry
Charity Cup Final	11/05/1889	Orion	City Rangers	8	1	Chanonry

Note: No score is known for the Orion-Ashley game on 15/09/1888 although it was reported that Orion won easily.

Aberdeenshire Cup - 1888-1889

	Date			F	A	Venue
First round	06/10/1888	Union	Rovers	0	15	Duthie Park
First round	06/10/1888	Caledonian	Britannia	1	4	Chanonry
First round	06/10/1888	Ellon	Albert	0	3	Ellon
First round	06/10/1888	St Crispin	Playfair	1	3	Duthie Park
First round	06/10/1888	Victoria	Orion	0	17	Central Park
First round	06/10/1888	St George	Rosebery	1	5	Links
First round	06/10/1888	Rangers	Granite City	4	2	Holburn
First round	06/10/1888	Vale of Dee	Froghall	1	13	Links
Second round	17/11/1888	Aberdeen	Rosebery	23	0	Chanonry
Second round	17/11/1888	Rovers	Rangers	4	3	Central Park
Second round	17/11/1888	Ashley	Crescent	5	1	Seafield
Second round	17/11/1888	Port Elphinstone	Britannia	3	3	Port Elphinstone
Second round	17/11/1888	Black Diamond	Albert	5	2	Inches
Second round	24/11/1888	Britannia	Port Elphinstone	6	1	Duthie Park
Third round	08/12/1888	Orion	Rovers	4	0	Central Park
Third round	08/12/1888	Aberdeen	Ashley	6	1	Chanonry
Third round	08/12/1888	Froghall	Playfair	1	3	Links

Competition	Date		Opposition	F	A	Venue
Third round	08/12/1888	Black Diamond	Britannia	4	5	Inches
Semi Final	19/01/1889	Aberdeen	Britannia	6	1	Chanonry
Semi Final	19/01/1889	Orion	Playfair	6	2	Central Park
Final	16/02/1889	Aberdeen	Orion	4	3	Chanonry

Aberdeen Charity Cup - 1888-1889

First round	23/02/1889	Aberdeen	Orion	1	4	Chanonry
First round	02/03/1889	City Rangers	Britannia	13	0	Central Park
First round	30/03/1889	Rovers	Playfair	4	0	Central Park
First round	30/03/1889	Black Diamond	Albert	4	2	Chanonry
Semi Final	27/04/1889	City Rangers	Black Diamond	5	3	Chanonry
Semi Final	27/04/1889	Orion	Rovers	4	1	Chanonry
Final	11/05/1889	Orion	City Rangers	8	1	Chanonry

1889-1890
Torry's football pioneers

J ust as Aberdeen and Orion were establishing themselves as the city's two premier clubs, a new force emerged on the South bank of the Dee at Torry. Victoria United, formed in the summer of 1889, set up home at the new Victoria Bridge Grounds located between what is now South Esplanade East and Crombie Road. The stadium was a substantial facility capable of holding crowds of 6,000 and upwards, and of hosting a variety of sporting events including cycling and athletics competitions. The new club publicised its emergence by holding a five-a-side football competition prior to the start of the season, then pulled off a major coup by attracting Glasgow Celtic to Torry for its first competitive match. Celtic had been formed in 1888 but the Parkhead side was already a major force in the game, having reached the final of the previous season's Scottish Cup, losing to Third Lanark. The Torry match was arranged for a Friday evening, 16th August 1889, and the Parkhead men travelled to Aberdeen that afternoon and checked into the Palace Hotel. Unfortunately, torrential rain greeted them and the poor weather deterred many people from going to the game. A small crowd assembled to watch the visitors dismantle the inexperienced home side in ruthless fashion. Celtic centre-forward Jake Madden helped himself to four goals as the visitors romped to a 10-0 victory. United managed just one shot on goal during the rain-sodden match which, perhaps fortunately for the homesters, was restricted to 30 minutes play each way. The Torry team had a lot to learn, but their backers didn't lack ambition. They employed a new trainer from Abercorn, a Mr McAulay, whose first instruction on arriving in Aberdeen was a strange recommendation that the players should get new boots with square toes instead of rounded ones! A couple of players from 'the south' were also persuaded to ply their trade in Torry.

United had joined the S.F.A and so found themselves in the Scottish Cup in which they were drawn away to Orion. The Central Park side won an ill-tempered match 3-1. In October 1889 Tom Leggat, later to play for Orion, scored the club's first hat-trick in a 6-4 defeat by Dundee's East End. United proceeded to enjoy a reasonably successful first season during which they reached the semi-final of the

Aberdeenshire Cup by brushing aside Britannia 8-0 and Ashley 6-0 before being narrowly beaten 2-1 by Aberdeen. The Whites also turfed United out of the Charity Cup but the Torry men got the better of their more experienced counterparts in a friendly. United also showed a willingness to invite a number of top Central Belt sides up to Aberdeen, Airdrie twice heading to the north east while Partick Thistle and Motherwell club Carfin Shamrock were all enticed to Torry. The Victoria Bridge team lost all of these matches but benefitted from the experience. Aside from the 10-0 hammering from Celtic, United's equal worst score of their inaugural campaign was a 10-0 loss to Arbroath at Gayfield.

Jim Gray – Victoria United's first goalkeeper.

The Third Lanark side which defeated Celtic in the Scottish Cup Final travelled north to play Aberdeen at the Chanonry a few weeks after Celtic's visit to Torry. It was the second year in a row that the Cathkin side had played the Whites at the Old Aberdeen venue and this time they ran out 9-4 winners. Aberdeen's Scottish Cup campaign got off to a stuttering start when drawn to play Lybster Portland. The Caithness club scratched from the competition, giving the Whites a walkover into the second round. The draw was made on a regional basis in the early rounds and the Whites were then paired with Orion who had beaten Victoria United in a feisty opening round match in which *"it seemed as if the players had made up their minds to be as disagreeable as possible, and to lay themselves out, not to give an exhibition of the science of the game, but to 'go' for each other as often as possible."* Two goals from 'Morley' Brown helped Aberdeen defeat the Orionites 2-1 to earn a Third Round home match against Forfar Athletic. The game wasn't without controversy, however, as there was a lengthy dispute as to whether Jarvis's second half goal for Orion should stand as the Aberdeen players claimed the ball had gone over the bar as opposed to under it, (there were no nets in these days). Forfar travelled to Aberdeen in confident mood as they had opened the season by crushing Orion 10-1 at Central Park. On the basis of that result, hopes of an Aberdeen victory weren't high. But the Whites produced an outstanding performance to win an exciting game 5-3 to set up a Fourth Round home tie with Scotland's oldest and arguably greatest team of the era, Queen's Park. The Hampden side had, of course, been at the Chanonry before, winning a friendly 6-1 on New Year's Day 1889. But this was now much more serious business and the Spiders, winners of the Cup eight times over the previous 15 years, were in no mood to show any mercy. So it proved, as the visitors, fielding six Scottish internationals, blew the home side off the park, winning 13-1 in front of 5,000 fans, to shatter Aberdeen hopes of making any further progress. The result prompted some Central Belt observers to suggest that there should be a qualifying competition held before the Cup got under way, to weed out weaker clubs and avoid the need for established sides such as Queen's Park having to make long journeys to places like Aberdeen just to go through the motions!

With Scottish Cup interest over for another year, the local clubs focussed on their own major competition, the Aberdeenshire Cup. Controversy was never in short supply in this tournament although the validity of some of the complaints was often very dubious. Stonehaven Primrose, for instance, lodged a protest after losing their fourth round tie 10-1 to Black Diamond. The Kincardineshire men claimed the pitch was in poor condition, it was far too muddy and slippery, and therefore the game should never have been played. The Aberdeenshire F.A. ordered a replay at Cowie and this time it ended 3-3. The Diamonds finally got through by winning the third match 2-0. There was a similar protest after Caledonian lost 8-6 to Orion at the Holburn grounds. The Caley claimed the outcome had been affected by the poor underfoot conditions and by the game finishing in darkness. Again a replay was ordered and Orion won 8-4. In January 1890 Aberdeen defeated Victoria United 2-1 in the semi final of the competition and the Torry outfit tried to use the 'wet conditions and game finished in darkness' excuse for a protest, but on this occasion the bid for a replay was thrown out. Ironically, the other semi-final, between Orion and Black Diamond, to be played the same day at Central Park, was called off because of the weather, but the sides played a friendly which Orion won 5-2. When the cup game was played seven days later Orion again won, 3-2.

The Final between Aberdeen and Orion ended in a 2-2 draw but the replay was a dramatic affair. It was 1-1 at the interval, but Orion led 3-2 with five minutes to go and seemed destined to lift the Cup. But Aberdeen fought to the bitter end and Campbell grabbed a late equaliser. The match moved into extra time and goals from Campbell, Key and Wallace gave the Whites a 6-3 lead at the halfway point of the extra 30minutes. As Orion went into meltdown, Aberdeen added a further two before the finish to win 8-3 and complete a hat-trick of Aberdeenshire Cup successes. Orion got an opportunity to avenge this defeat when the sides met again in the Charity Cup Final and this time the Central Park side came out on top, winning 2-1 at the Victoria Bridge Grounds to retain the trophy.

Disputes and controversy weren't confined to cup matches. Victoria United's friendly against Bon Accord in September 1889 was abandoned after 20 minutes with the Torry club leading 4-0. The Bon Accord players disputed one of the goals and, not for the first time in the club's history, they decided to walk off the pitch. United were also involved in another tempestuous encounter, with Orion, in a November friendly match. Two players had to be separated for fighting and frequent scuffles punctuated proceedings. The Bon Accord magazine stated: *"The game became of the roughest description, a portion of the players paying all their attention to the man, their idea seemingly being to grass their opponents in preference to playing the ball."*

The somewhat chaotic nature of the sport at times was reflected in the outcome of the match between Woodside and Bon Accord at Hayton in October when the clubs couldn't even agree on the scoreline at the end of the game. The Aberdeen Journal reported that Bon Accord had won 10-1 although both sides expressed amazement as to where this result had come from and the newspaper admitted it had no idea of the source. The Woodside club's version of affairs was that Bon Accord turned up with just seven players so the hosts suggested that the game should go ahead simply as a 'practice' match and not an official match. Woodside offered the Bons some of their players in order to even up the numbers. According to the hosts, this offer was refused, but the game went ahead, and the home side won 4-1. The Bon Accord secretary responded with a different version of events. He agreed that his side only had seven players, but a substitute goalkeeper was found and the match went ahead as a practice game with an understanding that the result wouldn't be reported. He admitted, however, that Bon Accord had lost, but only by 3-2 and certainly not by 4-1. Such disputes were not uncommon. It also seemed that players were free to move around clubs from one game to another. For instance, in September 1889 Aberdeen club Ashley travelled north to play Peterhead and fielded a strong team *"including Messrs Jarvis, Ewan, Farquharson and Gloag of Orion."* The visitors, strengthened by their imports, won 2-0.

An 'international select', which in reality was a Glasgow select, again came to Aberdeen to play the best of the locals at Victoria Bridge Grounds at the end of the season. A crowd of 3,000 turned up to watch the representative side which included a number of the Queen's Park team which crushed Aberdeen in the Scottish Cup. The visitors won 6-2 but there was a feeling that the fixture had lost some of the sparkle and interest of previous seasons. A few days before the international game, the Aberdeenshire select played the select reserves at the Chanonry in a game held in aid of former Orion player Tom Irvine who had sustained a serious injury which left him crippled for life. The select won 6-3. The Aberdeenshire FA select played three other games during the season, defeating Inverness-shire 2-0 at Torry but losing 3-1 to the North of Scotland side at Inverness. They also lost 6-1 to Perthshire at the St. Johnstone recreation grounds.

Notable Games

Victoria United 0, Glasgow Celtic 10
Victoria Bridge Grounds, Torry, Friday 16th August 1889
This was Victoria United's first game and the visitors certainly gave the new boys a harsh lesson. Celtic fielded a full strength side and it took them less than one minute to open the scoring through centre forward Jake Madden. Willie Groves made it 2-0 after eight minutes while a double from Johnny Coleman and another from Madden made it 5-0 by half-time. Madden took his personal tally to four after the break with Hugh Gallagher, Jimmy McLaren and Peter Dowds also getting on the scoresheet for the Celts. The Vics struggled to get out of their own half and in the whole game managed just one shot on target, an effort from Slater which gave the goalkeeper no trouble. The Torry men must have been glad the match was restricted to 30 minutes each way because of the poor weather. Peter Simpson, the United right back, would go on to have a long association with the

club. He later became a respected referee and was a trainer with the new Aberdeen club formed in 1903.

Victoria United – J. Gray, P. Simpson, J. McGregor, Mitchell, Kirkland, Gorman, J. Slater, W. Andrews, Morrison, Hogg, Robertson.

Celtic – McLaughlin, McKeowan, Reynolds, J. McLaren, P. Gallagher, Dowds, Cunningham, H. Gallagher, Groves, Madden, Coleman.

Referee – Mr Jaffray, Aberdeen.

Umpires, Mr Curtis (Celtic), Fred Reid (Aberdeen)

Orion 3, Victoria United 1
Scottish Cup 1st Round, Central Park, 7th September 1889
This was a notable game as it was Victoria United's first Scottish Cup tie although it was also only the club's third match coming on top of the 10-0 defeat by Celtic and a 7-0 win over Stonehaven Primrose at Cowie. It was also, obviously, the first meeting of the two Aberdeen clubs and it turned into a real cut and thrust derby with no shortage of crunching tackles and fearsome challenges. United played

Orion F.C. Second Eleven

down the hill in the first half but fell behind after 15 minutes when Fyfe scored. United claimed for offside but the referee didn't agree. In an increasingly exciting tussle both sides had chances but it was the Torry men, in their light blue shirts, who celebrated next when Robertson beat Diack for the equaliser. United pressed hard but couldn't break through the Orion defence and there was no further scoring before the interval. Both sides fought hard in the second period and *"the play became fast and rough, fouls being frequently given."* Orion gradually got on top and Fyfe notched his second goal of the game to give his side the lead. The rough play continued and an unnamed player was cautioned by the referee before Jarvis secured the tie for Orion with a third goal. Play was held up for a while towards the end to allow treatment to Orion's Ewen who was injured after colliding with an opponent.

Orion – Diack, Foote, McBean, Ewen, MacKay, Baird, Fyfe, Gloag, Jarvis, Mundin, Jopp.

Victoria United – J. Gray, P. Simpson, J. McGregor, J. Kirkland, J. Campbell, J. Slater, W. Hogg, E. Robertson, A.H. Morrison (captain), W. Andrews, A. Gorman.

Aberdeen 1, Queen's Park 13
Scottish Cup 4th Round, Chanonry, 9th November 1889

Queen's brushed aside Aberdeen's challenge en route to winning the Scottish Cup for the ninth time. It was 6-0 at half-time with Peterhead man William Sellar grabbing four and Hamilton getting the other two. The deadly duo added to their personal tallies in the second period, although not all the scorers were recorded. Jimmy Thompson got Aberdeen's consolation. Afterwards the teams were treated to tea in Hay's Restaurant. This would be the heaviest defeat in the history of the original Aberdeen club.

Aberdeen - D. Wood, T. Ketchen (captain), A. Wood, B. McCann, D. McVey, J. Thompson, J. Smith, C. Christie, W. A. Key, W. S. Brown, A. Whitehead.

Queen's Park - J. Tudhope, W. Arnott, R. Smellie, J. McAra, A. Stewart, J. Robertson, G. Hector, W.H. Berry, James Hamilton, Eccles, W. Sellar (Captain).

Aberdeen 2, Orion 2
Aberdeenshire Cup Final, Victoria Bridge Grounds, 8th February 1890

This was a disappointing game in which *"the science of the sport was conspicuous by its absence.* " Orion enjoyed the bulk of possession and should have won comfortably, but found themselves twice having to come from behind to force a replay. Reith gave Aberdeen the lead but Mundie equalised soon afterwards in a first half punctuated by a series of fouls, a feature which was common in many local derbies throughout the season. William Key put the Whites 2-1 ahead before the break but Orion levelled again in the second period.

Aberdeen – D. Wood, T. Ketchen (captain), A. Wood, D. McVay, A.D. Farnworth, J. Thompson, W. A. Key, M. Campbell, J. Reith, W. S. Brown, A. Whitehead.

Orion defender Edward Foote

Orion - Diack, Foote, Jarvis, Ewen, McBain, Baird, Whitehead, Fyfe, Gloag, Mundie, Jopp

Aberdeen 8, Orion 3 (after extra time, 2-2 at 90 minutes)
Aberdeenshire Cup Final Replay, Victoria Bridge Grounds, 22nd February 1890
The sides matched up for a second time in a fortnight. In between times both suffered heavy defeats, Orion losing 5-2 to Victoria United while Aberdeen went down 6-2 to Dundee Wanderers. Tom Ketchen fired Aberdeen into the lead with a powerful shot which beat Diack. Orion fought back and Davie Wood did well to prevent the stripes from scoring on a number of occasions. The pressure finally paid off, however, when Jopp notched an equaliser before the interval. Orion continued to dominate and it was no surprise when they went 2-1 ahead 10 minutes after the restart. But the Whites retaliated and 15 minutes from the end it was all square again. Then, with just five minutes remaining Orion swept into what most people felt would be a winning lead. But Aberdeen again hit back, Campbell

Aberdeen F.C. – Aberdeenshire Cup Winners.
Back Row - D. Wood, J. Reith, T. Ketchen, J.A. McHardy, R. Hyslop, A.D. Farnworth, J. Thomson, A. Wood, C. E. Glennie.
Front – A. Whitehead, M. Campbell, W.A. Key. W.S. Brown, P. Wallace

grabbing a last minute equaliser to send the game into extra time. Campbell was again on the mark to make it 4-3 for Aberdeen five minutes into the added period then Key and Wallace added to the Whites' score before the break. A dejected Orion completely capitulated and Aberdeen added a further two goals before the end to run out comprehensive 8-3 winners.

Aberdeen – D. Wood, J. Reith, A. Wood, T. Ketchen (Captain), A.D. Farnworth, J. Thompson, A. Whitehead, M. Campbell, W. A. Key, W.S. Brown, P. Wallace

Orion – Diack, Foote, Jarvis, Ewen, McBain, Baird, Whitehead, Fyfe, Gloag, Kelly, Jopp

Orion 2, Aberdeen 1
Charity Cup Final, Victoria Bridge Grounds,26th April 1890

This was a poor game, played in front of a large crowd, on a windy day when *"the number of fouls awarded against each side was abnormally large."* There was controversy over Orion's decision to field a player called Edwards, signed from Caledonian, who had apparently been banned by the Charity Committee. After a goalless first half, Baird put Orion 1-0 ahead. Frank Whitehead then sent a header beyond Wood for a second goal within the first 15 minutes of the second period. Tom Ketchen's strong run opened up a chance for Aberdeen to claw one back but there was no further scoring and Orion successfully retained the trophy.

Orion - Love, McBain, Jarvis, Ewen, Mackay, Baird, Fyffe, Gordon, Edwards, Jopp, Whitehead.

Wattie Baird – scored opening goal for Orion in Charity Cup Final

Aberdeen - D. Wood, J. Reith, A. Wood, T. Ketchen (captain), A.D. Farnworth, J. Thomson, A. Whitehead, G. Robertson, W. A. Key, M. Campbell, P. Wallace

Aberdeenshire F.A. Select 2, International Select 6
Victoria Bridge Grounds, Torry, 31st May 1890

Frank Whitehead gave the crowd plenty to cheer when he fired the home side ahead, but the Glasgow visitors hit back strongly to open up a 4-1 halftime lead. Whitehead pulled one back after the interval and missed a great opportunity to complete a hat-trick before the international side added two more goals to complete a comfortable victory.

Aberdeenshire F.A. Select - Gray, P. Simpson, Wood, Kirkland, T. Ketchen, Gordon, Turner, Leggat, Key, Jopp, F. Whitehead

International Select - Craig (Glasgow University), Arnott, Smellie, Russell, Hendry, T. Robertson, Wardle, Brown, Paull (Partick Thistle), McPherson, Sellar.

Aberdeen F.C - 1889-1890

Competition	Date		Opposition	F	A	Venue
	31/08/1889	Aberdeen	Third Lanark	4	9	Chanonry
Scottish Cup 1R	01/09/1889	Aberdeen	Portland Lybster	w	o	
	07/09/1889	Aberdeen	Bon Accord	7	2	Chanonry
	14/09/1889	Aberdeen	City Rangers	11	0	Chanonry
	21/09/1889	Aberdeen	Our Boys, Dundee	0	7	West Craigie,Dundee
Scottish Cup 2R	28/09/1889	Aberdeen	Orion	2	1	Chanonry
	05/10/1889	Aberdeen	Dunfermline	5	0	Chanonry
	07/10/1889	Aberdeen	Peterhead	2	0	Chanonry
	12/10/1889	Aberdeen	Dundee Strathmore	2	4	Chanonry
Scottish Cup 3R	19/10/1889	Aberdeen	Forfar Athletic	5	3	Chanonry
	26/10/1889	Aberdeen	Victoria United	2	3	Victoria Bridge Grounds
Scottish Cup 4R	09/11/1889	Aberdeen	Queen's Park	1	13	Chanonry
Aberdeenshire Cup 3R	16/11/1889	Aberdeen	Bon Accord	5	0	Chanonry
	30/11/1889	Aberdeen	Black Diamond	5	1	Chanonry
	07/12/1889	Aberdeen	Montrose	2	3	Chanonry
	14/12/1889	Aberdeen	Dundee Wanderers	2	4	Chanonry
	25/12/1889	Aberdeen	Aberdeen University	7	0	University Recreation Grounds
	28/12/1889	Aberdeen	Caledonian	1	1	Holburn
	04/01/1890	Aberdeen	Partick Thistle	2	5	Chanonry
Aberdeenshire Cup SF	11/01/1890	Aberdeen	Victoria United	2	1	Victoria Bridge Grounds
	18/01/1890	Aberdeen	St Johnstone	2	1	Chanonry
	01/02/1890	Aberdeen	Victoria United	3	0	Chanonry
Aberdeenshire Cup Final	08/02/1890	Aberdeen	Orion	2	2	Victoria Bridge Grounds
	15/02/1890	Aberdeen	Dundee Wanderers	2	6	Morgan Park,Dundee
Aberdeenshire Cup Final	22/02/1890	Aberdeen	Orion	8	3	Victoria Bridge Grounds
	15/03/1890	Aberdeen	Ashley	5	2	Chanonry
	22/03/1890	Aberdeen	Our Boys Dundee	2	5	Chanonry

Competition	Date		Opposition	F	A	Venue
	29/03/1890	Aberdeen	Montrose	2	10	Montrose
	05/04/1890	Aberdeen	Orion	2	6	Chanonry
Aberdeen Charity Cup 2R	12/04/1890	Aberdeen	Victoria United	2	1	Victoria Bridge Grounds
Aberdeen Charity Cup Final	26/04/1890	Aberdeen	Orion	1	2	Victoria Bridge Grounds

Orion F.C. - 1889-1890

Competition	Date		Opposition	F	A	Venue
	17/08/1889	Orion	Forfar	1	10	Central Park
	24/08/1889	Orion	Coupar Angus	7	5	Central Park
Scottish Cup 1R	07/09/1889	Orion	Victoria United	3	1	Central Park
	14/09/1889	Orion	Dundee Wanderers	3	3	Central Park
	21/09/1889	Orion	Black Diamond	4	3	Central Park
Scottish Cup 2R	28/09/1889	Orion	Aberdeen	1	2	Chanonry
	05/10/1889	Orion	Bon Accord	4	0	Central Park
	12/10/1889	Orion	Thistle	9	1	Central Park
	19/10/1889	Orion	Victoria United	2	0	Victoria Bridge Grounds
	26/10/1889	Orion	Clyde	3	8	Central Park
	02/11/1889	Orion	Fair City Athletic	1	4	Balhousie, Perth
	16/11/1889	Orion	Aberdeen University	7	0	University Recreation Grounds
	23/11/1889	Orion	Black Diamond	2	2	Central Park
	30/11/1889	Orion	Victoria United	1	2	Victoria Bridge Grounds
Aberdeenshire Cup 4R	07/12/1889	Orion	Caledonian	8	6	Holburn
Aberdeenshire Cup 4R	14/12/1889	Orion	Caledonian	8	4	Holburn
	21/12/1889	Orion	Ashley	6	4	Central Park
	28/12/1889	Orion	Britannia	5	0	Central Park
	01/01/1890	Orion	Cowlairs	3	7	Central Park
	02/01/1890	Orion	Royal Albert Athletic	1	8	Central Park
	11/01/1890	Orion	Black Diamond	5	2	Central Park

Competition	Date		Opposition	F	A	Venue
Aberdeenshire Cup SF	18/01/1890	Orion	Black Diamond	3	2	Central Park
	01/02/1890	Orion	Bishopmill	8	1	Elgin
Aberdeenshire Cup Final	08/02/1890	Orion	Aberdeen	2	2	Victoria Bridge Grounds
	15/02/1890	Orion	Victoria United	2	5	Central Park
Aberdeenshire Cup Final	22/02/1890	Orion	Aberdeen	3	8	Victoria Bridge Grounds
	01/03/1890	Orion	Forfar Athletic	3	5	Forfar
	15/03/1890	Orion	Bon Accord	8	0	Central Park
	22/03/1890	Orion	Caledonian	10	1	Central Park
Aberdeen Charity Cup 1R	29/03/1890	Orion	Black Diamond	4	1	Holburn
	05/04/1890	Orion	Aberdeen	6	2	Chanonry
	12/04/1890	Orion	Stonehaven Thistle	3	6	Urie
	19/04/1890	Orion	Brechin	5	3	Central Park
Aberdeen Charity Cup Final	26/04/1890	Orion	Aberdeen	2	1	Victoria Bridge Grounds
	03/05/1890	Orion	Montrose	1	4	Central Park

Note: A protest was lodged after the Orion-Caledonian match on 07/12/1889 and it was replayed on 14/12/1889

Victoria United F.C. - 1889-1890

Competition	Date		Opposition	F	A	Venue
	16/08/1889	Victoria United	Glasgow Celtic	0	10	Victoria Bridge Grounds
	24/08/1889	Victoria United	Stonehaven Primrose	7	0	Cowie
Scottish Cup 1R	07/09/1889	Victoria United	Orion	1	3	Central Park
	14/09/1889	Victoria United	Bon Accord	4	0	Victoria Bridge Grounds
	28/09/1889	Victoria United	Elgin Rovers	6	1	Elgin
	05/10/1889	Victoria United	City Rangers	2	1	Victoria Bridge Grounds
	12/10/1889	Victoria United	East End, Dundee	4	6	Victoria Bridge Grounds
	19/10/1889	Victoria United	Orion	0	2	Victoria Bridge Grounds

Competition	Date		Opposition	F	A	Venue
	26/10/1889	Victoria United	Aberdeen	3	2	Victoria Bridge Grounds
	02/11/1889	Victoria United	Arbroath	1	5	Victoria Bridge Grounds
	09/11/1889	Victoria United	Stonehaven Primrose	3	2	Cowie
Aberdeenshire Cup 3R	16/11/1889	Victoria United	Britannia	8	0	Victoria Bridge Grounds
	23/11/1889	Victoria United	Broughty Ferry	1	2	Victoria Bridge Grounds
	30/11/1889	Victoria United	Orion	2	1	Victoria Bridge Grounds
Aberdeenshire Cup 4R	07/12/1889	Victoria United	Ashley	6	0	Victoria Bridge Grounds
	14/12/1889	Victoria United	Montrose	1	3	Links Park, Montrose
	28/12/1889	Victoria United	Excelsior	4	0	Victoria Bridge Grounds
	02/01/1890	Victoria United	Partick Thistle	0	2	Victoria Bridge Grounds
	03/01/1890	Victoria United	Airdrieonians	2	5	Victoria Bridge Grounds
Aberdeenshire Cup SF	11/01/1890	Victoria United	Aberdeen	1	2	Victoria Bridge Grounds
	25/01/1890	Victoria United	Caledonian	7	1	Holburn
	01/02/1890	Victoria United	Aberdeen	0	3	Chanonry
	15/02/1890	Victoria United	Orion	5	2	Central Park
	22/02/1890	Victoria United	Brechin	1	8	Montrose St Park, Brechin
Aberdeen Charity Cup 1R	01/03/1890	Victoria United	Caledonian	3	1	Chanonry
	15/03/1890	Victoria United	Caledonian	5	2	Victoria Bridge Grounds
	22/03/1890	Victoria United	Arbroath	0	10	Gayfield, Arbroath
	05/04/1890	Victoria United	Thistle	6	1	Victoria Bridge Grounds
Aberdeen Charity Cup SF	12/04/1890	Victoria United	Aberdeen	1	2	Victoria Bridge Grounds
	19/04/1890	Victoria United	Airdrieonians	1	5	Victoria Bridge Grounds
	03/05/1890	Victoria United	Forfar Athletic	3	6	Victoria Bridge Grounds
	07/05/1890	Victoria United	Junior Association	2	4	Victoria Bridge Grounds
	07/06/1890	Victoria United	Carfin Shamrock	1	2	Victoria Bridge Grounds

Note: Bon Accord walked off the pitch after 20 minutes of the game with Victoria United on 14/09/1889

Aberdeenshire Cup 1889-1890

Competition	Date			F	A	Venue
Aberdeenshire Cup 1R	21/09/1889	Bon Accord	Thistle	1	0	Chanonry
Aberdeenshire Cup 1R	21/09/1889	Stonehaven Thistle	Vale of Dee	5	1	Stonehaven
Aberdeenshire Cup 1R	21/09/1889	Stonehaven Primrose	Inverurie	3	3	Stonehaven
Aberdeenshire Cup 1R	21/09/1889	Crescent	Ashley	1	4	Angusfield
Aberdeenshire Cup 1R	21/09/1889	Carlton	Gordon Highlanders	1	2	Links
Aberdeenshire Cup 1R	21/09/1889	Aberdeen Harp	Rubislaw Athletic	3	3	Bleachfield
Aberdeenshire Cup 1R	05/10/1889	Rubislaw Athletic	Aberdeen Harp	1	3	Rubislaw
Aberdeenshire Cup 2R	19/10/1889	Stonehaven Primrose	Stonehaven Thistle	4	0	Urie
Aberdeenshire Cup 2R	19/10/1889	Ashley	Gordon Highlanders	15	0	Bleachfield
Aberdeenshire Cup 2R	19/10/1889	Aberdeen Harp	Bon Accord	0	10	Central Park
Aberdeenshire Cup 3R	16/11/1889	Aberdeen	Bon Accord	5	0	Chanonry
Aberdeenshire Cup 3R	16/11/1889	Victoria United	Britannia	8	0	Victoria Bridge Grounds
Aberdeenshire Cup 4R	07/12/1889	Orion	Caledonian	8	6	Holburn
Aberdeenshire Cup 4R	07/12/1889	Victoria United	Ashley	6	0	Victoria Bridge Grounds
Aberdeenshire Cup 4R	07/12/1889	Black Diamond	Stonehaven Primrose	10	1	Inches
Aberdeenshire Cup 4R	14/12/1889	Orion	Caledonian	8	4	Holburn

Competition	Date			F	A	Venue
Aberdeenshire Cup 4R	14/12/1889	Stonehaven Primrose	Black Diamond	3	3	Cowie
Aberdeenshire Cup 4R	28/12/1889	Black Diamond	Stonehaven Primrose	2	0	Chanonry
Aberdeenshire Cup SF	11/01/1890	Aberdeen	Victoria United	2	1	Victoria Bridge Grounds
Aberdeenshire Cup SF	18/01/1890	Orion	Black Diamond	3	2	Central Park
Aberdeenshire Cup Final	08/02/1890	Aberdeen	Orion	2	2	Victoria Bridge Grounds
Aberdeenshire Cup Final	22/02/1890	Aberdeen	Orion	8	3	Victoria Bridge Grounds

Notes:

Not all results have been found.

A protest was lodged after the Orion-Caledonian match on 07/12/1889 and it was replayed on 14/12/1889.

Black Diamond thrashed Stonehaven Primrose 10-1 at the Inches on 28/12/1889. The ground, as was often the case, was in poor condition and the visitors lodged a protest which was sustained. The game was replayed the following week at Stonehaven and ended in a 3-3 draw. The tie was finally settled on 28th December, at Chanonry, the Blacks winning 2-0.

Aberdeen Charity Cup 1889-1890

Competition	Date			F	A	Venue
Aberdeen Charity Cup 1R	01/03/1890	Victoria United	Caledonian	3	1	Chanonry
Aberdeen Charity Cup 1R	29/03/1890	Orion	Black Diamond	4	1	Holburn
Aberdeen Charity Cup 2R	12/04/1890	Victoria United	Aberdeen	1	2	Victoria Bridge Grounds
Aberdeen Charity Cup Final	26/04/1890	Orion	Aberdeen	2	1	Victoria Bridge Grounds

1890-1891
Henry Flaws handball controversy

Football in the city was gradually becoming more organised and a natural order was establishing itself. The leading clubs, mainly but not yet exclusively those with their own grounds, became known as 'senior' sides while the smaller outfits formed themselves into 'junior' leagues and formed their own association. The number of senior clubs began to shrink while the juniors continued to grow. The main senior sides in the city at the start of 1890-1891 were Aberdeen, Caledonian, Orion and Victoria United.

It was a mixed season for Aberdeen whose Scottish Cup campaign got off to a promising start with a 5-1 win over local rivals Orion at Central Park. The Whites were expected to struggle as a significant number of newcomers had been brought into the side since the end of the previous season. But any thoughts Orion had of securing an easy win were quickly dispelled as the visitors raced into as 2-0 first half lead thanks to a double from Willie Key. It was a typical derby match during which *"an unnecessary amount of temper was infused into the proceedings, and consequently play was fast and furious, and of the kick and rush order."* Orion's hopes of a comeback were dashed when Willie Gloag was forced to retire with an injury at the start of the second period and Key soon completed his hat-trick before a fourth goal put the result beyond doubt. Tom Leggat grabbed a consolation for the Stripes but a fifth goal just before the end completed a comfortable Aberdeen win. Tom Ketchen was one of Aberdeen's stars. He was said to have been given *"some severe handling, but he behaved like a Hercules, wading through his opponents in grand style."* Orion complained *"of several of the Aberdeen (players) holding them with their hands, and planting their elbows in their sides, which is certainly very irritable and not at all conducive to a pleasant game."* No matter, it was Aberdeen who progressed to the next round to face Caledonian, another Aberdeen club which had eliminated Victoria United 2-1 in the previous round. The sides surprisingly agreed to play a friendly at the Chanonry just seven days before the Scottish Cup tie, and a weakened Aberdeen side which fielded 'veterans' Alec Clark, Charlie Glennie and Charlie Christie, edged home by 3-2. The following week, however, a much more one-sided game ended with a full strength Whites romping to an 8-0 success. Centre forward Willie Key was in great form, scoring four of the goals and having a hand in the other four. Caledonian were *"too light for their burly opponents"* and their goalkeeper, Main, who had performed so well in previous games, was below par. One local press report showed no mercy to the Caledonian forward, Gunn, who was described as being *"irritatingly bad – almost useless in fact."* The win earned Aberdeen a trip to the Highlands to play Inverness Caledonian in the next round. The match, played at Muirton, started at 1-30pm to allow Aberdeen to catch an early train home and the Chanonry side certainly seemed to be in a hurry as they sprinted into a two goal lead. The Highlanders pulled one back before the interval, but there was little indication of what was to come. In the second period Aberdeen *"went to pieces"* as Caley hit five without reply to send the visitors away with their tails between their legs.

Aberdeen's record against other city clubs was satisfactory throughout the season, although the club failed to win any silverware. In 16 games played against other Aberdeen sides, the Chanonry men lost just twice, 6-2 to Orion and 4-3 to Bon Accord, both in friendly matches. Aberdeen did, however, controversially lose out to Caledonian despite defeating their rivals in an Aberdeenshire Cup match. The Whites won the tie 6-4 at the Holburn Grounds, but a replay was ordered because of a Caledonian protest over some of the decisions of the referee, Mr P. Curran. The Chanonry side, which had won the competition for the previous three years, refused to turn up for the replay and the tie was awarded to Caledonian. A disgruntled Aberdeen didn't feature in the Charity Cup later in the season as the club was still at loggerheads with the Aberdeenshire F.A over this incident and was actually expelled for a while.

It was, however, against teams from other parts of the country that Aberdeen suffered most. It was rare for the club to travel south for such fixtures and when they did the outcome was depressing. A visit to Dunfermline ended in a 9-2 defeat while there were also defeats of 8-3 at Montrose and 8-2 at Dundee. The team sent to Montrose contained only a handful of regulars, the others coming on loan for the day from Bon Accord. Apparently the club committee had been too slow in letting the players know that a game had been arranged. In the New Year fixtures at the Chanonry, Dumbarton side Methlan Park won 5-1 while a Celtic reserve team won 4-2. At the tail end of the season Dumbarton, joint Scottish league champions with Rangers, travelled north and cruised to a 6-2 victory in front of a crowd estimated as being 5,000. Aberdeen also made a late season trip to Kintore, and handed out a 14-0 beating to the locals, but according to one account *"the Whites could have made it 40 if they had cared, but they simply amused themselves."* Fortunately for the home side, the ball burst during the second half, and because there was no replacement, the game came to an abrupt end.

A friendly fixture against Arbroath in February earned the Whites some plaudits from the visitors who were impressed by the surprisingly "genteel" approach of the hosts (a feature which seems to have been rather rare at this time). The Arbroath Guide reported on proceedings as follows: *" There was a lot of rather mixed work on the Arbroath side and they did not secure very great admiration from the Aberdonians who had gathered to see the great Red Lichties give their townsmen a thrashing. The Aberdeen men played a very fast and genteel game. They spent a good deal of time apologising and begging pardon when they collided with an Arbroath player and their overwhelming courtesy quite took some of the Maroons breath away. One or two of the Maroons were hardly so gentlemanly in their play. The Maroons were treated in a very generous way both during and after the match, and came away quite astonished at Aberdonian manners."* The match ended in an honourable 3-3 draw.

Although Aberdeen ended the season without winning either of the two major local trophies, the Aberdeenshire Cup or the Charity Cup, at the club's annual meeting it was declared that *"in the local matches the club had the advantage over all their opponents."* David Wood, Aberdeen's long serving goalkeeper, emigrated in February 1891 at the age of 26 to take up a post in Hong Kong. Educated at Gordon's College, he was described as *"the most popular athlete who has trod the classic turf of Chanonry for many a long day."* Wood had originally been a rugby player but joined Aberdeen FC in 1885 and made his mark between the sticks. The Bon Accord magazine's football writer said of Wood: *"As a goalkeeper we have never had his equal. Cool and collected under the most trying circumstances, he fists and kicks with equal ability.....We have often seen*

Davie Wood, Aberdeen F.C. goalkeeper

him tackled in goalmouth, so that it seemed almost impossible for him to get away, but he invariably succeeded in evading his opponents, who looked very crestfallen indeed on observing the sphere soaring away to the other end of the field." Wood was also an accomplished cricketer and gymnast, and he was well known in rowing and swimming circles.

Deliberate handball was still not outlawed in football at this time which meant some unscrupulous players would get away with the offence time and time again without punishment. The Aberdeen - Bon Accord game at the end of November highlighted how bad the problem had become. The Whites won the match 3-1, but Henry Flaws of Bon Accord fisted the ball off his goal line or indeed anywhere near his goal, on numerous occasions. In one instance he actually caught the ball and threw it up the park. Flaws behaved in this way on a regular basis. In the Charity Cup match between Orion and Bon Accord in February 1891 he was reported to have fisted the ball away from the goal on at least three occasions. Orion won the bruising tie 2-1 but felt aggrieved they had to play against two goalkeepers. In response, the Bon Accord club secretary, Mr A. Jaffray wrote to the local press to complain about the way in which Flaws was being criticised for handling. Mr Jaffray claimed that Flaws had only deliberately handled the ball once and he did so to prevent a goal, but if he had not handled the ball, then the goalkeeper would have been able to have saved it as he was standing right behind Flaws. Mr Jaffray didn't seem to feel, therefore, that there was any problem in Flaws' actions.

Orion's season was also a mixed bag. The Central Park men won the Aberdeenshire Cup for the first time after two previous Cup Final defeats, but lost in the Charity Cup Final after having won for the previous two years. The Scottish Cup brought no joy, as mentioned earlier, with a 5-1 loss to Aberdeen. The Stripes only ventured out of the city on four occasions, drawing a fiesty friendly 1-1 at Montrose, winning an Aberdeenshire Cup tie 9-2 at Ellon, thumping Stonehaven 7-1 in a friendly at Cowie and winning 7-5 against Brechin in another friendly at the Angus club's Montrose Street Park. The visit to Montrose, at the beginning of the season, was a somewhat unpleasant affair, the game being *"very rough"* with one home official being accused of

Henry Flaws,
Bon Accord F.C.
Persistent hand ball

"demonstrating his partisanship by throttling one of the Orion." The Aberdeen side described their opponents as *"demons"* and *"foul mouthed."* The Montrose version was that the trouble was started by Orion's Ewen who fouled the home side's star man, Keilor, on numerous occasions and was warned by the referee that he might be sent off. Ewen continued to scythe down Keilor and that sparked off a near riot amongst the fans.

Orion's 4-4 draw with Aberdeen in a friendly in late November was marked by more rough play which led to Orion's Ewen receiving a one month suspension. Throughout the match he was engaged in a constant battle with Morley Brown. At one point a spectator ran onto the pitch and tried to attack Ewen. After the match this same spectator assaulted Ewen in the nearby Riddell's Inn. Riddell's had become the Orion F.C. headquarters, the patron of the bar having given them the use of rooms and a hall for functions. Ewen left Orion shortly afterwards and joined Victoria United but returned to the Kittybrewster club after a few matches.

The furthest travelled visitors to Kittybrewster were Glasgow Thistle and Leith Athletic who headed north for the New Year holiday matches. Thistle won 6-1 on New Year's Day with Leith winning 5-2 just 48 hours later.

Victoria United did equally little travelling during the season. The Torry men won 7-0 at Inverurie and 6-4 at Stonehaven but were thrashed 11-1 at Montrose and 8-1

J. Gordon (Captain, Orion F.C.)

Jim Gordon, captain, Orion F.C.

at Brechin on their only expeditions beyond the city boundaries. It was, however, a successful campaign for the Blues who picked up their first trophy by winning the Charity Cup. They had to overcome some stubborn resistance from Caledonian in the semi final. Caley's centre forward, Forsyth, and Vics centre half Willie Stewart engaged in a tousy battle. The United player was accused of having *"a shady style of bringing up an opponent (which) called forth the intervention of the referee and the ire of the spectators on several occasions."* Vics, with a galeforce wind behind them in the first half, raced into a 3-0 lead. After the turnaround Caley pulled one back in a style which would not be tolerated today: *"The Caley goal was got after a regular rugby maul, the Vics goalkeeper, backs, and about half a dozen of the Caley (players) going through the goal in a heap."*

The Vics season was peppered with bouts of controversy and colourful incidents. There was almost a riot at Torry on the first Saturday in December when Dundee Wanderers visited the Victoria Bridge Grounds. United had taken a 3-2 lead when Dundee's Lewis hauled down Victoria's Rab Turner and a fight broke out between the two players. The home crowd decided to join in, and a number of local worthies broke onto the pitch and began attacking the visiting defender. Police were on hand to help the Wanderers player make his way to the dressing room and the visitors continued the game with 10 men. With the angry crowd still baying for blood, Lewis had to be smuggled out of the ground and was transported back across the Dee by ferry boat to avoid the masses. United went on to win this 'friendly' encounter by 5-2.

J. Burnett took over as Vics trainer in 1890-1891 having previously fulfilled the same role for Orion and Caledonian. In his younger days he had been a runner, competing at the Recreation Grounds in 10 mile races, one hour races and 'go-as-you please' events held over a number of days. He at one point was Aberdeen 10 mile champion, having set a time of 59 minutes although he claimed to have clocked 55 minutes 'in private.'

J. Burnett, trainer, Victoria United

Facilities were gradually improving at Aberdeen's football venues but changing accommodation remained fairly primitive. The Aberdeen Reserve team got changed for their match against Telephone F.C. in a wash house close to the Chanonry while the visitors just stripped off in the open.

Travel was also, on occasion, rather novel. Teams generally journeyed out of town by train, but when Aberdeen went to Stonehaven in February 1891, they did so in style, using a carriage drawn by four horses.

The city's premier clubs were still lacking in the wider experience needed to make an impact at a higher level, but moves were afoot to change all that. Aberdeen, Orion and Victoria United all took part in discussions about the formation of a Northern League which would involve sides from the North-east, Angus, Tayside and Fife. After considerable debate, agreement was reached to progress with this competition the following season, although there was considerable discomfort about which clubs would be allowed to participate and which would be left out of the competition. At one point it seemed that the League would include 12 clubs: Our Boys, East End, Johnstone Wanderers, Harp (all Dundee); Arbroath; Forfar Athletic; Montrose; St. Johnstone, Fair City (both Perth); Victoria United, Orion, Aberdeen (all Aberdeen).

A subsequent decision was taken to reduce this to eight with Johnstone Wanderers, Fair City, Orion and Victoria United all missing out. Orion and Victoria United both felt aggrieved to have been dumped from the competition especially as they had better records than Aberdeen in that season's local cup competitions. Aberdeen did, however, make more progress in the Scottish Cup than their local rivals and in overall head-to-head meetings the Whites arguably had the best record.

The Aberdeen F.C. sports, held at the Chanonry at the end of the season attracted a record entry of 676 competitors with 3,000 spectators turning up for the last of the four days. When first held in August 1886, there were 223 competitors.

ABERDEEN FOOTBALL CLUB—ANNUAL SPORTS.

INSTRUCTOR MUNRO
(General Referee).

"TICKETS, PLEASE?"
(The Ground Man.)

MR WILLIAM CORBET
(Trainer to the Club).

Aberdeen Football Club Sports at the end of the season were very popular, attracting big crowds to the Chanonry

Notable Games

Aberdeenshire 3 Perthshire 4
Inter County Match, Victoria Bridge Grounds, 11th October 1890

A crowd of 3,000 witnessed a seven goal thriller in this first Inter County representative match. Aberdeenshire were without Ketchen, A. Wood and MacKay who would all normally have been selected. A. Whitehead put the home side ahead but the visitors hit back with two quick goals before Jopp levelled the scores. Leggat gave Aberdeenshire the lead again early in the second half but Henderson soon equalised. Back came the north east men and they thought they had scored only for the referee to call for offside. A

Bill Jopp, Orion and Aberdeenshire Jopp emigrated to the USA in February 1891

draw seemed on the cards until Gray in the home goal made an error which resulted in Perthshire getting the winner. The home keeper's performance was described as *"weak and nervous."*

Aberdeenshire – Gray, Edwards, Ririe, Kirkland, Fraser, Gordon, Turner, Leggatt, Key, Jopp, A. Whitehead.

Perthshire – Tulloch, Robertson, Elliot, Watson, Winton, Reekie, Smith, Henderson, Wilson, Burnfield, Anderson

Orion 4, Caledonian 1
Aberdeenshire Cup Final, Victoria Bridge Grounds, 14th February 1891,

Perhaps it was because of the absence of one or other of the city's big clubs (Aberdeen and Victoria United) but the Cup Final attracted *"a rather small crowd of spectators."* In fact, there was some criticism of Aberdeen for arranging to play a match against Arbroath at the Chanonry at the same time as the Cup Final, a clash which was considered to have had an impact on the attendance at Torry Caledonian had thrashed Stonehaven 11-0 in the semi final, and survived a protest

Charles Annand – opened scoring for Caledonian. He was also known as a good cricketer

from the Cowie side who complained that the ground was too hard. Charles Annand, who had started his career with Bon Accord, gave Caledonian an eighth minute lead but Whitehead soon equalised for Orion. After that it was all one way traffic and Whitehead grabbed another goal from a corner to give the Central Park side a 2-1 lead at the interval. Orion totally dominated the second half with Whitehead completing his hat-trick while Kelly added a fourth to conclude a rather one-sided affair. Despite his goalscoring achievement, the Bon Accord magazine's report on the match unforgivingly declared that Orion's Kelly *"appeared too nervous and is no use against heavy opponents, parting with the ball immediately he gets it, and very seldom trying to score."* Centre half John Mackay was described as the best centre half in the town but Wattie Baird was castigated for his rough play.

Orion - Low, Edwards, Foote, Baird, Mackay, Gordon, Gloag, Leggat, Andrews, Kelly, Whitehead.

Caledonian - Main, Milne, Sutherland, Mitchell, B. Fraser, Slater, Reid, Annand, Fyfe, Fraser, Mackay

Victoria United 2, Orion 2
Charity Cup Final, Victoria Bridge Grounds, 25th April 1891

Orion swept into a 2-0 first half lead in front of a large crowd which attracted gate receipts of £50. There was a little disquiet, however, over the fact that prices had been raised for the match. Gloag got Orion's opener after just two minutes and Vics goalkeeper Cannon had to be on top form to prevent Orion going further ahead. Watson then missed a great chance for the Torry men before a Jarvis shot took a deflection off United's Stewart and flew past Cannon to make it 2-0. Victoria fought back in the second half and managed to pull level to force a replay

thanks to goals from Duffus and Turner.
Victoria United – Cannon, Simpson, Ririe, Ross, Stewart, Duffus,Turner, Sinclair, Watson, Duffus, Ferries
Orion – Low, Edwards, Foote, Jarvis, Mackay, McBain,Gloag, Leggatt, Gordon, Andrews, Whitehead.

James Ririe, Victoria United

Victoria United 2, Orion 1
Charity Cup Final, Victoria Bridge Grounds, 9th May 1891.

The Vics thoroughly deserved their victory although Orion took an early lead through Leggat, but goals from Watson and Sandy Wallace gave the Torry side a 2-1 half-time lead. The Vics continued to press in the second period but there was no further scoring and so the Torry side collected its first major trophy. The United men all played well but Ririe and Cannon were picked out as being among the best at the back while Wallace and Turner were a constant threat up front.
Victoria United – Cannon, Simpson, Ririe, Ross, Stewart, Duffus,Turner, Sinclair, Watson, Wallace, Ferries
Orion – Low, Foote, Ross, Jarvis, Mackay, Gordon,Edwards, Leggat, Gloag, Andrews, Whitehead.

Aberdeen 2 Dumbarton 6
Chanonry, 23rd May 1891

Aberdeen pulled in some top players from other local clubs to strengthen their side ahead of this meeting with Dumbarton who had tied with Rangers for the Scottish Fist Division league title.

The match attracted a crowd of 5,000 spectators who bathed in the early summer sunshine. Aberdeen made a bright start but the visitors got the first goal midway through the first half, Galbraith scoring with a low shot.Centre-half Boyle made it 2-0 with a scorching shot, a third followed quickly then Mallor made it 4-0 at the interval. The home side rallied in the second period and following a spell of pressure they reduced the leeway when Watson turned a Key header beyond his own goalkeeper.Leggat then grabbed another to rouse the home support but

J. Duffus, Victoria United – played for Aberdeen against Dumbarton	Mr John Stewart, one of the founders of Bon Accord F. C., was presented with a gold medal by his team-mates at the end of the season prior to his emigration to the USA.	J. W. Caithness, Aberdeen F.C. Caithness started off with Ashley then played as a full back for Orion before moving to Aberdeen.

Dumbarton responded again by scoring a fifth. The Chanonry men claimed another goal following a scramble in the Dumbarton goal area but the referee turned down their claim.before the end Dumbarton secured a sixth. The teams enjoyed a post match meal in the Atheneum after which several toasts were celebrated and many songs were sung.

Aberdeen - Caithness, Ketchen, Wood, Gordon, Thomson, Duffus, Turner, Leggat, W. Key, Sinclair, Whitehead.

Dumbarton - McLeod, Watson, Miller, McMillan, Boyle, Lang, Taylor, Galbraith, Mallor, McNaught, Black

Aberdeen F.C. - 1890-1891

Competition	Date		Opposition	F	A	Venue
	23/08/1890	Aberdeen	Victoria United	7	3	Chanonry
	30/08/1890	Aberdeen	Dunfermline	2	9	Dunfermline
Scottish Cup 1R	06/09/1890	Aberdeen	Orion	5	1	Central Park
	20/09/1890	Aberdeen	Caledonian	3	2	Chanonry
Scottish Cup 2R	27/09/1890	Aberdeen	Caledonian	8	0	Chanonry
	04/10/1890	Aberdeen	Dunfermline Athletic	2	2	Chanonry

Competition	Date		Opposition	F	A	Venue
Scottish Cup 3R	18/10/1890	Aberdeen	Inverness Caledonian	2	6	Inverness
	25/10/1890	Aberdeen	Thistle	10	0	Chanonry
	01/11/1890	Aberdeen	Our Boys,Dundee	2	8	West Craigie Park,Dundee
	08/11/1890	Aberdeen	Victoria United	4	1	Victoria Bridge Grounds
	15/11/1890	Aberdeen	Bon Accord	3	2	Chanonry
	22/11/1890	Aberdeen	Orion	4	4	Chanonry
	29/11/1890	Aberdeen	Bon Accord	3	1	Chanonry
Friendly	06/12/1890	Aberdeen	Aberdeen University	8	1	University
Aberdeenshire Cup 4R	13/12/1890	Aberdeen	Caledonian	6	4	Holburn
Aberdeenshire Cup 4R	27/12/1890	Aberdeen	Caledonian	*	*	Chanonry
	01/01/1891	Aberdeen	Methlan Park (Dunbartonshire)	1	5	Chanonry
	03/01/1891	Aberdeen	Glasgow Celtic Reserves	2	4	Chanonry
	10/01/1891	Aberdeen	Arbroath	2	3	Gayfield
	17/01/1891	Aberdeen	Edinburgh University	3	2	Chanonry
	24/01/1891	Aberdeen	Montrose	3	8	Montrose
	31/01/1891	Aberdeen	Orion	2	1	Chanonry
	07/02/1891	Aberdeen	Stonehaven	5	0	Chanonry
	14/02/1891	Aberdeen	Arbroath	3	3	Chanonry
	21/02/1891	Aberdeen	Caledonian	2	1	Holburn
	28/02/1891	Aberdeen	Stonehaven	8	2	Stonehaven
	07/03/1891	Aberdeen	Inverness Caledonian	4	5	Chanonry
	14/03/1891	Aberdeen	Orion	2	6	Chanonry
	21/03/1891	Aberdeen	Montrose	0	4	Chanonry
	27/03/1891	Aberdeen XI	Culter	3	3	Culter
	28/03/1891	Aberdeen	Kintore	14	0	Kintore
	04/04/1891	Aberdeen	Bon Accord	3	4	Chanonry
	11/04/1891	Aberdeen	Our Boys Dundee	4	7	Chanonry

Competition	Date		Opposition	F	A	Venue
	18/04/1891	Aberdeen	Victoria United	5	5	Chanonry
	02/05/1891	Aberdeen	Cameron Highlanders	4	4	Chanonry
	23/05/1891	Aberdeen	Dumbarton	2	6	Chanonry

Note: Caledonian submitted a protest over their defeat by Aberdeen in an Aberdeenshire Cup tie on 13th December. A replay was scheduled for 27th December but Aberdeen refused to play and were thereby eliminated from the tournament.

Orion F.C. - 1890-1891

Competition	Date		Opposition	F	A	Venue
	16/08/1890	Orion	Forfar Athletic	4	6	Central Park
Friendly	23/08/1890	Orion	Montrose	1	1	Links Park,Montrose
Scottish Cup 1R	06/09/1890	Orion	Aberdeen	1	5	Central Park
	13/09/1890	Orion	Brechin	3	2	Central Park
	17/09/1890	Orion	Hawthorn,Peterhead	12	2	Central Park
	20/09/1890	Orion	Victoria United	3	2	Central Park
	04/10/1890	Orion	Stonehaven	7	1	Stonehaven
	18/10/1890	Orion	Harp,Dundee	4	0	Central Park
	01/11/1890	Orion	Caledonian	6	1	Central Park
	15/11/1890	Orion	Cameron Highlanders	4	3	Central Park
	22/11/1890	Orion	Aberdeen	4	4	Chanonry
	06/12/1890	Orion	Broughty Ferry	1	2	Central Park
Aberdeenshire Cup 4R	13/12/1890	Orion	Ellon	9	2	Ellon
	01/01/1891	Orion	Glasgow Thistle	1	6	Central Park
	03/01/1891	Orion	Leith Athletic	2	5	Central Park
	10/01/1891	Orion	Victoria United	3	1	Victoria Bridge Grounds
Aberdeenshire Cup SF	24/01/1891	Orion	Victoria United	3	1	Victoria Bridge Grounds
	31/01/1891	Orion	Aberdeen	1	2	Chanonry
	07/02/1891	Orion	University	3	2	Old Aberdeen
Aberdeenshire Cup Final	14/02/1891	Orion	Caledonian	4	1	Victoria Bridge Grounds
	21/02/1891	Orion	Thistle	7	0	Central Park

Competition	Date		Opposition	F	A	Venue
Charity Cup	28/02/1891	Orion	Bon Accord	2	1	Victoria Bridge Grounds
	07/03/1891	Orion	Coupar Angus	3	2	Central Park
	14/03/1891	Orion	Aberdeen	6	2	Chanonry
	28/03/1891	Orion	Brechin	7	5	Montrose St Park, Brechin
	04/04/1891	Orion	Montrose	3	3	Central Park
Charity Cup Final	25/04/1891	Orion	Victoria United	2	2	Victoria Bridge Grounds
Charity Cup Final Replay	09/05/1891	Orion	Victoria United	1	2	Victoria Bridge Grounds

Victoria United F.C. - 1890-1891

Competition	Date		Opposition	F	A	Venue
	23/08/1890	Victoria United	Aberdeen	3	7	Chanonry
	30/08/1890	Victoria United	Arbroath	1	5	Victoria Bridge Grounds
Scottish Cup 1R	06/09/1890	Victoria United	Caledonian	1	2	Victoria Bridge Grounds
	13/09/1890	Victoria United	Bon Accord	3	2	Victoria Bridge Grounds
	20/09/1890	Victoria United	Orion	2	3	Central Park
	27/09/1890	Victoria United	Inverurie	7	0	Inverurie
	18/10/1890	Victoria United	Caledonian	3	2	Holburn
	25/10/1890	Victoria United	Cowdenbeath	3	5	Victoria Bridge Grounds
	01/11/1890	Victoria United	East End,Dundee	1	4	Victoria Bridge Grounds
	08/11/1890	Victoria United	Aberdeen	1	4	Victoria Bridge Grounds
	15/11/1890	Victoria United	Montrose	9	1	Victoria Bridge Grounds
	22/11/1890	Victoria United	Bon Accord	2	1	Victoria Bridge Grounds
	29/11/1890	Victoria United	Kings Park Stirling	3	4	Victoria Bridge Grounds
	06/12/1890	Victoria United	Dundee Wanderers	5	2	Victoria Bridge Grounds
Aberdeenshire Cup 4R	13/12/1890	Victoria United	Bon Accord	4	1	Victoria Bridge Grounds
Friendly	27/12/1890	Victoria United	Stonehaven	6	4	Stonehaven
	02/01/1891	Victoria United	East Stirlingshire	1	9	Victoria Bridge Grounds
	03/01/1891	Victoria United	Dykebar,Paisley	3	5	Victoria Bridge Grounds
	10/01/1891	Victoria United	Orion	1	3	Victoria Bridge Grounds

Competition	Date		Opposition	F	A	Venue
	17/01/1891	Victoria United	Our Boys Dundee	3	6	West Craigie Park
Aberdeenshire	24/01/1891	Victoria United	Orion	1	3	Victoria Bridge Grounds
Cup SF						
	31/01/1891	Victoria United	Caledonian	5	0	Victoria Bridge Grounds
	07/02/1891	Victoria United	Montrose	1	11	Montrose
	21/02/1891	Victoria United	Forfar Athletic	2	5	Victoria Bridge Grounds
	07/03/1891	Victoria United	Our Boys Dundee	2	6	Victoria Bridge Grounds
	14/03/1891	Victoria United	Caledonian	8	0	Victoria Bridge Grounds
	21/03/1891	Victoria United	Brechin	1	8	Montrose St Park
Charity Cup1R	28/03/1891	Victoria United	Caledonian	3	1	Victoria Bridge Grounds
	04/04/1891	Victoria United	Dunblane	3	1	Victoria Bridge Grounds
	11/04/1891	Victoria United	Thistle	12	0	Victoria Bridge Grounds
	18/04/1891	Victoria United	Aberdeen	5	5	Chanonry
Charity Cup	25/04/1891	Victoria United	Orion	2	2	Victoria Bridge Grounds
Final						
Charity Cup	09/05/1891	Victoria United	Orion	2	1	Victoria Bridge Grounds
Final Replay						
	16/05/1891	Victoria United	Brechin	4	1	Victoria Bridge Grounds
	30/05/1891	Victoria United	Raith Rovers	2	7	Victoria Bridge Grounds

Aberdeenshire Cup 1890-1891

Competition	Date			F	A	Venue
Aberdeenshire		Aberdeen	Aberdeen University	*	*	
Cup 1R						
Aberdeenshire	18/10/1890	Inverurie	Vale of Dee	1	1	Inverurie
Cup 2R						
Aberdeenshire	18/10/1890	1st Batt Gordon	Ellon	0	1	Ellon Cricket Ground
Cup 2R		Highlanders				
Aberdeenshire	25/10/1890	Inverurie	Vale of Dee	3	2	
Cup 2R						
Aberdeenshire	22/11/1890	Caledonian	Inverurie	8	0	Holburn
Cup 3R						

Competition	Date			F	A	Venue
Aberdeenshire Cup 4R	13/12/1890	Caledonian	Aberdeen	4	6	Holburn
Aberdeenshire Cup 4R	13/12/1890	Stonehaven	Aberdeen Thistle	8	1	Stonehaven
Aberdeenshire Cup 4R	13/12/1890	Victoria United	Bon Accord	4	1	Victoria Bridge Grounds
Aberdeenshire Cup 4R	13/12/1890	Orion	Ellon	9	2	Ellon
Aberdeenshire Cup 4R	27/12/1890	Aberdeen	Caledonian	*	*	Chanonry
Aberdeenshire Cup SF	17/01/1891	Caledonian	Stonehaven	11	0	Holburn
Aberdeenshire Cup SF	24/01/1891	Victoria United	Orion	1	3	Victoria Bridge Grounds
Aberdeenshire Cup Final	14/02/1891	Orion	Caledonian	4	1	Victoria Bridge Grounds

Notes: (1) The First Round tie between Aberdeen and University never took place because the students failed to raise a team.

(2) Caleldonian submitted a protest over their defeat by Aberdeen in an Aberdeenshire Cup tie on 13th December. A replay was scheduled for 27th December but Aberdeen refused to play and were thereby eliminated from the tournament.

Charity Cup 1890-1891

Competition	Date			F	A	Venue
Charity Cup 1R/SF	28/02/1891	Orion	Bon Accord	2	1	Victoria Bridge Grounds
Charity Cup 1R/SF	28/03/1891	Victoria United	Caledonian	3	1	Victoria Bridge Grounds
Charity Cup Final	25/04/1891	Victoria United	Orion	2	2	Victoria Bridge Grounds
Final Replay	09/05/1891	Victoria United	Orion	2	1	Victoria Bridge Grounds

1891-1892
Key's historic penalty

Aberdeen's entry to the Northern League gave the Chanonry club a clear focus for the season ahead, but before that competition got underway there was business to see to in the Scottish Cup. The Whites were drawn against city rivals Caledonian in the First Round, but Aberdeen didn't have to break sweat as their opponents scratched from the contest. At the same stage Bon Accord thumped Stonehaven 9-0 to earn a place in the second round while Victoria United and Orion played out a goalless draw at Torry, with the Stripes eventually winning through to the next round by winning the replay 5-1 on their own patch. The regionalised draw for the second round paired Aberdeen with Bon Accord, while Orion received a bye. For Aberdeen player William Key, the match against the Bons would prove to be an historic occasion as he claimed his place in local football history by becoming the first man to score from a penalty kick in the city. SFA officials had become increasingly frustrated by the amount of fouling and deliberate hand balls taking place within the goal areas at games across the country. There was little to deter the perpetrators of such crimes, so the Association decided to introduce 'the penalty kick' at the start of season 1891-1892. The rule was somewhat different to that we know today, and for interest, it is worth describing it here in full: 'If any player should intentionally trip or hold an opposing player, or deliberately handle the ball within 12 yards of his own goal-line, the referee shall, on appeal, award the opposing side a penalty kick, to be taken from any point 12 yards from the goal-line, under the following conditions:- All players, with the exception of the player taking the penalty kick and the opposing goalkeeper (Who should not advance more than six yards from the goal-line) shall stand at least six yards behind the ball. The ball shall be in play when the kick is taken. A goal may be scored from the penalty kick.'

Key's big moment came in the second half of the tie with Bon Accord at the Holburn Grounds. Aberdeen had established a 2-1 first half lead, Key and Brown scoring for the Whites before James Flaws pulled one back just before the interval. No details of the penalty exist other than that Key had the honour of scoring from the spot. Aberdeen went on to win 5-2 thanks to further goals from

William Key, Aberdeen F.C. – scorer of the first penalty kick in the city

Whitehead and Thomson. Key, who was raised in Montrose before moving to the Grammar School in Aberdeen, left the city at the end of the season to further his law studies at Edinburgh University.

Aberdeen moved into the Third Round and defeated Orion 3-1. The city club's progress continued when they came back from 1-0 down at halftime to defeat Dunbartonshire's Dalmuir Thistle 2-1 to set up a Fifth Round tie with Mid Annandale. The game was played at Stirling where an aggrieved Aberdeen lost 6-2. The Whites weren't too happy with the outcome and lodged an unsuccessful protest which focussed on the *"state of the ground and the rough play of their opponents."* The Chanonry men weren't too impressed either by the foul language coming from their adversaries. The Whites contributed to their own downfall, the Bon Accord magazine reporting that goalkeeper Ritchie *"was awfully nervous and terribly mixed, seemingly being unable to make up his mind what to do in an emergency."*

Aberdeen's Northern League season had, in the meantime, got off to a difficult start with the Whites losing three and drawing one of their first four matches during which they scored eight goals and conceded 22. The elusive first win came, unexpectedly, with a 4-0 thumping of Arbroath at the Chanonry on 14th November, the goals coming from Thomson, Key, Whitehead and Brown. The celebrations were short-lived, however, as the Angus side successfully claimed that the fixture should be replayed. Arbroath officials complained that the match was 13 minutes late in starting due to the later arrival onto the pitch of the Aberdeen team and that because of this the referee was forced to stop the game seven minutes short of the regulation time because the pitch was in darkness.

Victoria United - Aberdeenshire Cup Winners 1891-1892

The League Committee agreed and ordered a replay. When it was played, the visitors won 4-1, but Aberdeen took their revenge at Gayfield later in the season when a last minute goal gave them a 4-3 victory. A 6-2 defeat from St. Johnstone at Perth at the beginning of October could be put down in part to the chaotic preparations for the game. The Aberdeen train was late in arriving with the result that the players got changed in a railway carriage then rushed to the ground and immediately started the game.

The Whites had to wait until 30th January for their first league win, a 4-2 success against Forfar Athletic. It was to be one of just five wins as Aberdeen ended the season in sixth position from the eight competing clubs. Dundee rivals East End and Our Boys shared the inaugural title, but not after some controversy. East End had been deducted two points for fielding an ineligible player in a win over Montrose which meant that they and Our Boys both had 19 points. The League Committee decided that a play-off should be held to determine the destiny of the title, but East End refused to play and threatened legal action unless they were declared champions. A compromise was eventually negotiated which led to the

Sandy Wallace in his
Sheffield United strip

title being shared. The Committee also decided to extend the league to ten clubs for the following season with Victoria United and Johnstone Wanderers being elected. For some reason a subsequent change was made, however, and United's place was taken by Fair City Athletic.

The Torry side may not have been able to participate in the Northern League but they did dominate the main local competitions during the season, winning both the Aberdeenshire Cup and the Charity Cup. United defeated Aberdeen 2-0 in the Aberdeenshire Cup Final to lift the trophy for the first time and they retained the Charity Cup with a comfortable 3-0 win over Orion.

The Vics continued to show great enterprise by inviting a string of notable big name clubs to Torry for challenge matches throughout the season, none more so than Heart of Midlothian who finished in third position in the Scottish League. The Edinburgh side won 3-1 at the Victoria Bridge Grounds in a Friday evening game at the end of the season. A weakened Queen's Park also paid a visit and were sent away with a 7-0 thrashing. The season's Scottish champions, Dumbarton, maintained their links with Aberdeen by visiting the Chanonry in January and winning 6-1.

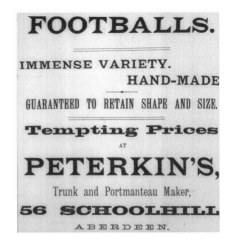

Advert for footballs, 1891

Last photograph of Bon Accord F.C. April 1892
Players Back Row (Left to right) – James Lamont, Dod Thomson (goalkeeper), Henry Flaws (Captain).
Middle Row (left to right) - Morren, McBain, Ewen.
Front row (left to right) James Flaws, MacFarlane, John Forsyth, Hay, Black.
Henry Flaws, James Flaws and James Lamont had been capped at County level.

Sandy Wallace, who played for the Vics for a couple of seasons and scored the winning goal in the previous season's Charity Cup Final, left to join Paisley's Abercorn but was quickly signed up as a full time professional by top English side Sheffield United where he made his mark.

Orion's season was somewhat disappointing as they failed to win any silverware. The highlights included hitting double figures on three occasions - a 15-2 annihilation of Peterhead in the Aberdeenshire Cup, a 10-2 win over Fraserburgh Wanderers and a 10-0 victory over Aberdeen Thistle. Off the field, the club was well known for its social evenings in Miss Riddell's New Inn at Kittybrewster where, apparently, many a fine night was spent.

More generally, the playing of football in the city streets still wasn't being tolerated at this time and four youngsters - Thomas Johnston, James Clark, George Duguid and William Milne - found themselves in front of Aberdeen Police Court after being found kicking a ball in Mount Place. Baillie Mearns expressed concern that this was a problem which was getting worse and threatened to jail the lads unless they promised not to commit this crime again. The promise was made and they were released. There were also conflicts between footballers and others down at the Links, prompting one local worthy to write to the Aberdeen Journal with a plea that football should be restricted to the area north of Broad Hill and south of Cotton Street, leaving the central area free for others. Concerns were also expressed about the loss of pitches at the Recreation Grounds, Inches, where industrial developments were taking over the open spaces. Meanwhile the infamous Bon Accord F.C. decided to call it a day, because a few of their leading players were leaving the town, some emigrating to the USA. Most of the remaining players joined Aberdeen. A farewell supper for club members was held in the Waverley Hotel when some expressed a desire to reform the club at a future date should there be enough interest. Popular captain, Henry Flaws, was presented with *"a handsome dressing case"* by his fellow players. It was reported that in this, their final season, the Bons played 23 matches, winning 16, losing four and drawing three. They scored 134 goals and conceded 88.

Notable Games

Aberdeen 1, East End, Dundee 5
Northern League, Chanonry, 21st September 1891
Aberdeen entertained Dundee's East End in the first Northern League match played in the city. A crowd of 3,000 turned up at the Chanonry. Aberdeen took the lead in the first half following some enterprising play from Frank Whitehead. East End responded with some rough play which upset the home crowd but it proved effective as the visitors grabbed two goals before the interval. Aberdeen put an almighty effort into the opening period of the second half but ultimately ran out of steam and the Dundonians added three late goals to win 5-1. East End went on to share the title with local rivals Our Boys.

Aberdeen - Ritchie, Ketchen, Wood, Ross, McDonald, Cobban, Robinson, Thomson, Key, Sands, F. Whitehead.

East End - Fotheringham, Ramsay, Brown, Petrie, Longair, Knowles, Reid, Webster, Craik, Coupar, Gilligan.

Aberdeen 5, Bon Accord 2
Scottish Cup, 2nd Round, Holburn Grounds, 26th September 1891

This game was significant because it featured the first penalty kick to be awarded in Aberdeen following the introduction of the new law at the beginning of the season. Aberdeen's William Key scored from the award. It was perhaps ironic that the penalty should be awarded against Bon Accord as their captain, Henry Flaws, was one of the best known characters for deliberately handling the ball in his own goalmouth to prevent the opposition scoring. Until now he was never penalised for his actions. Key had also given Aberdeen an early lead which was added to by W.S. Brown before James Flaws scored for Bons before the interval. Key's penalty made it 3-1 and further goals followed from Whitehead and Thomson. Bons grabbed a late second, but they were outclassed. Bon Accord's rough play was noted in the press: *"Fouls for infringements were numerous against the Bon Accord who should at once remedy the defects."*

Aberdeen – Ritchie, Ketchen, Wood, Reith, Ross, Cobban, F. Brown, Thomson, Key, W.S. Brown, Whitehead.

Bon Accord – Thomson, Lamont, H. Flaws, Ingram, McBain, Black, Rice, Macfarlane, Forsyth, Hay, J. Flaws.

Referee – Mr. Aitchison, Victoria United

Aberdeen 0, Victoria United 2
Aberdeenshire Cup Final, Chanonry 13th February 1892

A record crowd of 7,000 packed into the Chanonry for the final. Vics were without their captain, Rab Turner, because of a family bereavement, and his place was taken by Wallace. The Whites were at full strength, although an injury to Willie Key during the game didn't help their cause. Vics were also handicapped by an injury to Peter Simpson who missed most of the second half. It was a tense and untidy encounter in which the balance of play swung from one side to the other. At

J. Sinclair – scorer of Victoria United's second goal in Cup Final.

129

the end of the day it was United's better finishing, combined with some fine goalkeeping from Cannon, which decided the outcome. Binks give the Torry men the lead after 30 mins and shortly before halftime former Arbroath player J. Sinclair added a second. There was no further scoring and so United lifted the Cup for the first time. It was also the first time Aberdeen had been beaten in the competition.

Aberdeen - Low, Ketchen, Wood, Ross, Reith, Thomson, Cobban, Brown, Key,Thomson, Whitehead

Victoria United - Cannon, Thomson, Ririe, Ross, Stewart, Duffus, Wallace, Sinclair, Binks, Simpson, Ferries

Victoria United 3, Orion 0
Charity Cup Final, Chanonry, 30th April 1892

Vics completed a local Cup double by winning the trophy for the second year in a row with a comfortable win. Annand gave the Torry men a first minute lead and they missed several chances before Orion came close with a shot which hit the crossbar. Orion made a positive start to the second half and Cannon had to be in good form to prevent the Central Park side from equalising. But United settled again and gradually took control. Binks, who also scored in the Aberdeenshire Cup Final, put them 2-0 ahead then Rab Turner made it three.

Orion - Lumsden, Mackay, Foote, Wight, Low, Baird, Fraser, Leggat, Gloag, Ruxton, Mitchell.

Victoria United - Cannon, Ririe, Thomson, Duffus, Stewart, Ross, Turner, Sinclair, Binks, Annand, Ferries.

Aberdeen 2, London Caledonians 3
Chanonry, 16th April 1892

Technically the Caledonians were the first English-based side to play in Aberdeen. The team was made up of Scots living in the capital. They played in the F.A. Cup around this time but never made it beyond the qualifying

Rab Turner, Captain of Victoria United

London Caledonians F.C.
Back Row (left to right) - Laing, Howie, Williamson, W. Stirling, P. Hunter, MacPherson (Hon Sec).
Middle Row (left to right) Menzie, A. Whitehead, W. Hay (Captain), J. Barbour, J. Barclay.
Front (left to right) - J. Key, Brown.

stages. The London side included Arthur Whitehead, a former Aberdeen player, and Joss Key, the brother of Aberdeen's Willie Key. The visitors dominated the opening period and soon established a three goal lead and had another disallowed. Aberdeen gradually worked their way into the game and Frank Whitehead reduced the deficit before halftime. Colin Ross sustained an injury early in the second half and Aberdeen had to play with ten men for a long spell. When Ross was able to return to the game the home side again began to press forward and, following a scrimmage, scored a second goal. The Whites continued to apply pressure but couldn't get an equaliser before the final whistle.

Aberdeen - Ramsay, Ketchen, Wood, C. Ross, Thomson, Cobban, Flaws, Macfarlane, Forsyth, Brown, Whitehead.

Caledonians - William Stirling, H. Gaylord, J. Barbour, J.D. Menzies, J.M. Barclay, G.M. Key, R.H. Howie, A. Whitehead, R.H. Clark, W. Williamson, C.H. Brown

Northern League 1891-1892

		P	W	D	L	F	A	Pts
1	East End *	14	10	1	3	41	24	19
2	Our Boys	14	9	1	4	56	39	19
3	Montrose	14	5	4	5	49	45	14
4	Harp	14	5	3	6	43	53	13
5	Arbroath	14	5	2	7	43	44	12
6	Aberdeen	14	5	2	7	39	62	12
7	Forfar Athletic	14	4	2	8	35	47	10
8	St Johnstone *	14	4	3	7	41	41	9

Title shared by Dundee clubs Our Boys and East End

* Two points deducted for fielding ineligible players

Aberdeen F.C - Northern League 1891-1892

Competition	Date		Opposition	F	A	Venue
Northern League	19/09/1891	Aberdeen	East End, Dundee	1	5	Chanonry
Northern League	03/10/1891	Aberdeen	St Johnstone	2	6	Perth
Northern League	10/10/1891	Aberdeen	Forfar Athletic	2	2	Chanonry
Northern League	24/10/1891	Aberdeen	Montrose	3	9	Links Park,Montrose
Northern League	19/12/1891	Aberdeen	Montrose	3	3	Chanonry
Northern League	30/01/1892	Aberdeen	Forfar Athletic	4	2	Forfar
Northern league	20/02/1892	Aberdeen	Harp Dundee	5	4	Chanonry
Northern League	05/03/1892	Aberdeen	Our Boys Dundee	4	5	Dundee
Northern League	19/03/1892	Aberdeen	East End, Dundee	0	8	Carolina Port,Dundee
Northern League	02/04/1892	Aberdeen	Arbroath	1	4	Chanonry
Northern League	09/04/1892	Aberdeen	Our Boys Dundee	6	4	Chanonry
Northern League	23/04/1892	Aberdeen	Harp Dundee	1	6	East Dock St Dundee
Northern League	07/05/1892	Aberdeen	Arbroath	4	3	Gayfield,Arbroath
Northern League	14/05/1892	Aberdeen	St Johnstone	3	1	Chanonry

Notes: The two games shown below were played as Northern League fixtures but on both occasions the League ordered replays. Arbroath had protested that their match at Chanonry was called to a halt seven minutes early because of darkness. The Angus side claimed that the problem occurred when Aberdeen were late in taking the field for the start of the game and the League Committee agreed there should be a rematch. The St Johnstone game was replayed as both sides agreed the original match should only be given 'friendly' status because of poor ground conditions.

				F	A	
Northern League	14/11/1891	Aberdeen	Arbroath	4	0	Chanonry
Northern league	12/03/1892	Aberdeen	St Johnstone	2	4	Chanonry

Aberdeen Captain Tom Ketchen depicted celebrating his club's 5-2 Aberdeenshire Cup Semi Final win over Orion.

Aberdeen F.C. - Other Games 1891-1892

Competition	Date		Opposition	F	A	Venue
Friendly	29/08/1891	Aberdeen	Orion	5	2	Chanonry
Scottish Cup	05/09/1891	Aberdeen	Caledonian	w	0	
Friendly	12/09/1891	Aberdeen	Stonehaven	9	3	Stonehaven
Scottish Cup	26/09/1891	Aberdeen	Bon Accord	5	2	Holburn
Scottish Cup	17/10/1891	Aberdeen	Orion	3	1	Central Park
Aberdeenshire Cup 1R	31/10/1891	Aberdeen	Stonehaven	4	2	Chanonry
Scottish Cup	07/11/1891	Aberdeen	Dalmuir Thistle	2	1	Chanonry
Scottish Cup	05/12/1891	Aberdeen	Mid Annandale	2	6	Stirling
Aberdeenshire Cup 2R	12/12/1891	Aberdeen	Bon Accord	6	4	Chanonry
Friendly	02/01/1892	Aberdeen	Victoria United	5	6	Victoria Bridge Grounds
Friendly	04/01/1892	Aberdeen	Dumbarton	1	6	Chanonry
Friendly	16/01/1892	Aberdeen	Orion	2	5	Chanonry

Competition	Date		Opposition	F	A	Venue
Aberdeenshire Cup SF	23/01/1892	Aberdeen	Orion	5	2	Chanonry
Friendly	06/02/1892	Aberdeen	Cameron Highlanders	5	2	Chanonry
Aberdeenshire Cup Final	13/02/1892	Aberdeen	Victoria United	0	2	Chanonry
Charity Cup	26/03/1892	Aberdeen	Orion	0	2	Victoria Bridge Grounds
Friendly	16/04/1892	Aberdeen	London Caledonians	2	3	Chanonry
Friendly	12/05/1892	Aberdeen	Orion	3	1	Central Park

Note: Caledonian scratched from their Scottish Cup tie with Aberdeen on 05/09/1891.

Orion F.C. - 1891-1892

Competition	Date		Opposition	F	A	Venue
Friendly	29/08/1891	Orion	Aberdeen	2	5	Chanonry
Scottish Cup	05/09/1891	Orion	Victoria United	0	0	Victoria Bridge Grounds
Scottish Cup	12/09/1891	Orion	Victoria United	5	1	Central Park
	26/09/1891	Orion	Fraserburgh Wanderers	10	2	Fraserburgh Links
	03/10/1891	Orion	Montrose	1	2	Central Park
	10/10/1891	Orion	Stonehaven	6	4	Stonehaven
Scottish Cup	17/10/1891	Orion	Aberdeen	1	3	Central Park
	24/10/1891	Orion	Victoria United	2	3	Central Park
	07/11/1891	Orion	Strathmore, Dundee	0	1	Central Park
	14/11/1891	Orion	Johnstone Wanderers	1	6	Clepington Park, Dundee
	21/11/1891	Orion	Peterhead	4	4	Recreation Park, Peterhead
	28/11/1891	Orion	Aberdeen Thistle	10	0	Central Park
Aberdeenshire Cup 2R	12/12/1891	Orion	Peterhead	15	2	Peterhead
	19/12/1891	Orion	Bon Accord	1	1	Central Park
	26/12/1891	Orion	Our Boys, Blairgowrie	4	1	Central Park
	01/01/1892	Orion	East Stirlingshire	3	6	Central Park
	02/01/1892	Orion	Leith Athletic	1	8	Central Park
	16/01/1892	Orion	Aberdeen	5	2	Chanonry

Competition	Date		Opposition	F	A	Venue
Aberdeenshire Cup SF	23/01/1892	Orion	Aberdeen	2	5	Chanonry
	30/01/1892	Orion	Johnstone Wanderers	3	3	Central Park
	06/02/1892	Orion	East End, Dundee	2	1	Central Park
	27/02/1892	Orion	Stonehaven	2	1	Urie Stonehaven
	05/03/1892	Orion	Victoria United	1	5	Victoria Bridge Grounds
	12/03/1892	Orion	Bon Accord	1	4	Holburn
	19/03/1892	Orion	Brechin	6	4	Montrose St Park Brechin
Charity Cup	26/03/1892	Orion	Aberdeen	2	0	Victoria Bridge Grounds
	02/04/1892	Orion	Victoria United	1	5	Victoria Bridge Grounds
	16/04/1892	Orion	Montrose	0	5	Links Park,Montrose
Charity Cup Final	30/04/1892	Orion	Victoria United	0	3	Chanonry
	02/05/1892	Orion	Brechin	1	4	Victoria Bridge Grounds
Friendly	12/05/1892	Orion	Aberdeen	1	3	Central Park
	14/05/1892	Orion	Port Glasgow Athletic	1	8	Central Park

Tam Leggat, Orion F.C. Captain

Victoria United F.C. - 1891-1892

Competition	Date		Opposition	F	A	Venue
	01/08/1891	Victoria United	Mossend Swifts	2	4	Victoria Bridge Grounds
	15/08/1891	Victoria United	Johnstone Wanderers	1	1	Victoria Bridge Grounds

Competition	Date		Opposition	F	A	Venue
	22/08/1891	Victoria United	Lochee United	2	1	Victoria Bridge Grounds
Scottish Cup 1R	05/09/1891	Victoria United	Orion	0	0	Victoria Bridge Grounds
Scottish Cup 1R	12/09/1891	Victoria United	Orion	1	5	Central Park
	19/09/1891	Victoria United	Black Diamond	6	3	Victoria Bridge Grounds
	26/09/1891	Victoria United	Forfar Athletic	3	1	Victoria Bridge Grounds
	03/10/1891	Victoria United	Dunfermline	2	1	Victoria Bridge Grounds
	10/10/1891	Victoria United	Coupar Angus	5	1	Victoria Bridge Grounds
	17/10/1891	Victoria United	Brechin	3	6	Montrose St Park, Brechin
	24/10/1891	Victoria United	Orion	3	2	Central park
	07/11/1891	Victoria United	Harp,Dundee	6	3	Victoria Bridge Grounds
	14/11/1891	Victoria United	Cambuslang	2	1	Victoria Bridge Grounds
	28/11/1891	Victoria United	Cowlairs	2	4	Victoria Bridge Grounds
Aberdeenshire Cup 2R	12/12/1891	Victoria United	Ellon	*	*	
	19/12/1891	Victoria United	Brechin	5	0	Victoria Bridge Grounds
Aberdeenshire Cup SF	26/12/1891	Victoria United	Black Diamond	13	0	Victoria Bridge Grounds
	02/01/1892	Victoria United	Aberdeen	6	5	Victoria Bridge Grounds
	09/01/1892	Victoria United	Inverurie	9	0	Inverurie
	16/01/1892	Victoria United	Johnstone 7 Wanderers	1		Clepington Park, Dundee
	23/01/1892	Victoria United	Peterhead	9	2	Recreation Park, Peterhead
	30/01/1892	Victoria United	Raith Rovers	1	2	Victoria Bridge Grounds
	06/02/1892	Victoria United	Dunblane	8	2	Victoria Bridge Grounds
Aberdeenshire Cup Final	13/02/1892	Victoria United	Aberdeen	2	0	Chanonry
Charity Cup	27/02/1892	Victoria United	Bon Accord	3	2	Chanonry
	05/03/1892	Victoria United	Orion	5	1	Victoria Bridge Grounds
	12/03/1892	Victoria United	Stonehaven	13	1	
	19/03/1892	Victoria United	Our Boys Dundee	5	4	Victoria Bridge Grounds
	26/03/1892	Victoria United	Montrose	0	4	Links Park Montrose

Competition	Date		Opposition	F	A	Venue
	02/04/1892	Victoria United	Orion	5	1	Victoria Bridge Grounds
	23/04/1892	Victoria United	Montrose	4	2	Victoria Bridge Grounds
Charity Cup Final	30/04/1892	Victoria United	Orion	3	0	Chanonry
	07/05/1892	Victoria United	Cowdenbeath	1	3	Victoria Bridge Grounds
	20/05/1892	Victoria United	Hearts	1	3	Victoria Bridge Grounds
	21/05/1892	Victoria United	Kings Park	0	5	Victoria Bridge Grounds
	28/05/1892	Victoria United	Queen's Park	7	0	Victoria Bridge Grounds

* Note: Ellon pulled out of the Aberdeenshire Cup tie scheduled for 12th December 1891, so United progressed

Aberdeenshire Cup 1891-1892

	Date				F	A	Venue
Aberdeenshire Cup	31/10/1891	Aberdeen	Stonehaven		4	2	Chanonry
Aberdeenshire Cup	31/10/1891	Peterhead	Aberdeen Thistle		7	0	Peterhead
Aberdeenshire Cup	12/12/1891	Aberdeen	Bon Accord		6	4	Chanonry
Aberdeenshire Cup	12/12/1891	Orion	Peterhead		15	2	Peterhead
Aberdeenshire Cup	12/12/1891	Victoria United	Ellon				Ellon scratched
Aberdeenshire Cup	19/12/1891	Black Diamond	Inverurie		3	0	
Aberdeenshire Cup SF	26/12/1891	Victoria United	Black Diamond		13	0	Victoria Bridge Grounds
Aberdeenshire Cup SF	23/01/1892	Aberdeen	Orion		5	2	Chanonry
Aberdeenshire Cup Final	13/02/1892	Aberdeen	Victoria United		0	2	Chanonry

Charity Cup 1891-1892

	Date			F	A	Venue
Charity Cup	27/02/1892	Victoria United	Bon Accord	3	2	Chanonry
Charity Cup	26/03/1892	Aberdeen	Orion	0	2	Victoria Bridge Grounds
Charity Cup Final	30/04/1892	Victoria United	Orion	3	0	Chanonry

Representative Games

Date			F	A	Venue
31/10/1891	Aberdeenshire	Perthshire	3	7	Victoria Bridge Grounds
21/11/1891	Aberdeenshire	Inverness-shire	10	2	Central Park

05/12/1891	Aberdeen Select	Glasgow Select	0	6	Chanonry
12/03/1892	Aberdeenshire	Inverness-shire	5	1	Inverness
09/04/1892	Aberdeenshire	Fifeshire	4	3	Dunfermline

1892-1893
First floodlit match follows tragic death of Culter player

A berdeen's footballing community was plunged into mourning in October 1892 when young paper mill worker William Wallace died from injuries sustained playing for Culter against Victoria Athletic in a junior match. The full-back, who was also vice-captain his club, had been badly hurt when colliding with an opposition player, but he was able to complete the game. Sadly, however, he collapsed and died the following day. Local clubs rallied round and arranged to play a benefit match in aid of Wallace's family. Mr Worling, the Orion President arranged for the game to be played under an experimental floodlighting system at Central Park. The match took place on a Thursday evening in November, and featured Orion and an Aberdeenshire F.A. select made up of players from Aberdeen and Victoria United. A crowd of 3,000 turned up for the 7-30pm kick-off but despite the gate money going to a very worthy cause, a good number of spectators, possibly as many as 1,000, disgracefully took advantage of the darkness to sneak into the ground without paying. It appears that the floodlighting – *"six Well's patent lights kindly lent by several firms in the city for the occasion"* – were not too powerful and *"play was naturally very loose in the darkness."* Some rival players also took the opportunity of *"settling their little affairs"* under cover of darkness. The game was keenly fought with Orion winning 3-2 thanks to a late goal from their centre forward, Willie Gloag.

Orion's initiative in testing out floodlights has to be commended, but the club's enterprise wasn't matched by too many outstanding on-field performances during the season. Indeed, it was for an off-field incident that one of Orion's players attracted attention. Vice captain John Forsyth, who was cautioned for his wild behaviour during the 3-2 Aberdeenshire Cup Final defeat to Victoria United, almost lost his life a few months later after getting involved in a drunken brawl with a seaman by the name of John Leys. Forsyth, an iron moulder to trade, who lived in Frederick Street, was stabbed by Leys in a late night fight in Charlotte Street which landed the footballer in hospital. He lost a lot of blood and his life was

John Forsyth - Orion

considered to be in danger had he not received prompt and proper treatment. The subsequent court case ended, however, with Leys being found not guilty of the assault. The seaman claimed he used the knife in self defence to protect himself from Forsyth and that the footballer had thrown himself onto the weapon whilst attacking Leys.

Forsyth, who was 19 at the time of this incident, was known to have a temper but he was a popular player. His career started with Bon Accord, the club he helped form. After the Bons disbanded at the end of the 1891-1892 season he joined Aberdeen but quickly moved on again to sign up with the Orion. He would later play for Victoria United.

The highlight of Orion's season was reaching the Aberdeenshire Cup Final, even although it ended in defeat. En route to the final, the Central Park side travelled to Ellon, in early December, for a tie against the local club. The game was played in heavy snow but the Aberdeen men soon built up a 6-0 lead. After 35 minutes, however, the ball burst and the game had to be abandoned as the home side claimed not to have a replacement.

For some reason Victoria United could not get the use of the Victoria Bridge Grounds at Torry for season 1892-1893 so the club moved across the river to a new venue close to Wellington Suspension Bridge. A deal was reached with the landowners, Aberdeen Harbour Board, whose Land and Fishing Committee agreed to let the ground, on the south side of Old Ford Road, for one year at a rent of £50, 'payable in advance.' The Vics called their new home the Wellington Bridge Grounds and the facility was opened with a friendly against Brechin City on Saturday October 22nd.

Vics President and sponsor, Bob Durward of the Exchange Street Restaurant, got proceedings underway and the home side strolled to a comfortable 9-1 victory.

The Vics who were now known by the nickname of 'the Iron Dukes' (The nickname is thought to come from the fact that the Duke of Wellington was known as 'the Iron Duke' and Victoria's new ground was named after the nearby bridge bearing Wellington's name) enjoyed a rather mixed season which started poorly with a 7-2 Scottish Cup defeat by local rivals Orion. United's fortunes picked up with a 3-2 win over the Central Park side in the Aberdeenshire Cup Final, but the campaign ended in shame when the team sparked a near riot by walking off the park during the Charity Cup Final with Aberdeen. In between these major events the Blues fans had to settle for a series of friendlies, most of which were played on home territory. United scored 10 straight wins on their new ground between October 1892 and March 1893 when Port Glasgow Athletic ended the unbeaten run with a 3-2 victory. The furthest the Vics ventured for an away game was Arbroath's Gayfield Park where the Aberdeen men endured a

A comic sketch of Bob Durward opening the new Wellington Bridge Grounds

10-1 thrashing at the hands of the Angus side who would go on to win the Northern League title. This was United's heaviest defeat of the season but to counteract that, some impressive scalps were taken at the Wellington Bridge Grounds, with Falkirk being dumped 7-3 and Stenhousemuir edged out 6-5.

The 4-1 victory over Cowlairs in April 1893 was, however, described as *"one of the fiercest and roughest games witnessed in the city,"* the play being *"replete with all that is vile and disgusting in unfair tactics."* Referee Simpson was accused of

141

being far too lenient. It was, however, the end-of-season Charity Cup match that grabbed everyone's attention. Vics thumped Orion 4-0 in the semi final and faced Aberdeen in the Final. Aberdeen got off to a flying start with a fourth minute goal from Wilf Toman. Shortly afterwards Frank Whitehead made it 2-0 despite strong claims for offside from the Vics defenders. There was further drama a few minutes later when the Ayrshire referee, Mr McLean, sent off United's centre half Willie Stewart for swearing. The rest of the Vics team then decided they too would leave the park. Vics supporters amongst the large crowd were enraged by what they were seeing and the atmosphere turned decidedly hostile. The situation became increasingly bizarre when, despite now having no opponents, Aberdeen kicked off, walked the ball down the field and tapped it into the empty net to make it 3-0. This was too much for many of the fans who then burst onto the field and began to threaten the referee. Mr McLean was escorted to the safety of the pavilion where he offered to let someone else take over the refereeing of the game. In the absence of any volunteers it was apparent the game couldn't continue, so United left the ground. Angry spectators became increasingly frustrated, and, when it was announced there would be no refund of entrance fees, the atmosphere became even more tense. Police had to use their batons to clear the approaches to the clubhouse and disperse the crowd. As a consequence the Blues were banished from the competition and Aberdeen claimed the trophy. United fans may not have been too pleased to learn that Mr McLean had been a guest at the Aberdeen club's annual night out the previous month!

The Vics were, however, involved in another charitable venture earlier in the season when they played a combined Aberdeen-Orion select at the Chanonry in a game to raise funds to assist clearing off the debt on the Aberdeen Trades Council Buildings in Belmont Street. United won the game 4-3.

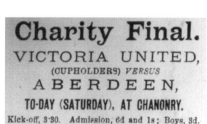

At the start of the season Aberdeen F.C held a testimonial dinner to mark the departure of William Key who was moving to Edinburgh. The man who the previous season scored from the first penalty ever awarded in the city received three books – 'Trayners Maxims and Phrases', 'Bells Dictionary of Law' and 'Craigie's Conveyancing.' He was also presented with *"a pretty tennis racket."* Key's departure was one of a number of changes within the ranks of the Whites who nevertheless went on to enjoy a decent run in the Scottish Cup, defeating Peterhead 9-2, Orion 4-2 (after a 3-3 draw) and Inverness Caledonian 5-2 in the preliminary rounds. In the First Round they were then drawn at home against St Mirren who that season would go on to finish third behind Celtic and Rangers in the Scottish League First Division. The Paisley side were firm favourites to progress, but Aberdeen gave them a harder test than they might have been expecting in front of a 5,000 Chanonry crowd. The visitors won 6-4 but Aberdeen were far from disgraced.

The Whites pulled off a major coup by attracting Notts County to the Chanonry for the big New Year game. This was the first time an English league club had visited the city. County were the oldest club in the country, having been founded in 1862. They were founder members of the English Football League in 1888 and reached the F.A. Cup Final in 1890-1891, losing 3-1 to Blackburn Rovers. County also finished third in the First Division that season. In 1893-1894 they would win the F.A. Cup by defeating Bolton Wanderers 4-1 in

William Davidson – a sponsor of Victoria United. Davidson had been involved in the company which laid out the Victoria Bridge Grounds. He remained a backer of United when they moved to the Wellington Bridge Grounds.

the Final. The Notts team that lined up in the Chanonry included Scottish international Jimmy Oswald, who scored County's goal in the 1890-1891 Cup Final. The side also featured two other Scottish internationals, Daniel Bruce and David Calderhead. Calderhead went on to manage Chelsea for a record 966 games between 1907 and 1933. English internationals George Toone and Alf

Aberdeen goalkeeper Archie Ramsay, a medical student at Marischal College. He was from Stonehaven and earned the distinction of representing the North select at rugby and the Aberdeenshire F.A. in football. When he first joined Aberdeen he played as a forward.

Shelton also faced the Whites. Aberdeen may have been up against some formidable opponents, but they did well and were considered unlucky to lose by 4-0. Bruce got a double with the other goals coming from Wilkinson and Burke.

Aberdeen's Northern League campaign got off to a stuttering start with four defeats and two draws in the opening six matches. The reigning champions, Dundee's East End, visited the Chanonry for the opening game of the campaign and escaped with a victory courtesy of a last minute goal. That was followed by a crushing 10-2 loss to Harp in Dundee. Aberdeen had travelled to Tayside without several regulars who were involved in important cricket games that same day. The club captain, Tom Ketchen, for instance, was playing for Mugiemoss in a Bon Accord Trophy game against Wellington. That was little consolation for one observer who wrote: *"From start to finish it was a mere farce, the boys in green simply making rings round the Whites, whose bewildered movements astonished and amused the crowds."'* Arbroath, who would go on to lift the championship, then visited Aberdeen for what proved to be a 13 goal thriller, the Angus side coming out on top by 7-6. Fans of the home side felt aggrieved by the performance of the referee, Mr McIntosh from Montrose, who was regularly *"assailed with loud hissing, the opinion of the crowd being that he was particularly smart in discerning when a foul should be given against Aberdeen, while he nearly always failed to see the same thing on the Arbroath side."* There was little to cheer over the long winter

Colin Ross, Aberdeen F.C.
Colin Ross, one of Aberdeen's most consistent players during the season, announced he was moving to Birmingham for business reasons. Ross, like quite a few players at this time, did well despite never training! He started his career with Orion but got few first team opportunities. He joined Aberdeen after impressing during an Orion 6-2 victory over the Chanonry club. He gained county honours, representing Aberdeenshire against Inverness-shire.

Robert Hyslop, who played in the first Aberdeen side in 1881, died during the season. He was science and maths master at Aberdeen High School for Girls for 11 years. He had been president of the football club and remained involved in an official capacity until season 1891-1892. As a player he occupied numerous positions, including goalkeeper and full back. After his playing days were over he even took a turn as a referee. Hyslop played a major role, along with William Stewart, in setting up and organising the club's annual sports.

months of the league campaign but the Whites staged a remarkable recovery from the beginning of March until the end of the season, winning six of their final seven games to finish in sixth position.

Harry Wylie - Prominent businessman and Aberdeen F.C. Vice President

Notable Games

Victoria United 9, Brechin 1
Wellington Bridge Grounds, 22nd October 1892

Victoria United opened their new ground, the Wellington Bridge Grounds, with a match against Brechin. United kicked off towards the north goal and Annand put them ahead in the opening minute *"amid deafening cheers"*. Sutherland then made it 2-0 and Benzie came close to adding a third. Milne soon make it 3-0 then Sutherland (2), Ferries and Benzie all added to the tally by half time. Sutherland grabbed his fourth and United's eighth shortly after the interval and Ferries made it nine. Ferrier grabbed a late consolation for the visitors.

Victoria United - Gray, Thomson, Ririe, Milne, Stewart, Cruickshank, Turner, Benzie, Sutherland, Annand, Ferries.

Brechin - Hendry, J. Johnstone, Fowler, Bowman, Ferrier, Gray, Henderson, Richardson, G Johnstone, Donaldson, Hetherington.

Orion 3, Aberdeenshire F.A. Select 2
William Wallace Benefit Match, Central Park, 10th November 1992

This was the first game played under floodlights in the north east. It was held as a benefit match for the family of Culter player William Wallace who died some weeks earlier after sustaining injuries in a junior match against Victoria Athletic. Six Well's patent lights, kindly lent by several firms in the city for the occasion, were used with dubious success. A crowd of over 3,000 turned up to see Sutherland open the scoring for the AFA. Turner made it 2-0 but Willie Gloag pulled one back for Orion before the interval. In the second half Ferries of the AFA had a goal chalked off for offside and soon afterwards Fraser equalised for Orion. Centre-forward Gloag then grabbed a late winner for Orion.

Orion - Edwards, Foote, Mackay, Wight, Low, Baird, Fraser, Macfarlane, Gloag,Forsyth, Leggat.

AFA Select - Gray, Thomson, Hickie, Colin Ross, W Stewart, A. L. Cobban, Turner, Benzie, Sutherland, Annand, Ferries.

Ref - Mr. Jaffray.

Aberdeen 4, St Mirren 6
Scottish Cup First Round, Chanonry, 26th November 1892.

Brash opened the scoring for Saints amid great cheering, suggesting that the visitors had a sizeable support. McPhee made it 2-0 but White pulled one back with a header which went in via a post. Brown then equalised to send the home crowd wild with delight. After the interval the Paisley men went 3-2 ahead, but White soon equalised. Saints responded again, going 4-3 in front through McPhee, then Shaw made it 5-3 and soon after it was 6-3. Cobban gave the home side some

ABERDEEN FOOTBALL CLUB.—
GRAND SCOTTISH CUP TIE MATCH,
To-Day (Saturday)—
ST MIRREN
(PAISLEY), *VERSUS*
A B E R D E E N,
AT CHANONRY.
Kick off 2·30. Admission, 6d and 1s ; Boys, 3d.

S.S. Singleton, Aberdeen F.C
Singleton joined Aberdeen from Accrington. A versatile player, he appeared in almost every position except goalkeeper.

hope when shooting home a fourth, but there was to be no further scoring.

Aberdeen - Ramsay, Ketchen, Wood, Ross, Cobban, Ewan, Black, White, Toman, Brown, Singleton.

St Mirren - Patrick, Crawford, Mirk, Douglas, Brown, McBain, Brash, Wyllie, McPhee, Shaw, McLean.

Ref J Williamson, Edinburgh

Aberdeen 0, Notts County 4
Chanonry, 2nd January 1893

Aberdeen fielded a very colourful forward line of White, Black, F. Whitehead, A. Whitehead and Brown against the highly rated English side. The Chanonry men more than held their own during the opening 45 minutes and were considered unlucky to lose a goal near the interval, Wilkinson

Toone, the Notts County and England goalkeeper

getting on the scoresheet, Even then, the home side retaliated strongly and on one occasion the ball bobbled along the Notts bar before going behind. Scottish international Daniel Bruce put the English side 2-0 ahead early in the second half and further goals from Burke and Bruce, who completed his hat-trick, sealed victory for the visitors as Aberdeen tired.The teams were given tea in the Waverley Hotel after the match before County caught the 5-25pm train for Glasgow.

Aberdeen - Ramsay, Ketchen, Wood, Anderson, Cobban, Ross, White, Black, F Whitehead, Arthur Whitehead, Brown

Notts County - Toone, Calderhead, Hendry, Shelton, Wilkinson, Bramley, Burke, McGregor, Oswald, Docherty, Bruce

Ref Charles Glennie (ex Aberdeen player)

Victoria United 3, Orion 2

Aberdeenshire Cup Final, Chanonry, 25th February 1893

United retained the trophy by winning a five goal thriller in front of 5,000 spectators. After an even opening spell, Orion gradually intensified the pressure which paid dividends when Fraser gave them the lead after Vics goalkeeper Gray slipped. But Vics responded quickly and within a few minutes they were level thanks to Sutherland. United then enjoyed a spell on top and Orion keeper Edwards had to be on top form. At one point he made a great save and showed guts and determination by fending off Annand and Ferries who together *"brought him to the ground."* The Orion man, however, *"held onto the ball with all the tenacity of a bull dog."*

It was level pegging at the interval but Vics were soon ahead in the second half, Turner netting a fine goal. The Torry side continued to dominate and Annand added a third. This seemed to stir Orion into action and Fraser quickly made it 3-2 to set up an exciting finish. The game became increasingly tense and Orion's Forsyth had to be warned by the referee *"for seizing Stewart and trying to strike him."* There was no further scoring, however, and United claimed the trophy.

The Cup was presented that evening by Mr Litster, the A.F.A. President, at a supper in the Waverley Hotel.The trophy was received by Mr Durward, President of the Vics. All the players all received *"a handsome medal."*

Victoria United - Gray, Anderson, Ririe, Hickie, Stewart, Ross, Turner,Benzie, Sutherland, Annand, Ferries.

Orion - Edwards, Foote, Mackay, Wight, Low, Baird, Fraser, MacFarlane, Forsyth, Gloag, Leggat.

Ref - Mr Johnston, Kings Park, Stirling

John Low
At the end of the season Orion's John Low became the latest North east player to seek his fortune in the USA. Low first played football for a club called Rovers in Peterhead. On returning to his native Aberdeen he joined Britannia before moving to Orion.

Alec Macfarlane (Orion F.C.). Started his career with Bon Accord. Moved to Aberdeen for a brief spell before joining Orion.

Aberdeen 3, Victoria United 0 (Match abandoned)
Charity Cup Final, Chanonry, Saturday 27th May 1893

Victoria United's hopes of completing a double trophy win fell apart during one of the most bizarre games ever held in the city. The match had to be abandoned early in the first half after the whole United team walked off the park following the dismissal of their battling centre half Willie Stewart. Police had to be deployed to disperse the angry crowd. Goals from Wilf Toman and Frank Whitehead had given Aberdeen an early 2-0 lead before the Blues took the huff and walked off. The Whites, with no opposition, then rolled in a third goal before the pitch invasion brought proceedings to a halt. Aberdeen kept the trophy.

Victoria United - Gray, Anderson, Ririe, Ross, Stewart, Ritchie, Turner, Benzie,

Sutherland, Annand, Ferries.
Aberdeen - Ramsay, Ketchen, Wood,
Morren, Singleton, Cobban, Fred
Whitehead, White, Toman, McArthur,
Frank Whitehead.

Willie Stewart, Victoria United

Northern League 1892-1893

		P	W	D	L	F	A	Pts
1	Arbroath	18	14	1	3	70	40	29
2	East End, Dundee	18	13	2	3	61	31	28
3	Montrose	18	10	2	6	80	48	22
4	Forfar Athletic	18	9	2	7	66	60	20
5	Harp, Dundee	18	9	1	8	74	54	19
6	Aberdeen	18	8	2	8	60	66	18
7	Johnstone Wanderers, Dundee	18	6	4	8	50	62	16
8	Our Boys, Dundee	18	7	1	10	61	72	15
9	St Johnstone	18	5	2	11	52	69	12
10	Fair City Athletic	18	0	1	17	24	95	1

Aberdeen F.C - Northern League 1892-1893

Northern League	20/08/1892	Aberdeen	East End, Dundee	0	1	Chanonry
Northern League	27/08/1892	Aberdeen	Harp,Dundee	2	10	Dundee
Northern League	10/09/1892	Aberdeen	Arbroath	6	7	Chanonry
Northern League	17/09/1892	Aberdeen	St Johnstone	3	3	Chanonry
Northern League	12/11/1892	Aberdeen	Johnstone Wanderers	2	2	Dundee
Northern League	03/12/1892	Aberdeen	Montrose	2	5	Links Park Montrose
Northern League	24/12/1892	Aberdeen	Fair City Athletic	3	2	Balhousie Park Perth
Northern League	28/01/1893	Aberdeen	Our Boys Dundee	2	4	Chanonry
Northern League	04/02/1893	Aberdeen	Montrose	4	3	Chanonry
Northern League	11/02/1893	Aberdeen	Arbroath	2	5	Gayfield, Arbroath
Northern League	18/02/1893	Aberdeen	Forfar Athletic	4	8	Forfar
Northern League	04/03/1893	Aberdeen	Fair City Athletic	5	1	Chanonry
Northern League	11/03/1893	Abedeen	Johnstone Wanderers	6	1	Chanonry
Northern League	18/03/1893	Aberdeen	East End, Dundee	2	1	Dundee
Northern League	01/04/1893	Aberdeen	Forfar Athletic	6	2	Chanonry
Northern League	08/04/1893	Aberdeen	St Johnstone	5	3	Perth
Northern League	15/04/1893	Aberdeen	Harp,Dundee	4	2	Chanonry
Northern League	22/04/1893	Aberdeen	Our Boys Dundee	2	6	West Craigie Park, Dundee

Aberdeen F.C. 1892-1893 – Other Games

Scottish Cup	24/09/1892	Aberdeen	Peterhead	9	2	Chanonry
	08/10/1892	Aberdeen	Orion	2	6	Central Park
Scottish Cup	15/10/1892	Aberdeen	Orion	3	3	Central Park
Scottish Cup	22/10/1892	Aberdeen	Orion	4	2	Chanonry
	29/10/1892	Aberdeen	Victoria United	5	4	Chanonry
Scottish Cup	05/11/1892	Aberdeen	Inverness Caledonian	5	2	Chanonry
Aberdeenshire Cup1R	19/11/1892	Aberdeen	Peterhead	12	0	Peterhead
Scottish Cup 1R	26/11/1892	Aberdeen	St Mirren	4	6	Chanonry
	31/12/1892	Aberdeen	Orion	7	1	Chanonry
	02/01/1893	Aberdeen	Notts County	0	4	Chanonry

Aberdeenshire Cup SF	21/01/1893	Aberdeen	Victoria United	2	3	Wellington Grounds
	25/02/1893	Aberdeen	Fraserburgh Thistle	14	0	Fraserburgh
Charity Cup	25/03/1893	Aberdeen	County Select	7	1	Central Park
	29/04/1893	Aberdeen	Orion	2	2	Chanonry
	13/05/1893	Aberdeen	King's Park	2	1	Chanonry
Charity Cup Final	27/05/1893	Aberdeen	Victoria United	3	0	Chanonry
Local Charities Match	01/06/1893	Aberdeen	Orion	5	1	Chanonry

Orion F.C. - 1892-1893

	20/08/1892	Orion	Ellon	13	0	Ellon
	27/08/1892	Orion	Strathmore Dundee	3	7	Logie Park Dundee
Scottish Cup	03/09/1892	Orion	Victoria United	7	2	Chanonry
	17/09/1892	Orion	Mossend Swifts	6	0	Central Park
	24/09/1892	Orion	Our Boys Dundee	2	4	Central Park
	26/09/1892	Orion	Montrose	2	5	Central Park
	01/10/1892	Orion	Dunfermline Athletic	1	1	Central Park
	08/10/1892	Orion	Aberdeen	6	2	Central Park
Scottish Cup	15/10/1892	Orion	Aberdeen	3	3	Central Park
Scottish Cup	22/10/1892	Orion	Aberdeen	2	4	Chanonry
	29/10/1892	Orion	Stonehaven	6	4	Stonehaven
	05/11/1892	Orion	Arbroath Wanderers	8	2	Central Park
Wallace Benefit Match	10/11/1892	Orion	AFA Select	3	2	Central Park
	12/11/1892	Orion	Coupar Angus	8	0	Central Park
Aberdeenshire Cup1R	19/11/1892	Orion	Stonehaven	13	0	Central Park
	26/11/1892	Orion	Montrose	2	5	Montrose
Aberdeenshire Cup SF	10/12/1892	Orion	Ellon	6	0	Ellon
	17/12/1892	Orion	Victoria United	5	7	Wellington Grounds
	24/12/1892	Orion	Orion Reserves	3	1	Central Park
	31/12/1892	Orion	Aberdeen	1	7	Chanonry
	02/01/1893	Orion	Victoria United	2	2	Central Park
	14/01/1893	Orion	Vale of Athole,Pitlochry	7	4	Central Park
	04/02/1893	Orion	Brechin	3	3	Brechin

	11/02/1893	Orion	Glasgow Wanderers	10	0	Central Park
	18/02/1893	Orion	Edinburgh University	6	4	Central Park
Aberdeenshire	25/02/1893	Orion	Victoria United	2	3	Chanonry
Cup Final						
	04/03/1893	Orion	Strathmore Dundee	4	1	Central Park
	11/03/1893	Orion	Lochee	2	2	South Road Park Dundee
	18/03/1893	Orion	Brechin	3	4	Central Park
	01/04/1893	Orion	Battlefield	2	2	Central Park
	08/04/1893	Orion	Edinburgh Adventurers	6	1	Central Park
	20/04/1893	Orion	Victoria United	0	2	Central Park
	22/04/1893	Orion	Alva	3	4	Central Park
	29/04/1893	Orion	Aberdeen	2	2	Chanonry
Charity Cup Semi Final	06/05/1893	Orion	Victoria United	0	4	Chanonry
	18/05/1893	Orion	Victoria United	1	7	Wellington Grounds
Local Charities Match	01/06/1893	Orion	Aberdeen	1	5	Chanonry

Victoria United – 1892-1893

Scottish Cup	03/09/1892	Victoria United	Orion	2	7	Chanonry
	10/09/1892	Victoria United	Stonehaven	13	2	Urie
	17/09/1892	Victoria United	Montrose	1	2	Montrose
	26/09/1892	Victoria United	Arbroath	1	10	Gayfield, Arbroath
Aberdeenshire Cup	15/10/1892	Victoria United	Fraserburgh Buchan Wanderers	7	3	Bellslea Park
	22/10/1892	Victoria United	Brechin	9	1	Wellington Grounds
	29/10/1892	Victoria United	Aberdeen	4	5	Chanonry
	05/11/1892	Victoria United	Montrose	7	1	Wellington Grounds
	12/11/1892	Victoria United	Our Boys Blairgowrie	10	0	Wellington Grounds
	19/11/1892	Victoria United	Forfar Athletic	4	1	Wellington Grounds
	03/12/1892	Victoria United	University	5	1	Wellington Grounds
	17/12/1892	Victoria United	Orion	7	5	Wellington Grounds
	24/12/1892	Victoria United	Johnstone Wanderers	4	2	Wellington Grounds
	02/01/1893	Victoria United	Orion	2	2	Central Park

Aberdeenshire Cup SF	21/01/1893	Victoria UnitedAberdeen	3	2	Wellington Grounds
	28/01/1893	Victoria United	Montrose	3	7	Links Park
Montrose						
	04/02/1893	Victoria United	Dunblane	5	1	Wellington Grounds
	18/02/1893	Victoria United	Campsie	8	1	Wellington Grounds
Aberdeenshire	25/02/1893	Victoria United	Orion	3	2	Chanonry
Cup Final						
	04/03/1893	Victoria United	Port Glasgow Athletic	2	3	Wellington Grounds
	11/03/1893	Victoria United	Broxburn Shamrock	6	1	Wellington Grounds
	18/03/1893	Victoria United	Raith Rovers	2	4	Wellington Grounds
	25/03/1893	Victoria United	Peterhead	3	0	Peterhead
	01/04/1893	Victoria United	Cowdenbeath	4	2	Wellington Grounds
	07/04/1893	Victoria United	Montrose	3	3	Wellington Grounds
	08/04/1893	Victoria United	Cowlairs	4	1	Wellington Grounds
	15/04/1893	Victoria United	Falkirk	7	3	Wellington Grounds
	20/04/1893	Victoria United	Orion	2	0	Central Park
	22/04/1893	Victoria United	Arbroath	5	2	Wellington Grounds
Benefit Match	27/04/1893	Victoria United	Combined Aberdeen-Orion	4	3	Chanonry
	29/04/1893	Victoria United	Stenhousemuir	6	5	Wellington Grounds
Charity cup	06/05/1893	Victoria United	Orion	4	0	Chanonry
Semi Final						
	13/05/1893	Victoria United	Camelon	4	3	Wellington Grounds
	18/05/1893	Victoria United	Orion	7	1	Wellington Grounds
	20/05/1893	Victoria United	Our Boys Dundee	7	4	Wellington Grounds
Charity Cup final	27/05/1893	Victoria United	Aberdeen	0	3	Chanonry

Aberdeenshire Cup 1892-1893

Aberdeenshire Cup	15/10/1892	Victoria United	Fraserburgh Buchan Wanderers	7	3	Bellslea Park
Aberdeenshire Cup	19/11/1892	Orion	Stonehaven	13	0	Central Park
Aberdeenshire Cup	19/11/1892	Aberdeen	Peterhead	12	0	Peterhead
Aberdeenshire Cup SF	10/12/1892	Orion	Ellon	6	0	Ellon

Aberdeenshire Cup SF	21/01/1893	Victoria United	Aberdeen	3	2	Wellington Grounds
Aberdeenshire Cup Final	25/02/1893	Victoria United	Orion	3	2	Chanonry

Notes: I have not been able to confidently identify all the Aberdeenshire Cup ties played this season. The Ellon v Orion game was abandoned when the ball burst but it seems that Orion were allowed to progress in the competition without a replay.

Charity Cup 1892-1893

Charity Cup Semi Final	25/03/1893	Aberdeen	County Select	7	1	Central Park
Charity Cup Semi Final	06/05/1893	Victoria United	Orion	4	0	Chanonry
Charity Cup Final	27/05/1893	Aberdeen	Victoria United	3	0	Chanonry

Notes: The Final was abandoned after Victoria United left the field. It seems that the trophy was awarded to Aberdeen.

Representative Matches 1892-1893

01/10/1892	Aberdeenshire	Perthshire	2	2	Perth
03/12/1892	Aberdeenshire	Inverness-shire	4	2	Chanonry
29/04/1893	Aberdeenshire	North of Scotland	2	6	Telford Street, Inverness

1893-1894
Northern league chaos

Victoria United finally got their wish by being accepted into the Northern League, but within a few months the season was tumbling into chaos as the Dundee clubs, Strathmore and Johnstone Wanderers, announced they were withdrawing from the competition. League officials wanted to continue with the remaining six clubs but Victoria objected and said they too would withdraw. A compromise was reached and it was decided to continue with the remaining fixtures. It all became a bit of a farce as the campaign ended with clubs playing varying numbers of matches. In a highly unsatisfactory conclusion, Arbroath finished top of the table, but the title wasn't awarded because of the large number of incomplete fixtures. It seems that the problems all stemmed from state of flux within Dundee footballing circles. During the close season East End and Our Boys amalgamated to form Dundee FC. The new Dundee club was also admitted to the Scottish League. Dundee's Irish community club, Harp, chose to resign from the Northern League on the eve of the season over financial concerns and worries about the impact of professionalism which had been legalised in Scotland. Then came the withdrawal of Strathmore and Johnstone Wanderers who ultimately merged with the aim of calling themselves Dundonians. Dundee FC objected to this name and so the new club became known as Wanderers.

Yet it had all started so promisingly for Victoria United who got the league season off to a great start with a 7-3 victory over Forfar Athletic at the Wellington Bridge Grounds. United's most bizarre league performance,however, came in mid-January when they travelled to Gayfield to face Arbroath. The Blues raced into a 3-1 lead but were pegged back to 3-3 by the interval as the title-holders got into their stride. No-one could have anticipated what was to happen after such an evenly balanced first half, but the home side went wild by scoring eleven goals in the second half to run out 14-3 winners. It would be the heaviest defeat suffered in the history of Victoria United. This setback didn't seem to demoralise the Vics as seven days later they routed Orion 6-3 at the Chanonry to win the Aberdeenshire Cup for the third year in a row.

The Scottish Cup campaign also started well with a narrow 3-2 win over Peterhead being followed by an 8-0 hammering of Aberdeen in a game played at the Victoria Bridge Grounds

Scottish Cup—2nd Round.
ABERDEEN
v.
VICTORIA UNITED
At Victoria Bridge Grounds, Torry.
Kick-off, 3·30 p.m.
Admission, 3d ; Grand Stand. 6d ; Boys, 1½d.

which appears to have been made available to United on a one-off basis. Progress in the national competition was, however, halted at the next hurdle with Orion winning 6-1 at the Wellington Bridge Grounds at which United opened a new grandstand which was packed for the occasion. United also made it to the Final of the Charity Cup for the fourth year in a row but Orion again proved to be too good, winning 5-3 at the Chanonry.

The Iron Dukes also caused a bit of a stir by becoming the first local club to adopt professionalism by making legal payments to players. This was thought to be a key factor in persuading controversial local player John Forsyth to switch his allegiance from Orion to United. Forsyth would later be made Victoria's club captain.

At the end of the season United revealed they would be returning to the Victoria Bridge Grounds after securing a new lease on their original Torry home for three years beginning on 1st September. The club also announced with some regret that its swashbuckling centre half, William Stewart, would be leaving to concentrate on business interests.
Stewart was no stranger to controversy, having been sent off in the previous season's notorious Charity Cup Final, but nevertheless

William Stewart, Victoria United

he was described as being the *"greatest centre half Aberdeen football had seen."* Furthermore, one observer wrote that Stewart *"more than anyone else, has been the means of raising the club from comparative obscurity to an eminence of which all connected with it are justly proud."* Willie started his career in the mid 1880's with a junior side, Battlefield, in Arbroath. He then joined Waverley, but soon moved on to the senior ranks with Arbroath as a left back. After two years at Gayfield he relocated to Aberdeen in search of work and joined United. In his final game for Arbroath, on 30th August 1890, he helped the Lichties defeat United 5-1 at Torry. The following week he made his debut for the Blues in a Scottish Cup defeat by Caledonian. He made such rapid progress, however, that by the following March he was named captain of the Aberdeenshire select for a representative game against Fife.

Orion, despite now being the only one of Aberdeen's three senior clubs not to be admitted to the ill-fated Northern league, would emerge as the city's most successful side during the season. With 250 members and five teams being fielded in various leagues, the Kittybrewster outfit was certainly thriving. On 26th August they celebrated the opening of their refurbished ground by losing 4-2 to Victoria United in a friendly after having held a 2-1 lead. Vics included former Orion stalwarts Edwards and Foote in their line-up.

Orion, described as *'the stripes'* or *'the reds'* in match reports, made it to the First Round of the Scottish Cup after defeating Victoria United 6-1 and Kilsyth Wanderers 4-2 in the qualifying stages. Scottish First Division side Leith Athletic headed North for the tie and gave the home side a lesson in the finer arts of the game by winning 11-2. The Orion men were left to focus on the local tournaments in which they were to be remarkably successful. They reached the Aberdeenshire Cup Final for the fifth time in six years but, despite being favourites, failed to add to their solitary one success in the competition, Victoria United running out 6-3 winners after the Stripes threw away a 3-2 halftime lead. The same sides contested the Charity Cup Final but on this occasion Orion, led by the impressive Willie Gloag, scored twice in the closing ten minutes to win 5-3. The Stripes goalkeeper, Dick Edwards, had been castigated in the local press following Orion's 11-0 win over Peterhead in the Semi Final of the competition.

Mr A. J. Gershon

Edwards was accused of *"clowning"* during the one-sided match. The keeper was obviously bored by having so little to do *"but he might have borne the ordeal with some degree of consideration for his weaker brethren."*

Orion also triumphed in a new competition, the Gershon Cup, which was set-up during the season. This was a round robin tournament in which United, Orion and Aberdeen played each other home and away. The trophy was presented by Mr A.J. Gershon, a director of the Glasgow Clothing Company who operated an Aberdeen branch at 87 Broad Street.

With Orion and Victoria United sharing the local glory and silverware, the city's oldest club, Aberdeen, looked for different ways of securing some of the limelight and that was done by inviting some top sides to the city. The Whites suffered the embarrassment of an 8-0 Scottish Cup drubbing from Victoria United and went down 5-1 to Orion in the First Round of the Aberdeenshire Cup. They finished bottom of the table in the Gershon Cup and were again heavily beaten by Victoria United, 6-3, in the Charity Cup semi final. The Northern League campaign was equally demoralising with Arbroath handing out an 11-1 hiding on the opening day of the season. Aberdeen would fulfil just seven league fixtures and when the curtailed competition ended, the Whites were at the foot of the table with just one win under their belts. The Chanonry side lost the services of highly regarded club captain Alex Wood who decided that football would have to take a back seat as he wanted to concentrate on his studies at Aberdeen University. Wood had been one of the city's top full backs who gained county representative honours.

Aberdeen played Scottish Cup winners Queen's Park at Chanonry on the second weekend of the season, losing 8-1 with Scottish international Thomas Wallace scoring six for the visitors. The club secured a major coup in April 1894 by attracting to the north-east two of Britain's top sides, Rangers and Sunderland, within the space of five days in early April. Rangers had won the Scottish Cup a couple of months earlier, beating Celtic 3-1 in the Final at Hampden Park. Sunderland had been English champions in 1892-1893, finished runners-up in 1893-1894 and would be champions again in 1894-1895. The Wearsiders included Scottish international goalkeeper Ned Doig, formerly of Arbroath, in their star-studded line-up. The Whites went down 2-1 to Rangers and 7-1 to Sunderland.

Alex Wood, Aberdeen F.C. captain

All three senior clubs in the city took their social responsibilities seriously and twice during January 1894 they pooled their efforts to show support for local joiners on strike in Aberdeen. On 3rd January players from Victoria United and Orion played a benefit game to raise funds for the strikers. The match took place at Wellington Bridge Grounds and Willie Stewart's Victoria United select defeated Tom Leggat's Orion select 4-2 and £15 was raised. Victoria United then met a combined Aberdeen and Orion select team in a second benefit game for the joiners on Thursday 25th January 1894. The match was again played at the Wellington Bridge Grounds which were *"illuminated by the electric light."* The game, which ended in a 1-1 draw, was a momentous occasion, being preceded by a march through the city streets by striking joiners and their supporters. At 6-30pm a group of around 400 men congregated in Golden Square and proceeded to march in orderly fashion along Union Street and down Market Street to the Victoria club's pitch located on the reclaimed land south of Old Ford Road. The men carried torches and were preceded by a couple of pipers *"who blew a merry chant."* The experiment with floodlighting was, however, no more successful than the previous venture at Central Park as the game was played in semi-darkness. The Bon Accord magazine described the match as *"a delightful game of hide-and-seek, and if the spectators didn't see much of the play, they had the satisfaction of knowing that they had assisted the strikers to the tune of £15."*

Long serving Aberdeen player Tom Ketchen ended his days with the Whites after being injured in a friendly against St Bernard's at Chanonry in March. Saints, who finished third behind Celtic and Hearts in the First Division, fielded a strong side which included internationals Walter Arnott and Jimmy Oswald. The visitors strolled to an 8-1 win while Ketchen's involvement ended early when he had to leave the field with a twisted knee and Wilf Toman was allowed to come on as a substitute.

Ketchen was one of the most successful players in the history of the club. He seems to have made his first appearance in early 1886 when he moved to the city to take up the post of chief engineer with Messrs. Davidson and Sons, Mugiemoss Works. He scored the first goal at the Chanonry in Aberdeen's 10-2 win over Our Boys in February 1888 and was on the mark four times for the Whites in their 7-1 victory over Aberdeen Rangers in the first Aberdeenshire Cup

Final. Tom scored the Aberdeen Select's only goal in the 6-1 defeat by Scotland at the Chanonry in 1888 and he also represented the local select against Scotland selects in 1889 and 1890.

Ketchen featured in the first official inter county match played by the Aberdeenshire F.A. against Perthshire in October 1888 at Chanonry and scored twice as the north east side lost 7-3. He captained Aberdeen in the late 1880's and initially played as a centre

Tom Ketchen

forward but converted to a full back in later years. In September 1888 he scored nine goals in the 23-0 win over Rosebery in the Aberdeenshire Cup, which was the biggest win in the history of the Whites. He was an Aberdeenshire Cup winner three years in a row,1887-1888, 1888-1889 and 1889-1890 and helped the Whites win the Charity Cup in 1892-1893. Ketchen may have played one match for Victoria United in 1895. He also played cricket, quoiting, draughts and whist. Tom died at his home in Bucksburn on 29th February 1924. He was survived by his wife, three sons and a daughter.

Notable Games

Aberdeen 1, Queen's Park 8
Chanonry, 26th August 1893
Queen's fielded six of the team that had beaten Celtic 2-1 in the Scottish Cup Final in March. The Glasgow club also included six Scottish internationals. Aberdeen recalled old favourite Tom Ketchen for the occasion. Scotland centre forward Tom Waddell tore Aberdeen apart scoring six goals, four in the first half, as the Spiders cruised to a comfortable victory while White got Aberdeen's consolation goal just before halftime.
Aberdeen - Ramsay, Ketchen, Wood, Shepherd, Thomson, Ewan, Cumming, White, Toman, Fred Whitehead, Frank Whitehead.
Queen's Park - Baird,Sillars, Smellie, Gillespie, Robertson, Stewart, Frazer, Brand, Waddell, Muir, Cleland.

Victoria United 7, Forfar Athletic 3
Northern League, Wellington Bridge Grounds, 9th September 1893
United's first Northern League fixture ended with the Blues scoring a fine victory, Sutherland gave the Vics an early lead *"amidst the cheers of the onlookers."* Clark soon added a second. Then Sutherland made it 3-0 but Shepherd got one back for Forfar before the interval. Soon after the restart Clark restored United's three goal advantage and a fifth goal followed. Scrimgeour then scored two for the visitors but Clark grabbed another two to take his tally to four to give Vics an impressive win.
Victoria United - Edwards, Foote, Ririe, Morrice, Annand, Duffus, Turner, Benzie, Sutherland, Meldrum, Clark.

Forfar Athletic - Muckersie, Scott, Cable, Milne, Taylor, Mann, Anderson, Scrimgeour, Petrie, Booth, Shepherd.

Victoria United 6, Orion 3
Aberdeenshire Cup Final, Chanonry,
20th January 1894

FOOTBALL.

Northern League Match.

AT Wellington Grounds, Inches, TO-DAY (Saturday), Kick-off 3 30,

FORFAR ATHLETIC
v.
VICTORIA UNITED.

Admission, 4d ; Reserved, 3d extra ; Boys, 2d.

Orion, described as 'the Reds', probably on account of their red and white striped shirts, were deemed to be favourites having already beaten United twice earlier in the season. Perfect weather conditions and a crowd of 5,000, created a wonderful atmosphere.Within five minutes Orion were ahead courtesy of Willie Gloag. Smith quickly equalised but Orion again surged forward, scoring on two occasions. United pulled one back to make it 3-2 for Orion at the interval. Vics grabbed two quick goals after the restart to gain the ascendancy and although Orion tried to fight back it was the Blues who added another two before the end to run out comfortable winners.Orion could point to the fact that their half back Currie twisted his leg early in the game and was *"practically useless"*. Jim Ririe was United's star man while Orion keeper Dick Edwards and striker Gloag did well for the losers. Orion had now reached the final five times but won just the once. The Cup and gold badges were awarded in the Waverley Hotel later in the day.

Victoria United - Cannon, Anderson, Ririe, Morrice, Stewart, Annand, Turner, Smith, Sutherland, Forsyth, Ferries.

Orion - Edwards, Mackay, Ross, Wight, Low, Currie, Anderson, James, Williams, McBain, Leggat.

Aberdeen 1, Glasgow Rangers 2
Chanonry, Saturday 7th April 1894

Despite its significance this game was given scant attention in the local press, perhaps because it was held on the same day as the Scotland v England international. I couldn't even find details of the Aberdeen team line-up.

What is known is that White gave Aberdeen the lead after 15 minutes and the home side held on to this advantage until the interval. After the break Rangers took control and scored twice to secure victory. Aberdeen goalkeeper Smyth was in outstanding form. According to one source *"the Glasgow Rangers gave a*

capital exposition of scientific play."
Aberdeen – Not known.
Glasgow Rangers - Mckenzie, Smith, Drummond, Marshall, Blyth, Muir, Steele, McReadie, Gray, Boyd, Baxter

Aberdeen 1, Sunderland 7
Chanonry,10th April 1894

The English champions strolled to a comprehensive victory which had spectators and reporters enraptured from start to finish: *"A finely balanced or more accomplished set of players have never set foot on Chanonry,"* wrote one observer about Sunderland. Gillespie put the English side ahead after five minutes while Miller, D. Hannah, Hyslop and another un-named player made it 5-0. Realising that Aberdeen had no chance of winning, the spectators *"settled down to the enjoyment of the pretty tactics of the visitors."* The home fans did get something to cheer just before the break when Orion's Willie Gloag, one of a number of players guesting for Aberdeen, beat Ned Doig to make it 5-1. Doig's former Arbroath team-mate Willie Stewart, now with Victoria United, was also playing for Aberdeen as a guest.

Two further Sunderland goals in the second period completed the scoring. It could have been more: *"The score indicates only to a meagre extent the one-sided nature of the play. Sunderland's play was thought to have been the best ever seen in these parts. The passing was beautifully timed, the dribbling most bewildering, the kicking stylish and strong, while the shooting was as straight as an arrow and quite unholdable."*
Aberdeen - T. Smyth, Edwards (Orion), Joe

Sunderland's Ned Doig. The Scottish international goalkeeper started his career with Arbroath.

165

Davidson, Reith, Stewart (Victoria United), Morren, Allott, White, Gloag (Orion), Mcfarlane, Whitehead.

Sunderland - Doig, Gow, Gibson, Dale, Hyslop, Wilson, Gillespie, J. Hannah, Miller, D. Hannah, Scott.

Orion 5, Victoria United 3
Charity Cup Final, Chanonry, 28th April 1894

Played on a hot day, the first half provided the crowd of between 3,000 and 4,000 with as high a level of entertainment as any game that season, the sides sharing six goals in and end to end battle. The heat seemed to take its toll on the players during the second period, however, and play became more disjointed. Orion's Johnston made it 4-3 with 10mins to go and Openshaw added a fifth two minutes later to clinch the trophy.

Hard tackling full-back Hugh Mackay was one of the Orion heroes *"blocking, tackling and kicking in a way that his closest friends were not prepared for."* Gloag led the forwards well and *"little Openshaw did some remarkably clever things."* Mr. W. Litster, chairman of the Charity Committee presented the cup to Mr W. Walker of Orion at the Waverley Hotel that evening.

Orion - Edwards, Ross, Mackay, Wight, Low, Currie, Johnston, James, Gloag, Openshaw, Stopani

Victoria United - Cannon, Thomson, Ririe, Morrice, Stewart, Annand, Turner, Benzie, Clark, Forsyth, Ferries.

Northern League 1893-1894 - Unfinished

		P	W	D	L	F	A	Pts
1	Arbroath	11	9	0	2	64	32	18
2	Forfar Athletic	11	7	0	4	41	43	14
3	Montrose	10	3	2	5	23	30	8
4	Victoria United	10	3	2	5	31	43	8
5	Strathmore, Dundee	8	3	1	4	22	22	7
6	Johnstone Wanderers,Dundee	5	2	1	2	19	17	5
7	St Johnstone	7	1	2	4	27	26	4
8	Aberdeen	7	1	2	4	18	34	4

Note: Many fixtures were not fulfilled and the title wasn't awarded.

Aberdeen F.C - Northern League 1893-1894

Competition	Date		Opposition	F	A	Venue
Northern League	09/09/1893	Aberdeen	Arbroath	1	11	Gayfield Park, Arbroath
Northern League	30/09/1893	Aberdeen	St Johnstone	4	4	Chanonry
Northern League	11/11/1893	Aberdeen	Victoria United	2	5	Chanonry
Northern League	02/12/1893	Aberdeen	Forfar Athletic	6	4	Chanonry
Northern League	13/01/1894	Aberdeen	Montrose	1	4	Chanonry
Northern League	03/02/1894	Aberdeen	Arbroath	3	5	Chanonry
Northern League	10/03/1894	Aberdeen	Victoria United	1	1	Wellington Bridge Grounds

Note: 10th March 1894 match doubled up as a Gershon Cup game

Aberdeen F.C. – 1893-1894 – Other Games

Competition	Date		Opposition	F	A	Venue
	19/08/1893	Aberdeen	Orion	1	6	Chanonry
	26/08/1893	Aberdeen	Queen's Park	1	8	Chanonry
Scottish Cup 1R	02/09/1893	Aberdeen	Fraserburgh Wanderers	11	1	Chanonry
	16/09/1893	Aberdeen	Montrose	2	6	Montrose
Scottish Cup 2R	23/09/1893	Aberdeen	Victoria United	0	8	Victoria Bridge Grounds
	07/10/1893	Aberdeen	Peterhead	4	0	Recreation Park, Peterhead
Aberdeenshire Cup 1R	28/10/1893	Aberdeen	Orion	1	5	Chanonry
	04/11/1893	Aberdeen	Raith Rovers	3	4	Chanonry
	09/12/1893	Aberdeen	Stonehaven	9	4	Stonehaven
Gershon Cup	16/12/1893	Aberdeen	Orion	4	4	Central park
	23/12/1893	Aberdeen	Montrose	2	5	Chanonry
	30/12/1893	Aberdeen	Johnstone Wanderers	3	2	Chanonry
	01/01/1894	Aberdeen	Victoria United	3	4	Wellington Bridge Grounds

Competition	Date		Opposition	F	A	Venue
Striking Joiners Benefit	31/01/1894	Aberdeen-	Victoria United Orion Select	1	1	Wellington Bridge Grounds
Gershon Cup	10/02/1894	Aberdeen	Orion	1	4	Chanonry
	03/03/1894	Aberdeen	Linthouse	7	4	Chanonry
Gershon Cup	10/03/1894	Aberdeen	Victoria United	1	1	Wellington Bridge Grounds
	17/03/1894	Aberdeen	St Bernard's	1	8	Chanonry
Gershon Cup	24/03/1894	Aberdeen	Victoria United	2	9	Chanonry
Charity Cup SF	31/03/1894	Aberdeen	Victoria United	3	6	Chanonry
	07/04/1894	Aberdeen	Glasgow Rangers	1	2	Chanonry
	10/04/1894	Aberdeen	Sunderland	1	7	Chanonry
	14/04/1894	Aberdeen	Dundee	1	3	Chanonry
	21/04/1894	Aberdeen	Orion	2	4	Central Park
	03/05/1894	Aberdeen	Victoria United	3	5	Chanonry
	05/05/1894	Aberdeen	Orion	4	4	Chanonry
	17/05/1894	Aberdeen	Victoria United	6	3	Wellington Bridge Grounds

Orion - 1893-1894

Competition	Date		Opposition	F	A	Venue
	19/08/1893	Orion	Aberdeen	6	1	Chanonry
	26/08/1893	Orion	Victoria United	2	4	Central Park
	02/09/1893	Orion	Hawthorn, Inverurie	9	1	Central Park
	09/09/1893	Orion	Broxburn	5	1	Central Park
	16/09/1893	Orion	Cowdenbeath	2	4	Central Park
	23/09/1893	Orion	Elgin Association	2	5	Elgin
	25/09/1893	Orion	Hawthorn, Fraserburgh	9	2	Fraserburgh
	30/09/1893	Orion	Lochee United	2	0	Central Park
	07/10/1893	Orion	Kirkcaldy	4	0	Central Park
Scottish Cup	14/10/1893	Orion	Victoria United	6	1	Wellington Bridge Grounds
Aberdeenshire Cup 1R	28/10/1893	Orion	Aberdeen	5	1	Chanonry

Competition	Date		Opposition	F	A	Venue
Scottish Cup	04/11/1893	Orion	Kilsyth Wanderers	4	2	Central Park
	11/11/1893	Orion	Arbroath Wanderers	8	1	Central Park
Aberdeenshire Cup 2R	18/11/1893	Orion	Peterhead	8	1	Central Park
Scottish Cup 1R	25/11/1893	Orion	Leith Athletic	2	11	Central Park
	02/12/1893	Orion	Dundee A	0	2	Central Park
	09/12/1893	Orion	Brechin	4	2	Central Park
Gershon Cup	16/12/1893	Orion	Aberdeen	4	4	Central Park
	23/12/1893	Orion	Victoria United	3	2	Wellington Bridge Grounds
	30/12/1893	Orion	Dunblane	3	1	Central Park
	01/01/1894	Orion	Battlefield, Glasgow	2	3	Central Park
Striking Joiners	03/01/1894	Orion	Victoria United	2	4	Wellington Bridge Grounds
Benefit	06/01/1894	Orion	Mossend Swifts	3	2	Central Park
	13/01/1894	Orion	Edinburgh University	4	1	Central Park
Aberdeenshire Cup Final	20/01/1894	Orion	Victoria United	3	6	Chanonry
	27/01/1894	Orion	Fraserburgh	5	2	Central Park
Striking Joiners Benefit	31/01/1894	Orion-Aberdeen Select	Victoria United	1	1	Wellington Bridge Grounds
Gershon Cup	10/02/1894	Orion	Aberdeen	4	1	Chanonry
	17/02/1894	Orion	Elginshire	1	1	Central Park
Charity Cup	24/02/1894	Orion	Peterhead	11	0	Wellington Bridge Grounds
Gershon Cup	03/03/1894	Orion	Victoria United	3	2	Central Park
	10/03/1894	Orion	Banchory	6	0	Burnett Park,Banchory
	24/03/1894	Orion	Montrose	3	0	Central Park
	31/03/1894	Orion	Fraserburgh Association	8	1	Fraserburgh
Gershon Cup	07/04/1894	Orion	Victoria United	6	0	Wellington Bridge Grounds
	14/04/1894	Orion	Forfar Athletic	3	4	Central Park
	21/04/1894	Orion	Aberdeen	4	2	Central Park
Charity Cup Final	28/04/1894	Orion	Victoria United	5	3	Chanonry

Competition	Date		Opposition	F	A	Venue
	05/05/1894	Orion	Aberdeen	4	4	Chanonry
	12/05/1894	Orion	Culter	10	1	Culter

Victoria United – Northern League 1893-1894

Competition	Date		Opposition	F	A	Venue
Northern League	09/09/1893	Victoria United	Forfar Athletic	7	3	Wellington Bridge Grounds
Northern League	16/09/1893	Victoria United	Johnstone Wanderers	3	4	Wellington Bridge Grounds
Northern League	30/09/1893	Victoria United	Montrose	2	2	Montrose
Northern League	07/10/1893	Victoria United	Arbroath	2	3	Wellington Grounds
Northern League	11/11/1893	Victoria United	Aberdeen	5	2	Chanonry
Northern League	25/11/1893	Victoria United	Johnstone Wanderers	1	9	Clepington Park, Dundee
Northern League	09/12/1893	Victoria United	Strathmore, Dundee	6	3	Wellington Grounds
Northern League	13/01/1894	Victoria United	Arbroath	3	14	Gayfield Park, Arbroath
Northern League	17/02/1894	Victoria United	Montrose	1	2	Wellington Bridge Grounds
Northern League	10/03/1894	Victoria United	Aberdeen	1	1	Wellington Bridge Grounds

Note: 10th March 1894 match doubled up as a Gershon Cup game

Victoria United – 1893-1894 – Other Games

Competition	Date		Opposition	F	A	Venue
	05/08/1893	Victoria United	Port Glasgow Athletic	2	6	Wellington Bridge Grounds
	12/08/1893	Victoria United	Greenock Morton	6	3	Wellington Bridge Grounds
	19/08/1893	Victoria United	Harp, Dundee	1	3	Wellington Bridge Grounds
	26/08/1893	Victoria United	Orion	4	2	Central Park

Competition	Date		Opposition	F	A	Venue
Scottish Cup	02/09/1893	Victoria United	Peterhead	3	2	Recreation Park, Peterhead
Scottish Cup	23/09/1893	Victoria United	Aberdeen	8	0	Victoria Bridge Grounds
	25/09/1893	Victoria United	Montrose	1	3	Wellington Bridge Grounds
Scottish Cup	14/10/1893	Victoria United	Orion	1	6	Wellington Bridge Grounds
Aberdeenshire Cup 1R	28/10/1893	Victoria United	Fraserburgh Wanderers	13	1	Fraserburgh
	04/11/1893	Victoria United	Montrose	4	2	Wellington Bridge Grounds
	18/11/1893	Victoria United	King's Park	4	2	Wellington Bridge Grounds
	02/12/1893	Victoria United	Brechin	1	4	Brechin
Aberdeenshire Cup 2R	16/12/1893	Victoria United	Aberdeen University	6	1	Wellington Bridge Grounds
	23/12/1893	Victoria United	Orion	2	3	Wellington Bridge Grounds
	30/12/1893	Victoria United	Partick Thistle	4	5	Wellington Bridge Grounds
	01/01/1894	Victoria United	Aberdeen	4	3	Wellington Bridge Grounds
	02/01/1894	Victoria United	Renton	2	6	Wellington Bridge Grounds
Striking Joiners Benefit	03/01/1894	Victoria United	Orion	4	2	Wellington Bridge Grounds
Aberdeenshire Cup Final	20/01/1894	Victoria United	Orion	6	3	Chanonry
	27/01/1894	Victoria United	Brechin	5	2	Wellington Bridge Grounds
Striking Joiners Benefit	31/01/1894	Victoria United	Aberdeen-Orion Select	1	1	Wellington Bridge Grounds

Competition	Date		Opposition	F	A	Venue
	03/02/1894	Victoria United	Dundonians	3	1	Wellington Bridge Grounds
	10/02/1894	Victoria United	Heart of Midlothian	1	8	Wellington Bridge Grounds
Gershon Cup	03/03/1894	Victoria United	Orion	2	3	Central Park
Gershon Cup	10/03/1894	Victoria United	Aberdeen	1	1	Wellington Bridge Grounds
	17/03/1894	Victoria United	Argyll & Sutherland H'landers	5	2	Wellington Bridge Grounds
Gershon Cup	24/03/1894	Victoria United	Aberdeen	9	2	Chanonry
Charity Cup SF	31/03/1894	Victoria United	Aberdeen	6	3	Chanonry
Gershon Cup	07/04/1894	Victoria United	Orion	0	6	Wellington Bridge Grounds
	13/04/1894	Victoria United	Montrose	1	1	Wellington Bridge Grounds
	21/04/1894	Victoria United	Junior Select	6	4	Wellington Bridge Grounds
	26/04/1894	Victoria United	Rosemount Comb Works			Wellington Bridge Grounds
Charity Cup Final	28/04/1894	Victoria United	Orion	3	5	Chanonry
	02/05/1894	Victoria United	Culter	9	3	Culter
	03/05/1894	Victoria United	Aberdeen	5	3	Chanonry
	05/05/1894	Victoria United	Fair City Athletic	4	4	Wellington Bridge Grounds
	10/05/1894	Victoria United	Albert			Wellington Bridge Grounds
	12/05/1894	Victoria United	Arbroath	5	2	Wellington Bridge Grounds
	17/05/1894	Victoria United	Aberdeen	3	6	Wellington Bridge Grounds
	19/05/1894	Victoria United	Forfar Athletic	2	2	Wellington Bridge Grounds

Aberdeenshire Cup 1893-1894

Competition	Date			F	A	Venue
First Round	28/10/1893	Victoria United	Fraserburgh Wanderers	13	1	Fraserburgh
First Round	28/10/1893	Aberdeen	Orion	1	5	Chanonry
First Round	28/10/1893	Peterhead	Faithlie Thistle	9	0	Peterhead
Second Round	18/11/1893	Orion	Peterhead	8	1	Central Park
Second Round	16/12/1893	Victoria United	Aberdeen University	6	1	Wellington Grounds
Cup Final	20/01/1894	Victoria United	Orion	6	3	Chanonry

Charity Cup 1893-1894

Competition	Date			F	A	Venue
Charity Cup	24/02/1894	Orion	Peterhead	11	0	Wellington Bridge Grounds
Charity Cup	31/03/1894	Aberdeen	Victoria United	3	6	Chanonry
Charity Cup Final	28/04/1894	Victoria United	Orion	3	5	Chanonry

Gershon Cup Final Table 1893-1894

	P	W	D	L	F	A	Pts
Orion	4	3	1	0	17	7	7
VU	4	1	1	2	12	12	3
Aberdeen	4	0	2	2	8	18	2

1894-1895
Opening of Cattofield Park

After the problems of the previous season there was no Northern League in 1894-1895 so the local clubs again focussed on the Scottish Cup and the usual diet of local cup matches and friendlies. Orion relocated up the hill from their Central Park ground to a new facility leased from Aberdeen Town Council at Cattofield, immediately next to the reservoir. The ground was described as *"one of the best in the north"* with the club spending £200 in levelling and enclosing it. The Central Park grandstand was also moved to sit alongside the new pitch. The Stripes opened the ground, sometimes also referred to at this time as Orion Park, with a match against Scottish League side Dundee in front of a crowd of 2,000. Councillor Glass kicked off *"amid loud cheers"* but it was the visitors who took the plaudits by winning 4-2. However, not everyone was pleased with the ground. At the end of the season local residents held a public meeting to voice their concerns about the disruption caused by football matches. They were particularly worried by the foul and abusive language used by many football fans, especially youths who congregated in the surrounding streets on match days and evenings. The locals called on the Town Council to cancel Orion's lease, but no action was taken.

The severe winter weather also caused Orion problems. A game scheduled against Victoria United on 22nd December had to be cancelled after gale force winds blew the roof of the grandstand into adjoining fields and the wooden enclosure was all but destroyed. Despite such difficulties Orion set out their stall as the top club in the city by winning the Aberdeenshire Cup and the Gershon Cup. They progressed further in the Scottish Cup than their city rivals, eventually going out to Dundee, and the only blemish on their season was a defeat by Aberdeen in the Charity Cup semi final. The advent of professionalism had touched all the senior clubs in the city who started paying their players. Orion's wage bill was close to £78 which was roughly 10% of the club's turnover. Orion attracted Scottish First Division champions Hearts of Midlothian to Cattofield for a challenge game towards the end of the season. The Edinburgh club sent a second eleven up to Aberdeen and won the game 5-4 in front of a crowd of 3,000.

Victoria United were also on the move early in the season when relocating back to their Torry roots at the old Victoria Bridge Grounds after two years at the Wellington Bridge Grounds. Peterhead provided the opposition for the first game back at the old venue, but the home side ran out easy 8-1 winners in what was a Scottish Cup tie. United went out of the competition in the next round, however, losing 5-0 to Orion at Cattofield after a 4-4 draw at Torry. The replay was an ill-tempered affair: *"It was apparent from the commencement that the players had lost their heads somewhat and there was much wild kicking and loose ineffective play,"* is how one reporter described the action. United were handicapped by the loss of John Annand for much of the game because of injury.

Victoria's three-year domination of the Aberdeenshire Cup also came to an end when they were beaten by Aberdeen in the semi final. The tie had been postponed five times because of the wintry weather which left the city covered in snow and ice for weeks on end. The Blues did get their hands on some silverware, however, when winning the Charity Cup for the third time in five years by beating Aberdeen 6-2 in the Final after a 1-1 draw. United's biggest win of the season came in February when they thumped Aberdeen University 11-0 in a benefit match which raised £4 for the fund which had been set up to help unemployed people during the winter. Aberdeen F.C. also donated £2 to the fund.

Aberdeen endured a pretty miserable season which ended with a bare trophy cabinet and very little to celebrate. The Whites fell at the first hurdle in the Scottish Cup, losing to Orion in a replay. They did manage to get to the Final of the Aberdeenshire Cup but once again Orion brushed them aside by handing out a 5-0 drubbing. The Charity Cup Final was also reached but Victoria United swept to victory in that contest. And they finished bottom of the table in the Gershon Cup competition.

There were nevertheless a few interesting talking points for Chanonry fans. Former Aberdeen player W.S. Brown, for instance, caused a minor sensation when refereeing the Whites game against Our Boys of Blairgowrie at the Chanonry in December. Brown sent off Aberdeen's John Davidson and Blair's Sinclair *"for disgracing the rules of propriety."* A sending off was still a remarkable rare event and a double sending off was almost unique.

At the end of the season the local press was able to report that the Northern League was to be revived for season 1895-1896 and would comprise the following eight clubs: Dundee Wanderers, Fair City Athletics, Montrose, Arbroath, Forfar Athletic, Aberdeen, Orion and Victoria United. United declined to take up their place, however, no doubt still feeling aggrieved over the way the league operated the previous year.

Before the footballers packed away their gear for the summer one final game attracted great interest in the city. On 27th May a crowd of 6,000 packed into the Victoria Bridge Grounds to watch women players in action. *"Ten players dressed in red blouses and dark blue knickers represented the north and nine members attired in blue blouses and blue knickers represented the south,"* was how the line-ups were described. The Reds featured a mother and daughter who the crowd, for some unknown reason, chose to call *"Tommy"* and *"Charlie."* The Blues keeper, a Mrs Graham, was described as a *"tall, well-built woman."* The Reds won 2-1 and at the end of the game many of the spectators invaded the pitch and crowded round the players who required a police escort back to the pavilion. The curious crowds stayed outside the gates for a considerable period afterwards but eventually the women were escorted out and driven to their hotel.

Sunderland won the English First Division title and Aberdeen's Bon Accord magazine, in an effort to share information with the city's footballers, published dietary advice and instructions for exercise which was given out to the Sunderland players by the club trainers. Many local players didn't bother training, so may have been interested in following the professional's regime. Here it is:

7-30am   - To rise. Half an hour's stroll.

8-30am   - Breakfast, consisting of weak tea, chops, toast or stale bread.

9-45am   - Walking exercise, with bath to follow.

1pm   - Dinner, consisting of plain roast joints, mutton and beef, with vegetables, toast or stale bread, tapioca pudding, and half-a-pint of beer.

3-30pm - Running exercise.

6pm   - Tea, consisting of fresh fish or light boiled eggs, with toast or stale
        bread and watercress.

7-30pm - One hour's stroll.

9pm   - Supper; half-a-pint of bitter beer and bread.

10-30pm - retire to rest.

N.B - Butter, sugar and milk to be used sparingly. Smoking to be moderate.
Nothing to be eaten or drunk between meals.

Notable Games

Orion 2, Dundee 4
Cattofield, Saturday 4th August 1894

Orion opened their new Cattofield ground with a friendly against Scottish league
side Dundee in front of a crowd of 2,000. Orion had the best of the opening
stages but the visitors soon assumed control. Dundee *"with wind, sun and incline
in their favour, worked down to the home goal and before halftime they had three
points - all from the foot of Gilligan."* Orion rallied at the start of the second half
and two goals from John Stopani brought the Aberdeen side back into the game.
Dundee weathered the storm however and added a fourth goal before the end.

Orion - Edwards, Dawson, Ross, Wight, Low, Currie, Openshaw, James,
Johnston, Stopani, Leggat.

Dundee - Barratt, Ferrier, Campbell, Darroch (late Sheffield Wednesday), Longan,
Fleming (late Sheffield United), Thomson, Gilligan, Sawers (late Blackburn
Rovers), Dickson, Keillor.

Aberdeen 2, London Corinthians 2
Chanonry , 31st December 1894

The famous Corinthians were Aberdeen's New Year visitors to the Chanonry. The
London club boasted numerous England internationals amongst its members
although many of them also played for other clubs. In the 1880's it was mainly
Corinthian members who represented England in international matches against
Scotland. In 1894 and 1895 the entire England teams for the games against Wales
were made up of Corinthians. For the Chanonry match the visitors fielded two

England internationals, Norman Cooper and Cuthbert 'Pinky' Burnup. Conditions at the Old Aberdeen venue were atrocious with a strong wind blowing across the field from the west and frequent driving showers leaving the pitch coated in several inches of snow. After an even opening 20 minutes the visitors took the lead through F. Street and 'Pinky' Burnup made it 2-0 before the interval. But five minutes after the restart Aberdeen equalised through Mackie.After intense Aberdeen pressure Mackie thought he had scored a deserved equaliser but his effort was chalked off because of offside. The Whites continued to press and finally earned the draw their efforts merited when Thompson scored right at the death.

Aberdeen - Smyth, John Davidson, Gall, Ritchie, Joe Davidson, Thomson, Smith, Taylor, Toman, Gray, Mackie.

Corinthians - A.G.S. Lawrence, E. H. Bray, H. K.Foster, W. L. Foster, N.C. Cooper, E.C. Bliss, Boaworth Smith, E. D. Compton, F. Street, G.S. Wilson, C. Burnup

Orion 5, Aberdeen 0
Aberdeenshire Cup Final, Victoria Bridge Grounds,
Saturday 16th March 1895

The attendance given for this game was a very precise 3,991 – this is the first exact attendance figure I have found, all others reported until now were estimates.

Reports of the match suggest, however, that as many as 4,500 people were in the ground once 'free' places were taken into account. Orion totally dominated the game with Thom and Leggat giving them a comfortable 2-0 halftime lead while Stopani came close with an effort which hit the post. Toman twice came close for Aberdeen in the second half before Orion

George Benzie, Orion F.C.
Benzie started his senior career with Victoria United and won the Aberdeenshire Cup with the Blues in 1892-1893. He pocketed a second winner's medal with Orion in 1894-1895. He also played for Vics in two losing Charity Cup Finals.

had another effort disallowed for offside. The Stripes soon added a third, however, with Willie Gloag heading home after a great run and cross from Stopani. A Thom header made it 4-0 then John Low bundled the ball, his team-mate Gloag and Aberdeen goalkeeper Tom Smyth into the net for number five. The players were presented with their gold medals in the Northern Hotel after the match.

Orion - Morrison, Mackay, Ross, Wright, Low, Currie, Gloag, Benzie, Thom, Leggat, Stopani

Aberdeen - Smyth, John Davidson, Gall, C.W. Mackie, Joe Davidson, Thomson, Turner, Taylor, Toman, Gray, J. Mackie

Ref: J. McLaughlin, Celtic F.C

Victoria United 2, Hibernian 9
Friendly, Victoria Bridge Grounds, Monday 6th May 1895

Edinburgh's Hibernian visited the city for the first time and gave United a thorough beating. Smith gave Hibs the lead after 30min and five minutes later United's Jim Ririe unfortunately headed a corner beyond his own goalkeeper to give the visitors a 2-0 halftime lead. Further goals from Smith, Murray and Martin extended the Hibernian lead, but there was great excitement when John Forsyth pulled one back for the home side. Martin grabbed two more for Hibs to complete his hat-trick, a feat then matched by Smith when putting the Edinburgh men 8-1 ahead. Near the end Ritchie got United's second before Martin took his personal tally to four by completing the rout.

Victoria United: Inch, Anderson, J. Ririe, Easton, W. Ririe, Annand, G. McFarlane, A McFarlane, Forsyth, Clark, Ritchie

Hibernian: Cameron, Neill, Macfarlane, Breslin, Murphy, Smith, Murray, Kennedy, Martin, Smith, Tullie.

Ref: Peter Simpson

Victoria United 6, Aberdeen 2
Charity Cup Final replay, Cattofield Park, Monday 20th May 1895

Aberdeen's last chance of landing some silverware ended as Victoria United secured the trophy for the third time in five years. The Whites had managed to take the Final to a replay thanks mainly to a great goalkeeping display by Tom Smyth in the first game which ended in a 1-1 draw. But the Torry men showed no mercy in the rematch at Cattofield. Playing 'up the hill', G. Mcfarlane put United ahead after just two minutes. This was followed by a *"spell of rough play"* which ended with Aberdeen equalising with a brilliant 30 yard freekick by Taylor. It was all square at the interval but after the restart United charged ahead with goals from Mcfarlane and Ritchie. Mcfarlane added a fourth then a fifth was scored. Taylor reduced the leeway as Aberdeen made a late fightback before A. Mcfarlane wrapped things up with United's sixth.

Tom Smyth – Aberdeen F.C. captain and goalkeeper.

Victoria United: Insch, Anderson, Burgess, Morrice, Ririe, Annand, G. Mcfarlane, A. Mcfarlane, Clark, Forsyth, Ritchie.

Aberdeen: Smyth, John Davidson, Gall, C.W. Mackie, Joe Davidson, Thomson, Turner, Taylor, Toman, Gray, Mackie.
Ref: Mr Black, Forfar.

Orion 4, Hearts 5
Cattofield Park 18th May 1895

A crowd of 3,000 turned up to see Orion face the Scottish champions but the Edinburgh side fielded very much a second string with only a couple of players having had regular first team experience. Orion, with a strong wind at their backs, made a bright start and Hearts goalkeeper Gardiner was put under immediate pressure. With just two minutes played, Willie Gloag gave the home side the lead and shortly afterwards John Low made it 2-0 with a great header. Orion continued to dominate but great goalkeeping by Gardiner kept the Cattofield men at bay. Just before the interval Atherton gave Hearts some hope by netting a fine goal. The visitors were playing up the hill in the second half but now had wind advantage and it wasn't long before Walls equalised. But Orion fought back and

The Aberdeen and Victoria United teams pose for the cameras prior to the Charity Cup Final at Cattofield. Note the press box in the background. It's thanks to the efforts of these unidentified gentlemen that we have any meaningful record of early football in the city.

John Stopani put them ahead again. The game was now opening up and Hearts stormed back with Walls firing home a powerful shot to make it 3-3. A fourth soon followed then Atherton grabbed a fifth, but Orion still refused to give in and Gloag netted to set up an exciting finish. The Stripes tried hard to get the equaliser but Hearts held on for a narrow win.

Orion - Morrison, Mackay, Ross, Wight, Low, Currie, Gloag, Leggat, Thom, Stopani, Moultrie

Hearts - Gardiner, Turner, Phillips, Paterson, Gray, Hall, Taylor, Atherton, Walls, Fairbairn, Black

Ref: James Philip, Aberdeen

Aberdeen 1894-1895

Competition	Date		Opposition	F	A	Venue
	16/08/1894	Aberdeen	Culter	4	1	Chanonry
	25/08/1894	Aberdeen	Orion	3	3	Orion Park,Cattofield
Scottish Cup	01/09/1894	Aberdeen	Orion	3	3	Chanonry
Scottish Cup	08/09/1894	Aberdeen	Orion	1	5	Orion Park,Cattofield

Competition	Date		Opposition	F	A	Venue
	15/09/1894	Aberdeen	Montrose	4	2	Chanonry
	22/09/1894	Aberdeen	Culter	4	1	Culter
	29/09/1894	Aberdeen	Brechin	4	4	Montrose St Park,
Brechin						
	13/10/1894	Aberdeen	Victoria United	2	8	Chanonry
	20/10/1894	Aberdeen	St Johnstone	6	3	Chanonry
	27/10/1894	Aberdeen	Stonehaven	10	2	Chanonry
	03/11/1894	Aberdeen	Cowlairs	5	3	Chanonry
Aberdeenshire Cup	10/11/1894	Aberdeen	Peterhead	3	1	Recreation Park, Peterhead
	17/11/1894	Aberdeen	Orion	3	2	Chanonry
	24/11/1894	Aberdeen	Aberdeen University	4	3	Kings College
Gershon Cup	01/12/1894	Aberdeen	Victoria United	3	2	Chanonry
	08/12/1894	Aberdeen	Montrose	0	7	Links Park Montrose
	15/12/1894	Aberdeen	Our Boys Blairgowrie	4	2	Chanonry
	29/12/1894	Aberdeen	Partick Thistle	4	1	Chanonry
	31/12/1894	Aberdeen	London Corinthians	2	2	Chanonry
	01/01/1895	Aberdeen	Victoria United	4	4	Chanonry
	05/01/1895	Aberdeen	Orion	4	4	Chanonry
	12/01/1895	Aberdeen	Peterhead	6	2	Peterhead
Aberdeenshire Cup	19/01/1895	Aberdeen	Victoria United	2	2	Victoria Bridge Grounds
	26/01/1895	Aberdeen	Victoria United	2	2	Chanonry
Aberdeenshire Cup SF	02/03/1895	Aberdeen	Victoria United	5	3	Chanonry
	09/03/1895	Aberdeen	Banchory	15	0	Burnett Park,Banchory
Aberdeenshire Cup Final	16/03/1895	Aberdeen	Orion	0	5	Victoria Bridge Grounds
Gershon Cup	23/03/1895	Aberdeen	Orion	0	2	Chanonry
	30/03/1895	Aberdeen	Fraserburgh	7	3	Fraserburgh
Gershon Cup	06/04/1895	Aberdeen	Victoria United	1	2	Victoria Bridge Grounds
	13/04/1895	Aberdeen	Clachnacuddin	4	2	Chanonry
Gershon Cup	20/04/1895	Aberdeen	Orion	0	6	Orion Park,Cattofield

Competition	Date		Opposition	F	A	Venue
	25/04/1895	Aberdeen	Junior Select	5	2	Chanonry
Charity Cup SF	27/04/1895	Aberdeen	Orion	3	2	Victoria Bridge Grounds
	04/05/1895	Aberdeen	Clachnacuddin	0	1	Inverness
Charity Cup Final	11/05/1895	Aberdeen	Victoria United	1	1	Orion Park,Cattofield
Charity Cup Final Replay	20/05/1895	Aberdeen	Victoria United	2	6	Orion Park, Cattofield

Orion 1894-1895

Competition	Date		Opposition	F	A	Venue
	04/08/1894	Orion	Dundee	2	4	Cattofield
	11/08/1894	Orion	Alloa Athletic	2	2	Cattofield
	18/08/1894	Orion	Montrose	4	0	Montrose
	25/08/1894	Orion	Aberdeen	3	3	Orion Park, Cattofield
Scottish Cup	01/09/1894	Orion	Aberdeen	3	3	Chanonry
Scottish Cup	08/09/1894	Orion	Aberdeen	5	1	Orion Park, Cattofield
	15/09/1894	Orion	Forfar Athletic	5	2	Orion Park, Cattofield
Scottish Cup	22/09/1894	Orion	Victoria United	4	4	Victoria Bridge Grounds
Scottish Cup	29/09/1894	Orion	Victoria United	5	0	Orion Park, Cattofield
Scottish Cup	13/10/1894	Orion	Inverness Thistle	3	1	Orion Park, Cattofield
	20/10/1894	Orion	Arbroath	3	1	Orion Park, Cattofield
	27/10/1894	Orion	Elginshire	5	1	Orion Park, Cattofield
	03/11/1894	Orion	Brechin	8	2	Orion Park, Cattofield
Gershon Cup	10/11/1894	Orion	Victoria United	0	3	Victoria Bridge Grounds
	17/11/1894	Orion	Aberdeen	2	3	Chanonry
Scottish Cup	24/11/1894	Orion	Dundee	1	5	Orion Park,Cattofield
	01/12/1894	Orion	Peterhead	0	0	Recreation Park, Peterhead
	08/12/1894	Orion	Mossend Swifts	1	5	Orion Park, Cattofield
	15/12/1894	Orion	Edinburgh University	3	1	Orion Park, Cattofield
	29/12/1894	Orion	Montrose	3	4	Montrose
	05/01/1895	Orion	Aberdeen	4	4	Chanonry
	12/01/1895	Orion	Victoria United	2	2	Orion Park, Cattofield

Competition	Date		Opposition	F	A	Venue
Aberdeenshire Cup SF	19/01/1895	Orion	Culter	7	0	Orion Park, Cattofield
	02/02/1895	Orion	Dundee A	4	0	Orion Park, Cattofield
	16/02/1895	Orion	Dunfermline	3	2	Orion Park, Cattofield
	23/02/1895	Orion	St Andrews University	4	1	Orion Park, Cattofield
	09/03/1895	Orion	Victoria United	2	4	Orion Park, Cattofield
Aberdeenshire Cup Final	16/03/1895	Orion	Aberdeen	5	0	Victoria Bridge Grounds
Gershon Cup	23/03/1895	Orion	Aberdeen	2	0	Chanonry
	30/03/1895	Orion	Ellon	10	0	Ellon
	06/04/1895	Orion	Culter	6	0	Culter
	13/04/1895	Orion	Junior Select	5	1	Orion Park, Cattofield
Gershon Cup	20/04/1895	Orion	Aberdeen	6	0	Orion Park, Cattofield
Charity Cup SF	27/04/1895	Orion	Aberdeen	2	3	Victoria Bridge Grounds
	04/05/1895	Orion	Dumbarton	3	2	Orion Park,Cattofield
	18/05/1895	Orion	Heart Of Midlothian	4	5	Orion Park,Cattofield
Gershon Cup	23/05/1895	Orion	Victoria United	3	0	Central Park
	25/05/1895	Orion	Clyde	2	2	Orion Park,Cattofield

Victoria United 1894-1895

Competition	Date		Opposition	F	A	Venue
	04/08/1894	Victoria United	Bo'ness	3	3	Wellington Bridge Grounds
	11/08/1894	Victoria United	Kirkcaldy	10	2	Wellington Bridge Grounds
	18/08/1894	Victoria United	Dundee Wanderers	5	2	Wellington Bridge Grounds
	24/08/1894	Victoria United	Culter	3	0	Culter
	25/08/1894	Victoria United	Arbroath Wanderers	11	2	Wellington Bridge Grounds
Scottish Cup	01/09/1894	Victoria United	Peterhead	8	1	Victoria Bridge Grounds

Competition	Date		Opposition	F	A	Venue
	08/09/1894	Victoria United	Lochee United	6	2	Victoria Bridge Grounds
	15/09/1894	Victoria United	Hearts Reserves	5	3	Victoria Bridge Grounds
Scottish Cup	22/09/1894	Victoria United	Orion	4	4	Victoria Bridge Grounds
	24/09/1894	Victoria United	Fraserburgh Hawthorn	8	4	Bellslea Park, Fraserburgh
Scottish Cup	29/09/1894	Victoria United	Orion	0	5	Orion Park, Cattofield
	06/10/1894	Victoria United	Culter	6	2	Culter
	13/10/1894	Victoria United	Aberdeen	8	2	Chanonry
	27/10/1894	Victoria United	Dundee A	1	1	Victoria Bridge Grounds
	03/11/1894	Victoria United	Montrose	10	1	Victoria Bridge Grounds
Gershon Cup	10/11/1894	Victoria United	Orion	3	0	Victoria Bridge Grounds
Aberdeenshire Cup 2R	17/11/1894	Victoria United	Faithlie Thistle Fraserburgh	10	1	Bellslea Park, Fraserburgh
	24/11/1894	Victoria United	Arbroath	8	1	Victoria Bridge Grounds
Gershon Cup	01/12/1894	Victoria United	Aberdeen	2	3	Chanonry
	08/12/1894	Victoria United	Brechin	2	0	Victoria Bridge Grounds
	15/12/1894	Victoria United	Gordon Highlanders Glasgow	7	1	Victoria Bridge Grounds
	31/12/1894	Victoria United	Port Glasgow	1	3	Victoria Bridge Grounds
	01/01/1895	Victoria United	Aberdeen	4	4	Chanonry
	02/01/1895	Victoria United	Partick Thistle	1	4	Victoria Bridge Grounds
	05/01/1895	Victoria United	Peterhead	6	2	Recreation Park, Peterhead
	12/01/1895	Victoria United	Orion	2	2	Orion Park, Cattofield
Aberdeenshire Cup	19/01/1895	Victoria United	Aberdeen	2	2	Victoria Bridge Grounds
	26/01/1895	Victoria United	Aberdeen	2	2	Chanonry
Unemployed Benefit Match	16/02/1895	Victoria United	Aberdeen University	11	0	Victoria Bridge Grounds

Competition	Date		Opposition	F	A	Venue
Aberdeenshire Cup SF	02/03/1895	Victoria United	Aberdeen	3	5	Chanonry
	09/03/1895	Victoria United	Orion	4	2	Orion Park,Cattofield
	16/03/1895	Victoria United	Montrose	0	10	Links Park, Montrose
Charity Cup	30/03/1895	Victoria United	County	10	0	Victoria Bridge Grounds
Gershon Cup	06/04/1895	Victoria United	Aberdeen	2	1	Victoria Bridge Grounds
	12/04/1895	Victoria United	Montrose	3	0	Victoria Bridge Grounds
	13/04/1895	Victoria United	Dundee A	7	0	Victoria Bridge Grounds
	18/04/1895	Victoria United	Victoria United Reserves			Victoria Bridge Grounds
	27/04/1895	Victoria United	Culter	8	1	Culter
	02/05/1895	Victoria United	Rosemount Combworks			Victoria Bridge Grounds Victoria Bridge Grounds
	04/05/1895	Victoria United	Queen's Park	2	2	Victoria Bridge Grounds
	06/05/1895	Victoria United	Hibernian	2	9	Victoria Bridge Grounds
Charity Cup Final	11/05/1895	Victoria United	Aberdeen	1	1	Orion Park, Cattofield
	16/05/1895	Victoria United	Junior Select			Victoria Bridge Grounds
	18/05/1895	Victoria United	Raith Rovers	3	3	Victoria Bridge Grounds
Charity Cup Final Replay	20/05/1895	Victoria United	Aberdeen	6	2	Orion Park, Cattofield
Gershon Cup	23/05/1895	Victoria United	Orion	0	3	Central Park
	30/05/1895	Victoria United	Dundee	1	4	Victoria Bridge Grounds

Aberdeenshire Cup 1894-1895

Competition	Date			F	A	Venue
First Round	27/10/1894	Aberdeen University	Fraserburgh Hawthorn	4	6	Links, Fraserburgh
First Round	27/10/1894	Culter	Our Boys Turriff	10	2	Culter
Second Round	10/11/1894	Aberdeen	Peterhead	3	1	Recreation Park, Peterhead
Second Round	17/11/1894	Victoria United	Faithlie Thistle, Fraserburgh	10	1	Bellslea Park, Fraserburgh

Competition	Date			F	A	Venue
Semi-Final	19/01/1895	Victoria United	Aberdeen	2	2	Victoria Bridge Grounds
Semi-Final	19/01/1895	Orion	Culter	7	0	Orion Park, Cattofield
Semi-Final	02/03/1895	Aberdeen	Victoria United	5	3	Chanonry
Cup Final	16/03/1895	Orion	Aberdeen	5	0	Victoria Bridge Grounds

Note: not all results known

Charity Cup 1894-1895

Competition	Date			F	A	Venue
Semi-Final	30/03/1895	Victoria United	County	10	0	Victoria Bridge Grounds
Semi-Final	27/04/1895	Aberdeen	Orion	3	2	Victoria Bridge Grounds
Cup Final	11/05/1895	Aberdeen	Victoria United	1	1	Orion Park, Cattofield
Final Replay	20/05/1895	Victoria United	Aberdeen	6	2	Orion Park, Cattofield

Gershon Cup 1894-1895

Competition	Date			F	A	Venue
Gershon Cup	10/11/1894	Victoria United	Orion	3	0	Victoria Bridge Grounds
Gershon Cup	01/12/1894	Aberdeen	Victoria United	3	2	Chanonry
Gershon Cup	23/03/1895	Aberdeen	Orion	0	2	Chanonry
Gershon Cup	06/04/1895	Victoria United	Aberdeen	2	1	Victoria Bridge Grounds
Gershon Cup	20/04/1895	Orion	Aberdeen	6	0	Orion Park,Cattofield
Gershon Cup	23/05/1895	Orion	Victoria United	3	0	Orion Park,Cattofield

	P	W	D	L	F	A	Pts
Orion	4	3	0	1	11	3	6
Victoria United	4	2	0	2	7	7	4
Aberdeen	4	1	0	3	4	12	2

The Gershon Cup was presented by Mr A J Gershon, the local representative of the Glasgow Clothing Company. A new Cup was presented every year to the winners of a round-robin competition featuring Orion, Victoria United and Aberdeen. The 1894-1895 Cup was manufactured by Mr Benjamin Duffus, watchmaker and jeweller, Upperkirkgate, Aberdeen.

1895-1896
Innovative Orion launch matchday programme

The number of clubs entering the Scottish Cup had mushroomed to such an extent that the Scottish Football Association decided to introduce a preliminary competition called the Scottish Qualifying Cup. For a number of seasons prior to this a series of regionalised preliminary rounds had been held, but now there was to be a tangible reward for clubs involved at this stage. All teams reaching the last 16 of the Qualifying Cup would be entered into the first round of the Scottish Cup. The Qualifying Cup itself, would be become a much prized trophy. Aberdeen, Victoria United, Orion and Culter all entered the first Qualifying Cup, and, as the First Round draw was still made on a regional basis, they found themselves drawn against each other. Vics thrashed Aberdeen 9-1 while Orion despatched Culter by 8-0. Peterhead received a bye into the Second Round in which they lost 5-2 to Orion. This was a particularly turbulent match, played at the Blue Toon's Recreation Park. The home side ended the game with nine men while the visitors were reduced to ten. Peterhead left winger May was dismissed for disputing a decision while his team-mate Davidson was given his marching orders along with Orion's right winger Campbell after the pair squared up to each other. The Blue Toon's players were described as being *"blessed with a fine physique"* but showed *"a commensurate lack of science in their movements."* Victoria United received a bye to the Third Round in which they travelled to the village of Polton, south of Edinburgh, where they lost 3-1 to Polton Vale. Orion took the train to Perth where they lost 3-1 to St Johnstone, although again there was a minor degree of controversy. Stripes captain John Low lodged a protest on the grounds that 14 yards in front of one of the goalmouths there was an uncovered iron water hydrant which posed a threat to the safety of the players. His appeal fell on deaf ears. So none of the north-east's clubs made it to the last 16 of the competition and therefore all failed to progress into the Scottish Cup itself.

The Northern League had started up again, however, with Aberdeen and Orion both taking their places while Victoria United declined the opportunity of being involved. This was Orion's first experience of the League and they opened up the campaign by travelling to Forfar on 7th September for a match against the Angus side. Forfar led 4-1 at the interval but Orion pegged them back to 4-3 before the finish. It was a decent result against the team that would go on to win the title. Indeed, Orion produced one of the biggest upsets of the season in the return fixture at Cattofield on 23rd November when they thrashed Forfar 8-1. It was Orion's first league win in their fifth game of the campaign. The stunned visitors lodged a protest on the basis that the first half was too long and the second half was ten minutes too short, but no further action was taken over the matter.

The Forfar club was involved in further controversy at the end of the League game against Aberdeen at the Chanonry in April. As the match moved into its closing stages, with Forfar leading 2-1 and the home side chasing an equaliser, referee Mr Davie, from Perth, blew his whistle to announce full-time. However, a linesman told the referee there were still five minutes to play. The referee acknowledged that he had made a mistake and tried to restart the game. The Forfar players had rushed off the field, however, and would not return. Aberdeen's players had also left the park and the referee subsequently claimed that they refused to come back on. Tom Smyth, the Aberdeen captain denied this was the case and lodged a protest. The game was eventually replayed at the end of May with Forfar winning 5-2, a result which took them to the top of the table, pipping Arbroath by a single point to claim the championship.

Orion's only league victory away from home was impressive as they shocked Arbroath 4-3 at Gayfield. It was goal-less at the interval but the visitors took an early lead in the second period and went on to upset the home side with a fine display. Arbroath also endured a surprise when they visited the Chanonry for a league game in November. The Red Lichties were leading 5-2 with little more than ten minutes remaining when a large number of spectators invaded the pitch causing the game to be abandoned. The result was, however, allowed to stand.

The issuing of protests seemed to become a regular occurrence at games throughout the season as teams attempted to find excuses for losing. Dundee Wanderers tried claiming that the game they lost 7-1 to Aberdeen at the Chanonry, again in November, should be replayed because it ended in darkness.

This claim was rejected.

The Northern League would not turn out to be particularly memorable for either Aberdeen or Orion with the city clubs finishing fourth and seventh respectively from the eight teams taking part.

Football Shirts.

HENDERSON BROTHERS,

THE LEADING HOUSE FOR

FOOTBALL GOODS.

Shirts, Knickers, and Belts.

HENDERSON BROTHERS

ATHLETIC AND FOOTBALL
OUTFITTERS,

33 and 35 BROAD STREET,

ABERDEEN.

Victoria United, meanwhile, kept active by arranging a series of friendlies, or challenge matches, against teams from near and far. The visit of Kilmarnock Athletic in September was notable for two reasons. Firstly, despite being described as *"a thrilling match"* it ended in a goalless draw, which was a very rare feature in 19th Century football. And secondly the game enjoyed a rather boisterous conclusion during which, remarkably, no-one was sent off even although at one stage the referee, Mr. Beaton, was thrown to the ground by a player and later had the ball thrown at him, as, in the words of the Aberdeen Journal *"roughness began to show itself in a marked degree and fights became of frequent occurrence."* United's decision to avoid the Northern League didn't mean the club lacked ambition. Far from it. In fact, during the season the committee decided to apply for membership of the Scottish League First Division. Just how that was treated by the powers-that-be in Glasgow is not clear, but the Torry men's hopes never materialised. By the Spring of 1896 they were reconsidering their options and decided to apply for readmission to the Northern league for the following season.

United proved to be the best of the bunch in local competitions, winning the Aberdeenshire Cup for the fourth time in five years by hammering Aberdeen 6-2 in the Final at Cattofield while they also enjoyed a first Gershon Cup victory by winning all four games in the round robin contest. The Gershon Cup was given to the club's loyal defender Jim Ririe who appears to have retired at the end of the season in order to move to Dublin to take up employment. United also proudly boasted of winning another trophy during the season. This was the Allan Cup

Victoria United and their trophies April 1896

presented by Mr. J. Allan of the Victoria Restaurant in Torry. There were, however, only two teams in the competition, Victoria United and Victoria United Reserves. The reserves were given a four goal start but the first eleven still ran out 6-4 winners. The Torry side ended the season on a high by defeating Scottish champions Celtic 4-2 at the Victoria Bridge Grounds. Wilf Toman, who had joined the Blues from Aberdeen, made his debut and scored twice, while United's other impressive striker, Sandy Caie, got the other two as the home side humbled a lethargic visiting outfit. The Vics also clocked up their record victory, a 21-0 thumping of the unfortunate Our Boys from Turriff in the first round of the Aberdeenshire Cup in a game described as *"a fiasco."*

It was yet another disappointing season for Aberdeen. For the third year in a row the Chanonry trophy cabinet remained empty despite the club reaching the final of both the Aberdeenshire Cup and the Charity Cup. The Northern League campaign started brightly with five wins from the first six matches. But just one victory in the other eight fixtures saw the Chanonry men slide down to finish fourth in the table. The heaviest defeat came in the second last match of the season, a 7-2 thumping at Arbroath. This game summed up Aberdeen's season. They travelled south with just 10 men as full-back Gall missed the train. The player managed to catch a later service to Arbroath but it made little difference. The visitors lost Joe Davidson with an injury early in the second half, then goalkeeper Tom Smyth also left the field, although by then the damage had been done. One reporter commented that the Aberdeen 'keeper had been at fault for a number of the goals and was clearly *"off colour."* The White's did, however, perform admirably in a friendly against a powerful Glasgow Celtic side, one report claiming: *"seldom have the Aberdeen played with such dash."* The visitors, who would go on to win the Scottish First Division title, still did enough, however, to escape with a 3-2 win. Smyth also did well enough to be called up to play in the Scotland international trials held at Cathkin Park, Glasgow in early March. Four trial teams were picked and Smyth turned out for the 'D' team which was beaten 3-2 in front of a crowd of 15,000 spectators. Immediately after this game, the 'A' and 'B' sides played out a 2-2 draw. Smyth was, unfortunately, not subsequently called up to play for his country.

Aberdeen's biggest win of the season came with an 18-0 thrashing of Brechin at the Chanonry, when Charlie Mackie was tried out at centre forward to great effect: *"He simply rollicked in the fun, scoring seven goals and bundled the custodian through on another occasion."*

Orion started the season with an innovative decision to produce a match day programme. It was edited by Mr James Russell and the first of these was prepared for the friendly against Port Glasgow on 3rd August. The document contained *"club notes of interest to members and adherents, names of the day's teams in 'field' order, fixtures."* It was described as being: *"a leaflet of six pages, is well got-up and will be retailed at the modest sum of one half-penny. Portraits of the respective members of the team will be run weekly, beginning with the captain, John Low."* The programme took the name of the "Orion Observer" and was published on a regular basis for a number of seasons. Only one surviving copy is known to exist and that is in a private collection. Perhaps other copies languish in the corner of someone's attic!

Mr James Russell – Originator of the Orion Observer

For that match against Port Glasgow, Orion officials invited members of the Town Council to be their guests in an effort to persuade the local politicians that the anti social behaviour associated with crowds at matches at Cattofield, which was concerning local residents, was capable of being controlled. A large police presence in the streets helped keep any trouble-makers at bay. There were reports, however, of people climbing onto the roofs of neighbouring houses to watch the game to avoid paying to get in.

Orion invited some of Scotland's top clubs to Cattofield during the season and took a notable scalp when defeating First Division Third Lanark 3-2 in August. The Stripes also attracted eventual Scottish league runners-up Glasgow Rangers to Cattofield in November, the visitors winning 7-2. Not to be outdone, Victoria United persuaded Scottish Cup finalists Hibernian to visit Torry for the second year in a row, the Edinburgh men winning 1-0 on this occasion. Hibs had been beaten 3-1 by Hearts in the national Cup Final.

Orion's Northern League campaign was pretty dismal, but they took some consolation by winning the Charity Cup by defeating Aberdeen 3-1 in the Final. There were signs of discontent among the Orion ranks, however, and in April 1896 the Evening Express speculated that the club was in danger of being taken over by a syndicate keen to establish a single powerful club in the city. According to the newspaper, a number of people connected with Orion were *"dissatisfied with the current working of the club"* and were preparing to leave and join the new set-up. The Evening Express concluded: *"There is one thing for certain – that three professional elevens cannot be maintained in the city for long."* It was, however, to be a further seven years before that statement became fact. As it was, a proposal was put to the Orion committee suggesting that the club be wound up and its debts cleared by the new syndicate who would establish a new club. Although some members supported the idea, others rejected it and nothing happened.

People seemed to be willing to turn up in decent numbers to watch any sporting event involving local footballers. On Monday 23rd September, for instance, a crowd of 4,000 showed up at the Chanonry grounds to watch a 660 yards race open only to members of Aberdeen Football Club. The players were competing for a Challenge Cup presented by Dr Maitland Moir. Four men started, Charles W. Mackie, Joseph Davidson, J. Gauld and W. Ritchie. Mackie won the trophy with Ritchie and Davidson next to finish.

There was tragedy at the Links in a junior match between Caledonian and Aberdeen Athletics when Caley's Samuel Sharp was accidently kicked in the abdomen by a player called William Mann. Sharp was administered some brandy on the field and this seemed to revive him, but later that night he became unwell again and died.

Meanwhile, in April, Orion player Tom Leggat was lucky to survive a boating accident when his small fishing vessel was capsized by two steamers at the entrance to Aberdeen harbour.

Notable Games
Forfar Athletic 4, Orion 3
Northern League, Station Park, Forfar, 7th September 1895

Orion made their debut in the Northern League by travelling to Angus to meet Forfar Athletic. On a stormy day the home side played with the wind at their backs in the first half and went ahead through Mcfarlane. Orion hit back and soon equalised. Forfar responded and Morrison did well to save a Cable shot but before the 'keeper could get rid of the ball he was bundled into the net by Mcfarlane for Forfar's second goal. Cable then made it 3-1 and Scrymgeour added a fourth before the interval. Orion applied pressure in the second half when the wind was behind them and on the hour mark they reduced the deficit. Leggat then picked up an injury and had to leave the field. Despite being down to 10 men Orion still controlled the game and clawed back another goal. The Aberdeen side

battled gamely to the finish but couldn't get the equaliser their efforts deserved.
Orion - Morrison, Mackay, Ross, Stopani, Low, Currie, Gloag, Robertson, Thom,Leggat, Clark.
Forfar Athletic - Thom, James, Scott, J. Cable, Thomson, Mann, Taylor, Scrymgeour, Booth, Mcfarlane, Cable.

Orion 8, Forfar Athletic 1
Northern League, Cattofield, 23rd November 1895

Orion endured a miserable league season but somehow pulled off an amazing 8-1 victory over eventual league champions Forfar Athletic at Cattofield. Goals from Clark (2) , Benzie, Leggat and Stopani had the home side 5-1 ahead at the interval, Craik grabbing Forfar's sole counter. After the break Stopani added another couple to complete his hat-trick with Thom also adding to the tally. Athletic lodged a protest on the grounds that the first period was unduly prolonged and that in the second half about 35 minutes was played instead of 45 minutes. This wasn't accepted by league officials.
Orion - Edwards, Mackay, Ross, Wight, Low, Currie, Benzie, Leggat, Thom, Clark, Stopani
Forfar Athletic - Dalgetty, Black, James, Cable, Anderson, J Taylor, Taylor, Scrymgeour, Craik, McFarlane, Booth.

Aberdeen 2, Glasgow Celtic 3
Chanonry, 23rd September 1895

The Aberdeen Journal called Celtic "the Irishmen" and described how their *"smart, short passing completely baffled the Aberdeen at times."* Goalkeeper Tom Smyth was in great form, however, and he kept the Glasgow side at bay for 20 minutes when McMahon opened the scoring. Mcfarlane then made it 2-0 and most people seemed to think it was all over. The Whites battled back into the game, however, and scored to a background of *"deafening cheers."*
The Chanonry men kept up the good work in the second period and J. Mackie grabbed an equaliser after a spell of good pressure. This stung the visitors into action and they retaliated by grabbing a decisive third before the end.
Aberdeen - Smyth, John Davidson, Low, Alexander, Joseph Davidson, Thomson, Toman, Taylor, C.W. Mackie, Milne, J. Mackie.

Celtic - Cullen, Battles, Doyle, McEleney, Maley, Crossan, Mcfarlane, Blessington, Martin, McMahon, Divers. Referee: Peter Simpson.

Orion 2, Glasgow Rangers 7
Cattofield, 16th November 1895
Rangers led 3-0 at halftime despite Edwards in the Orion goal having a good game. The visitors added another four in the second half before two late goals gave Orion some consolation. The Rangers team featured Jimmy Oswald who had played for Notts County against Aberdeen in January 1893. The talented centre-forward won three Scotland caps, the first coming in

George Alexander, Aberdeen F.C.

a 3-2 win over England 1889 when he was with Third Lanark. Oswald scored the second goal in front of 10,000 at the Oval. He then captained the side in a 3-0 defeat by England at Goodison Park in 1895, and his final appearance was in a 2-2 draw with Wales in 1897 at Wrexham. He also played for the Scotland team that crushed an Aberdeen select 10-0 at the Chanonry in 1889, scoring two goals.

Orion - Edwards, Mackay, Ross, Wight, Low, Currie, Thom, Benzie, Gloag, Leggat, Stopani.
Rangers - Bell, Smith, Drummond, Marshall, Burns, Gibson, Miller, McCreadic, Oswald, McPherson, A. Smith.
Ref: Peter Simpson

Victoria United 6, Aberdeen 2
Aberdeenshire Cup Final, Cattofield, 22nd February 1896
Wilf Toman gave Aberdeen a 17th minute lead but in the final four minutes before the interval United hit back with two goals from Sandy Caie. Within 60 seconds of the restart Aberdeen were level, Joe Mackie scoring from the penalty spot after a foul by Gordon. The game could have gone either way until Vics unleashed a

devastating final effort which generated
four goals in the last 25 minutes.
Aberdeen - Smyth, John Davidson,
Low, Alexander, Joseph Davidson,
Thomson, J. Mackie, C.W. Mackie,
Toman, Milne, Little.
Victoria United - Gillespie, Anderson,
Ririe, Morrice, Gordon, Annand,
MacConnachie, Forsyth, Caie, Burnett,
Ritchie.
Referee - Mr Mcfarlane, Port Glasgow

John Annand, Captain Victoria United,
February 1896

Victoria United 0, Hibernian 1
Victoria Bridge Grounds, 2nd
November 1895

Hibernian crushed United 9-2 on their
first visit to Torry the season before but
it was a much tighter affair on this
occasion. The Edinburgh side finished third in the First Division and they also
reached the Scottish Cup Final, losing to Edinburgh rivals Hearts. A hard fought
game watched by 3,000 spectators, ended with the visitors edging home by 1-0.
The only goal came in the first half but *"to most people it seemed very doubtful
whether the ball had gone through the posts or not, and much dissatisfaction was
expressed at the referee's decision."*
Victoria United - Gillespie, Thomson, Ririe, Morrice, Gordon, Annand,
McConnachie, Forsyth, Caie, Burnett, Ritchie
Hibernian - McGinn, Neil, Robertson, Breslin, Murphy, Leighton, B Murray,
McCann, Ferguson, Tullis, P Murray.

Orion 3, Aberdeen 1
Charity Cup Final, Victoria Bridge Grounds, 25th April, 1896

This was described as a poor game: *"the play was of a wretched character."* Not
for the first time in a local Cup Final, there was a serious lack of quality on view;
"Too frequently, rough play asserted itself, and the referee would have been justified

in expelling several of the players who persisted in such tactics." Orion took the lead with a *"fluke"* goal. Willie Gloag, who was *"clearly offside"* rushed into the goal area but missed the ball which fell into the path of Jim Thom who smashed it home. Aberdeen 'keeper Tom Smyth made no attempt to stop it as he was claiming for offside but the referee ignored his pleas. Orion went 2-0 ahead when Aberdeen's McIntosh conceded a penalty from which Thom scored by putting the ball through Smyth's legs. Tom Leggat got Orion's third while Aberdeen's Wilf Toman, *"the best player on the field"* grabbed his side's consolation.

Aberdeen - Smyth, John Davidson, Low, Alexander, Joseph Davidson, Thomson, J. Mackie, McIntosh,Toman, Hamilton, A.N. Other

Orion - McBean, Mackay, Ross, Wight, Low, Currie, Stopani, Thom, Gloag, Leggat, Hogg.

Referee - Mr Baillie, St Bernards

Victoria United 4, Glasgow Celtic 2
Victoria Bridge Grounds, 29th May 1896

The Scottish League champions were defeated at Torry. Wilf Toman, who had played for Aberdeen against Celtic earlier in the season, gave United an early lead when he evaded Dan Doyle and slotted the ball into the net. The home side continued to press and Toman added a second. This seemed to spur the champions into action and following fine build up play involving John Henderson (who would join the Vics in 1897) and Willie Ferguson, the visitors pulled one back. But the Torry men upped the tempo again in the second half and two goals from Sandy Caie put them firmly in the driving seat. Barney Battles got another for Celtic but there was to be no further scoring.

Victoria United - Gillespie, Gordon, Allan, Morrice, Joseph Davidson, Annand, Forsyth, Toman, Caie, Burnett, Ritchie.

Celtic - McArthur, Meechan, Doyle, McEleney, Maley, Battles, Madden, Blessington, McMahon, Henderson, Ferguson.

Referee - Mr James Philip, Aberdeen

At the end of season 1895-1896 Victoria United's Jim Ririe was presented with that season's Gershon Cup in recognition of his services to the Blues. Ririe, who had been captain of the club, was emigrating to Ireland. His football career

James Ririe, Victoria United F.C.

started in his native Mugiemoss where he played for the local junior club. Ririe's talents were courted by all the senior clubs in the city and it was widely expected that he would join Aberdeen, but he chose the bright lights of Torry instead. He made his debut in October 1889 against City Rangers and went on to make at least 184 appearances for the Blues.* He was described as a player who *"rushes in where few would dare to go, tackles cleverly and his returns are invariably well placed and powerfully parted with."* Ririe enjoyed a lot of success helping United win the Aberdeenshire Cup four times and the Charity Cup once. He was also twice on the losing side in the Charity Cup Final, including the notorious abandoned game in 1892-1893. Ririe was also capped by the Aberdeenshire F.A. in inter county matches.

*Ririe's appearance against City Rangers is the first game he is recorded as having played. However, records of team line-ups have not been found for every United game, some of those missing are for the matches immediately before the City Rangers fixture. Ririe's debut may therefore have been slightly earlier. Also, Ririe's total number of appearances is probably slightly higher than 184 for the same reason. He is most likely to have made more appearances for United than any other player.

Northern League 1895-1896

		P	W	D	L	F	A	Pts
1	Forfar Athletic	14	10	1	3	62	31	21
2	Arbroath	14	9	2	3	50	26	20
3	Dundee Wanderers	14	7	1	6	34	42	15
4	Aberdeen	14	6	2	6	41	38	14
5	Lochee United	14	6	2	6	36	31	14
6	Montrose	14	4	3	7	30	41	11
7	Orion	14	4	2	8	42	45	10
8	Fair City Athletic	14	3	1	10	19	63	7

Aberdeen F.C. - Northern League 1895-1896

	Date		Opposition	F	A	Venue
Northern League	07/09/1895	Aberdeen	Montrose	5	3	Chanonry
Northern League	05/10/1895	Aberdeen	Fair City Athletic	4	1	Balhousie Park, Perth
Northern League	02/11/1895	Aberdeen	Arbroath	2	5	Chanonry
Northern League	30/11/1895	Aberdeen	Dundee Wanderers	7	1	Chanonry
Northern League	07/12/1895	Aberdeen	Orion	4	3	Cattofield
Northern League	11/01/1896	Aberdeen	Lochee United	4	0	Chanonry
Northern League	01/02/1896	Aberdeen	Orion	1	5	Chanonry
Northern League	08/02/1896	Aberdeen	Montrose	2	2	Links Park, Montrose
Northern League	14/03/1896	Aberdeen	Forfar Athletic	1	1	Station Park,Forfar
Northern League	04/04/1896	Aberdeen	Fair City Athletic	6	0	Chanonry
Northern League	18/04/1896	Aberdeen	Forfar Athletic	1	2	Chanonry
Northern League	02/05/1896	Aberdeen	Dundee Wanderers	1	5	Dundee
Northern League	09/05/1896	Aberdeen	Arbroath	2	7	Gayfield Park, Arbroath
Northern League	23/05/1896	Aberdeen	Forfar Athletic	2	5	Chanonry

Notes: The result of Aberdeen's away fixture with Lochee United isn't known. I have some doubts as to whether the match took place as there is no reference to it in either the Aberdeen Journal or the Dundee Courier. It is possible that Aberdeen forfeited the match as Lochee seem to have been awarded the points. Aberdeen played Forfar Athletic twice at the Chanonry. The first game ended too early with Forfar leading 2-1. Aberdeen protested and the game was replayed with the visitors winning 5-2. The result secured the league title for Forfar.

Aberdeen F.C. - Other Games 1895-1896

	Date		Opposition	F	A	Venue
	17/08/1895	Aberdeen	Culter	1	1	Culter?
	24/08/1895	Aberdeen	Dundee Hibernian	2	0	Chanonry
Scottish	31/08/1895	Aberdeen	Victoria United	1	9	Chanonry
Qualifying Cup						
	14/09/1995	Aberdeen	Brechin	18	0	Chanonry
	21/09/1895	Aberdeen	Arbroath Wanderers	4	0	Chanonry
	23/09/1895	Aberdeen	Celtic	2	3	Chanonry
Friendly	28/09/1895	Aberdeen	Leith Athletic	1	5	Chanonry
Aberdeenshire	19/10/1895	Aberdeen	Peterhead	5	1	Chanonry
Cup1R						
Gershon Cup	26/10/1895	Aberdeen	Orion	2	2	Chanonry
Gershon Cup	09/11/1895	Aberdeen	Victoria United	2	6	Chanonry
Aberdeenshire	16/11/1895	Aberdeen	Aberdeen University	7	0	Chanonry
Cup 2R						
	23/11/1895	Aberdeen	Peterhead	2	1	Peterhead
	14/12/1895	Aberdeen	Aberdeen University	4	1	Kings College
	28/12/1895	Aberdeen	Fraserburgh	13	0	Chanonry
Friendly	01/01/1896	Aberdeen	Orion	6	0	Chanonry
	02/01/1896	Aberdeen	Airdrie	3	3	Chanonry
	04/01/1896	Aberdeen	Partick Thistle	2	1	Chanonry
Aberdeenshire	18/01/1896	Aberdeen	Culter	5	0	Chanonry
Cup SF						
	15/02/1896	Aberdeen	Peterhead	7	1	Chanonry
Aberdeenshire	22/02/1896	Aberdeen	Victoria United	2	6	Cattofield
Cup Final						
Aberdeen	29/02/1896	Aberdeen	Peterhead	7	0	Victoria Bridge Grounds
Charity Cup						
Gershon Cup	07/03/1896	Aberdeen	Orion	2	2	Cattofield
Gershon Cup	21/03/1896	Aberdeen	Victoria United	1	4	Victoria Bridge Grounds
Aberdeen Charity	25/04/1896	Aberdeen	Orion	1	3	Victoria Bridge Grounds
Cup Final						

Orion - Northern League 1895-1896

	Date		Opposition	F	A	Venue
Northern League	07/09/1895	Orion	Forfar Athletic	3	4	Station Park,Forfar
Northern League	05/10/1895	Orion	Arbroath	1	2	Cattofield
Northern League	02/11/1895	Orion	Dundee Wanderers	2	5	Clepington Park, Dundee
Northern League	23/11/1895	Orion	Forfar Athletic	8	1	Cattofield
Northern League	07/12/1895	Orion	Aberdeen	3	4	Cattofield
Northern League	11/01/1896	Orion	Montrose	3	3	Links Park,Montrose
Northern League	25/01/1896	Orion	Fair City Athletic	3	3	Cattofield
Northern League	01/02/1896	Orion	Aberdeen	5	1	Chanonry
Northern League	08/02/1896	Orion	Dundee Wanderers	2	4	Cattofield
Northern League	29/02/1896	Orion	Lochee United	1	7	Dundee
Northern League	21/03/1896	Orion	Arbroath	4	3	Gayfield Park,Arbroath
Northern League	18/04/1896	Orion	Fair City Athletic	0	3	Balhousie Park,Perth
Northern League	02/05/1896	Orion	Lochee United	2	5	Cattofield
Northern League	09/05/1896	Orion	Montrose	5	0	Cattofield

Orion - Other Games 1895-1896

	Date		Opposition	F	A	Venue
Friendly	03/08/1895	Orion	Port Glasgow Athletic	4	0	Cattofield
Friendly	10/08/1895	Orion	Third Lanark	3	2	Cattofield
Friendly	17/08/1895	Orion	Alloa Athletic	2	1	Cattofield
Friendly	24/08/1895	Orion	Dundee A	4	1	Cattofield
Scottish Qualifying Cup	31/08/1895	Orion	Culter	8	0	Culter
Scottish Qualifying Cup	12/09/1895	Orion	Peterhead	5	2	Recreation Park, Peterhead
Scottish Qualifying Cup	28/09/1895	Orion	St Jonstone	1	3	Perth
Gershon Cup	12/10/1895	Orion	Victoria United	2	5	Victoria Bridge Grounds
Friendly	19/10/1895	Orion	Montrose	2	1	Cattofield
Gershon Cup	26/10/1895	Orion	Aberdeen	2	2	Chanonry
Friendly	16/11/1895	Orion	Glasgow Rangers	2	7	Cattofield

	Date		Opposition	F	A	Venue
Friendly	14/12/1895	Orion	Black Watch	4	1	Cattofield
Gershon Cup	21/12/1895	Orion	Victoria United	2	3	Cattofield
Friendly	28/12/1895	Orion	Arbroath Wanderers	2	1	Cattofield
Friendly	01/01/1896	Orion	Aberdeen	0	6	Chanonry
Friendly	02/01/1896	Orion	Kilmarnock	0	7	Cattofield
Aberdeenshire Cup SF	18/01/1896	Orion	Victoria United	1	4	Cattofield
Friendly	15/02/1896	Orion	Victoria United	2	0	Victoria Bridge Grounds
Gershon Cup	07/03/1896	Orion	Aberdeen	2	2	Cattofield
Friendly	14/03/1896	Orion	Victoria United	6	3	Cattofield
Aberdeen Charity Cup SF	28/03/1896	Orion	Victoria United	4	2	Chanonry
Aberdeen Charity Cup Final	25/04/1896	Orion	Aberdeen	3	1	Victoria Bridge Grounds
Friendly	04/05/1890	Orion	East Stirlingshire	3	4	Cattofield
Friendly	16/05/1896	Orion	Victoria United	3	0	Victoria Bridge Grounds

Victoria United - 1895-1896

Competition	Date		Opposition	F	A	Venue
	03/08/1895	Victoria United	Dundee	0	6	Victoria Bridge Grounds
	10/08/1895	Victoria United	Kings Park	6	2	Victoria Bridge Grounds
	17/08/1895	Victoria United	Clackmannan	4	0	Victoria Bridge Grounds
	24/08/1895	Victoria United	Cowdenbeath	3	4	Victoria Bridge Grounds
Scottish Qualifying Cup	31/08/1895	Victoria United	Aberdeen	9	1	Chanonry
	07/09/1895	Victoria United	Blairgowrie	6	0	Victoria Bridge Grounds

New Year Holidays.

GREAT FOOTBALL MATCHES

AT

VICTORIA BRIDGE GROUNDS.

TO-DAY (THURSDAY), JANUARY 2ND, AT 12 NOON—
DUMBARTON v. VICTORIA UNITED.

SATURDAY JANUARY 4, 1896 AT 2 30—
ANNBANK v. VICTORIA UNITED.

Admission, 3d—Reserve Side, 3d extra. Boys, 1½d.

Competition	Date		Opposition	F	A	Venue
	14/09/1995	Victoria United	Kilmarnock Athletic	0	0	Victoria Bridge Grounds
	21/09/1895	Victoria United	St Johnstone	4	2	Victoria Bridge Grounds
	23/09/1895	Victoria United	Our Boys Turriff	4	0	Market Mill, Turriff
Scottish	28/09/1895	Victoria United	Polton Vale	1	3	Polton
Qualifying Cup						
	05/10/1895	Victoria United	Dunfermline Athletic	5	2	Victoria Bridge Grounds
Gershon Cup	12/10/1895	Victoria United	Orion	5	2	Victoria Bridge Grounds
Aberdeenshire	19/10/1895	Victoria United	Our Boys, Turriff	21	0	Victoria Bridge Grounds
Cup1R	26/10/1895	Victoria United	Peterhead	4	3	Peterhead
	02/11/1895	Victoria United	Hibernian	0	1	Victoria Bridge Grounds
Gershon Cup	09/11/1895	Victoria United	Aberdeen	6	2	Chanonry
	16/11/1895	Victoria United	Peterhead	8	0	Victoria Bridge Grounds
	23/11/1895	Victoria United	Hearts A	3	4	Victoria Bridge Grounds
	07/12/1895	Victoria United	Montrose	1	4	Links Park, Montrose
	14/12/1895	Victoria United	Denny Athletic	3	5	Victoria Bridge Grounds
Gershon Cup	21/12/1895	Victoria United	Orion	3	2	Cattofield
Allan Challenge	28/12/1895	Victoria United	Victoria United A	6	4	Victoria Bridge Grounds
Cup						
	02/01/1896	Victoria United	Dumbarton	8	0	Victoria Bridge Grounds
	04/01/1896	Victoria United	Annbank	2	2	Victoria Bridge Grounds
	11/01/1896	Victoria United	Dunblane	7	2	Victoria Bridge Grounds
Aberdeenshire	18/01/1896	Victoria United	Orion	4	1	Cattofield
Cup SF						
	25/01/1896	Victoria United	Arbroath Wanderers	6	1	Victoria Bridge Grounds
	08/02/1896	Victoria United	Motherwell	2	0	Victoria Bridge Grounds
Friendly	15/02/1896	Victoria United	Orion	0	2	Victoria Bridge Grounds
Aberdeenshire	22/02/1896	Victoria United	Aberdeen	6	2	Cattofield
Cup Final						
	29/02/1896	Victoria United	Stonehaven	2	4	Stonehaven
	07/03/1896	Victoria United	Inverness Thistle	3	2	Kingsmills,Inverness
Friendly	14/03/1896	Victoria United	Orion	3	6	Cattofield
Gershon Cup	21/03/1896	Victoria United	Aberdeen	4	1	Victoria Bridge Grounds

Competition	Date		Opposition	F	A	Venue
Aberdeen Charity Cup SF	28/03/1896	Victoria United	Orion	2	4	Chanonry
Friendly	18/04/1896	Victoria United	Cowdenbeath	5	1	Victoria Bridge Grounds
	02/05/1896	Victoria United	Dundee A	2	4	Victoria Bridge Grounds
	04/05/1890	Victoria United	Falkirk	2	2	Victoria Bridge Grounds
	09/05/1896	Victoria United	Polton Vale	4	0	Victoria Bridge Grounds
	16/05/1896	Victoria United	Orion	0	3	Victoria Bridge Grounds
	29/05/1896	Victoria United	Celtic	4	2	Victoria Bridge Grounds

Aberdeenshire Cup 1895-1896

	Date			F	A	Venue
First Round	19/10/1895	Aberdeen	Peterhead	5	1	Chanonry
First Round	19/10/1895	Victoria United	Our Boys, Turriff	21	0	Victoria Bridge Grounds
First Round	19/10/1895	Culter	Fraserburgh Wanderers			
Second Round	16/11/1895	Aberdeen	Aberdeen University	7	0	Chanonry
Semi Final	18/01/1896	Orion	Victoria United	1	4	Cattofield
Semi Final	18/01/1896	Aberdeen	Culter	5	0	Chanonry
Cup Final	22/02/1896	Victoria United	Aberdeen	6	2	Cattofield

Note: No record of the Culter/Fraserburgh Wanderers game has been found

Charity Cup 1895-1896

	Date			F	A	Venue
Semi Final	29/02/1896	Aberdeen	Peterhead	7	0	Victoria Bridge Grounds
Semi Final	28/03/1896	Orion	Victoria United	4	2	Chanonry
Cup Final	25/04/1896	Aberdeen	Orion	1	3	Victoria Bridge Grounds

Gershon Cup 1895-1896

	Date			F	A	Venue
Gershon Cup	12/10/1895	Victoria United	Orion	5	2	Victoria Bridge Grounds
Gershon Cup	26/10/1895	Aberdeen	Orion	2	2	Chanonry
Gershon Cup	09/11/1895	Aberdeen	Victoria United	2	6	Chanonry
Gershon Cup	21/12/1895	Orion	Victoria United	2	3	Cattofield
Gershon Cup	07/03/1896	Orion	Aberdeen	2	2	Cattofield

	Date			**F**	**A**	**Venue**
Gershon Cup	21/03/1896	Victoria United	Aberdeen	4	1	Victoria Bridge Grounds

	P	**W**	**D**	**L**	**F**	**A**	**Pts**
Victoria United	4	4	0	0	18	7	8
Orion	4	0	2	2	8	12	2
Aberdeen	4	0	2	2	7	14	2

1896-1897
Orion win Northern League

This was to be Orion's most successful season so far, the highlight of which was winning the Northern League after an exciting battle with Dundee Wanderers. The Stripes also won the Aberdeenshire Cup for the second time in three years and the Gershon Cup was also taken to Cattofield. The Kittybrewster men also enjoyed an appearance in the Scottish Cup, reaching the First Round after negotiating the early stages of the Qualifying Cup.

Home form was the key to success in the Northern League with the Stripes winning all seven matches of their matches at Cattofield. Their only defeats came at Dundee Wanderers' Clepington Road Grounds (3-1) and to Victoria United at Torry (4-2). It was nip and tuck with the Dundee club throughout the season with the crunch game coming at Cattofield in late April. This was Wanderers last game of the season and they held a two point lead over Orion. The Aberdeen side had

Orion goalkeeper Duncan McBean

one further game to play after this one but needed to beat the Dundonians to ensure they had a chance of winning the title outright. Under the circumstances a close game was anticipated but it ended as a one-sided affair with Orion running out comfortable 7-2 winners. An injury to Wanderers goalkeeper Coventry a few minutes after the start certainly handicapped the visitors, but this was of no concern to the home men. This result left the sides level on points. Goal difference didn't count in these days which meant that Orion still had to take something from their final game to avoid sharing the title. That last game was against lowly Aberdeen at the Chanonry and a crowd of 2,000 turned out for the occasion.

Any thoughts that this might be a formality were soon put to bed as the Whites took a first half lead. Orion were strangely below par and struggled to find any rhythm as the game degenerated into a *"kick and rush"* affair. It looked as though the Stripes would slump to defeat until, with just 30 seconds remaining, they grabbed the title-winning equaliser. It was reported that *"there was a feeling that the game had been continued longer than it should have been,"* the implication being that the referee gave Orion every chance to grab the necessary goal.

Orion's John Low – criticised for fouling

Orion's Scottish Qualifying Cup run took them past Victoria United (5-2), Peterhead (7-0) and Bathgate (5-1) before they fell to Motherwell who won 3-1 at Cattofield. A crowd of more than 4,000 saw Alec Mcfarlane open the scoring for Orion but the Lanarkshire side hit back to win the tie. The Stripes had progressed far enough in the competition, however, to secure entry to the First Round of the Scottish Cup in which a trip to Falkirk ended with a 2-0 defeat. The Aberdeenshire Cup campaign started with a rumbustious encounter against Aberdeen. The Whites did well to hold Orion to a 1-1 draw in the first game at the Chanonry but the return at Cattofield degenerated

Orion's Donald Currie – sent off against Aberdeen.

A sketch in the Bon Accord magazine gives a slightly exaggerated artists impression of the aftermath of the Orion – Aberdeen County Cup tie at Cattofield.

into something of a kicking match. One reporter noted that *"no fewer than 19 fouls were awarded in the second period - 13 against the Aberdeen, divided between Milne and Cadger, and six against the Orion, nearly all by John Low."* Midway through the second period Aberdeen's Milne and Orion's Donald Currie were sent off. Currie had the ball and was making for the Aberdeen goal when Milne's leg, *"accidentally or otherwise"*, got in contact with the Orion man who fell to the ground. Currie got up and struck Milne who then retaliated. As to the game itself, two first half goals from Mcfarlane put Orion in the driving seat while Gray pulled one back for Aberdeen after each side had been reduced to ten men. There was no further scoring and Aberdeen went out of the competition.

Orion then thumped Culter 18-0 in the semi final, prompting one scribe to advise the Deeside club to: *"take our tip and join the junior association next season, ye villagers."* This would remain the biggest victory in Orion's history. The Final pitted Orion against Cup-holders Victoria United and it took two games to determine the outcome, the Orionites winning 5-2 after a 2-2 draw.

Ambitious Victoria United had made their intentions clear during the summer by making a number of major signings, many of whom were tempted to move to

Torry by the prospect of joining the professional ranks. Top of the signing list was Wilf Toman who joined the Blues from Aberdeen after starring in a friendly against Celtic at the tail end of the previous season. United's backers were keen to strengthen the side in order to make a serious bid for the Northern League title and other players who joined up included Alec Allan (Montrose), John Stopani (Orion) and Joe Davidson (Aberdeen). The Vics weren't always successful, however, in trying to lure players from other local sides. On one occasion it was rumoured that an Aberdeen player who was considering a move to United was warned by one his club's backers that if he signed for the Torry outfit he would lose his job.

There was so much interest in Victoria's prospects for the season that a crowd of 300 turned up to watch the club's first training session, more than 100 of whom paid to get in.

English scouts were beginning to take notice of the improved standard of player in Aberdeen and Victoria United's Torry ground was regularly visited by 'agents' from the South. In December 1897, Vics' 23 year-old centre forward Wilf Toman was persuaded to sign for English First Division side Burnley. Toman had been born in Bishop Auckland but his football career began with Aberdeen at the Chanonry. He enjoyed success as a regular with the Whites before moving to the Blues of Torry at the tail end of the 1895-1896 season,scoring twice on his debut in a 4-2 win over Celtic. Toman had been educated at St Cuthbert's Grammar School in Newcastle and later at a college in Berkshire. He moved to Aberdeen in 1891 at the age of 17, to attend Mr Stewart Thomson's Civil Service classes, and for two years he attended the North Silver Street School. He made his north east footballing debut for Aberdeen Strollers (Aberdeen's reserves) at Stonehaven and the following week was called up for the Aberdeen first team. He was a regular for the Whites up until the end of the 1895-96 season when he moved to Victoria United. Toman did, however, play one Scottish League match for Dundee against Rangers and travelled to England with the Dark Blues for their 1896 Easter tour. Away from football, he was a member of the Aberdeen Lyric Society during his stay in the city. Toman's transfer to Burnley earned him a £10 fee plus wages of £3 per week (£1-10s in the close season). He also got a bonus of 10s for every

Wilf Toman earned a big money transfer to Burnley

League win, a sum which was increased for Cup victories. Burnley also wanted to sign Victoria's Sandy Caie but the offer was turned down.

In Toman's first season at Turf Moor he made eight appearances, scoring four goals, but Burnley were relegated to the Second Division. He enjoyed better luck the following year as the Lancashire club won the Second Division title. Toman played in all but one game and scored 15 goals. He scored another four goals in the end of season play-offs which led to Burnley going back up to the First Division. Toman again excelled in the top flight, being Burnley's top scorer with 11 goals as the club finished in third position. His fine play earned him a place in the English League team for a match against the Scottish League in Glasgow, which the visitors won 4-2. Toman then joined Everton where he stayed until 1900 before moving again, this time to Southampton. He helped the Saints win the Southern League title but then rejoined Everton.In his second game back on Merseyside he suffered a serious injury which all but ended his career. He was out of action for more than two years but tried to make a comeback with Stockport County then had short spells at Oldham and Newcastle United. After his retirement from playing he moved back to Scotland. He was killed on 2nd May 1917 when fighting for the King's Regiment (Liverpool) on the Western front during the First World War.

Toman's striking partner at Torry, Sandy Caie, wasn't long in following Wilf down the road to England when, aged just 19, he signed for English Second Division side Woolwich Arsenal. The Torry man was propelled into the high life with the promise of a weekly wage of £2 10s (£2.50) plus substantial win bonuses. His club also received a whopping transfer fee of *"close to £100"* in a deal which had Aberdeen's

football fans enthralled for weeks.
According to the Bon Accord magazine,
Sandy was the first Aberdeen-born and-
bred footballer to earn a move to a
professional club in England (as his
mate Toman had been born south of the
border).
Caie first played for local clubs Orient,
Rosebud, Albert, Vale of Dee and
Victoria Rangers before being called up
for the Victoria United first eleven. He is
said to have played in every position
except goalkeeper, but his best
performances came as a centre forward
"where his fine turn of speed and dash
has led his side to victory times
innumerable."

Sandy Caie

He was a member of the side which won the Aberdeenshire cup in 1895-1896
and the Gershon cup in 1896-1897. His only representative honour, however, was
for Aberdeenshire against Perthshire in 1895-1896. Caie resisted offers from a
number of English clubs, including Burnley, before signing for Arsenal in early
1897. He put pen to paper on Saturday 11th February, travelled by train to London
late on the Sunday afternoon *"with two agents"* and made his debut for the
Londoners in a 5-4 defeat by Celtic in a friendly on the Monday. The following
Saturday he scored on his league debut, a 3-0 win over Burton Swifts, at Arsenal's
Manor Ground in Plumstead. Sandy made a further seven league appearances
for Arsenal before the end of the season, scoring four goals. During the summer
of 1897, however, Arsenal manager Sam Hollis moved to Bristol City and took
Caie and a number of other Woolwich players with him. Sandy stayed at Bristol
until 1900 when he returned to London to play for Millwall. A season later he was
on the move again, this time to Newcastle United where he spent two seasons,
making 31 appearances but scoring just once. Sandy moved to London for a
third time to play for Brentford before heading back to Scotland for the 1904-1905
season which he spent with Motherwell. The Lanarkshire side finished bottom of

213

the First Division and Sandy was released. It's not clear what happened after that, although it seems he may have appeared on Aberdeen's books for a while, without playing any first team games. He later moved to the United States where, in 1914, he was killed in a railway accident.

Alec McConnochie also moved south to join First Division Notts County. The Vics man made his name as a good forward with the English side and in 1898-1899 he was the club's top scorer with 14 goals and bagged another 12 the following year. The loss of such top class players certainly seemed to impact on United's hopes for success. The Vics made an early exit from the Scottish Qualifying Cup, losing to Orion in the Second Round after hammering Culter 8-0 in the opening stage of the competition. The Aberdeenshire Cup started with a comfortable 9-0 victory over Fraserburgh Wanderers but the semi-final produced a frustrating encounter with a red-shirted Peterhead side. United huffed and puffed their way to a 1-0 victory but had goalkeeper Findlay to thank for making a number of good saves. The Torry men, nevertheless, dominated the second half of the game during which Peterhead's defensive tactics upset the crowd to such an extent that when the Blue Tooners left the ground they were *"assailed with quite a fusillade of stones and mud."* United's hopes of retaining the County Cup were, however, dashed by Orion who won the trophy following a replay. United took some consolation at the end of the season by winning the Charity Cup for the second time in three years. The Northern League campaign produced mixed results with Vics losing just once at home but winning only twice on their travels. A shared third position with the previous season's champions, Forfar Athletic, might have been considered satisfactory had it not been for the fact that local rivals Orion won the title. Away from league and Cup fixtures United maintained their tradition of inviting top clubs up to Aberdeen. Liverpool, St Bernards, St Mirren and Hibernian were among the big attractions at Torry during the season.

Aberdeen decided not to compete with Orion and Victoria United in offering big wages to their players and as a result the Chanonry club found it difficult to compete with their city rivals. The Whites endured another miserable campaign which got off to a disastrous start when losing 6-3 to Peterhead in the opening round of the Scottish Qualifying Cup. Whites goalkeeper Tom Smyth was criticised for his performance while his opposite number in the Blue Toon goal, Mackie, a former Aberdeen player, put in an outstanding performance.

The Charity Cup gave the Whites the opportunity of taking revenge on Peterhead and this was achieved with a clearcut 6-1 victory on the neutral Victoria Bridge Grounds. There was disappointment for Aberdeen in the Final, however, as they lost 2-1 to Victoria United. The Northern League campaign was also very poor with the Whites winning just three of their 14 games and finishing second bottom of the table.

In April Aberdeen played a game against the cast of 'Old Kentucky,' appearing as the Picanniny Boys, who were touring at the time. Aberdeen won 6-2. Also, on 15th April, the Whites decided to engage in a marathon session of playing two games within a few hours of each other. In the afternoon the Chanonry side lost 5-1 to Orion in the final Gershon Cup match of the season. Later in the day, nine of the eleven who featured in the Orion match, lined up for a friendly against the mighty Queen's Park. Not surprisingly, the visitors ran out easy 8-1 winners in a match watched by a small crowd.

Notable Games
Orion 18, Culter 0
Aberdeenshire Cup, Cattofield, 12th December 1896,

This would turn out to be the biggest win in Orion's history. Unfortunately not all the scorers were listed in the local press as the reporter probably got fed up watching the one-sided encounter. All we know is that it was 5-0 at half-time and four of the goals came from Thom (2), A. Mcfarlane, and Gordon. Culter had been given the choice of grounds for the tie and opted to travel to Cattofield where they hoped for a better financial return. The atrocious weather didn't prevent *"a fair turnout of spectators."* The pitch was in poor condition, being covered with large puddles of water. Culter's performance was described as being *"miserable"* while Orion apparently *"took matters easy and played a faultless game."*

Culter - Coutts, G. Smith, Esson, J. Ritchie, Macdonald, Davidson, McIntosh, Ririe, Watson, P. Smith, T. Ritchie.

Orion - McBean, Ross, James Low, Gordon, John Low, Dawson, M. Mcfarlane, A. Mcfarlane, Thom, Leggat, Hogg

Victoria United 0, Liverpool 1
Friendly, Victoria Bridge Grounds, 28th April 1897

A crowd of 2,000 turned up and the gate receipts more than covered the £25 guarantee offered to the touring visitors. Liverpool had won the English Second Division title the previous season and in the 1896-1897 campaign they finished a creditable fifth in the First Division. United were without regulars Morrice, Annand and Thornton, which gave the Torry side a major handicap against a near full strength opposition line-up. Liverpool dominated the early stages and at times *"the United were completely bewildered."* England international Thomas Bradshaw was particularly impressive and it was little surprise when he set up Frank Becton for Liverpool's opening goal. United suffered a further blow before the interval when Davidson had to go off with an injury, leaving the Torry men one man short. The home side did well in the second period with goalkeeper Findlay one of the top performers, and there was no further scoring. Liverpool impressed throughout by giving *"an exhibition of scientific play such as we but seldom see here."*

Victoria United - Findlay, McNeil, Allan, Russell, Davidson, Grant, McPherson, Murison, G. Burnett, J. Burnett, Stopani

Liverpool - Storer, Dunlop, Goldie, McCartney, Neil, Cleghorn, Hannah, Becton, Michael, Geary, Bradshaw

Ref - Mr. J. Thomson

Orion 2, Victoria United 2
Aberdeenshire Cup Final, Chanonry, 20th February 1897

More than 5,000 people crammed into the Chanonry filling every possible space including tree branches and the tops of the boundary walls. It was great news for the charity committee which saw record takings of £110 generated at the gate. Youngsters tried to climb over the wall to get free entry but many were chased away by officials and police. The sides were evenly matched in the opening stages but Orion seemed to get the upperhand when George Hogg hit the ball home only for his effort to be chalked off for being offside. Ten minutes before the break, however, Vics took the lead, team captain Morrice converting after good approach play by Forsyth. Straight from the kick-off Thornton made it 2-0 after the award of a penalty. The goal was scored in what would now be deemed a bizarre fashion as Ritchie took the penalty by passing to Thornton who then converted. The Torry fans celebrated with loud cheering. But Orion fought back and Thom gave them a lifeline with a goal on the stroke of half-time. The Stripes made a bright start to the second half and Alec Macfarlane soon levelled the scores. With 18 minutes remaining, Orion lost Wight with an injury which was so bad it was reckoned he wouldn't play again that season. Despite this setback the Stripes held on to force a replay.

Victoria United - Findlay, McConnochie, McNeill, Stopani, Davidson, Annand, Murison, Morrice, Forsyth, Thornton, Ritchie.

Orion - McBean, Gordon, Ross, Wight, Low, Currie, A. Mcfarlane, M. Mcfarlane, Thom, Leggat, Hogg.

Referee – Mr Banks, Bathgate

William Murison, Victoria United

Orion 5, Victoria United 2
Aberdeenshire Cup Final Replay, Chanonry, 27th February 1897

Another bumper crowd of close to 5,000 turned up for the second instalment of the Cup Final. Orion dropped Gordon who had a poor game in the first game a week earlier and his place was taken by James Low. Wright was also out due to the serious injury he sustained in the first game and he was replaced by Dawson. Vics were unchanged. With a strong wind at their backs United dominated the opening 45 minutes and the 2-1 lead they earned by the turnaround hardly reflected the way the game had gone. Thom's goal for Orion gave the Stripes some hope for the second half however and the Cattofield club went on to totally control proceedings. George Hogg set up a great chance which Tom Leggat headed home for the equaliser. From that point on there was no doubt about which side would win and Orion duly added three more goals to secure the trophy. John Low was considered to be the best player for the winners while Vics outside left Ritchie

George Hogg, Orion

was their top performer.

Orion - McBean, James Low, Ross, Dawson, John Low, Currie, A. Mcfarlane, M. Mcfarlane, Thom, Leggat, Hogg.

Victoria United - Findlay, McConnochie, McNeill, Stopani, Davidson, Annand, Murison, Morrice, Forsyth, Thornton, Ritchie.

Orion 7, Dundee Wanderers 2
Northern League, Cattofield, 24th April 1897

Dundee Wanderers travelled to Cattofield for what was effectively a league decider. This was the Dundee side's final game of the season and they held a two point lead over Orion who had one further game to play (against Aberdeen). A close match was expected but Orion swept into a 5-1 lead by the interval, although it should be mentioned that the Wanderers 'keeper, Coventry, was injured early in the game and eventually had to go off. Orion then lost Mcfarlane with a broken collarbone at the start of the second half but the Aberdeen men went on to win 7-2. Orion clinched the title the following week,but it was nerve-wracking affair. Aberdeen led 1-0 at the interval and it took a last minute equaliser from Orion to secure the point needed to win the championship outright

Orion - McBean, Jones, Low, Ross, Currie, Low, Dawson, M. Mcfarlane, Thom, Leggat, Hogg.

Dundee Wanderers - Coventry,Allan, Irons, Smart, Ireland, McColl, Betsworth, Graham, Aimers, Williamson, Ford.

Referee - Mr Davidson, Arbroath.

Victoria United 2, Aberdeen 1
Charity Cup Final, Cattofield, 22nd May 1897

The attendance was low *"due no doubt to the counter attractions of other pastimes such as cricket and cycling."* The season had to be extended to allow

Orion (stripes) and Victoria United players and officials pose for a photograph prior to the Aberdeenshire Cup Final replay at Chanonry on 27th February 1897. Orion won 5-2.

the game to take place and the lack of interest was reflected in the standard of play which was described as being *"of a very mediocre character"*. Aberdeen missed a hatful of chances in the first half which ended goal-less. Vics took the lead early in the second half with a *"soft shot"* then added another before the Whites grabbed a late consolation in what was a very disappointing game.

Victoria United – Findlay, McNeill, Allan, Morrice, Thomson, McPherson, Law, Burnett, Stopani, Ritchie (only ten names listed).

Aberdeen – Smyth, Gall, Davidson, Thomson, Henderson, J. Mackie, Gray, Milne, Fullarton, Jenkins, Thomson

Northern League 1896-1897

		P	W	D	L	F	A	Pts
1	Orion	14	9	3	2	55	27	21
2	Dundee Wanderers	14	8	4	2	40	24	20
3	Victoria United	14	8	1	5	43	36	17
4	Forfar Athletic	14	7	3	4	45	38	17
5	Arbroath	14	7	1	6	35	35	15
6	Montrose	14	4	3	7	19	37	11
7	Aberdeen	14	3	3	8	33	42	9
8	Lochee United	14	1	1	12	20	53	3

Aberdeen – Northern League 1896-1897

	Date		Opposition	F	A	Venue
Northern League	05/09/1896	Aberdeen	Dundee Wanderers	1	4	Clepington Park, Dundee
Northern League	19/09/1896	Aberdeen	Arbroath	4	2	Chanonry
Northern League	17/10/1896	Aberdeen	Victoria United	1	2	Victoria Bridge Grounds
Northern League	31/10/1896	Aberdeen	Montrose	2	2	Links Park, Montrose
Northern League	07/11/1896	Aberdeen	Forfar Athletic	3	4	Station Park,Forfar
Northern League	26/12/1896	Aberdeen	Orion	2	3	Cattofield
Northern League	09/01/1897	Aberdeen	Lochee United	3	1	Chanonry
Northern League	13/02/1897	Aberdeen	Dundee Wanderers	1	6	Chanonry
Northern League	27/02/1897	Aberdeen	Arbroath	1	5	Gayfield Park,Arbroath
Northern League	06/03/1897	Aberdeen	Forfar Athletic	3	4	Chanonry
Northern League	13/03/1897	Aberdeen	Lochee United	3	3	Lochee
Northern League	20/03/1897	Aberdeen	Montrose	5	0	Chanonry
Northern League	10/04/1897	Aberdeen	Victoria United	3	5	Chanonry
Northern League	01/05/1897	Aberdeen	Orion	1	1	Chanonry

Note: The game against Orion on 05/12/1896 was stopped early due to darkness and was replayed.

Aberdeen - Other Games 1896-1897

	Date		Opposition	F	A	Venue
	22/08/1896	Aberdeen	Culter	9	0	Culter
Scottish Qualifying Cup	29/08/1896	Aberdeen	Peterhead	3	6	Peterhead
	12/09/1896	Aberdeen	Stonehaven	13	0	Stonehaven
Friendly	26/09/1896	Aberdeen	Victoria United	3	3	Chanonry
Friendly	28/09/1896	Aberdeen	Dundee	0	4	Chanonry
	10/10/1896	Aberdeen	Orion	0	3	Cattofield
Aberdeenshire Cup	14/11/1896	Aberdeen	Orion	1	1	Chanonry
Aberdeenshire Cup	21/11/1896	Aberdeen	Orion	1	2	Cattofield
Gershon Cup	28/11/1896	Aberdeen	Victoria United	2	6	Victoria Bridge Grounds
	12/12/1896	Aberdeen	Mossend Swifts	4	4	Chanonry
	01/01/1897	Aberdeen	Victoria United	8	3	Victoria Bridge Grounds

	Date		Opposition	F	A	Venue
	02/01/1897	Aberdeen	Elgin			Elgin
	16/01/1897	Aberdeen	Montrose	4	2	Chanonry
Charity Cup	27/03/1897	Aberdeen	Peterhead	6	1	Victoria Bridge Grounds
	17/04/1897	Aberdeen	Morrison	4	0	Chanonry
	24/04/1897	Aberdeen	Piccanniny Boys	6	2	Chanonry
Gershon Cup	07/05/1897	Aberdeen	Orion	3	2	Cattofield
Gershon Cup	13/05/1897	Aberdeen	Victoria United	4	3	Chanonry
Gershon Cup	15/05/1897	Aberdeen	Orion	1	5	Chanonry
Friendly	15/05/1897	Aberdeen	Queen's Park	1	8	Chanonry
Charity Cup Final	22/05/1897	Aberdeen	Victoria United	1	2	Cattofield

Orion – Northern League 1896-1897

	Date		Opposition	F	A	Venue
Northern League	15/08/1896	Orion	Montrose	8	1	Cattofield
Northern League	22/08/1896	Orion	Arbroath	2	2	Gayfield Park,Arbroath
Northern League	05/09/1896	Orion	Forfar Athletic	7	3	Cattofield
Northern League	19/09/1896	Orion	Montrose	4	2	Montrose
Northern League	17/10/1896	Orion	Dundee Wanderers	1	3	Dundee
Northern League	31/10/1896	Orion	Arbroath	4	0	Cattofield
Northern League	05/12/1896	Orion	Aberdeen	5	2	Chanonry
Northern League	19/12/1896	Orion	Victoria United	6	3	Cattofield
Northern League	26/12/1896	Orion	Aberdeen	3	2	Cattofield
Northern League	13/02/1897	Orion	Forfar Athletic	2	2	Station Park, Forfar
Northern League	13/03/1897	Orion	Victoria United	2	4	Victoria Bridge Grounds
Northern League	20/03/1897	Orion	Lochee United	4	0	Cattofield
Northern League	10/04/1897	Orion	Lochee United	4	2	Lochee
Northern League	24/04/1897	Orion	Dundee Wanderers	7	2	Cattofield
Northern League	01/05/1897	Orion	Aberdeen	1	1	Chanonry

Orion - Other Games 1896-1897

Competition	Date		Opposition	F	A	Venue
Scottish Qualifying Cup	12/09/1896	Orion	Victoria United	5	2	Victoria Bridge Grounds

Competition	Date		Opposition	F	A	Venue
Scottish Qualifying Cup	26/09/1896	Orion	Peterhead	7	0	Cattofield
	10/10/1896	Orion	Aberdeen	3	0	Cattofield
Scottish Qualifying Cup	24/10/1896	Orion	Bathgate	5	1	Cattofield
Scottish Qualifying Cup	07/11/1896	Orion	Motherwell	1	3	Cattofield
Aberdeenshire Cup	14/11/1896	Orion	Aberdeen	1	1	Chanonry
Aberdeenshire Cup	21/11/1896	Orion	Aberdeen	2	1	Cattofield
Aberdeenshire Cup Semi Final	12/12/1896	Orion	Culter	18	0	Cattofield
	02/01/1897	Orion	Linthouse	10	3	Cattofield
Scottish Cup 1R	09/01/1897	Orion	Falkirk	0	2	Falkirk
	16/01/1897	Orion	St Andrews University	5	1	Cattofield
	23/01/1897	Orion	Dundee Wanderers	5	2	Cattofield
	30/01/1897	Orion	Lochee United	5	1	Lochee
Aberdeenshire Cup Final	20/02/1897	Orion	Victoria United	2	2	Chanonry
Aberdeenshire Cup Final	27/02/1897	Orion	Victoria United	5	2	Chanonry
Charity Cup	27/03/1897	Orion	Culter	11	0	Culter
Gershon Cup	03/04/1897	Orion	Victoria United	5	2	Victoria Bridge Grounds
	17/04/1897	Orion	London Caledonians	6	0	Cattofield
Charity Cup SF	29/04/1897	Orion	Victoria United	1	3	Victoria Bridge Grounds
Gershon Cup	07/05/1897	Orion	Aberdeen	2	3	Cattofield
Gershon Cup	11/05/1897	Orion	Victoria United	4	3	Cattofield
Gershon Cup	15/05/1897	Orion	Aberdeen	5	1	Chanonry

Victoria United – Northern League 1896-1897

	Date		Opposition	F	A	Venue
Northern League	22/08/1896	Victoria United	Lochee United	6	2	Victoria Bridge Grounds
Northern League	05/09/1896	Victoria United	Montrose	6	3	Victoria Bridge Grounds
Northern League	19/09/1896	Victoria United	Forfar Athletic	3	5	Station Park,Forfar

Date		Opposition	F	A	Venue
Northern League 17/10/1896	Victoria United	Aberdeen	2	1	Victoria Bridge Grounds
Northern League 31/10/1896	Victoria United	Dundee Wanderers	1	1	Victoria Bridge Grounds
Northern League 07/11/1896	Victoria United	Arbroath	2	1	Gayfield Park,Arbroath
Northern League 05/12/1896	Victoria United	Lochee United	6	2	St Margaret's Grounds, Lochee
Northern League 19/12/1896	Victoria United	Orion	3	6	Cattofield
Northern League 26/12/1896	Victoria United	Dundee Wanderers	1	4	Clepington Park, Dundee
Northern League 09/01/1897	Victoria United	Forfar Athletic	0	2	Victoria Bridge Grounds
Northern League 23/01/1897	Victoria United	Montrose	1	2	Links Park, Montrose
Northern League 13/02/1897	Victoria United	Arbroath	3	2	Victoria Bridge Grounds
Northern League 13/03/1897	Victoria United	Orion	4	2	Victoria Bridge Grounds
Northern League 10/04/1897	Victoria United	Aberdeen	5	3	Chanonry

Victoria United - Other Games 1896-1897

	Date		Opposition	F	A	Venue
Scottish Qualifying Cup	29/08/1896	Victoria United	Culter	8	0	Victoria Bridge Grounds
Scottish Qualifying Cup	12/09/1896	Victoria United	Orion	2	5	Victoria Bridge Grounds
Friendly	26/09/1896	Victoria United	Aberdeen	3	3	Chanonry
	24/10/1896	Victoria United	Arbroath Wanderers	8	1	Victoria Bridge Grounds
Aberdeenshire Cup	14/11/1896	Victoria United	Fraserburgh Wanderers	9	0	Victoria Bridge Grounds
Gershon Cup	28/11/1896	Victoria United	Aberdeen	6	2	Victoria Bridge Grounds
Aberdeenshire Cup SF	12/12/1896	Victoria United	Peterhead	1	0	Recreation Park, Peterhead
	01/01/1897	Victoria United	Aberdeen	3	8	Victoria Bridge Grounds
	02/01/1897	Victoria United	St Mirren	2	4	Victoria Bridge Grounds
	16/01/1897	Victoria United	St Johnstone	4	1	Victoria Bridge Grounds
Aberdeenshire Cup Final	20/02/1897	Victoria United	Orion	2	2	Chanonry

	Date		Opposition	F	A	Venue
Aberdeenshire Cup Final	27/02/1897	Victoria United	Orion	2	5	Chanonry
	20/03/1897	Victoria United	Vale of Atholl	3	3	Victoria Bridge Grounds
Gershon Cup	03/04/1897	Victoria United	Orion	2	5	Victoria Bridge Grounds
	17/04/1897	Victoria United	St Bernards	2	1	Victoria Bridge Grounds
	24/04/1897	Victoria United	Hibernian	3	4	Victoria Bridge Grounds
	28/04/1897	Victoria United	Liverpool	0	1	Victoria Bridge Grounds
Charity Cup SF	29/04/1897	Victoria United	Orion	3	1	Chanonry
	01/05/1897	Victoria United	Dundee A	2	2	Victoria Bridge Grounds
Gershon Cup	11/05/1897	Victoria United	Orion	3	4	Cattofield
Gershon Cup	13/05/1897	Victoria United	Aberdeen	3	4	Chanonry
Charity Cup Final	22/05/1897	Victoria United	Aberdeen	2	1	Cattofield

Aberdeenshire Cup 1896-1897

	Date			F	A	Venue
Aberdeenshire Cup	14/11/1896	Aberdeen	Orion	1	1	Chanonry
Aberdeenshire Cup	14/11/1896	Victoria United	Fraserburgh Wanderers	9	0	Victoria Bridge Grounds
Aberdeenshire Cup	14/11/1896	Peterhead	Aberdeen University	8	2	Peterhead
Aberdeenshire Cup	21/11/1896	Orion	Aberdeen	2	1	Cattofield
Aberdeenshire Cup SF	12/12/1896	Orion	Culter	18	0	Cattofield
Aberdeenshire Cup SF	12/12/1896	Victoria United	Peterhead	1	0	Recreation Park, Peterhead
Aberdeenshire Cup Final	20/02/1897	Orion	Victoria United	2	2	Chanonry
Aberdeenshire Cup Final	27/02/1897	Orion	Victoria United	5	2	Chanonry

Charity Cup 1896-1897

	Date			F	A	Venue
Charity Cup	27/02/1897	Peterhead	Aberdeen University	7	2	Recreation Park, Peterhead
Charity Cup SF	27/03/1897	Aberdeen	Peterhead	6	1	Victoria Bridge Grounds
Charity Cup	27/03/1897	Orion	Culter	11	0	Culter
Charity Cup SF	29/04/1897	Victoria United	Orion	3	1	Chanonry
Charity Cup Final	22/05/1897	Victoria United	Aberdeen	2	1	Cattofield

Gershon Cup 1896-1897

	Date			F	A	Venue
Gershon Cup	28/11/1896	Aberdeen	Victoria United	2	6	Victoria Bridge Grounds
Gershon Cup	03/04/1897	Orion	Victoria United	5	2	Victoria Bridge Grounds
Gershon Cup	07/05/1897	Aberdeen	Orion	3	2	Cattofield
Gershon Cup	11/05/1897	Orion	Victoria United	4	3	Cattofield
Gershon Cup	13/05/1897	Aberdeen	Victoria United	4	3	Chanonry
Gershon Cup	15/05/1897	Aberdeen	Orion	1	5	Chanonry

	P	W	D	L	F	A	Pts
Orion	4	3	0	1	16	9	6
Aberdeen	4	2	0	2	10	16	4
Victoria United	4	1	0	3	14	15	2

1897-1898
Northern League winners Victoria United defeat the champions of England

Victoria United engaged in a major recruitment drive during the summer in a bid to strengthen their hopes of emulating Orion's success of the previous season in winning the Northern League. The Torry side made a number of signings with a mixed degree of success. Jim Carlin, a former Celtic player, was among the first to join up, but on his debut against Aberdeen on 11th September he was promptly sent off after striking a Whites player. In one of his other four appearances for the Blues, he missed a penalty. It was little surprise that he moved on, to Reading, in November. Goalkeeper Willie Allan was signed from Sheffield Wednesday, but despite having made over 100 appearances for the Yorkshire club, he only tuned out a little more than ten times for the Torry men. At the start of the season the Vics also lost former club captain John Forsyth who decided to emigrate to South Africa to seek his fortune in the gold mines. Forsyth, it will be

John Forsyth, Victoria United

recalled from earlier chapters, was a colourful character who almost lost his life in a street brawl. He had a remarkable playing career within Aberdeen footballing circles. Although he was now just 23 years of age, Forsyth had been playing senior football in Aberdeen for almost a decade. He started off with Bon Accord, playing with the Links team for four years until the club folded at which point he joined Aberdeen for a short spell before moving on to Orion. He played for the Cattofield men for two seasons. By then professionalism had been legalised and Victoria United became the first city club to pay players. Forsyth was among the first to sign pro forms for the Torry outfit and he became captain for the 1894-95 campaign. That season he won his first inter county 'cap' and in total he made five inter county appearances. He played in seven cup finals for Vics, picking up five winners badges. A number of top English sides were interested in signing him but he was happy to stay in Aberdeen. In the summer of 1897 he decided to move back to the amateur ranks but then chose to seek his fortune in South Africa. Before leaving he was treated to a night out in the Prince of Wales pub when club officials and players presented him with a number of gifts including *"a handsome gold albert and badge"* and *"a travelling bag and dressing case."* Forsyth sailed for Johannesburg from London on the 'Dunnottar Castle' in September 1897 and on arrival he was met by a number of exiled Vics fans who made him most welcome. He continued to play football, signing for Johannesburg Rangers.

The Principal Route of Communication

Between Chanonry Grounds and Victoria Bridge Grounds is by Market Street.

In Market Street is

THE NEW MARKET BAR,

Where you can find Spirits, Wines, and Ales of the very Best Quality—Guaranteed to be so by the Proprietor,

WM. M. CUMMING.

DAVID MIDDLETON,

Wine ∗ and ∗ Spirit ∗ Merchant,

⚓ NEW BAR. ⚓

96 High Street, Old Aberdeen.

THE FAVOURITE RESORT OF FOOTBALLERS.

Health to the lads the bat who wield,
Or, freed from labour's thrall,
With lightsome hearts hie to the field
And deftly kick the ball.

1898 Pub adverts. The top one is aimed at football fans whether they are watching Aberdeen at the Chanonry or Victoria United at Torry. The lower advert, for the New Bar in Old Aberdeen is targeting fans watching games at Aberdeen F.C.'s nearby Chanonry grounds.

The vital Northern League fixture between top of the table Victoria United and bottom side Aberdeen on 12th March 1898 was notable for three reasons. Firstly, this was more than likely the first senior football match in the city to be filmed. Before the match started the teams marched past the west goal and were *"taken"* by Messrs Walker and Co's cinematograph, *"which was also in operation at various points of the game."* Secondly, spectators entering the ground were asked to sign a petition supporting Aberdeen plasterer Charles Smith who was on death row in a Durham jail. But most importantly, from a footballing standpoint at any rate, Vics knew they had to win the game to have any hope of bringing the

Victoria United score against Aberdeen, at Torry, 12th March. United won this match 2-1 to clinch the Northern League title. Note the interesting shape of what is now the six yard box. In the background is the chimney stack of the Seaton brick works and behind that the vague silhouette of tenements on Victoria Road.

Northern League title to Torry. A hard fought 2-1 home victory put United in pole position, but the Blues had to wait until Dundee Wanderers completed their fixtures before the final outcome of the battle for the league title would be known. The Dundee side needed to win their final three games to pip United for top spot. If they dropped just one point they would share it with the Torry side, but if they dropped two points, then Vics would be outright champions. At this time two points were awarded for a win and one for a draw. It all started well for the Dundee side as they crushed Orion 5-3 at Clepington Road in the first of these fixtures. But they suffered a serious setback the following week when being held to a 3-3 draw by Aberdeen at the Chanonry. That meant Wanderers went into their last match of the season, on 2nd April, knowing they needed a victory on home ground over Forfar Athletic to share the title with Vics. Wanderers surged into a 2-0 lead by halftime, but in the second half the Loons fought back to secure a 3-3 draw. That left the Dundee side one point behind United, so the title remained in Aberdeen for a second season, albeit at Torry rather than Cattofield.

Surprisingly, the Vics made little progress in any other competitions. They were eliminated from the Scottish Qualifying Cup by Orion and were equally

Action from a Victoria United v Orion match at Torry in March 1898

surprisingly knocked out of the Aberdeenshire Cup by Aberdeen. United did get to the final of the Charity Cup but again lost to Orion. It was the first time since their first season, 1889-1890, that the Torry men had failed to win at least one of the main local trophies. They did, however, end the season with one major scalp under their belts. English champions Sheffield United were lured to Torry, no doubt by the promise of a fat cheque. The Yorkshire side travelled by train and stayed in the Douglas Hotel before heading across the Dee for the Tuesday evening game. Little was expected of the Vics, but the home side rose to the occasion and handed out a 1-0 defeat to the distinguished visitors, Bobby Ritchie scoring the decisive goal five minutes from time.

Orion opened their Northern League season by unfurling the championship flag before their home game against Arbroath on 18th September 1897. A 40ft pole had been assembled to carry the specially commissioned flag and the carnival atmosphere continued as the home side swept to an impressive 8-1 victory. There was even a bit of fun during the half-time interval when, in an effort to improve community relations, the sergeant of police took part in a sprint race against some local youngsters and won easily.

In the game, Jim Thom scored four times, including a penalty, with the other goals coming from Webster, Wilson and Mcfarlane. Jim Milne scored Arbroath's consolation. Despite his four goals, Thom's performance didn't satisfy everyone, one reporter writing that *"it was one of Jim's off days."* Thom's consistency during the season did however capture the attention of Scotland's selectors and he was invited to take part in the international trials, but unfortunately he was ill at the time

Northern League Flag unfurled at Cattofield Park in September 1897 in honour of Orion's success the previous season.

and couldn't attend, thereby possibly missing the opportunity to become the first Aberdeen-based player to win a Scotland cap. (Aberdeen goalkeeper Tom Smyth had appeared in the trials in 1896, but he wasn't successful).

The Red Lichties took revenge one month later in the return fixture at Gayfield, winning 7-1.

This was a setback for Orion but the club had made a decent start to the season, this being their only defeat in the opening seven league games. The Scottish Qualifying Cup campaign was also successful with wins over Peterhead, Victoria United, Inverness Caledonian, Lochee United and Polton Vale taking the north east side all the way to the semi final in which they were drawn at home to East Stirlingshire. The Stripes held high hopes of going all the way and winning the

trophy, but after an exciting game they were pipped 4-3 by the visitors. Reaching the latter stages of the competition did, however, earn Orion a place in the First Round of the Scottish Cup, but that ended in disappointment as well with a 3-1 loss to Dundee Wanderers. The earlier Qualifying Cup tie against Peterhead, scheduled for Saturday 4th September, was postponed

Jim Thom, Orion F.C
Illness prevented Thom for playing a trial for Scotland. He was also an excellent cricketer and played for Caledonian cricket club. A number of English clubs were interested in signing him, most notably Everton, but he preferred to stay in the city.

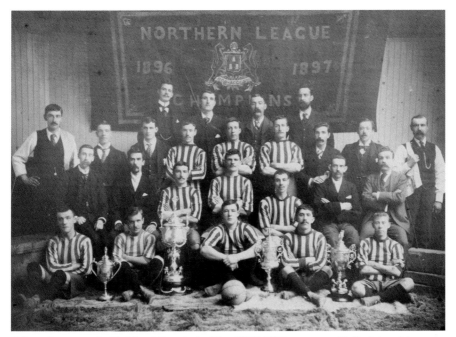

Orion players and officials at the start of the 1897-1898 season with their trophies.

after the Orion team kit was lost en route to the Blue Toon. The Great North of Scotland railway company, for some unknown reason, had offloaded the hampers at Auchnagatt. Both teams agreed to the postponement, although a large crowd had assembled, including around 100 Orion fans who had travelled north. The railway company later agreed to reimburse the Orion squad's train fares.

Orion's Northern League form deteriorated after the New Year and in the second half of the season they won just one of their seven games, and that was the final one of the season, a 3-1 victory preventing the Stripes from finishing bottom of the table just twelve months after being crowned champions. The wooden spoon went to Aberdeen. Nothing went right for Orion in their league game with Dundee Wanderers in February. It all started so well with Jim Thom netting from the penalty spot to give the Stripes the lead. But the scorer then twisted his knee and had to go off for a while. On returning he couldn't run freely so decided to swap places with McBean in goal. As the game progressed Orion lost the place and were losing 4-2 when a number of decisions went against them. Grant appeared to have scored, but the goal was chalked off for a foul on the goalkeeper. Then an Orion shot *"passed through the side of the goal and into the net,"* prompting the home side to again claim a goal. The referee, Mr Roebuck, was having none of it, however, much to the disgust of a section of the home support. At the end of the game the disgruntled Orion followers hustled the whistler and confronted him with a barrage of insults. There was a serious threat of violence and Mr Roebuck had to be escorted back to his hotel by police *"who were obliged to draw their batons to keep off the angry mob."*

Aberdeen finally decided to join the other two city clubs by offering full professional terms to players. The Whites may have been the longest established of the three senior clubs, but Orion and Victoria United had left them some way behind over the previous few seasons. The changes made little difference, however, as the Chanonry club ended the season joint bottom of the Northern League. They also went out of the Scottish Qualifying Cup at the first hurdle and lost out in the Charity Cup. Some consolation was achieved in the Aberdeenshire Cup, however, which was won for the first time since 1889-1890 with a 3-2 win over Orion in the Final at the Victoria Bridge Grounds.

Willie Corbett – the champion long distance runner who was Aberdeen's trainer for over a decade

Only the city's three senior clubs, Aberdeen, Orion and Victoria United, entered the Charity Cup. Peterhead wanted to participate but with all games scheduled for Thursday evenings the Blue Tooners said they would have found it difficult to get into town in time. So, a bizarre arrangement was put in place which resulted in Orion winning the trophy despite being beaten by Victoria United in the semi final. How was this possible? Let me try to explain it. United and Orion were drawn to meet in the first semi final and organisers decided that the losers of that game would play Aberdeen in the second

A rare picture of a game at The Chanonry taken in January 1898. Could it have been the Aberdeen (white shirts) v Dumbarton (striped shirts) match played on New Year's Day?

semi final. United duly defeated Orion 2-1 after a 2-2 draw to progress to the Final. Orion then dropped into the second semi final in which they defeated Aberdeen 2-1 to take their place in the Final where they would meet Victoria United once again. This time the Cattofield side won 6-4 to lift the trophy for the fifth time in the 10 year history of the competition.

On 11th April 1898 the Aberdeen Journal reported that this would probably be the last season that Aberdeen would play at the Chanonry as *"the ground has been acquired by the university authorities for a botanical garden. The buildings formerly occupied as Chanonry Gymnasium have also been purchased by the university in order to be converted into a hall of residence for lady students, and the second eleven pitch will be required as a recreation ground in connection with this institution. A peculiar circumstance is that the two pitches are on different estates."* The newspaper also indicated that the Whites were negotiating for a new ground *"in the vicinity of the Gallowhill."* Aberdeen's last game at the Chanonry appears to have been the 9-2 victory over Peterhead on 16th April. The final football match at the venue, however, was the Charity Cup Final between Orion and Victoria United on 28th April. At the end of the season the Aberdeen Catholic Association tried to arrange an exhibition game in the city between Celtic and Hibernian. Hibs weren't available but Celtic travelled north and played an Aberdeenshire select,

Aberdeen (white shirts) v Third Lanark (stripes) at The Chanonry, 2nd April 1898

winning 5-3 at the Victoria Bridge Grounds. The Celtic players also took part in a five-side competition that same weekend as part of a wider sports programme organised by the Catholic Association as a fund raiser for St Mary's Cathedral.

Notable Games

Orion 3 East Stirlingshire 4
Scottish Qualifying Cup Semi Final, Cattofield, 27th November 1897

This was the furthest an Aberdeen side had progressed in the Scottish Qualifying Cup and with the benefit of home advantage, local hopes were high that Orion might go on to win the trophy. An estimated 300 Shire fans made the journey north to support their side and the Cattofield ground was packed for the occasion. Orion kicked off playing up the slope with the low sun in their eyes, but despite these disadvantages, they managed to create a number of early chances. The visitors also looked dangerous, however, and on one of their attacks they took the lead in rather slapstick circumstances. Inside-left Alexander fired in a low shot which McBean seemed to have covered, but the goalkeeper, in moving across his line, slipped and fell, leaving the ball to trundle into the net. Orion responded positively, but it was the Shire who scored again through Jardine before half-time was called. Shortly after the interval, Orion's pressure paid off and Webster got on the scoresheet. Shire weathered the storm then came back into it with Alexander netting a third before McKie seemed to settle the outcome with a fourth. The Cattofield men refused to give up, however, and Webster was again on the mark to make it 2-4. Excitement reached fever pitch when the home side bundled home a third goal but, despite going all out for the equaliser, Orion couldn't quite break down their opponents again before the final whistle.

Orion - McBean, Ross, Scott, Currie, Low, Dawson,Webster, Grant, Thom, Wilson, Hogg.

East Stirlingshire - Shields, Steel, Johnston, Fish, Paterson, Prentice, McQueen, McDonald, McKie, Alexander, Jardine.

Referee - Mr Colville, Inverness.

Aberdeen 3, Orion 2
Aberdeenshire Cup Final, Victoria Bridge Grounds, 26th February 1898

Orion gave a debut to James Sword, signed from Arbroath, while Aberdeen also had a newcomer in their ranks with Jenkins making his first appearance after signing from Elgin City. On a very windy afternoon, Hogg gave Orion the lead with less than 60 seconds on the clock but Aberdeen hit back to score twice before the interval, the second coming from new man Jenkins. After a short break Clark put the Whites 3-1 ahead early in the second half. Hogg did well to reduce the deficit and Orion pressed for an equaliser but found Ritchie to be unbeatable in the Aberdeen goal. It was Aberdeen's first victory in the competition since season 1889-1890.

Aberdeen - Ritchie, John Davidson, McConnochie, James Mackie, Joe Davidson, Thomson, Livingstone, Gray, Jenkins, Clark, Shiach

Right: John Davidson,
Aberdeen captain
Far right: Donald
Currie, Orion captain

Orion - McBean, Ross, Scott, Currie, Low, Dawson, Webster, Grant, Sword, Wilson, Hogg.
Referee - Mr Tom Robertson, Queen's Park

Victoria United 2, Aberdeen 1
Northern League, Victoria Bridge Grounds, 12th March 1898

This was a vital game between table-topping United and bottom the league Aberdeen. The Torry men, playing their final league game of the season, needed a win to have any chance of winning the Northern title but Aberdeen had shown an upturn in form in the preceding weeks and the outcome was far from certain. A crowd of 3,000 turned up for the match which was also filmed by a local company, the first time this technology had been used at a football game in the city. Although United made a bright start, the visitors soon settled and began to assert themselves and on the half hour mark they took the lead through Livingstone.This setback stung United into action and they began to pressurise the Aberdeen defence. It seemed the Whites would hold out, but just before the interval United's Ritchie beat his namesake in the Aberdeen goal to secure the equaliser.United dominated the second period and McIlvenney grabbed the decisive winning goal. Aberdeen then did United a major favour the following Saturday when they held Wanderers to a 3-3 draw at the Chanonry. That result effectively ensured United would win the title unless Wanderers defeated Forfar Athletic in their final match. The Dundonians failed, throwing away a 2-0 lead to draw 3-3 with the Angus side, thereby leaving Victoria United as clear champions.
Victoria United - F. Findlay, C. Kilgour, D. McNeil, J. Dundas, J. Moffat, G. Mckenzie, George McPherson, George Burnett, Harry McIlvenney, J. Henderson, R. Ritchie.
Aberdeen - Ritchie, John Davidson, C.W. Mackie, J. Mackie, Henderson, Thomson, Livingstone, Mackay, Clark, Gray, Shiach.
Referee - Mr Black, Forfar Athletic

Victoria United 1, Sheffield United 0
Victoria Bridge Grounds,19th April 1898

The English champions ,Sheffield United, arrived in Aberdeen during their end of season tour which involved playing four games in five days against Celtic, Hearts, Victoria United and East Stirlingshire. It was a major achievement for the Vics to have attracted such a top class side to the north east , even although the Yorkshiremen could perhaps have been accused of going through the motions while picking up a big pay day cheque. That didn't matter to the home side who simply saw the chance of pitting their skills against what was arguably one of the world's top teams. The Victoria Bridge playing surface was specially rolled for the occasion and a big crowd turned out. The Blades fielded a strong line-up with the amazing 21 stone England international "Fatty" Foulke in

Fatty Foulke

goal. Foulke turned out to be the star of the show as he used his considerable bulk to shrug off the Vics challenges, while his amazing ability to throw the ball more than half the length of the pitch amazed the onlookers. He was described as *"the coolest man on the field, as well as the largest."* His considerable frame was put to good use as the attempts made by the Vics forward to *"rush the goalkeeper"* usually ended with the home players being *"recoiled on their backs."* Foulke's reputation was further enhanced in the second half when, after Vics had been awarded a dubious penalty, he *"saved grandly"* McNeill's spotkick. The big man was, however eventually beaten by a Bobby Ritchie shot five minutes from the end which earned the Torry men a memorable victory. The Blades overall performance didn't impress one commentator, who wrote: *"We were rather disappointed at Sheffield's display. From the English champions we expected to get a fine exhibition of the passing game; but no, in the open they were extremely smart, but finished wretchedly. They drew with Celtic, the Scottish league champions, but succumbed to the Northern League champions. Who says Aberdeen football is not improving?"*

Sheffield United - Foulke, Goudie, Cain, Morren, Howard, Beers, Jenkinson, Thacker, Almond, Cunningham, Needham

Victoria United - Findlay, Kilgour, McNeil, Russell, Anderson, Mckenzie, McPherson, Henderson, McIlvenney ,Burnett, Ritchie.

Referee - Mr P. Simpson

Orion 6, Victoria United 4
Charity Cup Final, Chanonry 28th
April 1898

This appears to have been the last game played at the Chanonry. United had scored with two minutes to go to defeat Orion 2-1 in the replayed Charity Cup Semi Final, but Orion still made it to the Final after beating Aberdeen in a second semi final. The Final received scant coverage in the press, probably due to it being held so late in the season and on a Thursday evening. Details are in short supply but it is known that Webster gave Orion the lead and Murphy made it 2-0, before "wee" John Henderson pulled one back for the Blues. Hogg then made it 3-1 but McIvenney replied for United. No other details are known.

John Henderson (Victoria United), who scored in the Charity Cup Final. Henderson joined the Torry side from Celtic at the beginning of the season but he was on his travels again by the end of the campaign, signing for Lincoln City along with clubmate Jim Moffat.

Victoria United - Findlay, Kilgour, McNeill, Russell, Anderson, Mckenzie, Riley, Henderson, McIvenney, Burnett, Ritchie.

Orion - Watson, Ross, Stopani, Currie, Low, Wilson, Wilson, Webster, Murphy, Hogg, Leggat Barron.

Aberdeenshire 3 Celtic 5
St Andrews Catholic Association Sports, Victoria Bridge Grounds,
21st May 1898

This fund raising game at Torry saw Celtic, the Scottish First Division Champions, take the lead through McCafferty after *"a sequence of see-saw passes tricked the back division of the locals."* The select responded and following some good work by Shiach, Gray netted an equaliser. McKay quickly restored Celtic's advantage before the interval. After the break, goals from Gray and Livingstone put the home side ahead but the visitors upped the tempo and goals from McKay, Moran and

McCafferty gave them a 5-3 victory. Afterwards the teams were treated to a meal in Mr Hay's Royal Atheneum restaurant when it was announced that the football and other sports had raised £100 for improvements to St Mary's Cathedral.

Aberdeenshire - Ritchie (Aberdeen), Kilgour (Victoria), Ross (Orion), Russell (Victoria), Low (Orion, captain), Currie (Orion), Livingstone (Aberdeen), Gray (Aberdeen), Hogg (Orion), Ritchie (Victoria), Shiach (Aberdeen).

Celtic - Docherty, Thomson, Goldie, Gilhooly, Hinds, king, Moran, McAulay, Campbell, Mckay, McCafferty

Referee - Mr P. Simpson, Victoria United

Aberdeen's Hugh Livingstone – scored against Celtic

Northern League 1897-1898

		P	W	D	L	F	A	Pts
1	Victoria United	14	8	3	3	33	27	19
2	Dundee Wanderers	14	7	4	3	32	28	18
3	Forfar Athletic	14	6	5	4	34	31	17
4	Arbroath	14	6	2	6	45	32	14
5	Montrose	14	5	2	7	25	28	12
6	Orion	14	5	2	7	40	41	12
7	Lochee United	14	5	1	8	20	29	11
8	Aberdeen	14	4	3	7	34	44	11

Aberdeen – Northern League 1897-1898

	Date	Opposition		F	A	Venue
Northern League	04/09/1897	Aberdeen	Lochee United	6	1	Chanonry
Northern League	18/09/1897	Aberdeen	Lochee United	2	2	Dundee
Northern League	02/10/1897	Aberdeen	Montrose	1	3	Links Park, Montrose

	Date		Opposition	F	A	Venue
Northern League	16/10/1897	Aberdeen	Victoria United	4	6	Chanonry
Northern League	23/10/1897	Aberdeen	Arbroath	1	6	Gayfield Park,Arbroath
Northern League	30/10/1897	Aberdeen	Dundee Wanderers	1	1	Clepington Park, Dundee
Northern League	13/11/1897	Aberdeen	Orion	1	4	Cattofield
Northern League	20/11/1897	Aberdeen	Forfar Athletic	4	3	Chanonry
Northern League	04/12/1897	Aberdeen	Arbroath	2	6	Chanonry
Northern League	29/01/1898	Aberdeen	Forfar Athletic	2	3	Station Park, Forfar
Northern League	19/02/1898	Aberdeen	Montrose	2	1	Chanonry
Northern League	12/03/1898	Aberdeen	Victoria United	1	2	Victoria Bridge Grounds
Northern League	19/03/1898	Aberdeen	Dundee Wanderers	3	3	Chanonry
Northern League	26/03/1898	Aberdeen	Orion	4	3	Chanonry

Aberdeen – Other Games 1897-1898

Competition	Date		Opposition	F	A	Venue
Scottish Qualifying Cup	11/09/1897	Aberdeen	Victoria United	1	2	Victoria Bridge Grounds
	25/09/1897	Aberdeen	Peterhead	2	4	Recreation Park, Peterhead
Friendly	27/09/1897	Aberdeen	Orion	4	4	Cattofield
	09/10/1897	Aberdeen	Bathgate	1	2	Chanonry
Friendly	27/11/1897	Aberdeen	Victoria United	2	1	Victoria Bridge Grounds
Aberdeenshire Cup 1R	11/12/1897	Aberdeen	Victoria United	4	3	Chanonry
	01/01/1898	Aberdeen	Victoria United	1	2	Victoria Bridge Grounds
	03/01/1898	Aberdeen	Dumbarton	0	2	Chanonry
	08/01/1898	Aberdeen	Dundee A	5	5	Chanonry
Aberdeenshire Cup SF	15/01/1898	Aberdeen	Aberdeen University	9	0	Chanonry
	22/01/1898	Aberdeen	St Johnstone	6	2	Chanonry
	12/02/1898	Aberdeen	Victoria United	5	5	Chanonry
Aberdeenshire Cup Final	26/02/1898	Aberdeen	Orion	3	2	Victoria Bridge Grounds

Competition	Date		Opposition	F	A	Venue
	05/03/1898	Aberdeen	Peterhead	4	7	Recreation Park, Peterhead
	02/04/1898	Aberdeen	Third Lanark	2	4	Chanonry
Friendly	09/04/1898	Aberdeen	Orion	3	2	Chanonry
Friendly	16/04/1898	Aberdeen	Peterhead	9	2	Chanonry
Charity Cup	23/04/1898	Aberdeen	Orion	1	2	Victoria Bridge Grounds
Friendly	30/04/1898	Aberdeen	Orion	3	2	Cattofield

Orion – Northern League 1897-1898

	Date		Opposition	F	A	Venue
Northern League	18/09/1897	Orion	Arbroath	8	1	Cattofield
Northern League	02/10/1897	Orion	Victoria United	2	4	Victoria Bridge Grounds
Northern League	16/10/1897	Orion	Arbroath	1	7	Gayfield Park,Arbroath
Northern League	30/10/1897	Orion	Forfar Athletic	3	3	Forfar
Northern League	13/11/1897	Orion	Aberdeen	4	1	Cattofield
Northern League	20/11/1897	Orion	Montrose	4	1	Links Park, Montrose
Northern League	04/12/1897	Orion	Montrose	2	1	Cattofield
Northern League	22/01/1898	Orion	Lochee United	2	4	Lochee
Northern League	29/01/1898	Orion	Victoria United	0	2	Cattofield
Northern League	05/02/1898	Orion	Forfar Athletic	3	3	Cattofield
Northern League	12/02/1898	Orion	Dundee Wanderers	2	4	Cattofield
Northern League	12/03/1898	Orion	Dundee Wanderers	3	5	Clepington Park, Dundee
Northern League	26/03/1898	Orion	Aberdeen	3	4	Chanonry
Northern League	02/04/1898	Orion	Lochee United	3	1	Cattofield

Orion – Other games 1897-1898

Competition	Date		Opposition	F	A	Venue
Scottish Qualifying Cup	11/09/1897	Orion	Peterhead	4	2	Peterhead
Scottish Qualifying Cup	25/09/1897	Orion	Victoria United	4	2	Cattofield
Friendly	27/09/1897	Orion	Aberdeen	4	4	Cattofield

Competition	Date		Opposition	F	A	Venue
Scottish Qualifying Cup	09/10/1897	Orion	Inverness Caledonian	2	0	Inverness
Scottish Qualifying Cup	23/10/1897	Orion	Lochee United	10	1	Cattofield
Scottish Qualifying Cup	06/11/1897	Orion	Polton Vale	5	0	Cattofield
Scottish Qualifying Cup SF	27/11/1897	Orion	East Stirlingshire	3	4	Cattofield
Friendly	18/12/1897	Orion	Dundee	2	7	Carolina Port, Dundee
	25/12/1897	Orion	Dunfermline	4	0	Cattofield
Scottish Cup 1R	08/01/1898	Orion	Dundee Wanderers	1	3	Clepington Park, Dundee
	15/01/1898	Orion	St Andrews University	9	4	Cattofield
Aberdeenshire Cup Final	26/02/1898	Orion	Aberdeen	2	3	Victoria Bridge Grounds
	05/03/1898	Orion	Falkirk	8	4	Cattofield
Friendly	19/03/1898	Orion	Victoria United	5	3	Victoria Bridge Grounds
Charity Cup	07/04/1898	Orion	Victoria United	2	2	Victoria Bridge Grounds
Friendly	09/04/1898	Orion	Aberdeen	2	3	Chanonry
Friendly	16/04/1898	Orion	Victoria United	2	1	Cattofield
Charity Cup	21/04/1898	Orion	Victoria United	1	2	Victoria Bridge Grounds
Charity Cup	23/04/1898	Orion	Aberdeen	2	1	Victoria Bridge Grounds
Charity Cup Final	28/04/1898	Orion	Victoria United	6	4	Chanonry
	29/04/1898	Orion	Hibernian	0	1	Cattofield
Friendly	30/04/1898	Orion	Aberdeen	2	3	Cattofield

Victoria United – Northern League 1897-1898

	Date		Opposition	F	A	Venue
Northern League	04/09/1897	Victoria United	Montrose	2	2	Montrose
Northern League	18/09/1897	Victoria United	Forfar Athletic	4	1	Victoria Bridge Grounds
Northern League	02/10/1897	Victoria United	Orion	4	2	Victoria Bridge Grounds
Northern League	16/10/1897	Victoria United	Aberdeen	6	4	Chanonry
Northern League	30/10/1897	Victoria United	Arbroath	1	1	Victoria Bridge Grounds

Date		Opposition	F	A	Venue
Northern League 13/11/1897	Victoria United	Lochee United	0	1	Lochee
Northern League 20/11/1897	Victoria United	Lochee United	4	1	Victoria Bridge Grounds
Northern League 18/12/1897	Victoria United	Dundee Wanderers	1	1	Victoria Bridge Grounds
Northern League 08/01/1898	Victoria United	Arbroath	0	7	Gayfield Park,Arbroath
Northern League 22/01/1898	Victoria United	Montrose	2	1	Victoria Bridge Grounds
Northern League 29/01/1898	Victoria United	Orion	2	0	Cattofield
Northern League 05/02/1898	Victoria United	Dundee Wanderers	1	2	Clepington Park, Dundee
Northern League 26/02/1898	Victoria United	Forfar Athletic	4	3	Station Park, Forfar
Northern League 12/03/1898	Victoria United	Aberdeen	2	1	Victoria Bridge Grounds

Victoria United – Other Games 1897-1898

Competition	Date		Opposition	F	A	Venue
Scottish Qualifying Cup	11/09/1897	Victoria United	Aberdeen	2	1	Victoria Bridge Grounds
Scottish Qualifying Cup	25/09/1897	Victoria United	Orion	2	4	Cattofield
Friendly	09/10/1897	Victoria United	Inverness Clachnacuddin	0	3	Victoria Bridge Grounds
	23/10/1897	Victoria United	Dundee A	6	1	Victoria Bridge Grounds
Friendly	27/11/1897	Victoria United	Aberdeen	1	2	Victoria Bridge Grounds
Friendly	04/12/1897	Victoria United	Forfar Athletic	2	5	Station Park, Forfar
Aberdeenshire Cup 1R	11/12/1897	Victoria United	Aberdeen	3	4	Chanonry
	25/12/1897	Victoria United	Mossend Swifts	4	4	Victoria Bridge Grounds
	01/01/1898	Victoria United	Aberdeen	2	1	Victoria Bridge Grounds
	03/01/1898	Victoria United	Kilmarnock	3	1	Victoria Bridge Grounds
	15/01/1898	Victoria United	Clackmannan	4	2	Victoria Bridge Grounds
	12/02/1898	Victoria United	Aberdeen	5	5	Chanonry
Friendly	19/02/1898	Victoria United	Peterhead	6	7	Peterhead
	05/03/1898	Victoria United	Inverness Caledonian	5	1	Victoria Bridge Grounds
Friendly	19/03/1898	Victoria United	Orion	3	5	Victoria Bridge Grounds
	26/03/1898	Victoria United	Raith Rovers	1	2	Victoria Bridge Grounds

Competition	Date		Opposition	F	A	Venue
Charity Cup	07/04/1898	Victoria United	Orion	2	2	Victoria Bridge Grounds
	09/04/1898	Victoria United	Cameron Highlanders	9	3	Victoria Bridge Grounds
	11/04/1898	Victoria United	Queen's Park	1	3	Victoria Bridge Grounds
Friendly	16/04/1898	Victoria United	Orion	1	2	Cattofield
	19/04/1898	Victoria United	Sheffield United	1	0	Victoria Bridge Grounds
Charity Cup	21/04/1898	Victoria United	Orion	2	1	Victoria Bridge Grounds
Charity Cup Final	28/04/1898	Victoria United	Orion	4	6	Chanonry
Friendly	30/04/1898	Victoria United	Arbroath	2	4	Victoria Bridge Grounds

Aberdeenshire Cup

	Date			F	A	Venue
Aberdeenshire Cup 1R	11/12/1897	Aberdeen	Victoria United	4	3	Chanonry
Aberdeenshire Cup SF	15/01/1898	Aberdeen	Aberdeen University	9	0	Chanonry
Aberdeenshire Cup Final	26/02/1898	Aberdeen	Orion	3	2	Victoria Bridge Grounds

Aberdeen Charity Cup

	Date			F	A	Venue
Charity Cup	07/04/1898	Victoria United	Orion	2	2	Victoria Bridge Grounds
Charity Cup	21/04/1898	Victoria United	Orion	2	1	Victoria Bridge Grounds
Charity Cup	23/04/1898	Orion	Aberdeen	2	1	Victoria Bridge Grounds
Charity Cup Final	28/04/1898	Orion	Victoria United	6	4	Chanonry

1898-1899
Orion domination

O rion bounced back as the city's premier club during the 1898-1899 season by winning the Northern league, the Aberdeenshire Cup and the Rhodesia Cup while Victoria United lifted the Charity Cup to leave Aberdeen F.C. trophy-less once again.

The Orionites made an encouraging start to the season by drawing 3-3 with Hibernian at Cattofield in a friendly match. Hibs had finished third behind Celtic and Rangers in the previous season's Scottish League First Division and would repeat that finishing position in the coming season. When the more serious business of Northern League matches got underway, however, Orion did not make the best of openings, losing 4-0 to Dundee Wanderers at Clepington Park. That, however, proved to be one of just two defeats the Cattofield side would endure throughout what turned out to be an exciting season in which the destiny of the league title would go down to the wire. For the second season in a row the Stripes battled neck-and-neck with Wanderers for the title and by the beginning of May, with just one fixture remaining, the rival clubs were tied together at the top of the table with 21 points apiece. Orion travelled to Arbroath for that final match knowing that a win or draw would give them the top prize. The home side, despite having little to play for other than pride, raced into a 2-0 lead by halftime. Orion dug deep into their reserves and Grant pulled one back in the second half, but then missed the chance to

Front cover of the only known surviving copy of the Orion Observer, published for a game against raith Rovers in October 1898

become a hero when he missed a late penalty, allowing the Red Lichties to hang on for victory. So, Orion and Wanderers were still locked together on the same points tally meaning that a play-off would be required to determine who would be champions. Orion argued for the match to be played in Aberdeen but Wanderers refused so Gayfield was again the chosen venue for the decider. This time the seaside location, which had been the scene of many maulings for Aberdeen clubs in the past, was to prove a happy hunting ground for Orion who won a hard fought game 1-0, James Kane grabbing the vital goal just before the interval.

The Rhodesia Cup

The Stripes also qualified for the First Round of the Scottish Cup in which they faced Second Division Kilmarnock at Cattofield. The Ayrshire visitors enjoyed a 2-0 victory but the Orion men were in no way disgraced.

A new trophy found its way into the Orion collection when the club lifted the Rhodesia Cup. This had been presented by an anonymous donor, a local businessman who had recently returned to the city from southern Africa. The Cup was intended to replace the Gershon Cup competition which had fallen by the wayside the previous season. The same format was to be used, namely, it would be a round robin competition between Orion, Victoria United and Aberdeen. Orion won all four of their matches to become the inaugural winners.

The Aberdeenshire Cup was won for the fourth time, but Orion needed a replay to dispose of Victoria United. By winning the trophy Orion qualified for the Dewar Shield, a competition which featured the county champions of Aberdeenshire, Forfarshire, Perthshire and Stirlingshire. The winners would be named

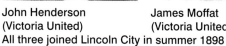

John Henderson   James Moffat   Billy Clark
(Victoria United)   (Victoria United)   (Aberdeen)
All three joined Lincoln City in summer 1898

"Champions of the Northern Counties." Orion were beaten 1-0 by Stirling's King's Park who went on to win the trophy by beating Arbroath 2-1 in the Final.

The only blemish on Orion's local cup record came in the Charity Cup semi final in which they went under by 1-0 to Aberdeen at Central Park.

Orion's success throughout the season was achieved despite having to do without the services of Jim Thom, one of their top players. Thom was suffering from a knee injury and he even travelled to Matlock at one stage to undergo treatment at a private clinic in a bid to cure the problem

After the euphoria of the previous season, Victoria United endured a torrid league campaign. During the summer, the Blues lost former Celtic man John Henderson and his Dumfries-shire colleague James Moffat who, along with Aberdeen's Willie Clark, moved south to join English Second Division Lincoln City. The north east trio seemed to experience mixed fortunes at Lincoln. Henderson scored 10 goals in 82 appearances over the next two seasons while Clark scored nine times in 37 outings. Moffat doesn't appear to have played at all.

United also gave serious consideration to joining the East of Scotland League, with the potential for having regular games against Hearts and Hibs, but decided not to proceed with the venture. The Northern League campaign got off to a promising

start for Vics, with a 3-0 home win over Forfar Athletic, the goals coming from Bobby Ritchie and a double from new signing Runcie who joined from one of the local Combworkers clubs. This match was due to kick-off at 3-30pm but was delayed by 70 minutes because Forfar's train arrived late. The Angus men had changed into their black and blue striped kit in their railway carriage so that there would be no further hold up. Many fans got bored waiting for the game to start, however, so they left the ground and headed for Duthie Park to watch the *"cavalry sports."*

Bobby Ritchie,
Victoria United

Moir,
Victoria United

United's impressive win was followed by two 5-3 defeats, at Montrose (this was the Links Park side's only league win of the season) and Lochee respectively. The next home league outing, on 1st October, was a carnival occasion, with Vics celebrating their previous season's championship victory by unveiling the Northern League flag. The blue banner, which cost £4-4s and was 16ft x 10ft in dimension, was unfurled by Mr Henry Ross, the club president. It was inscribed with the words *'1897-1898 Northern League Championship - Victoria United Football Club'* and in the centre there was a white cockerel standing on a football above a gaelic inscription which, when translated, read *'Cock of the North.'* Arbroath spoiled the celebrations by winning 2-1. The Vics slumped to finish second bottom of the league and had to seek re-election. The Torry men did, nevertheless, win the Charity Cup, crushing Aberdeen

7-1 in the Final at Cattofield. It was United's fifth success in the 11 year history of the competition. They also reached the final of the Aberdeenshire Cup for the fifth time in eight seasons, but lost 5-1 to Orion in a replay after the first game ended goalless.

Having been forced to vacate the Chanonry, Aberdeen moved to Central Park for the season. This was seen as a stop-gap measure until the Whites could find a more permanent home. Negotiations progressed on the possibility of taking over land leased by the Town Council from Mr Knight Erskine at Pittodrie. In the meantime, the club's Northern League campaign got underway with a visit to Arbroath. The north-east men made a promising start with former Dundee and Montrose player Bill Fullerton putting them ahead. The Red Lichties responded in emphatic fashion, however, ramming home seven goals without reply.

The beginning of September marked the first game at Aberdeen's new Central Park ground, previously home to Orion. Dundee Wanderers provided the opposition in a Northern League match. Fullerton again opened the scoring but once again Aberdeen collapsed to a 5-3 defeat. The bad news continued the following week in the opening round of the Scottish Qualifying Cup which ended with a 5-3 defeat by Victoria United at Torry. Vics' player Moir scored a hat-trick but this would ultimately count for nothing as the Whites discovered that United's new signing, Runcie, had played a game for his previous amateur side, the Combworkers, during the summer close season. Playing eleven-a-side games during the official close season was deemed to be a terrible infringement of footballing rules at this time, so Aberdeen lodged a protest which was upheld. The game was replayed at Torry the following Saturday and this time the Whites won 3-1. United were weakened by the absence of defender Kilgour whose father had died, while Aberdeen dropped goalkeeper Ritchie, who had conceded 17 goals in three games, replacing him with defender and former club captain Joe Davidson. The result only extended Aberdeen's stay in the competition by a couple of weeks as they were defeated 5-2 by Orion in the next round. Interestingly, Orion gave Aberdeen a dose of their own medicine by lodging a protest prior to the kick-off about the Whites fielding a player called Thomson, alleging that he, like Runcie, had been involved in an eleven-a-side game during the summer months. As Orion won the match, no further action was taken. The Whites then enjoyed an upsurge in form from the beginning of October until late January when they lost just once in ten games. Unfortunately their next defeat, again at the hands of Orion, came in the Aberdeenshire Cup semi final.

In February the Whites enjoyed an amazing tussle with Forfar Athletic in the Northern League at a muddy Central Park. The Angus men raced into a 3-1 halftime lead which was extended to 4-1 shortly after the break. But a Jim Mackie penalty gave the home supporters some hope. Mackie scored again then Davie Gray levelled the scores before two late goals gave the home side a dramatic victory. That mid-season surge soon dissipated although the Whites did manage to get to the final of the Charity Cup by defeating high-flying Orion 1-0 in a replay. The Final proved to be a total disaster, losing 7-1 to Victoria United. There was to be little joy either in the new Rhodesia Cup which Orion lifted with ease. Aberdeen had led the Orionites 4-2 at halftime but still contrived to lose 5-4 in a match played in a snowstorm.

Jim Mackie –
Aberdeen penalty scorer

Notable Games

Aberdeen 3, Dundee Wanderers 5
Northern League, Central Park, 3rd September 1898

Aberdeen's Bill Fullerton scored straight from the kick-off in this, their first game on their new pitch at Central Park. The match was played in front of *"a sizeable crowd"* who enjoyed Fullerton's early goal. But the home fans were stunned when the visitors equalised straight from the restart. After a spell of end-to-end attacking Wanderers again scored, although Ritchie in the Aberdeen goal thought he had scooped the ball clear before it crossed the line. A spell of rough play followed and it was something of a surprise that no-one was sent off. Wanderers began to dominate, however, and grabbed a third and could have added another but the ball rebounded off the crossbar and post before being cleared. Early in the second period the Dundee men went 4-1 ahead. Soon after it seemed to be all over as Durward netted a fifth for the visitors. Aberdeen responded and Livingston got one back before a scrimmage resulted in the ball again being bundled into the Wanderers net. The Whites continued to press and bombarded the visiting goalkeeper but *"the ball went everywhere but between the uprights"* and there was no further scoring.

Aberdeen - Ritchie, McConnochie, J. Davidson, Mackie, Henderson, Thomson, Livingstone, Cameron, Fullerton, Gray, Shiach.

Dundee Wanderers - Roberts, Robertson, Ferguson, McCulloch, Crawford, Waterson, Durward, Graham, McDonald, Ferguson, McInroy.

Referee - Mr. Peter Simpson

Orion 0, Kilmarnock 2
Scottish Cup First Round, Cattofield, 14th January 1899

Orion reached the First Round of the national competition via the Qualifying Cup and were drawn at home to Kilmarnock. The Ayrshire side would go on to win that season's Scottish Second Division title without losing a game all season, so the Aberdeen men knew they would be in for a stern challenge. Killie travelled north the day before the game and stayed overnight in Stonehaven, prompting one local reporter to speculate:*"would the temptations of our gay city have been too much for the men of Ayrshire?"* Orion kicked off playing towards the Cattofield House end of the ground in front of a *"record crowd"* which included a fair number of Killie fans who had travelled to Aberdeen by special train. The visitors took the lead through a Findlay effort which deceived Orion goalkeeper Watson who appeared to be blinded by the low sun. The home side showed great determination, however, and went on the offensive, but their efforts came to nothing as the ball hit the upright *"time after time."*Orion's failure to finish off their attacking moves proved costly as Findlay again scored for the visitors before the interval. There was controversy early in the second half when Orion's McPherson blasted beyond Craig in the Killie goal, but the ball hit the net and rebounded out with the goalkeeper then punching it behind. The referee awarded a corner much to Orion's disgust.

Orion - Watson, Livingstone, Ross, Currie, Low, Wilson, Webster, J. McPherson, Barron, Stopani, Hogg.

Kilmarnock - Craig, Busby, Brown, D. McPherson, Anderson, Johnstone, Maitland, Campbell, Reid, Muir, Findlay.
Referee - Mr King, Queen's Park

Orion 5. Victoria United 1
Aberdeenshire Cup Final Replay, Cattofield, 4th March 1899

Snow was falling but that didn't prevent a crowd of 4,000 packing into Cattofield for the Aberdeenshire Cup Final Replay. The first game had ended 0-0 and another close encounter was expected. Vics fielded the same team as in the first game the previous week while the only change in the Orion line-up was Barron's appearance at centre forward in place of Webster. Hogg gave Orion an early lead then Grant converted a penalty after McPherson was brought down by Thain. There was no more scoring before the interval. Orion continued to dominate after the break and Thain conceded another penalty when he handled the ball, Grant again converting. McPherson made it 4-0 before United finally broke clear and grabbed a consolation goal. Before the game restarted a spectator ran onto the field but he was apprehended by Orion's John Low and was removed from the ground. Orion added a fifth before the final whistle to secure the trophy which was presented to the winners in the Northern Hotel after the game.

Victoria United - Findlay, Kilgour, Thain, Dundas, Durie, Thomson, McHardy, Gardiner, Mckenzie, Watson, Ritchie.
Orion - Watson, Livingstone, Ross, Currie, Low, Wilson, McPherson, Grant, Barron, Kane, Hogg.
Referee - Mr. Dixon, Wishaw.

Victoria United 7, Aberdeen 1
Charity Cup Final, Cattofield , 6th May 1899,

Vics kicked off playing towards Cattofield Place and took the lead through Taylor within the opening 60 seconds. Taylor soon made it 2-0 then Dundas stretched United's lead to three. Ritchie made it 4-0 and Gardiner further demoralised Aberdeen with a fifth. The Whites responded and Livingstone got the ball between the posts only for his effort to be disallowed for offside. Further goals from Watson and McHardy finished the contest before halftime was reached. United eased off in the second period and Mackie grabbed a late consolation for the Whites when

scoring from the penalty spot.

Victoria United - Findlay, Kilgour, Thain, Dundas, Fraser, Thomson, McHardy, Gardiner, Watson, Taylor, Ritchie.

Aberdeen - Ritchie, McConnochie, Mackie, Cameron, Henderson, Thomson, Livingstone, Mackay, Fullerton, Gray, Shiach.

Referee - Mr. Blair, Glasgow.

Orion 1 Dundee Wanderers 0
Northern League Championship Play Off,
Gayfield Park, Arbroath, 13th May 1889
With both clubs tied on 21 points a play-off was necessary to decide which would become league champions. The match was played at Arbroath's Gayfield Park on a Monday evening and a crowd of between 3,000 and 4,000 turned out.

Wanderers applied some early pressure and James Watson in the Orion goal had to be on top form to keep the Dundonians at bay.

There was a moment of controversy when

Victoria United goalkeeper Findlay

Wanderer's full-back Allan fired a freekick into the Orion net but it was disallowed because the referee had indicated it was an indirect kick and no-one touched the ball. Both sides had their chances, but it was Orion who took the lead before the interval, John Kane netting to the great delight of the Aberdeen club's travelling support. After the break both sides continued to attack and at times tempers flared with Orion's John Low and Wanderer's Graham getting stuck into each other on one occasion. Wanderers piled on the pressure in the closing stages but Orion held on to claim the title for the second time in three seasons. Wanderers afterwards lodged a protest against some of the referee's decisions but this came to nothing.

Orion goalkeeper
James Watson

253

Orion - Watson, Livingstone, Ross, Currie, Low, Wilson, MacPherson, Grant, Thom, Kane, Hogg

Dundee Wanderers - Roberts, Allan, Ferguson, Neave, Crawford, McColl, McLean, Graham, Robertson, Donald, McInroy

Referee - J. Quarns, Glasgow

Northern League 1898-1899

		P	W	D	L	F	A	Pts
1	Orion	14	9	3	2	46	26	21
2	Dundee Wanderers	14	10	1	3	46	27	21
3	Arbroath	14	8	1	5	45	33	17
4	Forfar Athletic	14	7	2	5	44	33	16
5	Aberdeen	14	6	1	7	39	38	13
6	Lochee United	14	5	2	7	28	40	12
7	Victoria United	14	4	2	8	25	36	10
8	Montrose	14	1	0	13	24	64	2

Aberdeen – Northern League 1898-1899

	Date		Opposition	F	A	Venue
Northern League	20/08/1898	Aberdeen	Arbroath	1	7	Gayfield Park
Northern League	03/09/1898	Aberdeen	Dundee Wanderers	3	5	Central Park
Northern League	01/10/1898	Aberdeen	Montrose	4	0	Central Park
Northern League	29/10/1898	Aberdeen	Orion	3	3	Central Park
Northern League	12/11/1898	Aberdeen	Montrose	3	1	Links Park, Montrose
Northern League	19/11/1898	Aberdeen	Forfar Athletic *	4	1	Station Park,Forfar
Northern League	26/11/1898	Aberdeen	Lochee United	7	2	Central Park
Northern League	07/01/1899	Aberdeen	Arbroath	5	2	Central Park
Northern League	04/02/1899	Aberdeen	Victoria United	5	0	Central Park
Northern League	11/02/1899	Aberdeen	Orion	0	2	Cattofield
Northern League	18/02/1899	Aberdeen	Forfar Athletic	6	4	Central Park
Northern League	04/03/1899	Aberdeen	Dundee Wanderers	0	3	Dundee
Northern League	15/04/1899	Aberdeen	Lochee United	0	2	Lochee
Northern League	22/04/1899	Aberdeen	Victoria United	1	3	Victoria Bridge Grounds
Northern League	13/05/1899	Aberdeen	Forfar Athletic	1	4	Station Park,Forfar

* The League game between Aberdeen and Forfar at Station Park on 19/11/1898 was replayed on 13/05/1899 following a protest on the grounds of darkness.

Aberdeen – Other Games 1898-1899

Competition	Date		Opposition	F	A	Venue
	15/08/1898	Aberdeen	Victoria United	1	0	Victoria Bridge Grounds
	27/08/1898	Aberdeen	Peterhead	3	1	Recreation Park, Peterhead
Scottish Qualifying Cup	10/09/1898	Aberdeen	Victoria United	3	5	Victoria Bridge Grounds
Scottish Qualifying Cup	17/09/1898	Aberdeen	Victoria United	3	1	Victoria Bridge Grounds
Scottish Qualifying Cup	24/09/1898	Aberdeen	Orion	2	5	Central Park
Friendly	08/10/1898	Aberdeen	Orion	1	2	Cattofield
Friendly	15/10/1898	Aberdeen	Forres Mechanics	4	1	Forres
	22/10/1898	Aberdeen	Fair City Athletic	6	4	Central Park
Aberdeenshire Cup	10/12/1898	Aberdeen	Fraserburgh Wanderers	11	1	Central Park
Rhodesia Cup	24/12/1898	Aberdeen	Victoria United	5	0	Central Park
	05/01/1899	Aberdeen	Dundee			
Friendly	14/01/1899	Aberdeen	Montrose	0	4	Links Park,Montrose
	21/01/1899	Aberdeen	Orion	6	5	Cattofield
Aberdenshire Cup SF	28/01/1899	Aberdeen	Orion	1	2	Cattofield
Rhodesia Cup	11/03/1899	Aberdeen	Victoria United	2	4	Victoria Bridge Grounds
Rhodesia Cup	18/03/1899	Aberdeen	Orion	4	5	Central Park
Rhodesia Cup	01/04/1899	Aberdeen	Orion	1	5	Cattofield
Friendly	08/04/1899	Aberdeen	Victoria United	2	0	Victoria Bridge Grounds
Charity Cup	27/04/1899	Aberdeen	Orion	1	1	Cattofield
	01/05/1899	Aberdeen	Celtic	1	5	Central Park
Charity Cup	04/05/1899	Aberdeen	Orion	1	0	Central Park
Charity Cup Final	06/05/1899	Aberdeen	Victoria United	1	7	Cattofield

Orion – Northern League 1898-1899

	Date		Opposition	F	A	Venue
Northern League	20/08/1898	Orion	Dundee Wanderers	0	4	Clepington Road
Northern League	27/08/1898	Orion	Arbroath	3	2	Cattofield
Northern League	03/09/1898	Orion	Lochee United	2	2	St Margaret's Park
Northern League	17/09/1898	Orion	Forfar Athletic	3	2	Cattofield
Northern League	01/10/1898	Orion	Forfar Athletic	3	1	Forfar
Northern League	15/10/1898	Orion	Victoria United	4	2	Cattofield
Northern League	29/10/1898	Orion	Aberdeen	3	3	Central Park
Northern League	19/11/1898	Orion	Montrose	9	3	Cattofield
Northern League	07/01/1899	Orion	Lochee United	4	0	Cattofield
Northern League	04/02/1899	Orion	Montrose	7	3	Montrose
Northern League	11/02/1899	Orion	Aberdeen	2	0	Cattofield
Northern League	08/04/1899	Orion	Dundee Wanderers	4	1	Cattofield
Northern League	15/04/1899	Orion	Victoria United	1	1	Victoria Bridge Grounds
Northern League	01/05/1889	Orion	Arbroath	1	2	Gayfield Park, Arbroath
Northern League Play Off	13/05/1889	Orion	Dundee Wanderers	1	0	Gayfield Park, Arbroath

Orion - Other Games 1898-1899

Competition	Date		Opposition	F	A	Venue
	16/08/1898	Orion	Hibernian	3	3	Cattofield
	25/08/1898	Orion	Victoria United	0	2	Victoria Bridge Grounds
Scottish Qualifying Cup	10/09/1898	Orion	Peterhead	4	0	Peterhead
Scottish Qualifying Cup	24/09/1898	Orion	Aberdeen	5	2	Central Park
	26/09/1898	Orion	Victoria United	0	4	Cattofield
Friendly	08/10/1898	Orion	Aberdeen	2	1	Cattofield
	22/10/1898	Orion	Raith Rovers	5	1	Cattofield
Scottish Qualifying Cup	05/11/1898	Orion	Arbroath	0	1	Cattofield
Rhodesia Cup	12/11/1898	Orion	Victoria United	2	0	Victoria Bridge Grounds

Competition	Date		Opposition	F	A	Venue
	26/11/1898	Orion	Elgin City	2	3	Elgin
	03/12/1898	Orion	Victoria United	2	0	Victoria Bridge Grounds
	10/12/1898	Orion	St Andrews University	4	1	Cattofield
Scottish Cup 1R	14/01/1899	Orion	Kilmarnock	0	2	Cattofield
	21/01/1899	Orion	Aberdeen	5	6	Cattofield
Aberdeenshire Cup SF	28/01/1899	Orion	Aberdeen	2	1	Cattofield
	18/02/1899	Orion	Stonehaven	5	1	Urie
Aberdeenshire Cup Final	25/02/1899	Orion	Victoria United	0	0	Cattofield
Aberdeenshire Cup Final	04/03/1899	Orion	Victoria United	5	1	Cattofield
Rhodesia Cup	18/03/1899	Orion	Aberdeen	5	4	Central Park
Rhodesia Cup	01/04/1899	Orion	Aberdeen	5	1	Cattofield
Dewar Challenge Shield	22/04/1899	Orion	King's Park	0	1	Stirling
Charity Cup	27/04/1899	Orion	Aberdeen	1	1	Cattofield
Friendly	29/04/1899	Orion	Elgin City	7	1	Cattofield
Charity Cup	04/05/1899	Orion	Aberdeen	0	1	Central Park
Rhodesia Cup	10/05/1899	Orion	Victoria United	3	0	Cattofield

Victoria United - Northern League 1898-1899

	Date		Opposition	F	A	Venue
Northern League	20/08/1898	Victoria United	Forfar Athletic	3	0	Victoria Bridge Grounds
Northern League	27/08/1898	Victoria United	Montrose	3	5	Links Park,Montrose
Northern League	24/09/1898	Victoria United	Lochee United	3	5	St. Margaret's Park, Dundee
Northern League	01/10/1898	Victoria United	Arbroath	1	2	Victoria Bridge Grounds
Northern League	08/10/1898	Victoria United	Dundee Wanderers	2	2	Victoria Bridge Grounds
Northern League	15/10/1898	Victoria United	Orion	2	4	Cattofield
Northern League	22/10/1898	Victoria United	Montrose	2	1	Victoria Bridge Grounds
Northern League	29/10/1898	Victoria United	Dundee Wanderers	1	3	Clepington Road
Northern League	04/02/1899	Victoria United	Aberdeen	0	5	Central Park

Date		Opposition	F	A	Venue
Northern League 11/02/1899	Victoria United	Arbroath	1	5	Gayfield Park, Arbroath
Northern League 18/03/1899	Victoria United	Forfar Athletic	1	2	Station Park,Forfar
Northern League 15/04/1899	Victoria United	Orion	1	1	Victoria Bridge Grounds
Northern League 22/04/1899	Victoria United	Aberdeen	3	1	Victoria Bridge Grounds
Northern League 29/04/1899	Victoria United	Lochee United	2	0	Victoria Bridge Grounds

Victoria United - Other Games 1898-1899

Competition	Date		Opposition	F	A	Venue
	15/08/1898	Victoria United	Aberdeen	0	1	Victoria Bridge Grounds
	25/08/1898	Victoria United	Orion	2	0	Victoria Bridge Grounds
	03/09/1898	Victoria United	Inverness Thistle	1	4	Kingsmills
Scottish Qualifying Cup	10/09/1898	Victoria United	Aberdeen	5	3	Victoria Bridge Grounds
Scottish Qualifying Cup	17/09/1898	Victoria United	Aberdeen	1	3	Victoria Bridge Grounds
	26/09/1898	Victoria United	Orion	4	0	Cattofield
Rhodesia Cup	12/11/1898	Victoria United	Orion	0	2	Victoria Bridge Grounds
	03/12/1898	Victoria United	Orion	0	2	Victoria Bridge Grounds
	10/12/1898	Victoria United	Mossend Swifts	4	1	Victoria Bridge Grounds
Rhodesia Cup	24/12/1898	Victoria United	Aberdeen	0	5	Central Park
	03/01/1899	Victoria United	East Stirlingshire	2	2	Victoria Bridge Grounds
	04/01/1899	Victoria United	Port Glasgow	1	1	Victoria Bridge Grounds
Aberdenshire Cup SF	21/01/1899	Victoria United	Peterhead	6	3	Peterhead
Friendly	28/01/1889	Victoria United	Montrose	2	1	Victoria Bridge Grounds
	18/02/1899	Victoria United	Clachnacuddin	4	1	Victoria Bridge Grounds
Aberdeenshire Cup Final	25/02/1899	Victoria United	Orion	0	0	Cattofield
Aberdeenshire Cup Final	04/03/1899	Victoria United	Orion	1	5	Cattofield
Rhodesia Cup	11/03/1899	Victoria United	Aberdeen	4	2	Victoria Bridge Grounds
Friendly	08/04/1899	Victoria United	Aberdeen	0	2	Victoria Bridge Grounds
Charity Cup	26/04/1899	Victoria United	Peterhead	5	0	Victoria Bridge Grounds

Competition	Date		Opposition	F	A	Venue
Charity Cup Final	06/05/1899	Victoria United	Aberdeen	7	1	Cattofield
Rhodesia Cup	10/05/1899	Victoria United	Orion	0	3	Cattofield
Friendly	13/05/1899	Victoria United	Fair City Athletic	3	1	Victoria Bridge Grounds
Friendly	15/05/1899	Victoria United	Kilmarnock	0	4	Victoria Bridge Grounds

Notes: The Scottish Qualifying Cup tie on 10/09/1898 was replayed following a protest

Aberdeenshire Cup 1898-1899

	Date			F	A	Venue
Aberdeenshire Cup	10/12/1898	Aberdeen	Fraserburgh Wanderers	11	1	Central Park
Aberdenshire Cup SF	21/01/1899	Victoria United	Peterhead	6	3	Peterhead
Aberdenshire Cup SF	28/01/1899	Orion	Aberdeen	2	1	Cattofield
Aberdeenshire Cup Final	25/02/1899	Orion	Victoria United	0	0	Cattofield
Aberdeenshire Cup Final Replay	04/03/1899	Orion	Victoria United	5	1	Cattofield

Aberdeen Charity Cup 1898-1899

	Date			F	A	Venue
Charity Cup	15/04/1899	Peterhead	Fraserburgh	1	1	Recreation Park
Charity Cup	26/04/1899	Victoria United	Peterhead	5	0	Victoria Bridge Grounds
Charity Cup	27/04/1899	Orion	Aberdeen	1	1	Cattofield
Charity Cup	04/05/1899	Aberdeen	Orion	1	0	Central Park
Charity Cup Final	06/05/1899	Victoria United	Aberdeen	7	1	Cattofield

Note: No result found for the Peterhead-Fraserburgh replay

Rhodesia Cup 1898-1899

	Date			F	A	Venue
Rhodesia Cup	12/11/1898	Victoria United	Orion	0	2	Victoria Bridge Grounds
Rhodesia Cup	24/12/1898	Aberdeen	Victoria United	5	0	Central Park
Rhodesia Cup	11/03/1899	Victoria United	Aberdeen	4	2	Victoria Bridge Grounds

	Date			F	A	Venue
Rhodesia Cup	18/03/1899	Aberdeen	Orion	4	5	Central Park
Rhodesia Cup	01/04/1899	Orion	Aberdeen	5	1	Cattofield
Rhodesia Cup	10/05/1899	Orion	Victoria United	3	0	Cattofield

Rhodesia Cup		P	W	D	L	F	A	Pts
1	Orion	4	4	0	0	15	5	8
2	Aberdeen	4	1	0	3	12	14	2
3	Victoria United	4	1	0	3	4	12	2

1899-1900
Opening of Pittodrie

Thsis was a momentous season with Aberdeen moving into their new grounds at Pittodrie Park which soon afterwards hosted its first international match, while Victoria United threw away a wonderful opportunity to win the Northern League title for the second time in three years. On the eve of the season, however, the main talking point within the local footballing fraternity centred on the prospects of the city having a club in the Scottish First Division. The barrier to this goal was, according to sources in the Central Belt, as much a geographical one as anything to do with the footballing ability of the city's teams or the prospects for the financial success of an Aberdeen club within the national competition. It was, they said, simply too far for other league clubs to travel to the north east on a regular basis. That was the excuse being trotted out, no matter how feeble it was, as these same clubs seemed happy to travel North to pick up a healthy appearance fee for playing friendly matches, so what would be so much more difficult about making the same journey on league business? Aberdeen F.C. were, however, beginning to show serious signs of ambition by deciding to set up home on their new ground at Pittodrie in the east end of the city. The Aberdeen Journal described in detail the work that had been carried out to bring this plan into reality, stating: *"The ground has been secured on a 10 year lease from Mr Knight Erskine of Pittodrie - though on a sub-tenancy from the corporation at first. It is 4.5 acres in extent. An area of 156 yards by 85 yards has been levelled and the playing pitch measures 110 yards by 70 yards. An excellent cycle track and cricket pitch are in course of formation. The ground will also be admirably adapted for such gatherings as the Hospital Saturday and Police Sports. It has been enclosed by a strong wall and paling and the total cost of the work has been about £1,000. The engineers for the laying out of the ground were Messrs Beattie and Macdonald, Bridge Street, and the contractors were: for the laying out of the ground and erecting enclosing wall, Mr Peter Tawse; outside paling, Mr Thomson, Stonehaven; grandstand and paling round the pitch, Mr J. Farquhar, Broomhill Road, Aberdeen."*
The newspaper also carried a detailed report on the preparations for the first match

on the new ground, against Dumbarton on 2nd September 1899. It stated: *"Arrangements have now practically been completed for the opening, on Saturday first, of the new ground of the Aberdeen Football Club at Merkland Road East. For a number of years the club occupied ground at Chanonry, now acquired in connection with the botanic garden which is being laid out for the university. Having been obliged to seek new quarters, the club were fortunate in securing from the corporation a ten year lease of an extensive area at Merkland Road East, and this has been enclosed and laid out in the most approved fashion. A grandstand capable of accommodating 1,000 people has been erected, and the natural terraces that run round the ground are so admirably adapted for the convenience of a crowd that 10,000 spectators will be able to see every part of the field of play. By carrying out a certain amount of banking, which the club proposes to do ultimately, equally satisfactory accommodation will be provided for 35,000 spectators. Pittodrie Park, as the new ground has been named, will be opened by a friendly match between Dumbarton and the Aberdeen. The magistrates and Town Council have been invited to be present, and Baillie Lyon has consented to formally declare Pittodrie Park open. Invitations have also been sent to all the leading supporters of football in the city, each ticket admitting a lady and gentleman, and the ladies who are to take charge of the stalls at the club's bazaar are expected to be present. The services of the band of the 1st V.B. Gordon Highlanders, under Bandmate Killee, have been secured for the opening ceremony."*

Dumbarton were no longer the major force they had been in earlier years and Aberdeen easily won the opening game, 7-1, with Alex Shiach claiming his place

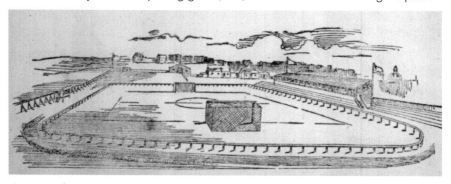

Sketch of Pittodrie as it was for its opening in 1899

in local footballing history by scoring the first goal on the new pitch. The following week saw the first competitive game at Pittodrie with Victoria United beating the home side 1-0 in a Scottish Qualifying Cup tie, McHardy grabbing the only goal of the match. Not everyone was delighted with the choice of name for the new ground, with the football reporter from Bon Accord magazine suggesting that surely a better name could be found. The same writer complained that the roof of the new grandstand sloped the wrong way: *"When standing at the back of the stand you can only see part of the playing field,"* he said. Nor was he too impressed by the positioning of the press box in the new stadium: *"What have we poor scribes done that all winter we will have to face a north wind?"* He also raised an issue which has come back into focus in more recent times regarding the provision of seating which until this point had been in short supply at local grounds. He stated: *"Of course the seats are for sitting on, but the football spectator is generally too excited to take things so calmly."*

The following month a bazaar, referred to in the newspaper report above, was held in the Music Hall as a fund-raiser to help offset the cost of acquiring and laying out Pittodrie. This bazaar featured *"stalls, marionettes, concerts, a shooting jungle, and Messrs Walker and Company's famous cinematograph."* The cinematograph showed pictures from the Aberdeen-Victoria United cup tie and was described in glowing terms: *"The picture is full of animation, with exciting incidents at goal, and brings out the fine play of the goalkeeper, while the play throughout the game can be followed with all its keenness on the part of the forwards, the half backs and backs, as well as the watchfulness of the referee."* The bands of the 1st Aberdeen Artillery Volunteers and 1st Aberdeenshire Royal Engineers (Volunteers) were to perform while the palmist 'the Original Gypsy Queen' was also to be there and a prize draw to win for a pony and trap and a bicycle was another major attraction.

So, Pittodrie was operational and there was tremendous excitement in the city in February when, thanks largely to the efforts of Aberdeen F.C. official Harry S. Wylie, the new stadium hosted the Scotland-Wales international. Mr James Philip, President of the Aberdeenshire F.A. later presented Wylie with an inscribed gold match in recognition of his services to football over many years.

Harry Wylie, Aberdeen F.C.

The Welsh team arrived in Aberdeen by train on the eve of the match and the players, who stayed at the Royal Hotel, were taken on a sight-seeing tour of the area. The Scotland squad, which was based at the Imperial Hotel, arrived later in the day. Both sides attended the Palace Theatre in the evening. A crowd of 12,000, the biggest for a football match in Aberdeen, turned up for the game which Scotland won 5-2.

The opening of Pittodrie was without doubt a key development in the history of football in the city, but it had minimal impact on Aberdeen F.C.'s level of performances. The Whites did enjoy their best season to date in the Northern League, and for a long time it looked as though they might have a chance of landing the title for the first time. It was not to be, however, and they finally had to settle for third position, two points behind Dundee Wanderers and a point adrift of Victoria United.

Aberdeen lost to Peterhead in the County Cup in circumstances which suggested a rift between some of the club's players and its committee. The Whites had to play with a weakened side following the non appearance of R. McKay, an amateur player on the club's books who, it was claimed *"plays when it suits him."* McKay didn't appear at Aberdeen station for the journey north but his replacement, McIntosh, was there and available to travel. The Whites officials decided they would buy McIntosh a ticket to Kittybrewster station, rather than for Peterhead. This was in the hope that McKay would show up and join the train at Kittybrewster, and if so, McIntosh would be sent back home as he would no longer be required. McIntosh wasn't too impressed by this arrangement so he stormed off. McKay, of course, wasn't at Kittybrewster, so the dispirited Whites had to draft in a non-playing member of the club to make up the eleven. It was little surprise they lost 3-2. The season was to end with Pittodrie's trophy cabinet sitting disappointingly empty.

At the beginning of November football fans were shocked to learn that Aberdeen F.C's centre half, Joe Davidson, had been sent to prison for assaulting a water bailiff. Davidson, a mechanic-engineer, who lived at 44 Canal Terrace, Woodside, committed the offence on the south bank of the River Don, opposite Mugiemoss paper mills. He was accused of throwing large stones at the bailiff, James Third. Davidson and three other men had been on the river bank at about midnight one night in October when they were seen 'sniggering' salmon. The bailiff challenged them, but the men ran off although Davidson stopped to throw stones, two of which struck Mr Third on the shoulder and chest. Davidson was imprisoned for 21 days.

Lord Provost Fleming seemed determined to get immersed in the local football scene and in August 1899 he offered to donate a cup or shield to be played for annually by the senior clubs in the city. The Aberdeenshire F.A. decided that the Charity Cup be withdrawn and that a competition for the Lord Provost's Shield would take its place. The Lord Provost immediately commissioned a trophy and by February 1900 an announcement appeared in the Aberdeen Journal stating that the shield was to be put on display in the window of Councillor Glass at 54 Union Street. A detailed description of the impressive trophy was given: *"The trophy is a circular embossed shield, mounted in a very handsome oak frame. The centre portion represents a field in play. The figures of the players are full of vigour and action and convey a lifelike picture of the game of football at an exciting period. Above the field is an admirable representation of the Market Cross in Castle Street and at the bottom are the arms of the city, flanked by figures of Charity supplying the wants of young and old. Encircling the field is a clear silver band setting forth that this is "*The Lord Provost Fleming Charity Football Trophy Aberdeen 1900. *"On the outer embossed circle encompassing the shield is a fringe of Scotch thistles, most admirably portrayed, and at intervals appear six representations of the head of Hercules, the god of strength. On the oak frame, set in a circle around the outer edge of the silver centre, are 12 circular bisses intended for the name of the winning team, which will be inscribed annually. In every respect the trophy is not only a work of art and a triumph of the* *silversmith's skill, but to the minutest detail is characterised by sound, honest workmanship. The members of the winning team will each be presented with a token of the victory by the Lord Provost. The shield will be under the control of the association and the Local Charity Committee who have been enabled in the past to allocate a considerable amount of money to different institutions in the city."* The Provost also raised his profile amongst the footballing public at the start of the season when he unfurled the Northern League championship flag before Orion's opening league match against Arbroath. Surprisingly this was the first time Mr. Fleming had attended a football match and it was reported that he left at half-time! The game ended 2-2, McKernan and Hogg scoring for Orion. It wasn't to be a great season for the champions as they slumped to finish in sixth position, winning just four of their 14 games. In quite a tight league it was drawn games, five in total, which proved to be Orion's ultimate undoing. Off the field there was also sad news for the Kittybrewster club's followers with the announcement in August 1899 of the death of Mr James Russell. Although he never played football, Russell, who was just 31, occupied almost every official position with Orion and he was the editor of the club's magazine, the Orion Observer, which was one of the pioneering club publications in Scottish football. Russell was a previous president of the Aberdeenshire F.A. and served as a delegate to the S.F.A.

Orion made some progress in the Scottish Qualifying Cup, defeating Peterhead 6-3, Victoria United 3-0 (after a 1-1 draw) and Forres Mechanics 3-2 to reach the quarter finals where they met Arbroath. The Aberdeen side, playing down the Cattofield slope and with the wind behind them, led 3-1 at the interval thanks to two own goals and a disputed penalty. The Red Lichties rallied in the second period, however, eventually running out 5-3 winners. Reaching the last eight of the competition was enough, nevertheless, for Orion to take up a place in the Scottish Cup in which they again faced Forres Mechanics. The Highland side, with home advantage, held the Aberdonians to a 1-1 draw but Orion skipped through to the next round by winning the return game 4-1. That earned them a daunting trip to Kilmarnock for a second round tie which ended in a predictable hammering. When Killie visited Kittybrewster the previous year, there was little between the sides and the visitors ran out narrow 2-0 victors. This time, Orion's long trip to Ayrshire seemed to drain their energy and enthusiasm and the home side romped to an embarrassingly easy 10-0 victory.

The Stripes were dumped out of the Aberdeenshire Cup by Victoria United and lost to Aberdeen in the Lord Provost Fleming Shield. There was to be some late season consolation, however, when they held on to the Rhodesia Cup following a protracted competition which ended with a 2-0 win over the Whites.
It is difficult to work out the format for this season's Rhodesia Cup competition but it appears this was played as a round robin competition as was the case in 1898-1899. After each side had played four games, however, all three were tied on four points. It then appears that a decision was taken for Aberdeen to play Victoria United in a play-off or semi final, the winners to meet Orion in the Final. Aberdeen and Vics drew 4-4 at Pittodrie but played again shortly afterwards at Cattofield. This was a bruising encounter and *"the game practically resolved itself into a series of free fights, the culminating point being reached when Mackie, the Aberdeen back, was hit on the head by a stone thrown by a spectator."* The sides again couldn't be separated, the score at 90 minutes being 3-3. A Kilgour penalty had given Vics the lead but Alex Shiach and Hugh Livingstone put the Whites in front before the interval. McHardy equalised then Burnett put Vics 3-2 ahead. Kilgour then had a chance to seal the match but shot wide from the penalty spot before Livingstone grabbed a late equaliser. A further 10 minutes of extra time was then played during which Livingstone completed his hat-trick to give Aberdeen victory. After all that effort, the Whites then lost 2-0 to Orion in the Final.

Orion's prospects during the season hadn't been helped by the intensification of the Anglo-Boer War which broke out in October 1899. Regular first team players John Kane and James Watson had to join their regiments (1st Battalion Gordon Highlanders) to fight in the African conflict. Both soldiers were sent warm underwear at Christmas as a gift from the football club. Among those reported wounded in action around this time was another former local footballer, Sgt H. G. Hickie who had played as a defender in the Victoria United side that won the Aberdeenshire Cup in 1892-1893. That same season he represented the Aberdeenshire select against Orion in the floodlit benefit match for the family of Culter player William Wallace who died as a result of an injury sustained in a local match. At the New Year's Day game between Victoria United and Aberdeen a collection was taken from the crowd in aid of the *"Those Left at Home Fund"* which looked after the dependents of Gordon Highlanders. Most local clubs showed support for the war effort by taking charitable collections at games. Another Orion stalwart, John Low, had also set sail for South Africa where it was reported he had joined the Cape mounted police.

Victoria United suffered an agonising end to a season which started so full of promise. The Torry Blues showed decent form throughout the Northern League campaign and by the middle of March had worked themselves into a wonderful position. The Vics sat second in the table, one point behind Dundee Wanderers who had completed all their games. Vics had two games to play, away to Lochee United and at home to Forfar Athletic. One win from these matches would give them the title and even one draw would ensure a tie with Wanderers and a possible play-off. As it was, they managed neither, losing 3-0 to Lochee and 2-1 to Forfar. Their only consolation was a victory over Peterhead in the Aberdeenshire Cup Final at Pittodrie. To reach the Final the Blues had to overcome a stuffy Orion side in a bad tempered game at Torry. United's scrappy 1-0 win attracted some scathing criticism in the Bon Accord magazine. The report of the game blasted both sides, saying: *"The amount of impotence displayed by both elevens we have only once seen equalled, and that was by the ladies football team. Aberdeen football is on the down grade and no mistake. There will have to be a vast improvement soon, for the public will get tired of wasting their money in paying to see such caricatures of the game as that which was served up to them on Saturday."* Vics had also crushed Fraserburgh Wanderers 7-1 in an earlier round. During the second half of that game United 'keeper Findlay played outfield and scored one of the Vics' goals.

In March there were rumours that Victoria United and Orion were discussing the possibility of a merger. That idea fell on stony ground, however, when it was alleged that the new club would still be called Orion! At the same time, there was also talk of United looking for a new ground in the vicinity of Holburn Street station as doubts emerged over the continued availability of the Victoria Bridge Grounds. The Lord Provost Fleming Shield charity competition was left undecided. In the first semi final at Torry, an Alex Shiach goal gave Aberdeen a 1-0 win over Orion. A railing round the pitch collapsed during the game but no-one was injured. Victoria United made heavy weather of defeating Peterhead 3-1 in the second semi final at Cattofield although the result made up for the disastrous 8-2 loss the Torry men suffered in a friendly match against the Blue Toon at Recreation Park a few weeks earlier. The final was scheduled for a date in April but Aberdeen then decided to invite Celtic to Pittodrie for a friendly on the appointed day. The Whites suggested an alternative date in late May but this wasn't acceptable to Victoria United, so the match wasn't played.

On a lighter note, a bizarre match was held at Pittodrie in April when Aberdeen and Victoria United players wore fancy dress costumes in a benefit for St Peter's Catholic Union. It ended 3-3.

There was some evidence, however, that local football fans were growing weary of seeing the local sides playing each other so often, no matter what the reason. There was a growing demand for greater variety and more excitement. Aberdeen and Victoria United had played each other 10 times during the season, Orion and Victoria United met eight times and Aberdeen and Orion clashed on six occasions. Such a frequency of meetings wasn't healthy. This might explain why no action appears to have been taken following an announcement in the local press, in October 1899, that a meeting of representatives of Aberdeen, Orion and Peterhead clubs in Ellon had concluded with a decision to form a county league to consist of the following clubs:-Aberdeen, Orion, Melrose, Peterhead and Fraserburgh Caledonian. Nothing seems to have come from this proposal.

Notable Games

Aberdeen 7, Dumbarton 1

Opening of Pittodrie Park, 2nd September 1899

Alex Shiach had the honour of scoring the first goal on the new park and shortly afterwards Fullerton made it 2-0. It was all going the home side's way and Gray added two more within the space of a couple of minutes to give the Whites a 4-0 halftime lead. Shiach made an amazing start to the second period with two quick goals to give him his hat-trick. Millar pulled one back for the visitors before Aberdeen grabbed a seventh thanks to an own goal by a Dumbarton defender.

Aberdeen - Bisset, Henderson, Mackie, Cameron, Wilson, Thomson, Livingstone, Mackay, Fullerton, Gray, Shiach.

Dumbarton - Millar, Thomson, Mitchell, Gillan, Richmond, Kennedy, McLasky,

Campbell, McCormack, G. Millar, Fullerton
Referee - Mr, James Philip

Aberdeen 0, Victoria United 1
Scottish Qualifying Cup First Round, Pittodrie Park, 9th September 1899

This was the first competitive match played at Pittodrie in front of *"an enormous concourse of spectators."* The game ebbed and flowed with both sides enjoying spells on top, but goalkeepers Bisset and Findlay were on top form. The Blues edged ahead early in the second half through McHardy and although the home side pressed hard, with Shiach in particular always threatening to score, the visitors held on for a fine win. Shiach's play, although delightful to the eye, was describes as being at times *"too fancy."*

Aberdeen – Bisset, Mackie, Skene, Henderson, Wilson, Thomson, Livingstone, Mackay, Fullerton, Gray, Shiach.

Victoria United – Findlay, Thain, Marshall, Dundas, Craig, Thomson, McHardy, Watson, Burnett, Taylor, Ritchie.

Referee – Mr Riddell, Edinburgh

Scotland 5 Wales 2
Pittodrie Park, 3rd February 1900,

A crowd estimated as being at least 12,000 packed into Pittodrie for the first full international to be played in the city. The game started with Scotland, who fielded seven Rangers men, playing towards the King Street end of the ground. Jack Bell and David Wilson soon had the home side two ahead before Bob McColl had another effort chalked off after being judged to be offside.The Scots continued to dominate but suffered a blow when Jacky Robertson had to leave the field with an injury. Despite being a man short the Scots continued to dominate and a great run by Wilson ended with the Queen's Park man shooting home a third goal. Bob Hamilton then made it 4-0 but Parry pulled one back for the Welshmen just before the interval. Wales made a bright start to the second half and Butler netted a second goal, hitting home a rebound after Matt Dickie blocked his first effort. The Scots looked rattled for a while but regained their composure and Alex Smith grabbed the fifth and final goal of an interesting match. Afterwards the teams were entertained with dinner at the Imperial hotel.

Scotland - Dickie (Rangers), Smith (Rangers), Crawford (Rangers), Irons (Queen's Park), Neil (Rangers), Robertson (Rangers), Bell (Celtic), Wilson (Queen's Park), McColl (Queen's Park), Hamilton (Rangers), Smith (Rangers).
Wales - F. Griffiths (Radnor and Blackpool), C. Thomas (Druids), C. Morrice (Chirk), Sam Meredith (Chirk), J. L. Jones (Rhuddian and Tottenham Hotspur), W.C. Harrison (Wrexham), D. H. Pugh (Wrexham and Lincoln), W. Butler (Druids), R. Jones (Bangor), T. D. Parry (Oswestry), A.F. Watkins (Carews and Aston Vila).
Referee - Mr Sutcliffe (Burnley).

David Wilson – scored twice for Scotland at Pittodrie

Victoria United 5, Peterhead 2
Aberdeenshire Cup Final, Pittodrie Park, 24th February 1900
Pittodrie hosted the Aberdeenshire Cup Final for the first time but there was a poor attendance although the fans from the Blue Toon were in good voice. Peterhead's bid to become the first club from outside the city to win the trophy looked like coming to fruition after the opening 45 minutes as the Buchan side took a 2-1 lead. Kemp and Thomson had the Blue Toon 2-0 ahead before Watson pulled one back before the interval. It could have been worse for the Torry side had goalkeeper Findlay not been in good form. United went on the rampage in the second half, however, with goals from Dundas and a McHardy hat-trick to give the Torry men the trophy for the fifth time. The Cup and badges were presented by Mr James Philip, president of the Aberdeenshire F.A. in the Waverley Hotel. Peterhead took revenge a few weeks later in a friendly match at Recreation Park, thumping the Vics 8-2.
Peterhead - Allardyce, Reid, J. Smith, Cowie, Davidson, Gray, Shand, Hall, G. Smith, Kemp, Thomson.
Victoria United - Findlay, Kilgour, Thain, Dundas, Stronach, Thomson, McHardy, R. Ritchie, Taylor, Watson, G. Ritchie.

Aberdeen 4, Glasgow Celtic 1
Pittodrie Park, 28th April 1900

Scottish Cup holders Celtic visited Pittodrie on their end of season tour. The visitors seemed somewhat disinterested in over-extending themselves and the Whites ran out easy winners. Livingstone opened the scoring for Aberdeen with a fine shot and Mckay added a second late in the first half. A rather lethargic Celtic brightened up a little at the start of the second period and after a period of sustained pressure the Glasgow men finally got on the scoresheet. But the Whites showed great courage and determination and raised their game once again. The visitors were gradually pushed back and Alex Shiach restored the Pittodrie side's two goal advantage. The game continued in an open fashion and just before the final whistle Fullerton set up Shiach for his second and Aberdeen's fourth. Two days later Celtic travelled to Inverness and defeated a North of Scotland select side 6-2.

Celtic - McArthur, Battles, Turnbull, Russell, Marshall, Orr, Hodge, Campbell, McMahon, Divers, Bell.

Aberdeen - Bisset, Mackie, Douglas, Cameron, Thomson, Wilson, Fullerton, A.S. Milne, Gray, Shiach, Livingstone.

Referee – Mr P. Simpson

Orion 1, Glasgow Rangers 4
Cattofield, 7th May 1900

Rangers, who won the Scottish first Division title for the second season in a row, fielded five of the seven players from the club who had turned out for Scotland against Wales at Pittodrie in February. Bob Hamilton put the Glasgow side 1-0 ahead and Millar made it 2-0 before McKay got one back for the home side. In the second half Gibson and Hamilton added to the Rangers tally.

Orion - Morrison, Grant, Ross, Livingston, Craigmyle, Currie, Low, McKay, Barron, Runcie, Grant

Rangers - Dickie, Smith, Drummond, Gibson, Robertson, Mitchell, Campbell, Wilkie, Hamilton, Millar, Smith.

Victoria United 1, Forfar Athletic 2
Northern League, Victoria Bridge Grounds, 12th May 1900

This was the deciding fixture in the League and United needed to win to lift the title. A draw meant they would share it with Dundee Wanderers and a defeat meant the flag would go to Dundee. Vics scored but it was disallowed because of offside. Jones then beat Findlay to give Forfar the lead. Immediately after that, Ritchie was tripped inside the box and Kilgour netted the equaliser from the spot. Then disaster struck Vics when Tarbet put the visitors 2-1 ahead before the interval. Vics bombarded the Forfar defence during the second half but couldn't make the breakthrough. This would turn out to be the last game United would play at the Victoria Bridge Grounds.

Northern League 1899-1900

		P	W	D	L	F	A	Pts
1	Dundee Wanderers	14	9	0	5	42	37	18
2	Victoria United	14	7	3	4	37	32	17
3	Aberdeen	14	7	2	5	36	30	16
4	Arbroath	14	6	3	5	40	32	15
5	Forfar Athletic	14	6	2	6	50	47	14
6	Orion	14	4	5	5	33	34	13
7	Lochee United*	14	5	4	5	30	26	10
8	Montrose	14	2	1	11	29	58	5

* Lochee United four points deducted- Two for playing an unregistered player called Bunce,(who had scored all five goals against Victoria United in a match the previous season) in a friendly with Dundee Wanderers. Two points were also deducted for playing a league match against the Wanderers later in the season than scheduled.

Aberdeen – Northern League Results 1899-1900

	Date	Opposition		F	A	Venue
Northern League	26/08/1899	Aberdeen	Arbroath	0	4	Gayfield Park,Arbroath
Northern League	16/09/1899	Aberdeen	Forfar Athletic	3	1	Station Park,Forfar
Northern League	07/10/1899	Aberdeen	Montrose	5	2	Montrose
Northern League	14/10/1899	Aberdeen	Orion	2	2	Pittodrie Park
Northern League	21/10/1899	Aberdeen	Montrose	3	2	Pittodrie Park
Northern League	04/11/1899	Aberdeen	Victoria United	1	2	Victoria Bridge Grounds
Northern League	18/11/1899	Aberdeen	Lochee United	4	2	Pittodrie Park
Northern League	09/12/1899	Aberdeen	Orion	0	2	Cattofield

	Date		Opposition	F	A	Venue
Northern League	23/12/1899	Aberdeen	Arbroath	3	2	Pittodrie Park
Northern League	30/12/1899	Aberdeen	Dundee Wanderers	1	5	Dundee
Northern League	10/02/1900	Aberdeen	Victoria United	2	3	Pittodrie Park
Northern League	10/03/1900	Aberdeen	Dundee Wanderers	6	1	Pittodrie Park
Northern League	17/03/1900	Aberdeen	Forfar Athletic	5	1	Pittodrie Park
		Aberdeen	Lochee United			

Note: Lochee United result (away) not found although it is believed to have been a 1-1 draw.

Aberdeen F.C – Other Games 1899-1900

Competition	Date		Opposition	F	A	Venue
Friendly	17/08/1899	Aberdeen	Victoria United	2	3	Victoria Bridge Grounds
Friendly	02/09/1899	Aberdeen	Dumbarton	7	1	Pittodrie Park
Scottish Qualifying Cup	09/09/1899	Aberdeen	Victoria United	0	1	Pittodrie Park
	25/09/1899	Aberdeen	St Bernard's	1	3	Pittodrie Park
	02/12/1899	Aberdeen	Royal Albert (Lanarkshire)	3	5	Pittodrie Park
Friendly	01/01/1900	Aberdeen	Victoria United	5	2	Victoria Bridge Grounds
Friendly	02/01/1900	Aberdeen	Alloa Athletic	2	0	Pittodrie Park
	13/01/1900	Aberdeen	Dundee Wanderers	3	1	Pittodrie Park
Friendly	20/01/1900	Aberdeen	Victoria United	3	1	Pittodrie Park
Fancy Dress Match	23/04/1900	Aberdeen	Victoria United	3	3	Pittodrie Park
	28/04/1900	Aberdeen	Celtic	4	1	Pittodrie Park
	02/05/1900	Aberdeen	Dundee	0	2	Pittodrie Park

Orion - Northern League Results 1899-1900

	Date		Opposition	F	A	Venue
Northern League	19/08/1899	Orion	Arbroath	2	2	Cattofield
Northern League	16/09/1899	Orion	Victoria United	1	5	Victoria Bridge Grounds
Norhern League	14/10/1899	Orion	Aberdeen	2	2	Pittodrie Park
Northern League	18/11/1899	Orion	Dundee Wanderers	0	2	Clepington Park, Dundee

	Date		Opposition	F	A	Venue
Northern League	25/11/1899	Orion	Victoria United	3	3	Cattofield
Northern League	02/12/1899	Orion	Montrose	4	1	Cattofield
Northern League	09/12/1899	Orion	Aberdeen	2	0	Cattofield
Northern League	16/12/1899	Orion	Dundee Wanderers	2	3	Cattofield
Northern League	30/12/1899	Orion	Forfar Athletic	5	3	Cattofield
Northern League	10/02/1900	Orion	Montrose	1	1	Links Park, Montrose
Northern League	17/02/1900	Orion	Lochee United	5	0	Cattofield
Northern League	24/02/1900	Orion	Forfar Athletic	5	5	Station Park,Forfar
Northern League	17/03/1900	Orion	Arbroath	0	4	Gayfield Park,Arbroath
Northern League	31/03/1900	Orion	Lochee United	1	3	Dundee

Orion – Other Games 1899-1900

Competition	Date		Opposition	F	A	Venue
Charity match	24/08/1899	Orion	Aberdeenshire F.A.	0	1	Victoria Bridge Grounds
	02/09/1899	Orion	Inverness Caledonian	1	0	Cattofield
Scottish Qualifying Cup	09/09/1899	Orion	Peterhead	6	3	Cattofield
Scottish Qualifying Cup	23/09/1899	Orion	Victoria United	1	1	Cattofield
Scottish Qualifying Cup	07/10/1899	Orion	Victoria United	3	0	Victoria Bridge Grounds
Scottish Qualifying Cup	21/10/1899	Orion	Forres Mechanics	3	2	Cattofield
	28/10/1899	Orion	Stonehaven	6	1	Glenury Park
Scottish Qualifying Cup	04/11/1899	Orion	Arbroath	3	5	Cattofield
	02/01/1900	Orion	Partick Thistle	3	8	Cattofield
	06/01/1900	Orion	Dundee A	1	1	Cattofield
Scottish Cup	13/01/1900	Orion	Forres Mechanics	1	1	Forres
Scottish Cup	20/01/1900	Orion	Forres Mechanics	4	1	Cattofield
Scottish Cup 2R	27/01/1900	Orion	Kilmarnock	0	10	Kilmarnock
	28/04/1900	Orion	Victoria United	1	1	Victoria Bridge Grounds
	07/05/1900	Orion	Glasgow Rangers	1	4	Cattofield

275

Competition	Date		Opposition	F	A	Venue
	12/05/1900	Orion	Peterhead	3	2	Recreation Park, Petehead

Victoria United – Northern League Results 1899-1900

	Date		Opposition	F	A	Venue
Northern League	26/08/1899	Victoria United	Montrose	6	2	Victoria Bridge Grounds
Northern League	16/09/1899	Victoria United	Orion	5	1	Victoria Bridge Grounds
Northern League	21/10/1899	Victoria United	Dundee Wanderers	1	4	Dundee
Northern League	04/11/1899	Victoria United	Aberdeen	2	1	Victoria Bridge Grounds
Northern League	25/11/1899	Victoria United	Orion	3	3	Cattofield
Northern League	02/12/1899	Victoria United	Arbroath	1	1	Gayfield Park,Arbroath
Northern League	09/12/1899	Victoria United	Forfar Athletic	1	6	Forfar
Northern League	13/01/1900	Victoria United	Montrose	4	2	Montrose
Northern League	27/01/1900	Victoria United	Dundee Wanderers	4	0	Victoria Bridge Grounds
Northern League	10/02/1900	Victoria United	Aberdeen	3	2	Pittodrie Park
Northern League	03/03/1900	Victoria United	Arbroath	4	3	Victoria Bridge Grounds
Northern League	17/03/1900	Victoria United	Lochee United	2	2	Victoria Bridge Grounds
Northern League	21/04/1900	Victoria United	Lochee United	0	3	Dundee
Northern League	12/05/1900	Victoria United	Forfar Athletic	1	2	Victoria Bridge Grounds

Victoria United – Other Games 1899-1900

Competition	Date		Opposition	F	A	Venue
Friendly	17/08/1899	Victoria United	Aberdeen	3	2	Victoria Bridge Grounds
Scottish Qualifying Cup	09/09/1899	Victoria United	Aberdeen	1	0	Pittodrie Park
Scottish Qualifying Cup	23/09/1899	Victoria United	Orion	1	1	Cattofield
Scottish Qualifying Cup	07/10/1899	Victoria United	Orion	0	3	Victoria Bridge Grounds
	18/11/1899	Victoria United	Dundee A	0	6	Dens Park,Dundee
	16/12/1899	Victoria United	Bishopmill Caledonian	8	1	Elgin
Friendly	01/01/1900	Victoria United	Aberdeen	2	5	Victoria Bridge Grounds

Competition	Date		Opposition	F	A	Venue
Friendly	02/01/1900	Victoria United	Leith Athletic	4	2	Victoria Bridge Grounds
Friendly	20/01/1900	Victoria United	Aberdeen	1	3	Pittodrie Park
Friendly	24/03/1900	Victoria United	Peterhead	2	8	Recreation Park, Petehead
Dewar Shield	14/04/1900	Victoria United	Stenhousemuir	0	2	Perth
Fancy Dress Match	23/04/1900	Victoria United	Aberdeen	3	3	Pittodrie Park
Friendly	28/04/1900	Victoria United	Orion	1	1	Victoria Bridge Grounds

Aberdeenshire Cup 1899-1900

	Date			F	A	Venue
Aberdeenshire Cup	14/10/1899	Victoria United	Fraserburgh Wanderers	7	1	Victoria Bridge Grounds
Aberdeenshire Cup	11/11/1899	Victoria United	Orion	1	0	Victoria Bridge Grounds
Aberdeenshire Cup	11/11/1899	Peterhead	Aberdeen	3	2	Recreation Park, Petehead
Aberdeenshire Cup Final	24/02/1900	Victoria United	Peterhead	5	2	Pittodrie Park

Rhodesia Cup 1899-1900

	Date			F	A	Venue
Rhodesia Cup	10/03/1900	Victoria United	Orion	1	2	Victoria Bridge Grounds
Rhodesia Cup	31/03/1900	Victoria United	Aberdeen	0	0	Victoria Bridge Grounds
Rhodesia Cup	14/04/1900	Aberdeen	Orion	2	1	Pittodrie Park
Rhodesia Cup	21/04/1900	Orion	Aberdeen	3	2	Cattofield
Rhodesia Cup	05/05/1900	Orion	Victoria United	0	2	Cattofield
Rhodesia Cup	07/05/1900	Aberdeen	Victoria United	4	4	Pittodrie Park
Rhodesia Cup	14/05/1900	Aberdeen	Victoria United	4	3	Cattofield
Rhodesia Cup Final	15/05/1900	Orion	Aberdeen	2	0	Victoria Bridge Grounds

	P	W	D	L	Pts
Orion	4	2	0	2	4
Aberdeen	4	1	2	1	4
Victoria United	4	1	2	1	4

All three clubs tied, so some form of play off was arranged with Orion eventually winning the trophy

Provost Fleming Shield

Date			F	A	Venue
24/03/1900	Aberdeen	Orion	1	0	Victoria Bridge Grounds
19/04/1900	Victoria United	Peterhead	3	1	Cattofield

Representative Matches

	Date			F	A	Venue
Inter County	28/10/1899	Aberdeenshire	Inverness-shire	2	5	Caledonian Park, Inverness
International	03/01/1900	Scotland	Wales	5	2	Pittodrie Park
Inter County	07/04/1900	Aberdeenshire	Forfarshire	2	0	Cattofield

1900-1901
Orion's agony

Orion suffered the agony of losing the Northern League title in a play-off against Dundee Reserves after both sides were level on points at the end of a roller coaster season. At one point it looked as though Aberdeen would lift the title for the first time, but the Pittodrie club fell apart over the final few games leaving Orion and the Dundee second string to battle it out for top spot. Ironically the clubs from the Granite City did themselves no favours at crucial stages during the campaign. For instance, Orion's title hopes were dented when they lost 2-1 to Aberdeen at Pittodrie on 9th March 1901. This match was originally played in December and ended in a 2-2 draw but because of bad light the game was stopped before the full 90 minutes had been played and a replay was ordered. Had the original result been allowed to stand, Orion would have had one extra point and, as a consequence, would have won the league. Similarly Aberdeen were forced to replay a game against Victoria United for the same reason. The Whites were leading the first match 3-0 when it was stopped, but then lost the replay 4-2. They also drew with United and lost to Orion in two of their final fixtures, but if these results had been more favourable, then the Whites might have been celebrating league success. The Play-Off was weighted in favour of the Dundee club with the game being played at Dens Park rather than at a neutral venue as was the case when Orion won the title under the same circumstances two seasons earlier. The Dundonians also strengthened their team by fielding a number of first team regulars including goalkeeper Tom Stewart and forwards Fred McDiarmid and David Steven. It was little surprise, therefore, that Orion lost 3-0. To be fair, the Dundee second string had beaten the north east men by the same scoreline at Dens during the regular season while the fixture at Cattofield ended 0-0.

Orion also enjoyed a great run in the Scottish Qualifying Cup, reaching the Semi Final in which they were beaten 1-0 by Scottish League Second Division side East Stirlingshire in a replay following a 1-1 draw at Cattofield. Orion's Cup run got off to a rocky start with a nervous 1-1 draw at Peterhead. The game was played on a pitch described as being so rough that it appeared *"to have a miniature hay crop on it."* The stripes survived, however, and had no trouble winning the replay 7-1 at

279

Cattofield. Victoria United proved to be stubborn opponents in the next round at Central Park. Within 60 seconds of the start the visitors were awarded a penalty which Burnett converted. Orion responded and Barron soon equalised. Barron was again on the mark right at the start of the second half when, with some help from Livingstone, he put the ball, and Vics keeper Ritchie, into the back of the net. But United refused to give up and Ritchie equalised from a suspiciously offside position to force a replay at neighbouring Cattofield. Vics failed to make home advantage count, however, and Orion cantered to a 5-2 win. Clachnacuddin were thrashed 4-0 in the next round, all the goals coming in the first half, Barron getting two and Livingstone the other two, one from a penalty. That earned the Orionites a home tie against St Johnstone. This was to be a memorable game for Orion's Livingstone who missed a penalty when the game was goalless but then he scored twice before Mailer grabbed a late consolation for the Perth side. And so the Cattofield men marched into the Quarter Finals where they travelled to Forfar and won 2-1 to set up a Semi Final clash with East Stirlingshire. Orion enjoyed home advantage against the Falkirk side and looked to be on their way to the Final when goal machine Barron blasted them into the lead. But a late goal from Harper forced a replay which Shire won 1-0 at Bainsford Park. Orion's Qualifying Cup run did at least earn them a place in the Scottish Cup in which they were drawn to meet another Scottish League side, Ayr. Having been trounced 10-0 by Kilmarnock the previous season, the Cattofield men must have had some fears about making another long trip to Ayrshire. On this occasion, however, they outcome was much better, Orion earning an honourable 2-2 draw. The Aberdonians twice led but were pegged back on both occasions by goals from Massey. The replay at Cattofield was disappointing as Massey gave Ayr an early lead and the visitors went on to win comfortably by 3-1. Orion's prospects weren't helped by an injury to Grant who had to leave the field.

A week after going out of the national tournament Orion bounced back to winning ways by defeating Aberdeen 3-2 to reach the final of the Aberdeenshire Cup. Victoria United awaited in the final and the Orion side showed their mettle by winning the trophy for the fifth time, a double from winger George Ritchie, a former Vics player (who, incidentally would return to the Blues the following season), giving them a 2-1 win at Pittodrie.

Victoria United v Orion 1901

Aberdeen's hopes of emerging as the city's most powerful side once more came to nothing as the Pittodrie men blew their chances of winning the Northern League, eventually finishing a disappointing fourth after topping the table just a few games before the end of the campaign. On 20th April the Whites led Dundee A by one point with Arbroath a further point behind and Orion three points further back. The sequence of events in the league has proved difficult to follow, however, as Aberdeen appear to have played only 16 games during the season. A number of matches finished early because of darkness and some of these were replayed, others weren't. I have, as a consequence, been unable to conclude precisely which games counted towards the league position and which didn't. Aberdeen's disappointment in the league was mirrored in other competitions as the Whites, for the third season in a row, failed to win any of the local trophies on offer. The Scottish Qualifying Cup campaign never got off the ground either as the Pittodrie side fell to Victoria United in the first round of the competition.

The Whites were near invincible on their home patch in the Northern League, winning seven and drawing one of their home fixtures. Unfortunately for them, the one defeat, at the hands of Victoria United in April 1901, seriously dented their title ambitions. The Vics also inflicted Aberdeen's heaviest defeat of the season when winning a Rhodesia Cup match 5-0 at Central Park.

The club remained unpopular with the city's other senior sides. This was a legacy from the previous season when Aberdeen arranged a friendly game against Celtic at Pittodrie when they should have been playing in the Final of the Provost Fleming Shield, a competition held to raise money for local charities. As a result, the charity game was never played. The Whites also refused to play in this season's competition, a decision which angered the Provost who threatened to withdraw the trophy unless Aberdeen played ball. The club also refused to make Pittodrie available for the final, claiming that on the prescribed date the ground was needed by St Clement's cricket club. The cricketers were also offered alternative facilities at either Duthie Park or Stewart Park for the day, but turned both down. These actions were seen as a deliberate snub towards the charity competition and maintained the ill will felt against the Whites. Despite all of this Aberdeen remained ambitious and at the end of the season the club submitted an unsuccessful application to join the Scottish League. Aberdeen ended their season with friendly games against Scottish League champions Rangers and beaten Scottish Cup finalists Celtic. Top English side, Everton, also arrived at Pittodrie. The Merseysiders scrambled home with a 3-2 victory while the game against the Light Blues ended in a 3-3 draw and Celtic went home with a 2-1 win. The Parkhead side, who stayed in the County Hotel, had enjoyed a tour of city and suburbs before the game and paid a visit to Blairs College. Some commentators expressed the view that big clubs visiting the city no longer took these games seriously and simply went through the motions, much to the frustration of paying customers.

Victoria United enjoyed a topsy turvy season during which the Blues performed poorly in the Northern League but won the Rhodesia Cup and the Provost Fleming Shield. United opened their Northern League campaign with a 2-2 draw against eventual champions Dundee A at Cattofield Park. The Vics no longer had the use of the Victoria Bridge Grounds in Torry and their new home, at Central Park, wasn't available, so Orion allowed them the use of their home patch. Vics first match at Central Park came the following week when they entertained Aberdeen and again the game ended in a draw, this time six goals were shared. Six defeats in a row between mid-October and mid-December put paid to any hopes of success in the league and the Scottish Qualifying Cup challenge had petered out by the end of

Victoria United pictured with the Rhodesia Cup and the Lord Provost Fleming Shield which the club won in 1900-1901. In the background is the Northern League flag from season 1897-1898.

September when, after defeating Aberdeen, United lost 5-2 to Orion in a replay.

Complete results from the Rhodesia Cup competition have been difficult to find but what's not in doubt is that United won the trophy by defeating Orion 2-1 in the Final at Cattofield. The Provost Fleming Shield competition was held as a straight Final because of Aberdeen's reluctance to take part and again United triumphed by defeating Orion 2-1 at Cattofield. Vics crushed Peterhead 7-3 to reach the Final of the Aberdeenshire Cup but Orion took the honours this time with another narrow 2-1 victory.

Notable Games
Orion 1, East Stirlingshire 1
Scottish Qualifying Cup Semi Final,Cattofield, 17th November 1900

A special train from Falkirk's Grahamston station brought 500 Shire fans north for the big game. The crowd was estimated to be the biggest in the city since the previous season's Scotland - Wales international at Pittodrie. Orion kicked off playing up the slope and enjoyed a lot of possession but failed to take any of the chances which came their way. Wilson missed the best opportunity after being set up by Barron. There was no score at halftime and home hopes were high given that the stripes would enjoy playing downhill in the second period. The crowd went wild when Orion took the lead with an excellent move. Ritchie started it with a pass to Wilson who crossed for Barron to fire powerfully past Allan . Livingstone and Prophet both came close to extending the Orion lead but there was bitter disappointment near the end when Harper snatched an equaliser which the visitors barely deserved.

East Stirlingshire 1, Orion 0
Scottish Qualifying Cup Semi Final Replay,Bainsford Park,
Falkirk, 24th November 1900

A goal from Rae after 18 minutes decided the tie which was notable for its scrappy play in a frantic first half. As time wore on, Orion became increasingly dominant and despite piling a huge amount of pressure on the Shire defence they couldn't make the breakthrough.

East Stirlingshire - Allan, Jonstone, Steel, Prentice, Fish, Rae, Gillespie, Laidlaw, Turnbull, Harper, Reid.

Orion - W. Ritchie, Thomson, Ross, Currie, Willox, Grant, Prophet, Livingstone, Barron, Wilson, G. Ritchie.

Referee - Mr W. McLeod, Glasgow

Ayr 2, Orion 2
Scottish Cup First Round,12th January 1901

A small band of fans travelled south with the team on the Friday evening although Wilson failed to show up at the station and his place was taken by Wright, a junior player. Orion survived an early scare when Ayr were awarded a penalty but Aitken sent the ball high over the crossbar and the first half ended goalless. Barron put Orion ahead in the second period but Massey quickly equalised.Livingston then made it 2-1 for the stripes but Massey again levelled. Orion keeper Ritchie was injured and the game was held up while he received treatment. There was no further scoring and Orion went home looking forward to the replay

Orion - Ritchie, Thomson, Ross, Craig, Willox, Wright, Prophet, Livingston, Barron, Grant, Ritchie.

Ayr - A. McDonald, J. McDonald,Wills, Stevenson, S. Aiten, Allan, Kennedy, Massey, A. Lounan, McAvoy, Lindsay.

Referee - Mr Marshall, Third Lanark

Orion 1, Ayr 3
Scottish Cup First Round Replay, Cattofield, 19th January 1901

On a miserable day a crowd of between 3,000 and 4,000 turned out, including 500 from Ayr. Massey, who scored both goals in the first game, was again on target to give the Honest Men an early lead. Orion's hopes were further dented when Grant had to go off with a knee injury and there was little surprise when Lindsay capitalised on a poor clearance by Ritchie to extend the visitors' lead before the interval. Grant attempted to return at the start of the second half but soon had to retire for good. Orion's misfortune continued when Thomson fouled Lindsay in the box and Wills converted the resultant penalty to make it 3-0. Wright fired home an angled shot to give the home side a consolation goal before the end.

Orion - Ritchie, Thomson, Ross, Wright, Willox, Wilson, Prophet, Livingston, Barron, Grant, G. Ritchie.

Ayr - A. McDonald, J. McDonald,Wills, Stevenson, S. Aiken, A. Aiken, Hamilton, Massey, Hughes, McAvoy, Lindsay.

Referee - Mr Gorman, Paisley

Orion 2, Victoria United 1
Aberdeenshire Cup Final, Pittodrie Park, 2nd March 1901

Two first half goals from George Ritchie gave Orion the Cup for the fifth time. Ritchie had put the stripes into an early lead but Burnett soon equalized. The Orion man scored again before the interval and although both sides had plenty of chances there was no further scoring. Vics dominated the second half but just couldn't get the better of Ritchie in the Orion goal.

Orion - Ritchie, Thomson, Ross, Currie, Willox, Wilson, Prophet, Livingston, Barron, Brebner,Ritchie

Victoria United - Findlay, Kilgour, Thain, Drummond, Stronach, Murray, Knowles, Duncan, Taylor, Burnett, Ritchie

Referee - Mr Nisbet, Edinburgh

Aberdeen 2, Everton 3
Pittodrie Park, 30th April 1901
Everton, the first English side to visit Pittodrie, had finished seventh in the English First Division and the following season they would be runners-up behind Sunderland. The visitors showed their class in the opening stages with *"the beautiful passing of the Everton forwards being much admired by the spectators."* But Aberdeen knuckled down and shocked the Liverpool outfit by taking the lead through Brown. There was more drama shortly afterwards when Shiach made it 2-0. This setback seemed to stir Everton into action and before the interval they had levelled the scores. Aberdeen continued to rattle the visitors who at times seemed uncomfortable. One report referred to: *"Settle, the internationalist, is a very nimble player, but he was somewhat chagrined by the way Brown and Thomson so often robbed him of the ball."* Aberdeen created numerous chances but couldn't convert them and paid the penalty when Turner scored a late winner for Everton.
Everton - Muir, Balmer, Eccles, Wolstenhome, Booth, Abbott, Taylor, MacDonald, Proudfoot, Settle, Turner.
Aberdeen - Ritchie, Douglas, J. Mackie, Thomson, Sangster, Brown, Fullerton, Davidson, C. Mackie, Shiach, Massey.
Referee - Mr J. Philip

Orion 1, Victoria United 2
Lord Provost Fleming Shield Final,
Cattofield, 4th May 1901
There was a *"large attendance"* and Provost Fleming was among the spectators.
Victoria United dominated the first half but failed to convert any of the chances created. *"An element of roughness crept into the game and not a few hard knocks were exchanged,"* and as a result of one incident, United's Burnett was hurt and had to leave the field for a while. Against the run of play, Orion edged in front just before the

Lord Provost Fleming

interval when Livingstone crossed for Prophet to head home. United made a bright start to the second half and Ritchie was kept busy as the Blues kept up the pressure. It was little surprise when they finally equalised through Kilgour who fired home a fine shot then Duncan scored what proved to be the winner to avenge the Aberdeenshire Cup Final result. At the end of the game Provost Fleming presented the Shield to Vics captain, Kilgour. The Provost said he was disappointed the shield had not been played for last year due to a *"misunderstanding"* and that even this year not all of the city clubs had participated. This was a quite open criticism of Aberdeen's failure to participate.He went on to indicate that if all three clubs didn't compete the following season he would consider withdrawing the Shield.

Orion - Ritchie, Thomson, Ross, Currie, Willox, Grant,Livingstone, Lindsay, Barron, Prophet, Thomson.

Victoria United – R. Murray, Kilgour, Craig, Drummond, Stronach, A. Murray, Knowles, Duncan, Walker, Burnett, Ritchie.

Dundee A 3, Orion 0
Northern League Play Off, Dens Park, Dundee 18th May 1901
A crowd estimated as being between 3,000 and 4,000 turned up for the title decider. Orion keeper Ritchie was in outstanding form in the first half, producing a string of fine saves to keep Dundee at bay.The white shirted Dundee side opened the second half strongly and W. Stewart finally headed them into the lead. Dave Macdonald then made it 2-0 and David Mackay put the outcome beyond doubt. Dundee eased back after that and Orion's Bremner had a chance to grab a consolation but, with the goal at his mercy, he *"bungled badly"* and the chance was lost.

Orion - Ritchie, Thomson, Ross, Currie, Willox, Esplin, Grant, Christie, Prophet, Lindsay,Bremner

Dundee A - Stewart, Bowman, Taylor, A. Halkett, W. Stewart, Gowans, McDiarmid, Steven, Mackay, MacDonald, J. Halkett.
Referee – Mr. McLeod, Cowlairs

Northern League 1900-1901

		P	W	D	L	F	A	Pts
1	Dundee A	18	12	4	2	61	16	28
2	Orion	18	13	2	3	45	21	28
3	Arbroath	18	10	4	4	54	41	24
4	Aberdeen	16	10	3	3	42	27	23
5	Dundee Wanderers	17	6	3	8	38	40	15
6	Victoria United	18	6	3	9	43	48	15
7	Forfar Athletic	17	5	0	12	41	55	10
8	Lochee United	17	4	2	11	34	57	10
9	Fair City Athletic	14	5	0	9	31	43	10
10	Montrose	17	1	4	12	20	69	6

Aberdeen – Northern League 1900-1901

	Date		Opposition	F	A	Venue
Northern League	25/08/1900	Aberdeen	Arbroath	2	1	Pittodrie
Northern League	01/09/1900	Aberdeen	Dundee Wanderers	2	2	Pittodrie
Northern League	13/10/1900	Aberdeen	Montrose	3	1	Pittodrie
Northern League	20/10/1900	Aberdeen	Dundee A	0	3	Dundee
Northern League	03/11/1900	Aberdeen	Lochee United	3	0	Pittodrie
Northern League	17/11/1900	Aberdeen	Forfar Athletic	3	2	Station Park, Forfar
Northern League	24/11/1900	Aberdeen	Dundee A	2	1	Pittodrie
Northern League	01/12/1901	Aberdeen	Orion	2	2	Pittodrie*
Northern League	08/12/1900	Aberdeen	Victoria United	3	0	Pittodrie*
Northern League	23/02/1901	Aberdeen	Fair City	5	1	Perth
Northern League	02/03/1901	Aberdeen	Dundee Wanderers	1	1	Clepington Park, Dundee
Northern League	09/03/1901	Aberdeen	Orion	2	1	Pittodrie
Northern League	16/03/1901	Aberdeen	Arbroath	6	3	Pittodrie
Northern League	30/03/1901	Aberdeen	Montrose	4	1	Montrose
Northern League	06/04/1901	Aberdeen	Forfar Athletic	4	1	Pittodrie
Northern League	20/04/1901	Aberdeen	Victoria United	2	4	Pittodrie
Northern League	27/04/1901	Aberdeen	Orion	1	3	Cattofield
Northern League	11/05/1901	Aberdeen	Victoria United	2	2	Central Park

Notes: The games against Orion and Victoria United on 01/12/1900 and 08/12/1900 respectively were stopped early because of darkness and replayed on 09/03/1902 and 20/04/1901.

Aberdeen F C – Other Games 1900-1901

Competition	Date		Opposition	F	A	Venue
Friendly	21/08/1900	Aberdeen	Victoria United	3	3	Central Park
Scottish Qualifying Cup	08/09/1900	Aberdeen	Victoria United	2	2	Central Park
Scottish Qualifying Cup	15/09/1900	Aberdeen	Victoria United	0	2	Pittodrie
Friendly	24/09/1900	Aberdeen	Queen's Park	1	4	Pittodrie
Aberdeenshire Cup	10/11/1900	Aberdeen	Fraserburgh Wanderers	9	0	Bellslea Park, Fraserburgh
Friendly	15/12/1900	Aberdeen	Aberdeen University	3	1	Pittodrie
Friendly	31/12/1900	Aberdeen	Partick Thistle	1	1	Pittodrie
Friendly	01/01/1901	Aberdeen	Victoria United	1	2	Pittodrie
Friendly	02/01/1901	Aberdeen	Stenhousemuir	3	6	Pittodrie
Rhodesia Cup	05/01/1901	Aberdeen	Orion	3	4	Cattofield
Aberdeenshire Cup	26/01/1901	Aberdeen	Orion	2	3	Pittodrie
Friendly	23/03/1901	Aberdeen	Free South Athletic	6	3	Pittodrie
Rhodesia Cup	13/04/1901	Aberdeen	Orion	1	1	Pittodrie
Friendly	30/04/1901	Aberdeen	Everton	2	3	Pittodrie
Friendly	06/05/1901	Aberdeen	Rangers	3	3	Pittodrie
Rhodesia Cup	08/05/1901	Aberdeen	Victoria United	0	5	Central Park
Friendly	14/05/1901	Aberdeen	Celtic	1	2	Pittodrie

Orion – Northern League 1900-1901

	Date		Opposition	F	A	Venue
Northern League	18/08/1900	Orion	Forfar Athletic	3	2	Forfar
Northern League	25/08/1900	Orion	Fair City	3	0	Cattofield
Northern League	24/09/1900	Orion	Arbroath	0	4	Cattofield
Northern League	13/10/1900	Orion	Dundee Wanderers	3	2	Clepington Park, Dundee
Northern League	20/10/1900	Orion	Victoria United	2	1	Central Park

	Date		Opposition	F	A	Venue
Northern League	10/11/1900	Orion	Dundee A	0	0	Cattofield
Northern League	01/12/1900	Orion	Aberdeen	2	2	Pittodrie *
Northern League	08/12/1900	Orion	Arbroath	0	0	Gayfield Park,Arbroath
Northern League	15/12/1900	Orion	Montrose	8	0	Cattofield
Northern League	22/12/1900	Orion	Victoria United	3	0	Cattofield
Northern League	29/12/1900	Orion	Forfar Athletic	6	1	Cattofield
Northern League	09/02/1901	Orion	Lochee United	4	2	Cattofield
Northern League	16/02/1901	Orion	Dundee Wanderers	2	0	Cattofield
Northern League	09/03/1901	Orion	Aberdeen	1	2	Pittodrie
Northern League	06/04/1901	Orion	Dundee A	0	3	Dundee
Northern League	20/04/1901	Orion	Montrose	3	1	Links Park,Montrose
Northern League	27/04/1901	Orion	Aberdeen	3	1	Cattofield
Northern League	06/05/1901	Orion	Fair City	4	2	Cattofield?
Northern League	18/05/1901	Orion	Dundee A	0	3	Dens Park, Dundee

Title Play Off

Note: The game against Aberdeen on 1/12/1900 was replayed on 09/03/1901

Orion – Other Games 1900-1901

Competition	Date		Opposition	F	A	Venue
Scottish Qualifying Cup	08/09/1900	Orion	Peterhead	1	1	Peterhead
Scottish Qualifying Cup	15/09/1900	Orion	Peterhead	7	1	Cattofield
Scottish Qualifying Cup	22/09/1900	Orion	Victoria United	2	2	Central Park
Scottish Qualifying Cup	29/09/1900	Orion	Victoria United	5	2	Cattofield
Scottish Qualifying Cup	06/10/1900	Orion	Clachnacuddin	4	0	Cattofield
Scottish Qualifying Cup	27/10/1900	Orion	St Johnstone	2	1	Cattofield
Scottish Qualifying Cup	03/11/1900	Orion	Forfar Athletic	2	1	Forfar

Competition	Date		Opposition	F	A	Venue
Scottish Qualifying Cup	17/11/1900	Orion	East Stirlingshire	1	1	Cattofield
Scottish Qualifying Cup	24/11/1900	Orion	East Stirlingshire	0	1	Bainsford Park
Rhodesia Cup	05/01/1901	Orion	Aberdeen	4	3	Cattofield
Scottish Cup 1R	12/01/1901	Orion	Ayr	2	2	Ayr
Scottish Cup 1R	19/01/1901	Orion	Ayr	1	3	Cattofield
Aberdeenshire Cup	26/01/1901	Orion	Aberdeen	3	2	Pittodrie
Friendly	23/02/1901	Orion	Dunfermline Athletic	1	0	Cattofield
Aberdeenshire Cup Final	02/03/1901	Orion	Victoria United	2	1	Pittodrie
Rhodesia Cup	23/03/1901	Orion	Victoria United	1	4	Central Park
Dewar Shield SF	30/03/1901	Orion	East Stirlingshire	0	3	Cattofield
Rhodesia Cup	13/04/1901	Orion	Aberdeen	1	1	Pittodrie
Fleming Shield Final	04/05/1901	Orion	Victoria United	1	2	Cattofield
Rhodesia Cup Final	13/05/1901	Orion	Victoria United	1	2	Cattofield

Victoria United – Northern League Results 1900-1901

Date		Opposition	F	A	Venue
Northern League 18/08/1900	Victoria United	Dundee A	2	2	Cattofield
Northern League 25/08/1900	Victoria United	Montrose	2	2	Links Park,Montrose
Northern League 06/10/1900	Victoria United	Dundee Wanderers	3	2	Dundee *
Northern League 13/10/1900	Victoria United	Arbroath	0	1	Central Park
Northern League 20/10/1900	Victoria United	Orion	1	2	Central Park
Northern League 03/11/1900	Victoria United	Dundee Wanderers	3	4	Central Park
Northern League 17/11/1900	Victoria United	Arbroath	1	2	Gayfield Park,Arbroath
Northern League 01/12/1900	Victoria United	Fair City	2	4	Perth
Northern League 08/12/1900	Victoria United	Aberdeen	0	3	Pittodrie *
Northern League 22/12/1900	Victoria United	Orion	0	3	Cattofield
Northern League 12/01/1901	Victoria United	Fair City	5	2	Central Park
Northern League 19/01/1901	Victoria United	Dundee A	0	7	Dundee
Northern League 23/02/1901	Victoria United	Forfar Athletic	5	4	Central Park

Date		Opposition	F	A	Venue
Northern League 09/03/1901	Victoria United	Montrose	7	0	Central Park
Northern League 16/03/1901	Victoria United	Lochee United	2	4	Dundee
Northern League 06/04/1901	Victoria United	Lochee United	5	3	Central Park
Northern League 20/04/1901	Victoria United	Aberdeen	4	2	Pittodrie
Northern League 27/04/1901	Victoria United	Dundee Wanderers	2	1	Clepington Park, Dundee
Northern League 06/05/1901	Victoria United	Dundee A	0	3	Dundee
Northern League 11/05/1901	Victoria United	Aberdeen	2	2	Central Park

Note: The game against Dundee Wanderers on 06/10/1900 was stopped due to heavy rain and replayed on 27/04/1901. The game against Aberdeen on 08/12/1901 was stopped early due to darkness and replayed on 20/04/1901

Victoria United – Other Games 1900-1901

Competition	Date		Opposition	F	A	Venue
Friendly	21/08/1900	Victoria United	Aberdeen	3	3	Central Park
Scottish Qualifying Cup	08/09/1900	Victoria United	Aberdeen	2	2	Central Park
Scottish Qualifying Cup	15/09/1900	Victoria United	Aberdeen	2	0	Pittodrie
Scottish Qualifying Cup	22/09/1900	Victoria United	Orion	2	2	Central Park
Scottish Qualifying Cup	29/09/1900	Victoria United	Orion	2	5	Cattofield
Friendly	10/11/1900	Victoria United	Cowdenbeath	4	2	Central Park
Friendly	24/11/1900	Victoria United	Aberdeen University	3	2	Central Park
Friendly	15/12/1900	Victoria United	Dundee A	0	0	Central Park
Friendly	01/01/1901	Victoria United	Aberdeen	2	1	Pittodrie
Friendly	02/01/1901	Victoria United	Raith Rovers	5	3	Central Park
Aberdeenshire Cup SF	16/02/1901	Victoria United	Peterhead	7	3	Central Park
Aberdeenshire Cup Final	02/03/1901	Victoria United	Orion	1	2	Pittodrie
Rhodesia Cup	23/03/1901	Victoria United	Orion	4	1	Central Park

Competition	Date		Opposition	F	A	Venue
Friendly	13/04/1901	Victoria United	Abergeldie	6	1	Central Park
Fleming Shield Final	04/05/1901	Victoria United	Orion	2	1	Cattofield
Rhodesia Cup	08/05/1901	Victoria United	Aberdeen	5	0	Central Park
Rhodesia Cup Final	13/05/1901	Victoria United	Orion	2	1	Cattofield

Aberdeenshire Cup 1900-1901

	Date			F	A	Venue
Aberdeenshire Cup	10/11/1900	Aberdeen	Fraserburgh Wanderers	9	0	Bellslea Park, Fraserburgh
Aberdeenshire Cup SF	26/01/1901	Aberdeen	Orion	2	3	Pittodrie
Aberdeenshire Cup SF	16/02/1901	Victoria United	Peterhead	7	3	Central Park
Aberdeenshire Cup Final	02/03/1901	Orion	Victoria United	2	1	Pittodrie

Rhodesia Cup 1900-1901

	Date			F	A	Venue
Rhodesia Cup	05/01/1901	Orion	Aberdeen	4	3	Cattofield
Rhodesia Cup	23/03/1901	Victoria United	Orion	4	1	Central Park
Rhodesia Cup	13/04/1901	Aberdeen	Orion	1	1	Pittodrie
Rhodesia Cup	08/05/1901	Victoria United	Aberdeen	5	0	Central Park
Rhodesia Cup Final	13/05/1901	Orion	Victoria United	1	2	Callofield

Lord Provost Fleming Shield

	Date			F	A	Venue
Final	04/05/1901	Orion	Victoria United	1	2	Cattofield

Representative Match

	Date			F	A
Inter County	27/10/1900	Aberdeenshire	Inverness-shire	1	1

1901-1902
Aberdeen's late collapse

Aberdeen lost one of their best players, Alex Shiach, who chose to sign for Orion before the start of the season, but he was replaced by Archie Brash, an experienced campaigner who had previously been with St Mirren, Sheffield Wednesday and Leicester Fosse. Brash played for the Sheffield Wednesday side that defeated Wolverhampton Wanderers 2-1 in the 1895-1896 F.A. Cup Final. One of his team-mates on that occasion was Dundonian Bob Petrie who would later play for Southampton and Arbroath.

The Whites got off to a flying start in the Northern League and for a long spell seemed destined to win the title for the first time, but a late season collapse saw them slump to fourth in the table. Raith Rovers and Dundee A tied for top spot with the Kirkcaldy side winning the resultant play-off 2-1 at Dens Park to claim the league flag in what was their first season in the competition. The other league newcomers, Cowdenbeath, also overhauled Aberdeen to finish third. Yet it could have been so different had the Whites not contrived to lose five of their last six league matches. In fact, they lost their last seven games in all competitions. This contrasted with the Pittodrie club's great opening to the campaign which saw them remain undefeated in their opening six league fixtures and lose only twice for the first 16 matches in the competition. This run included two victories over the powerful Dundee A. The decisive game of the season was on 26th April 1902, when Raith Rovers visited Pittodrie and won 2-0. Aberdeen's Brash put the ball into the net when it was 0-0, but he was judged to have been offside. Raith then scored twice within 60 seconds with just 10 minutes remaining to grab a vital two points and move ahead of Aberdeen at the top of the table. Aberdeen went on to lose their remaining two matches, 3-1 to Cowdenbeath and 5-2 to Victoria United.

There was a riot at the end of the Orion-Aberdeen Northern League match at Cattofield in early December 1901. The home side had gone 1-0 ahead after Aberdeen's O'Brien fouled former Whites star Shiach to concede a penalty which Willox converted. Brebner put Orion 2-0 ahead early in the second half and the buoyant Stripes fans decided to antagonise the visitors by constantly jeering the unfortunate O'Brien and his clubmate, Mackie, both of whom were being enticed into some rough play. Aberdeen responded positively to the hostile atmosphere, however, and Hugh Livingstone soon pulled a goal back before two late strikes from Fullerton stunned the home side and gave the visitors a sensational victory. At the final whistle hundreds of fans invaded the pitch, apparently with the aim of taking out their anger on O'Brien and Mackie. During the melee several people sustained light injuries while police escorted the players and officials to the relative safety of the nearby Northern Hotel.

What Local Football's

Coming To.

Cartoon in Bon Accord magazine after the riot at the Orion – Aberdeen game.

There was further crowd trouble at the end of a friendly between Victoria United and Dundee A at Central Park in February 1902. The home side won 2-0, but the antics of Dundee's Taylor upset the crowd. As one reporter described it: *"the right back of the Dundee was playing a brutal game, and, not content with hacking and tripping, he latterly struck out with his fists."* This so annoyed the home supporters that hundreds invaded the pitch and officials had their work cut out to restore order.

There was some consolation for Aberdeen on the home front, as the Whites won their first local trophy for four seasons when beating Victoria United 1-0 in the final of the Aberdeenshire Cup, Charlie Mackie grabbing the all-important goal in the second half of a hard fought encounter at Cattofield Park. That victory earned Aberdeen a place in the Dewar Shield in which they defeated Dundee Wanderers 1-0 in the semi final at Dens Park, Mackie again being on the mark with a late winner. The Final saw the Pittodrie side travel to Falkirk to meet Scottish Qualifying

Hugh Ross, Orion

Cup winners Stenhousemuir. Hopes of becoming the first Aberdeenshire club to win the trophy ended, however, as the Warriors ran out 2-1 winners. There was disappointment once again in the Scottish Qualifying Cup as the Whites were beaten by Victoria United in the opening round and the Rhodesia Cup also failed to give Aberdeen any cause for celebration. The Pittodrie side's lingering dispute with the local Charity Committee meant that once again the Whites didn't compete in the Lord Provost Fleming Shield but a number of top quality sides were induced to Pittodrie for friendly matches as the club sought to increase revenue. The most significant of these was the visit of top English side Blackburn Rovers who cruised to a 5-2 victory, while the previous season's Scottish Cup winners, Hearts, won by the same scoreline. Celtic made two trips to Pittodrie, winning 2-0 in April after losing 3-1 in March. The Celts also visited Peterhead on their latter trip to the north-east, beating the Recreation Park side 5-3.

Having been pipped at the post the previous season, Orion had high hopes of making an even stronger bid for the Northern League title on this occasion. It was not to be however, as the Cattofield Park side endured a rather miserable campaign, finishing seventh. The Stripes were also beaten by Aberdeen in a towsy Aberdeenshire Cup tie in which goalkeeper Ritchie was lucky not to be sent off after deliberately throwing the ball into the face of Aberdeen's Fullerton when the Whites player was appealing against a disallowed goal. There was further despair for Orion when, despite being given two chances to reach the final of the Lord Provost Fleming Shield , they lost out on both occasions, firstly to Peterhead then to Victoria United. Some silverware did come their way, however, when the Rhodesia Cup was won. Orion needed a replay to dispose of Peterhead in the

Orion F.C. 1901-1902
Players – Back row (Left to right) – Currie, Thompson, Ritchie, Ross, Esplin, Fitzpatrick (in uniform).
Front row: Prophet, Wilson, Campbell, Willox, Bremner, Shiach.

Scottish Qualifying Cup but were beaten 1-0 in the next round by Victoria United, former Orion player George Ritchie getting the only goal of the game.

Orion failed to win any of their four Northern League games against local rivals Aberdeen and Victoria United. The match between the Stripes and United at Central Park in November 1901, did, however, produce one of the most remarkable comebacks of the season as the sides served up an eleven goal thriller. Orion started the game with ten men as their goalkeeper was late in arriving, so Hugh Ross went between the sticks, and he immediately conceded a goal, Ferries ramming the ball home to put the Blues ahead. Orion soon settled, however, and a double from Wilson and another from Thomson soon had them 3-1 ahead. United went down to ten men when Craig had to leave the field with an injury and Orion went on the rampage with Bremner and Campbell putting them 5-1 ahead. It seemed to be all over but United began a storming fightback and a hat-trick from Burnett and a double from Bobby Ritchie gave them a stunning 6-5 victory.

Thomson, one of the Orion scorers, would soon after emmigrate to the USA, not on account of this result it must be said, and he was presented with a purse of sovereigns by his friends and clubmates prior to his departure.

The Stripes had been gradually improving their facilities at Cattofield Park, notably adding a roof to the grandstand during the summer months. Further improvements were planned, and to help with these, a concert and dance was held in the Albert Hall, Huntly Street at the end of February 1902. Officials from Victoria United and Aberdeen attended along with businessmen such as John Macgregor (Caledonian Railway), George Hay (Union Bar), John Worling (plumber) and John Mckay (Town and County Bank). Baillie Glass was also in attendance. The Indian club display by the Cleansing Department gymnastic team and the exhibition of dancing by the Pirie family apparently aroused much interest, and dancing took place to Miss Duncan's band during what appears to have been a happy evening. At the tail end of the season Orion invited Scottish Cup winners Hibernian to Cattofield Park, the Edinburgh side winning 2-0. The following week Aberdeen entertained the beaten Cup finalists, Celtic, at the Chanonry.

Orion's Donald Currie decided to hang up his boots after a long and hugely successful career during which he picked up more winner's medals than any other local player. Currie started playing football at Woodside before signing for Aberdeen in the early 1890's. He never progressed beyond the second string and so left to join Orion in 1893. He became a real favourite at Cattofield and was club captain for many years. Currie helped Orion win the Aberdeenshire Cup in 1894-1895,1896-1897,1898-1899 and 1900-1901 and the Charity Cup in 1893-1894,1895-1896 and 1897-1898. He was also in the squad that won the Gershon Cup in 1893-1894, 1894-1895 and 1896-1897 and the Rhodesia Cup in 1898-1899, 1899-1900 and 1901-1902. And, of course, he picked up two Northern League title wins, in 1896-1897 and 1898-1899.

Victoria United experienced a season of inconsistency which ended with the Blues finishing a lowly 10th in the Northern League, retaining the Lord Provost Fleming Shield and losing to Aberdeen in the Final of the Aberdeenshire Cup. The Central Park side also came unstuck in the Scottish Qualifying Cup. After

Aberdeen Football Club 1901-1902

disposing of Aberdeen and Orion in the opening rounds of the competition, United were drawn against Inverness Caledonian. The tie was meant to have been played in Inverness but United had difficulty in raising a team for the trip north so they offered the Highlanders guaranteed gate money of £40 if the match was played in Aberdeen. Caley obliged then thumped their hosts 4-0 at Central Park in front of a crowd which probably barely generated the income needed to pay off the visitors.

The severe winter weather played havoc with the fixture list but United and the others tried their hardest to ensure that games could go ahead. United's match against Aberdeen at the beginning of February was threatened by the arctic conditions so the Central Park side arranged for a snow clearing operation to be undertaken on the morning of the match. Someone got their wires crossed, however, and instead of clearing Central Park, the workmen moved into the adjacent Cattofield Park and began operations there. When Vics officials noticed what was happening they ordered the men to stop and move to Central Park. By this time it was too late to complete the task and by kick-off time the referee declared the pitch unplayable for a competitive game, so a friendly was played which the Blues won 2-0.

On 5th April 1902 Victoria United defeated Lochee United 3-0 at Central Park while Aberdeen and Peterhead played out a 3-3 draw at Pittodrie, but it was events elsewhere that day which had a profound impact on the arrangements for playing football in the city. At Ibrox Stadium in Glasgow, 26 people were killed and hundreds more injured when a section of wooden terracing collapsed during the Scotland – England international. Incredibly, despite this disaster, the game continued, with victims being carted away and hundreds of spectators spilling onto the pitch. Apparently the players occasionally had to dribble past the fans, as well as opponents, as the game progressed. It ended in a 1-1 draw. In the aftermath, concerns were rightly expressed about the safety of spectators at football grounds and inspections were carried out at all the Aberdeen grounds. The Town Council subsequently considered reports on the security and stability of the grandstands at Pittodrie, Cattofield and Central Park and instructed improvements to be carried out.

Notable Games

Aberdeen 1, Victoria United 0
Aberdeenshire Cup Final, Cattofield Park, 1st March 1902
An enormous crowd turned up on a day of fine weather although rain during the week beforehand left the pitch heavy and it was liberally covered in sand.Vics played down the slope in the first half and put the Aberdeen defence under some severe pressure, but centre half Thomson held the Blues at bay while full backs O'Brien and Dakers also played well. The Whites gradually worked their way into the game and Vics goalkeeper Murray had to remain alert. Vics Burnett and Aberdeen's O'Brien *"were sticking to one another like leeches"* and referee Baillie had to keep a close eye on them. The teams changed ends with the game goalless and Aberdeen made a brisk start to the second period, Hugh Livingston setting up a great chance for Brash who somehow missed. But the decisive goal came for the Whites on the hour mark following a great interchange of passes between McHardy and Livingston who set up an opportunity which Mackie gleefully took. United pressed for an equaliser but got caught time and again by Aberdeen's offside tactics which infuriated the Blues supporters. Whites 'keeper Bisset had to make a number of saves but his side held on to secure a narrow win. Mr David Gordon, President of the Aberdeenshire F.A. presented the trophy

and badges in the Northern Hotel after the game

Aberdeen - Bisset, O'Brien, Dakers, Sangster, Thomson, Robertson, Brash, C. Mackie, H. Livingston, Davidson, McHardy

Victoria United - Murray, Kilgour, Craig, Bremner, Arthur Murray, R. Ritchie, Knowles, Duncan, Burnett, Ferries, G. Ritchie.

Referee - Mr Baillie, Edinburgh.

Aberdeen 3, Celtic 1
Pittodrie Park, 8th March 1902

The Gordon Highlanders pipe band entertained the large crowd before the kick-off and the rousing tunes seemed to invigorate the home side who made a spritely start against a below full strength Celtic side. It was little surprise when Hugh Livingstone gave the Whites the lead after some fine attacking play. O'Brien extended Aberdeen's lead from the penalty spot and there was more glee for the home side when Celtic 'keeper Dan McArthur fumbled a Brash corner which ended up in the net. Heavy rain made conditions treacherous but both sides continued to battle hard in the second half. Tommy McDermott scored to give Celtic some hope but neither side was capable of adding to their tally before the end.

Aberdeen with the Aberdeenshire Cup 1902

Aberdeen - Bisset, O'Brien, Dakers, Sangster, Thomson, Robertson, Brash, C.Mackie, H. Livingstone, Davidson, Fullerton.
Celtic - McArthur, Watson, Davidson, Loney, Russell, Orr, Hamilton, McDermott, Mair, McMahon, Quinn.

Stenhousemuir 2, Aberdeen 1
Dewar Shield Final, Falkirk, 19th April 1902

The Dewar Shield was inaugurated in 1898-1899 and featured the county champions of Aberdeenshire, Forfarshire, Perthshire and Stirlingshire. The winners were crowned "Champions of the Northern Counties" but until this season no Aberdeenshire side had even reached the Final. Hopes were high that Aberdeen would actually win the trophy when they travelled to Falkirk to face Scottish Qualifying Cup champions Stenhousemuir. Stenny had lost 3-1 to the Whites in a friendly game at Pittodrie on New Year's Day, but sadly that result would not be repeated. A goal from 'farmer' Mackie had earned Aberdeen a 1-0 victory over Dundee Wanderers in the semi final at Dens Park a few weeks earlier and the Aberdeen men travelled south high in confidence. In front of a crowd of 4,000, Aberdeen made a bright start and Brash twice forced Stoddart to make good saves. The Whites thought they had taken the lead when Brash broke clear and crossed for Livingstone to fire a great shot against the crossbar and Charlie Mackie hit the rebound into the net. But the referee disallowed the goal as Bruce was deemed to have carried the ball over the line before centring. Aberdeen again had the ball in the net but this time Davidson was given offside. The north east side suffered a blow just one minute before the interval when W. Clarkson put Stenny ahead. McNair made it 2-0 in the second period. Hugh Livingstone gave Aberdeen some hope with a late goal and Mackie and Davidson also came close before the final whistle but Stenny held on to take the trophy.

Stenhousemuir - Stoddart, Mirk, McLeod, Fairley, McBride, Weir, McNair, Pollock, Baird, W. Clarkson, T. Clarkson.
Aberdeen - Bisset, O'Brien, Dakers, Sangster, Thomson, Robertson, Brash, C. Mackie, Livingstone, Davidson, A. Bruce.
Referee - Mr. Tom Robertson

Aberdeen 2, Blackburn Rovers 5
Pittodrie Park, 15th April 1902

Blackburn Rovers, who had finished fourth in the English First Division, visited Pittodrie for an evening fixture in April 1902. Heavy rain during the day seemed to deter fans from turning out and although the weather had improved by evening *"only a comparatively small number of spectators were present."*

Rovers played towards the beach end in the first half but were stunned when Livingston gave Aberdeen the lead. Dewhurst soon equalised and by the interval the Lancashire men were 3-1 ahead. Davidson reduced the leeway in the second half before Rovers added two more to secure a comfortable win.

Aberdeen - Bisset, O'Brien, J. Mackie, Sangster, Thomson, Robertson, Brash, C. Mackie, Livingston, Davidson, Bruce.

Blackburn Rovers - McIvor, Eastham, Darroch, Haworth, McClure, Houlker, Whittaker, Somers, Dewhurst, Blackburn, Swarbrick.

Referee – Mr. Ritchie, Aberdeen

Aberdeen 2, Hearts 5
Pittodrie Park, 5th May 1902

"A large crowd of spectators" turned out despite the awful weather. Hearts made a quickfire start and were a goal ahead inside the opening two minutes, Jamieson netting. Aberdeen hopes sank even deeper into the mire shortly afterwards when Bell's shot from the left flew past Bisset for to make it 2-0. The Whites eventually rallied and enjoyed a bit of pressure but it came to nothing. Thomson then broke away in a suspiciously offside position and coolly made it 3-0. Shortly before the break Bell added a fourth. The home fans were given something to cheer early in the second period when Inglis beat Don to make it 4-1 but Hearts responded with Thomson restoring the maroons' four goal advantage. Aberdeen grabbed another goal near the end when Charlie Mackie set up a chance for Inglis whose shot was pushed into the net by Don.

Aberdeen - Bisset, O'Brien, Dakers, Mackie, Thomson, Bell, Inglis, C. Mackie, Brash, Ruddiman, Douglas.

Hearts - Don, J. Hogg, Allan, Key, Buick, Baird, A.Walker, R. Walker, Thomson, Jamieson, Bell

Victoria United 0, Glasgow Rangers 7
Central Park, 5th May 1902

On the same day that Aberdeen entertained Hearts at Pittodrie, little more than a mile away, Victoria United hosted Scottish champions Glasgow Rangers. Two of Scotland's top three clubs were therefore playing in the city at the same time, but big crowds appeared at both venues. May and Wilkie gave Rangers a two goal lead in the early stages as United struggled to make much of an impact.The visitors, in total control, made it 3-0 before the interval. Vics made a bright start to the second half but the wind was taken from their sails when Speedie broke clear to make it 4-0. Wilkie then made it 5-0 with 15 minutes remaining and the visitors added two more before the end to complete an easy win.

Victoria United - Hamilton, Todd, Craig, Bremner, Murray, Ritchie, Knowles, Duncan, Thom, Ferries, G. Ritchie.

Rangers - Dickie, Smith, Drummond, Gibson, Stark, Robertson, Graham, Wilkie, May, Speedie, Smith.

Referee - Mr. Peter Simpson, Victoria United.

Orion 0, Hibernian 2
Cattofield, 8th May 1902

Just a few days after Hibs had defeated Celtic to win the Scottish Cup for the first time, the Edinburgh side travelled to Aberdeen to face Orion in front of an estimated crowd of 2,500 for an evening fixture. Hibs fielded eight of the Cup winning side but it was Orion who impressed in the early stages and the Scotland international goalkeeper Harry Rennie was forced to pull off a string of excellent saves. *"The game was exceptionally fast without being of the sprawling order"* and although the visitors gradually got into their stride, the home defence stood firm with 'keeper Ritchie thwarting Divers on a number of occasions. Hibs upped the pace in the second half and Orion defenders Willox and Brebner were given *"a hot time"* but they stood firm. In the closing stages, however, *"darkness fell rapidly"* and Hibs finally made the breakthrough with Divers scoring. Straight from the restart Breslin made it 2-0 to give the Cup winners a rather flattering margin of victory.

Orion – Ritchie, Willox, Brebner, Currie, Low, Wright, Prophet, Fraser, Burnett (Victoria United), Shiach, Jardine.

Hibernian – Rennie, Hogg, Robertson, Breslin, Atherton, Buchanan, McColl,

McGeachan, McGinnis, Callaghan, Divers.

Aberdeen 0, Glasgow Celtic 2
Pittodrie Park, 13th May 1902

The Celts fielded a stronger starting eleven than on their previous visit to Pittodrie in March when they were well beaten. The Parkhead men, beaten by Hibs in the Scottish Cup Final, applied pressure right from the start but poor finishing prevented them from scoring. Johnny Campbell eventually broke the deadlock then Willie McCafferty came close with an effort which struck a post and rebounded into play. In the second half, and with the wind at their backs, the Whites began to assert themselves and Brash came close with a shot which sailed over the bar. McCafferty then sealed the match for the visitors with a second goal.

Aberdeen - Ritchie, J. Mackie, Dakers, Sangster, Thomson, Robertson, McHardy, C.Mackie, Livingstone, Brash, Davidson

Celtic - MacPherson, Watson, Davidson, Battles, Marshall, Orr, Walls, McDermott, Campbell, Livingstone, McCafferty

Referee - Mr Peter Simpson, Victoria United

Victoria United 2, Peterhead 0
Lord Provost Fleming Shield Final, Cattofield Park, 22nd May 1902

The pipe band from Castlehill Barracks played before the game and at half-time. United goalkeeper Murray was unavailable so McBean of Orion Reserves took his place. Peterhead were somehow strengthened by the inclusion of Aberdeen players Ritchie, Sangster and Mackie. After an initial flurry of attacking moves by Peterhead, United took some degree of control and Ferries quickly netted. The referee disallowed the goal, however, as he had seen a foul in the lead-up. Vics continued to press and the on-loan Aberdeen keeper Ritchie made a string of fine saves to keep the Blues at bay. United finally took the lead early in the second half, George Ritchie blasting home, and there was no surprise when Duncan then made it 2-0. Lord Provost Fleming watched the game with a number of other dignitaries from reserved seats in the grandstand and it was from here that he presented the Shield to United captain C. Kilgour.

Victoria United - McBean, C. Kilgour, Craig, Bremner, A. Murray, R. Ritchie, Knowles, Ferries, Thom, Duncan, G. Ritchie.

Peterhead - Ritchie, Robinson, Reid, Sangster, Hall, Davidson, Shand, Mackie, Imlah, Buchan, Grant.

Referee - Mr Nisbet, Cowdenbeath

Northern League 1901-1902

		P	W	D	L	F	A	Pts
1	Raith Rovers	22	14	3	5	53	26	31
2	Dundee A	22	13	5	4	51	26	31
3	Cowdenbeath	22	13	3	6	51	27	29
4	Aberdeen	22	12	3	7	52	37	27
5	St Johnstone	19	10	3	6	40	33	23
6	Forfar Athletic	22	8	7	7	48	51	23
7	Arbroath	21	9	2	10	44	41	20
8	Orion	22	6	7	9	40	50	19
9	Dundee Wanderers	22	7	3	12	29	30	17
10	Victoria United	19	7	3	9	38	48	17
11	Montrose	21	4	1	16	33	70	9
12	Lochee United	22	4	0	18	26	68	8

Notes: Raith Rovers, Cowdenbeath, St Johnstone joined the league at the start of the season. Fair City Athletic dropped out. Raith Rovers beat Dundee 'A' 2-1 in a play-off at Starks Park

Aberdeen – Northern League 1901-1902

	Date		Opposition	F	A	Venue
Northern League	17/08/1901	Aberdeen	Arbroath	2	1	Pittodrie
Northern League	24/08/1901	Aberdeen	Raith Rovers	2	2	Kirkcaldy
Northern League	31/08/1901	Aberdeen	Forfar Athletic	2	2	Station Park, Forfar
Northern League	14/09/1901	Aberdeen	Lochee United	3	2	Dundee
Northern League	21/09/1901	Aberdeen	Montrose	3	2	Montrose
Northern League	28/09/1901	Aberdeen	Dundee A	3	0	Pittodrie
Northern League	19/10/1901	Aberdeen	Victoria United	2	3	Pittodrie
Northern League	02/11/1901	Aberdeen	Orion	3	1	Pittodrie
Northern League	09/11/1901	Aberdeen	Dundee A	1	0	Dens Park, Dundee
Northern League	30/11/1901	Aberdeen	St Johnstone	1	3	Perth
Northern League	07/12/1901	Aberdeen	Orion	3	2	Cattofield

	Date		Opposition	F	A	Venue
Northern League	28/12/1901	Aberdeen	Montrose	6	0	Pittodrie
Northern League	04/01/1902	Aberdeen	Dundee Wanderers	2	0	Pittodrie
Northern League	11/01/1902	Aberdeen	Lochee United	7	0	Pittodrie
Northern League	15/02/1902	Aberdeen	St Johnstone	3	1	Pittodrie
Northern League	22/02/1902	Aberdeen	Forfar Athletic	3	3	Pittodrie
Northern League	15/03/1902	Aberdeen	Cowdenbeath	1	3	Pittodrie
Northern League	29/03/1902	Aberdeen	Dundee Wanderers	1	2	Dundee
Northern League	12/04/1902	Aberdeen	Arbroath	1	0	Gayfield Park,Arbroath
Northern League	26/04/1902	Aberdeen	Raith Rovers	0	2	Pittodrie
Northern League	03/05/1902	Aberdeen	Cowdenbeath	1	3	Cowdenbeath
Northern League	10/05/1902	Aberdeen	Victoria United	2	5	Central Park

Aberdeen – Other Games 1901-1902

Competition	Date		Opposition	F	A	Venue
Scottish Qualifying Cup	07/09/1901	Aberdeen	Victoria United	0	1	Pittodrie
Rhodesia Cup	12/10/1901	Aberdeen	Victoria United	3	1	Central Park
Friendly	26/10/1901	Aberdeen	Aberdeen University	0	0	Pittodrie
Friendly	16/11/1901	Aberdeen	Orion	3	2	Pittodrie
Aberdeenshire Cup	23/11/1901	Aberdeen	Orion	2	1	
Friendly	01/01/1902	Aberdeen	Stenhousemuir	3	1	Pittodrie
Aberdeenshire Cup SF	18/01/1902	Aberdeen	Fraserburgh	4	0	Fraserburgh
Friendly	01/02/1902	Aberdeen	Victoria United	0	2	Central Park
Rhodesia Cup	08/02/1902	Aberdeen	Orion	1	4	Cattofield
Aberdeenshire Cup Final	01/03/1902	Aberdeen	Victoria United	1	0	Cattofield
Friendly	08/03/1902	Aberdeen	Celtic	3	1	Pittodrie
Dewar Shield SF	22/03/1902	Aberdeen	Dundee Wanderers	1	0	Dens Park, Dundee
Friendly	05/04/1902	Aberdeen	Peterhead	3	3	Pittodrie
Friendly	15/04/1902	Aberdeen	Blackburn Rovers	2	5	Pittodrie
Dewar Shield Final	19/04/1902	Aberdeen	Stenhousemuir	1	2	Falkirk
Rhodesia Cup	29/04/1902	Aberdeen	Victoria United	1	3	Pittodrie

Competition	Date		Opposition	F	A	Venue
Friendly	05/05/1902	Aberdeen	Hearts	2	5	Pittodrie
Friendly	13/05/1902	Aberdeen	Glasgow Celtic	0	2	Pittodrie

Orion – Northern League 1901-1902

	Date		Opposition	F	A	Venue
Northern League	17/08/1901	Orion	Raith Rovers	1	1	Cattofield
Northern League	24/08/1901	Orion	Arbroath	0	3	Gayfield Park,Arbroath
Northern League	31/08/1901	Orion	Lochee United	3	2	Cattofield
Northern League	28/09/1901	Orion	St Johnstone	1	5	Perth
Northern League	05/10/1901	Orion	Cowdenbeath	0	1	Cattofield
Northern League	12/10/1901	Orion	Forfar Athletic	1	1	Cattofield
Northern League	26/10/1901	Orion	St Johnstone	2	0	Cattofield
Northern League	02/11/1901	Orion	Aberdeen	1	3	Pittodrie
Northern League	09/11/1901	Orion	Victoria United	5	6	Central Park
Northern League	30/11/1901	Orion	Dundee A	0	0	Dundee
Northern League	07/12/1901	Orion	Aberdeen	2	3	Cattofield
Northern League	28/12/1901	Orion	Raith Rovers	0	6	Kirkcaldy
Northern League	18/01/1902	Orion	Dundee Wanderers	3	2	Cattofield
Northern League	25/01/1902	Orion	Montrose	2	1	Cattofield
Northern League	01/02/1902	Orion	Lochee United	6	1	Dundee
Northern League	15/02/1902	Orion	Dundee A	2	3	Cattofield
Northern League	08/03/1902	Orion	Cowdenbeath	0	0	Cowdenbeath
Northern League	15/03/1902	Orion	Forfar Athletic	1	4	Forfar
Northern League	22/03/1902	Orion	Montrose	3	1	Montrose
Northern League	29/03/1902	Orion	Victoria United	3	3	Cattofield
Northern League	05/05/1902	Orion	Dundee Wanderers	0	0	Dundee
Northern League	10/05/1902	Orion	Arbroath	4	4	Cattofield

Orion – Other Games 1901-1902

Competition	Date		Opposition	F	A	Venue
Rhodesia Cup	22/08/1901	Orion	Victoria United	2	1	Cattofield *
Scottish Qualifying Cup	07/09/1901	Orion	Peterhead	1	1	Peterhead

Competition	Date		Opposition	F	A	Venue
Scottish Qualifying Cup	14/09/1901	Orion	Peterhead	3	1	Cattofield
Scottish Qualifying Cup	21/09/1901	Orion	Victoria United	0	1	Cattofield
Friendly	16/11/1901	Orion	Aberdeen	2	3	Pittodrie
Aberdeenshire Cup	23/11/1901	Orion	Aberdeen	1	2	Pittodrie
Friendly	14/12/1901	Orion	Montrose	2	0	Cattofield
Friendly	21/12/1901	Orion	Victoria United	1	1	Cattofield
Provost Fleming Shield	04/01/1902	Orion	Peterhead	1	2	Cattofield
Rhodesia Cup	11/01/1902	Orion	Victoria United	1	0	Cattofield
Rhodesia Cup	08/02/1902	Orion	Aberdeen	4	1	Cattofield
Rhodesia Cup	22/02/1902	Orion	Victoria United	3	2	Central Park
Friendly	12/04/1902	Orion	Victoria United	1	1	Pittodrie
Friendly	19/04/1902	Orion	Dundee A	1	1	Cattofield
Provost Fleming Shield	24/04/1902	Orion	Victoria United	1	4	Pittodrie
Friendly	03/05/1902	Orion	Victoria United	3	2	Cattofield
Friendly	08/05/1902	Orion	Hibernian	0	2	Cattofield

Notes: Orion v Victoria United game on 22/08/1901 finished early and was replayed on 11/01/1902

Victoria United – Northern League 1901-1902

	Date		Opposition	F	A	Venue
Northern League	17/08/1901	Victoria United	Montrose	2	5	Montrose
Northern League	24/08/1901	Victoria United	Dundee A	0	0	Central Park
Northern League	31/08/1901	Victoria United	Cowdenbeath	0	3	Central Park
Northern League	14/09/1901	Victoria United	Forfar Athletic	1	5	Central Park
Northern League	28/09/1901	Victoria United	Arbroath	2	3	Central Park
Northern League	19/10/1901	Victoria United	Aberdeen	3	2	Pittodrie
Northern League	26/10/1901	Victoria United	Montrose	1	0	Central Park
Northern League	09/11/1901	Victoria United	Orion	6	5	Central Park
Northern League	23/11/1901	Victoria United	Lochee United	4	3	Dundee

309

	Date		Opposition	F	A	Venue
Northern League	30/11/1901	Victoria United	Dundee Wanderers	1	1	Central Park
Northern League	07/12/1901	Victoria United	Forfar Athletic	2	1	Forfar
Northern League	04/01/1902	Victoria United	St Johnstone	0	2	Perth
Northern League	25/01/1902	Victoria United	Dundee Wanderers	1	4	Dundee
Northern League	15/02/1902	Victoria United	Raith Rovers	0	1	Kirkcaldy
Northern League	15/03/1902	Victoria United	Dundee A	2	3	Dens Park,Dundee
Northern League	22/03/1902	Victoria United	Raith Rovers	1	2	Central Park
Northern League	29/03/1902	Victoria United	Orion	3	3	Cattofield
Northern League	05/04/1902	Victoria United	Lochee United	3	0	Central Park
Northern League	26/04/1902	Victoria United	Cowdenbeath	1	5	Cowdenbeath
Northern League	10/05/1902	Victoria United	Aberdeen	5	2	Central Park

Note: St Johnstone game on 04/01/1902 was abandoned and result didn't count

Victoria United – Other Games 1901-1902

Competition	Date		Opposition	F	A	Venue
Rhodesia Cup Charity match	15/08/1901	Victoria United	Aberdeen-Orion Select	2	6	Cattofield
Rhodesia Cup	22/08/1901	Victoria United	Orion	1	2	Cattofield
Scottish Qualifying Cup	07/09/1901	Victoria United	Aberdeen	1	0	Pittodrie
Scottish Qualifying Cup	21/09/1901	Victoria United	Orion	1	0	Cattofield
Scottish Qualifying Cup	05/10/1901	Victoria United	Inverness Caledonian	0	4	Central Park
Rhodesia Cup	12/10/1901	Victoria United	Aberdeen	1	3	Central Park
Friendly	21/12/1901	Victoria United	Orion	1	1	Cattofield
Friendly	28/12/1901	Victoria United	Brechin United	4	0	Central Park
Friendly	01/01/1902	Victoria United	Annbank	3	0	Central Park
Friendly	02/01/1902	Victoria United	Kilmarnock	2	0	Central Park
Rhodesia Cup	11/01/1902	Victoria United	Orion	0	1	Cattofield
Aberdeenshire Cup SF	18/01/1902	Victoria United	Peterhead	2	1	Peterhead
Friendly	01/02/1902	Victoria United	Aberdeen	2	0	Central Park

Competition	Date		Opposition	F	A	Venue
Friendly	08/02/1902	Victoria United	Dundee A	2	0	Central Park
Rhodesia Cup	22/02/1902	Victoria United	Orion	2	3	Central Park
Aberdeenshire Cup Final	01/03/1902	Victoria United	Aberdeen	0	1	Cattofield
Friendly	12/04/1902	Victoria United	Orion	1	1	Pittodrie
Friendly	19/04/1902	Victoria United	East End Juniors	2	2	Central Park
Provost Fleming Shield	24/04/1902	Victoria United	Orion	4	1	Pittodrie
Rhodesia Cup	29/04/1902	Victoria United	Aberdeen	3	1	
Friendly	03/05/1902	Victoria United	Orion	2	3	Cattofield
Friendly	05/05/1902	Victoria United	Glasgow Rangers	0	7	Central park
Provost Fleming Shield Final	24/05/1902	Victoria United	Peterhead	2	0	Cattofield

Aberdeenshire Cup 1901-1902

	Date			F	A	Venue
Aberdeenshire Cup	23/11/1901	Aberdeen	Orion	2	1	Pittodrie
Semi Final	18/01/1902	Victoria United	Peterhead	2	1	Peterhead
Semi Final	18/01/1902	Aberdeen	Fraserburgh	4	0	Fraserburgh
Final	01/03/1902	Aberdeen	Victoria United	1	0	Cattofield

Provost Fleming Shield 1901-1902

	Date			F	A	Venue
Provost Fleming Shield	04/01/1902	Orion	Peterhead	1	2	Cattofield
Provost Fleming Shield	24/04/1902	Orion	Victoria United	1	4	Pittodrie
Provost Fleming Shield Final	22/05/1902	Victoria United	Peterhead	2	0	Cattofield

Rhodesia Cup 1901-1902

	Date			F	A	Venue
Rhodesia Cup Charity match	15/08/1901	Victoria United	Aberdeen-Orion Select	2	6	Central Park
Rhodesia Cup	22/08/1901	Orion	Victoria United	2	1	Cattofield

	Date			F	A	Venue
Rhodesia Cup	12/10/1901	Victoria United	Aberdeen	1	3	Central Park
Rhodesia Cup	08/02/1902	Orion	Aberdeen	4	1	Cattofield
Rhodesia Cup	22/02/1902	Victoria United	Orion	2	3	Central Park
Rhodesia Cup	29/04/1902	Aberdeen	Victoria United	1	3	

1902-1903
Amalgamation - but no Scottish League status

As the 1902-1903 season progressed, the action on the football park took second place to the activity off it as protracted discussions took place over a proposed amalgamation of the city's three clubs in a bid to secure a place in the Scottish League First Division. It could be argued that the distraction caused by the merger talks resulted in playing standards slipping to an all-time low. That certainly seemed to be the case for the Whites of Pittodrie who spent most of the season bobbling around the foot of the Northern League, eventually finishing 12th of the 13 clubs, just one point ahead of bottom dogs Lochee United. Orion kept some degree of respectability by finishing fourth while Victoria United finished sixth equal (although they would have been eighth if goal difference was applied).

Aberdeen's league performances were truly awful, the Pittodrie side scoring a measly 24 goals in 23 matches. Just four games were won, all of them at Pittodrie, including a last day of the season win over Victoria United which prevented the Whites finishing bottom of the table. A meagre three points were garnished on the road. It was hardly inspiring stuff and did little to enhance the perception of the standard of football in the north east. There was to be no consolation in the Scottish Qualifying Cup as Victoria United trounced Aberdeen 4-1 in the opening round. Whites' goalkeeper Ritchie was described as playing *"a very shaky and unsafe game."* There was talk of a crisis at Pittodrie and certainly the results being churned out made for dismal reading. The team did at least reach the final of the Aberdeenshire Cup but went down 4-1 to Victoria United, albeit after a replay, the first game ending in a 2-2 draw. Then, in the final game of the season, and indeed the final game played by the original Aberdeen, the Pittodrie men lifted the Provost Fleming Shield by defeating Orion 2-0. This was the final game these two clubs would play. One of the Aberdeen goals was scored by Charlie Mackie, who would go on to enjoy a brief career with Manchester United. Mackie's time with Aberdeen almost overlapped with that of his namesake Charles W. Mackie who played for the Whites in the 1890's.

Charles Mackie (1) Charlie Mackie (2)

The two Charlie Mackies

Charles W. Mackie first played football for Aulton Rovers but joined Aberdeen in the early 1890's and spent two seasons in the reserves. He made his first team debut in season 1894-1895 as a right half. At the start of the next season he played right back for a short time before being moved to centre forward, a position in which he enjoyed a lot of success including scoring seven goals in an 18-0 rout of Brechin at the Chanonry. Mackie also held various committee posts with Aberdeen and co-edited the 1898 booklet summarising the history of the club. That same year he emigrated to Ceylon (now Sri Lanka) in connection with his work.

The second Charlie Mackie scored the only goal of the game when Aberdeen defeated Victoria United at Cattofield in the 1901-1902 Aberdeenshire Cup Final.
For some strange reason he also seems to have appeared as a guest in the Peterhead team beaten by Victoria United in the 1902-1903 Lord Provost Fleming Charity Shield Semi Final. Charlie was top scorer with the 'new' Aberdeen in 1903-1904 and at the end of that season he signed for Manchester United. He made a promising start to his career in the South but injuries hampered his progress and he moved on to West Ham before returning to Pittodrie midway through the 1905-1906 season. He ended his career with Lochgelly United. Neither of these Mackie's should be confused with long serving player Jim Mackie who also played for the Whites in the late 19th Century.

While Aberdeen stuttered through the season, Orion secured a place in the higher reaches of the Northern League. The Cattofield side went out of the Scottish Qualifying Cup, losing 2-1 to Inverness Caledonian in the Highland capital. The Stripes took the lead early in the second half through Burnett, then the hosts were reduced to ten men when Mair was sent off. But Orion lost two late goals to topple out of the competition. Orion still qualified for the Scottish Cup but found themselves drawn away to Nithsdale Wanderers, which required them to make an epic trip to Sanquhar in the south-west of the country. The team travelled to Glasgow on the Friday and stayed overnight before continuing their journey south. In all it was a disastrous affair with the home side recording a 1-0 victory in front of a small crowd which offered very little in the way of financial compensation for the dejected Orionites.

Orion's Northern League game against Dundee A at Cattofield in early October grabbed the headlines for all the wrong reasons. The Stripes went ahead through a first half penalty, Low scoring after Wilson was fouled in the box. After that *"an element of roughness crept into the play and one or two of the Dundee players had to be warned by the referee."* The aggression continued in the second period with Dundee full-back Bonthrone getting involved in a number of untidy episodes which antagonised the crowd to such an extent that fears grew of a potential pitch invasion. A boy in the crowd then threw a stone which hit Bonthrone on the leg. The Dundee side responded by scoring two late goals, both from winger Neil, to win the match.

A sign that Orion perhaps didn't hold out too much hope of the merger talks being successful, had carried out improvements to their ground at the start of the season. The grandstand was strengthened, raised gravel embankments were put in place and *"a commodious press box"* was built which was described as allowing for *"reporters to discharge their duties with comfort and freedom."*

Victoria United's unhappy existence at Central Park continued, and the once powerful Torry side slumped to joint sixth position in the Northern League. The Blues had, however, made a great start to the league campaign, losing just one of their opening 10 games up until mid-November. Then a remarkable slump set in with just two wins being achieved in the next 13 matches. United still demonstrated their usual battling qualities in local Cup competitions and succeeded in lifting the Aberdeenshire Cup for the sixth time. As county champions they qualified for the Dewar Shield and, after defeating East Stirlingshire in the semi final they faced Forfarshire champions Dundee in the Final at Pittodrie. The Dens Park side, who would finish second behind Hibernian in the Scottish First Division that season, proved too powerful and won 2-1. The Rhodesia Cup was also secured with a points victory after drawing with Aberdeen in the final fixture of this round robin competition. United's history ended with an honourable 2-2 draw in a friendly game against Scottish champions Hibernian at Central Park.

It was, however, away from the field of play that most of the action was taking place. In the autumn of 1902 rumours were spreading within the local footballing community that officials of Hibernian were considering relocating the Edinburgh club to Aberdeen. Speculation was rife that Hibs officials had even travelled to the north east to try to agree terms for leasing Pittodrie. Had this come to pass it would have given the city a ready-made place in the First Division of the Scottish League, but it is difficult to substantiate whether there was any truth in this at all. Could it possibly have been a story that one individual, or group of individuals, who supported the idea of merging the city's three senior clubs, set in motion to scare the doubters into action? Or was it really a bold move undertaken by enterprising Edinburgh men seeking to exploit an opportunity in Aberdeen? Whatever the truth of the matter, the Easter Road side was forced to make an official statement denying that they had even considered such a proposal. The Hibernian story did, however, stimulate and accelerate discussion in the city about a proposed merger of Aberdeen, Victoria United and Orion with a view to securing admission to the First Division of the Scottish League. Orion secretary George Alexander appears to have been the driving force behind the idea and he responded to *"the Hibernian question"* by submitting a passionate case for amalgamation in a letter to the Evening Express in November 1902. Alexander said: *"Rumours are floating around of the Edinburgh Hibernians transferring their quarters to Aberdeen. This is becoming a hardy annual, but may become absolute fact if local football legislators do not awaken and admit that something must be done to keep up the enthusiasm amongst the followers of the Association game in our city. My opinion of the matter is that the only remedy for this question is the amalgamation of the three senior clubs. It will be a sorry day indeed and also a slur on the intelligence and grit of our local sportsmen if they allow any outside parties to step in and monopolise the game in the Granite City. This is practically what it would mean. We have an instance of Dundee F.C. running out the other two Northern League clubs in that district, namely, Wanderers and Lochee. They are at their wits end how to arrange their fixture cards to keep clear of First Division matches at Dens Park, and are leading a starvation existence. This would act the same in Aberdeen - practically the survival of the fittest. A club or clubs may plume themselves with the idea that they are doing well financially and otherwise, and have no desire to link on with another in a less favoured position. But this is suicidal, for what is the luck of one this season may be with the other the next, and, as I have previously stated, if one is doing well, the other is between the devil and the deep seas to get ends to meet. Give up this antagonistic spirit, and have a friendly conference on the question of amalgamation. Don't tackle it with minds biased one way or another, but simply discuss the pros and cons of this matter which must be faced sooner or later. The longer this is left over the more difficult it will be to solve. Give up sentiment about names and other petty matters of an insignificant order. I have not the slightest hesitation in saying that we would obtain admission into the Scottish League. A larger guarantee may be asked, but that can be faced, and other matters of detail. Each team has a certain number of influential members and supporters, and if these three can be brought together in conference, I have not the slightest doubt but that the problem can be solved, notwithstanding that some assert that it would require the wisdom of Solomon. Dundee were admitted into the First Division without qualifying through the Second Division, as also were Queen's Park, and why not a team from the Granite City? We have gentlemen who have proved able members of the Scottish F.A. and of other councils conceived with the game, and shall it be said that we have not any of sufficient foresight and ability to tackle the question of amalgamation? Surely not. In the past we have wasted too much of our energy and finance in keeping an eye on one another. We have not been able to give our supporters the class of football worthy of our city, simply because our efforts are much too spread, instead of being concentrated in one good team. Other reasons could be given, but for the present I will refrain. Having kicked off, I trust the game will be taken up in a proper spirit by those interested; and that out of the three clubs we may form one capable of taking an honourable place in first class football."*

Alexander's plea was soon acted upon as a joint committee of representatives from the three clubs was set up to progress the idea and a key meeting of this committee took place on Wednesday 3rd December in the County Hotel, King Street . Mr Alexander presided and Mr James H. Wink (Victoria United) was appointed Secretary. The Chairman said that he strongly favoured amalgamation but admitted that the financial aspects of the project might be a problem. Mr H. S. Wylie (Aberdeen) said that a considerable sum of money would be required to wipe off the debts of the existing clubs and that a sufficient balance would be needed to enable them to procure players. He also warned that failure to gain admission to the First Division would do more harm than good. Generally, however, the representatives were in favour of the idea. Mr Gaudie (Victoria United) seconded by Mr Cable (Aberdeen) moved that Mr Wylie be sent to the following evening's Scottish League meeting in Glasgow to explain the idea and to gauge the views of League members. Wylie's remit was to inform League members that a new Aberdeen club would only be interested in joining the First Division as membership of the Second Division would be barely an improvement on playing in the Northern League and would more than likely be financially disastrous. Wylie set of full of hope and confidence but returned home in less than buoyant mood. The League officials, while not dismissing the Aberdeen approach, informed Wylie that he would have to put more detailed proposals in front of members before any decision could possibly be taken. Discussions in Aberdeen continued about where a new amalgamated club should play its games, with Pittodrie being favoured, but not unanimously, as there were concerns over whether or not a sufficiently long lease could be obtained for the ground.

After some deliberation, a new proposal was submitted to the Scottish League members over the Christmas-New Year period and this was considered by the League at a meeting in early January. But, again, the response was deflating in the extreme. On 3rd January 1903 the Evening Express reported that Victoria United's James H. Wink, the chairman of the amalgamation committee, had received a letter from the Scottish Football League Secretary. It read as follows:-

"Dear Sir - I duly received yours of 27th inst., and placed before the First Division Committee on Monday night. I am instructed to inform you that the committee cannot admit the amalgamation of the three leading clubs in Aberdeen to the First Division, as before doing so, drastic alteration would require to be made on the constitution of the League, and the representatives at present hold no mandate from their clubs to carry out these alterations. Yours truly, William MacAndrew." This was a devastating blow to the amalgamation committee who met again a few days later in the County Hotel to discuss what to do next. In some quarters concerns were being expressed about the way in which the committee was going about its work. There was a feeling that the efforts to secure League status were *"half hearted"* and it was widely believed that some members of the committee were still not fully supportive of a merger. There was also specific criticism of the delay in drafting and circulating the bid document which only arrived with League members a few days before their meeting, leaving them insufficient time to give it proper consideration.

But hope was not lost as the amalgamation committee decided to make a new approach to the League clubs. Messrs Wink, Alexander and Wylie were given the task of reviewing the bid document. So, in mid-January another letter was sent to the League clubs seeking their support. In this letter the Aberdeen clubs asked each of the League members to support the bid for First Division membership at the League's annual meeting later in the year. The letter indicated that if 10 league clubs supported the Aberdeen bid, then the amalgamation proposals would continue to be worked up in more detail. Meanwhile, the growing local interest in the affairs of the amalgamation committee prompted Orion's George Alexander to propose that a public meeting be held, but this was initially resisted by the Aberdeen F.C. representatives, Messrs Wylie and Ritchie. It was clear that, even at this stage, not all parties were altogether happy with the merger proposals. Mr Alexander in the meantime received a letter from a Glaswegian friend supporting the proposed merger of the three clubs and suggesting that the new team should play in tartan jerseys and white shorts. He suggested either Gordon tartan shirts or red tartan shirts should be worn. The letter stated: *"If Aberdeen adopt the tartan jersey they would be the only club in Britain who would wear the pure Scottish dress."* The writer also suggested that the club should be set up as a

Mr John Clarke, chaired vital amalgamation meeting in Trades Hall, Belmont Street.

limited liability company and should build a new ground with capacity for 30,000 fans and this new ground should be called Balmoral Park.

Discussions continued on a regular basis in the city and the idea of establishing a new club as a limited liability company was agreed. To gather public support, and more importantly, to attract investment, the amalgamation committee finally decided to hold a public meeting and this took place on Friday 20th March in the Trades Hall, Belmont Street. An estimated 1,600 people packed into the venue and each was issued with a piece of paper asking how many shares they would be interested in buying should it be decided to form a company. Mr John Clarke, a lecturer in Education at Aberdeen University, who lived in the Chanonry, was appointed to Chair the meeting and the others on the top table were:- Baillie Robertson, Dundee, Mr Wallace, Secretary of Dundee F.C, Councillor Milne, Messrs J.G. Cruickshank, SFA, H. Ross, H. Wylie, W. Cable, G. Alexander and Mr Wink, Secretary of the Amalgamation Joint Committee. The Dundee men had offered to come along to provide support and advice as the Tayside club had gone through a similar process a few years earlier.

The Chairman intimated that a crisis had been reached in the history of football in the city. He praised the work of the amalgamation committee as a merger was really the only way forward if Aberdeen was to take a prominent part in the football world. He suggested that if a first class team was to be established it would require significant investment and the committee was looking for people to invest in the new club. He was seeking the approval of the meeting to wind up the three existing clubs on consideration that Orion received £175-10s, Victoria United £101 and Aberdeen £800. Other assets and liabilities would need to be dealt with.

Bailie Robertson explained how matters had been dealt with in Dundee (who had been elected to the league in 1897-1898). Councillor Milne moved that the meeting proceed to *"form a company with a capital of £1500 in £1 shares."* The motion was unanimously carried. The Joint Committee was asked to prepare articles of association, appoint an interim law agent and prepare a list of names of gentlemen taking shares willing and qualified to act as interim directors of the company and make all the preliminary arrangements. It also became clear that the new club would be known as Aberdeen F.C. Limited and that its home ground should be Pittodrie. There's no doubt that the merger was now gathering unstoppable momentum but there was a slight hitch in early April when, at a meeting in the Good Templar Hall, George Street, committee members heard that Crescent Cricket Club had intimated that they didn't want to give up their tenancy of Pittodrie during May-August, although they would give up a fortnight at beginning of May and end of August for a reduction in rent. It was also intimated that the owners of Pittodrie might only agree to the new club being given a 10 year lease of the ground. As a result of this, Hugh Gaudie of Victoria United suggested that an alternative ground should be found. The committee disagreed with Gaudie and decided to remain on track as they felt the difficulties with the cricket club and the lease could be overcome, and so it proved. A bold approach to attract West Bromwich Albion to come to Pittodrie to play against a city select team fell through however as the English side was unavailable. The idea behind this venture was to show that a combined Aberdeen team could hold its own against a top English side.

Work continued towards setting up the new company and a prospectus was drawn up by mid-April and made available to the public. It stated the objectives of the new club. It said: *"To those who have closely studied the progress of association football in Aberdeen during several years past it is evident that the quality of the play of the leading city clubs has not been improving, and as a result the interest taken by the football public has been declining. The football talent in the city, broken up into too many different clubs, is wanting in effectiveness, and the general standard of Aberdeen football has been such that it is with difficulty the very best teams from the south can be induced to travel to Aberdeen. The solution of the difficulty lies in the amalgamation of the assets and*

of the talent of the three leading city clubs with the view of raising such a
combination as will secure admission to the First Division of the Scottish League."
It was decided to issue 3,000 shares of 10s each (5s on application and 5s on
allotment). The list was closed on 30th April and Councillor Milne was appointed
chairman of the interim board of directors. The other members of the interim
board were - Messrs H.S. Wylie, John MacKay, William Jaffray, James Philip and
James Rae. The company solicitor was Mr Alex Clark, 13 Bridge Street - he was a
former Aberdeen FC outside left.

At the beginning of May a friendly game was played between an Aberdeen select
with players drawn from all three local clubs, and Dundee. As with the West
Bromwich idea, this was a to be a demonstration of how a combined Aberdeen
team would fare against a top League club. Dundee agreed to provide the
opposition because of their support for an Aberdeen bid for First Division
membership. To accommodate the game, Aberdeen's Northern League match
against Montrose, scheduled for the same date, was brought forward to an 11-
15am kick-off while the Dundee match was played in the afternoon. Montrose
won the league match 4-2 although Aberdeen didn't field any of the players who
would turn out in the later game which Dundee won 4-1 in front of a crowd of
3,000. Charlie Mackie had given the select a 1-0 halftime lead, but the visitors
upped the tempo in the second period and ran out comfortable winners.
Meanwhile, the League membership bid seemed to be progressing perfectly until
May 18th 1903 when the Scottish Football League's annual meeting was held in
Glasgow. The meeting agreed to increase membership of the First Division from
12 to 14 clubs, which the new Aberdeen wanted. There were, however, three
clubs applying for membership – Motherwell, Airdrie and Aberdeen. Members
then proceeded to vote to decide which two of the three applicants should be
elected. A large crowd gathered outside the offices of the Aberdeen Free Press to
hear the outcome of the meeting and loud jeering started when the
announcement was made. It was:-

Motherwell 11 votes   **Airdrieonians 8 votes**   **Aberdeen 5 votes.**

At the same time Albion Rovers, Raith Rovers and Ayr Parkhouse were all elected
to the Second Division (but St Johnstone's bid was rejected).

The decision came as a bombshell for the north east men. Aberdeen had, of course, placed all their eggs in the one basket. They had applied only for membership of the First Division as the Second Division wasn't considered a viable option. The Aberdeen directors were totally deflated. They had been confident that their application would be successful. Extensive lobbying of clubs had been undertaken with the Aberdeen side offering to provide each club with 15 railway tickets to travel to matches in the city in addition to giving them one third of the gate money as was required by the League. Despite this major setback the directors decided to proceed with the formation of the new amalgamated club, which would, however, have to confine itself to playing in the Northern League and Scottish Cup. They vowed to submit a new application for League membership the following season. So the amalgamation was completed and the names of Orion and Victoria United passed into the history books.

Although the new Aberdeen Football Club's first official game was against Stenhousemuir in the Northern League on 15th August 1903, some of the Whites were in action the previous week when they took part in the Aberdeen Police Sports at Pittodrie. The Sports included a five-a-side football competition in which Aberdeen, Dundee, Celtic and Hibernian all entered teams. Aberdeen defeated Dundee 1-0 in the first round while Celtic defeated Hibs by the same score after extra time. The Celts edged out Aberdeen 3-2 in an exciting final to collect the £10 prize money. Pittodrie was packed for the occasion. The teams were:-
Aberdeen - Ritchie, Willox, Mckay, Strang and McAulay.
Celtic - Lonie, McMenemy, McLeod, Muir, Adams.
Dundee - Darroch, Jeffrey, Halkett, Wilson, McDermott. Hibernian - Rennie, Gray, MacConnachie, Stewart, Campbell

The Aberdeen team for the Stenhousemuir match featured just two men – John Sangster and Charlie Mackie – who had played for any of the three merged clubs the previous season (and both had played for the old Aberdeen club). Three members of Orion – Willie Ritchie, Sam Willox and Henry Low – didn't play in the first game but made appearances for Aberdeen in its inaugural season, 1903-04. Robert Ritchie was the sole Victoria United player to join the new club. The new Aberdeen's first manager was Jimmy Philip and the club's trainer was former Victoria United

First manager Jimmy Philip (first left, back row) and first trainer, Peter Simpson, extreme right, back row) pictured with the 'new' Aberdeen F.C, Scottish Qualifying Cup winners 1904-05

stalwart Peter Simpson. Both had a long involvement in north east football.

Jimmy Philip doesn't seem to have been a player at any stage, but he was first treasurer of the Aberdeenshire F.A. when it was formed in 1888. He had also been a founder member of the Britannia F.C. in October 1886, and was the club's first secretary-treasurer. He was appointed Aberdeenshire F.A. President in 1893-1894 and again six years later. When Britannia folded he became the Peterhead F.C. representative on the A.F.A. and maintained a connection with the Blue Toon club for the rest of his life. He was appointed secretary of the 'new' Aberdeen in 1903 and a year later when the club joined the Scottish League Second Division he became secretary-manager. He remained as manager until 1924. In 1927 he was co-opted onto the Board of Directors and remained a member until his death in 1930. During his time at Pittodrie, Philip was seen as the driving force behind much of the progress the club made. He oversaw the acquisition of Pittodrie (the ground originally being leased) and he secured many improvements to the facilities, including the construction of a large new grandstand. His side won the Scottish Qualifying Cup in 1904-5 and in the following year, admission was secured to the First Division. His pioneering ideas led to Aberdeen undertaking ambitious European tours and he served on the S.F.A. Council and the Scottish

League Management Committee for many years. Philip was also a keen follower of cricket and apparently was a daily sea swimmer. He gave up the manager's post in 1924, became a Town Councillor for the St Machar ward and was convenor of the Housing Committee. Philip died at home, 13 Erskine Street, on Sunday 11th October 1930, aged 68. He had attended the Aberdeen-St Mirren game the previous afternoon and was at the Pittodrie club's Board meeting at the Douglas Hotel on the Saturday evening. He had been injured in a road traffic accident while visiting Ireland earlier in the year. Initially it was believed his injuries weren't severe, but he never seemed to fully recover.

A little more than six months after Philip's death, another link between the old and new football regimes in the city was lost when Peter Simpson passed away. He had been Aberdeen's trainer for 20 years. A native of Peterhead, Simpson spent most of his life in Aberdeen and started playing football with Gladstone F.C. at the Links in the late 1880's. He then moved to the Rovers before becoming the first player to sign for Victoria United when the club was formed in 1889. He went on to captain the club, then held many committee positions. He was also a President of the Aberdeenshire F.A. Simpson subsequently became a Scottish League referee and also refereed a Scottish Cup Final. He died on 23rd April 1931, aged 66, at his home, 1 Nelson Street.

When the new Aberdeen opened the 1903-1904 season there remained a number of people who still didn't support the amalgamation. Indeed, some opponents of the project went so far as to form another new club which took on the name of Bon Accord Amateurs. This outfit applied, but failed, to obtain membership of the Northern League. They did, however, gain entry to the Scottish Qualifying Cup in which they were drawn to play the new Aberdeen. The Whites won 5-1.
Bon Accord 's aspirations to become the city's top club were doomed to fail due to a wholesale lack of interest from the footballing public. In October 1903 they invited Arbroath Reserves to Aberdeen for a friendly. The weather was atrocious, the pitch was *"in a horrible state"* and postponement was considered. After some debate it was decided to proceed with the match which, according to the Bon Accord magazine, attracted a crowd of *"absolutely nil."* Bon Accord won 2-0.

Notable Games

Victoria United 4, Aberdeen 1
Aberdeenshire Cup Final Replay, Cattofield Park, 14th March 1903

United played up the hill in the first half and for the first ten minutes they dominated but failed to score. Aberdeen broke away and a Woodlock shot scraped past the United post. The Whites settled into the game and enjoyed a long spell of pressure but a combination of good goalkeeping and poor finishing prevented them from taking the lead. The game swung from end to end and United finally broke the deadlock in the 35th minute, George Ritchie netting after Bisset saved his first effort. Aberdeen responded immediately with Charlie Mackie capping a brilliant solo run with a 30 yard shot from an oblique angle which beat Murray. It was all square at halftime but soon after the restart the Blues took the lead. George Ritchie broke clear on the wing and crossed for Steven to hit the ball beyond Bisset.Vics then took total control and Ferries made it 3-1 after a Lindsay shot was beaten away by Bisset. Steven notched a fourth shortly before full-time.

Victoria United - R. Murray, Kilgour, Craig, R. Ritchie, Jenkins, Robertson, Duncan, Steven, Lindsay, Ferries, G. Ritchie.

Aberdeen - Bisset, Walker, Ross, Sangster, Thomson, Murphy, J. Mackie, C. Mackie, Barron, Woodlock, Shiach.

Referee - Mr J. McCorquodale, Dalmuir

Victoria United 1, Dundee A 2
Dewar Shield Final, Pittodrie Park, 2nd May 1903

Vics were keen to become the first Aberdeenshire side to win the Shield but their hopes were upset in the first half when slack play allowed Joe Kerr to give the visitors the lead. Worse was to follow when Kerr was again on the mark when capitalising on a mistake by Robertson. The men from 'Juteopolis' continued to press but failed to add to

Aberdeen F.C. captain John Sangster

their tally before the interval. Vics came out for the second half in a rejuvenated mood and bombarded the visitors' goal but luck was not on their side. The Dens Park men defended stoutly, often blasting the ball out of the ground simply to relieve the pressure. Eventually, with three minutes remaining, United got some reward for their efforts when Knowles scored. The home team continued to attack but despite coming close on a few occasions,they couldn't break the Dundee rearguard for a second time.

Victoria United - R. Murray, Craig, McHardy, R. Ritchie, A. Murray, Robertson, Knowles, Duncan, Laurie, Ferries, G. Ritchie.

Dundee A - Muir, Bonthrone, Jeffrey, Halkett, Morris, Gowans, Grant, Kerr, Dickson, Wilson, Gibson.

Referee - Mr Tom Robertson, Queen's Park

Aberdeen Select 1, Dundee 4
Pittodrie Park, 4th May 1903

The select featured players from Aberdeen, Victoria United and Orion. This match was arranged to show how an amalgamated local side would fare against Scottish League opposition. Even playing against Dundee, a club which was sympathetic towards Aberdeen's aspirations for League membership, the result did little to enhance the city's footballing reputation as the visitors cantered to a comfortable win. Dundee started poorly and *"for the first half hour the First Leaguers did not rise above the usual Aberdeen standard."* Charlie Mackie upset the visitors by firing the Aberdeen select ahead but there was little else to excite the crowd as the *" rain sodden heavy ground accounted for a good deal of miskicking and muddling."* There was no further scoring before halftime was called. Dundee looked more alert in the second period and their centre half, Peter Robertson, equalised with an effort which trundled past the unsighted Ritchie. Robertson got his second of the game not long afterwards and Dundee added two more before the end to secure a comfortable if uninspiring win.

Dundee - Muir, Darroch, Sharp, Halkett, Robertson, McDiarmid, Bell, White, Wilson, McFarlane, T. Robertson.

Aberdeen Select - Ritchie, Walker, McHardy, Willox, A. Murray, Robertson, Knowles, C. Mackie, Lindsay, Henderson, Hogg

Victoria United captain, Arthur Murray

Victoria United 2, Hibernian 2
Central Park, 13th May 1903

Scottish First Division champions Hibernian visited Central Park for what was to be the last game played by Victoria United. Despite playing up the slope, the Edinburgh men wasted no time in showing their class, McGeachan netting with less than a minute on the clock, although reports suggest home 'keeper Douglas might have done better. Hibs kept the pressure up and Douglas was again judged to be at fault when Atherton scored with a rather soft shot. Vics had a chance to claw their way back into the game when they were awarded a penalty, but McHardy's effort was sent wide of the post. (Incredibly, a few days earlier it was reported that Vics had been awarded 14 penalties during the season, but managed to score from just three of them). The home side was, however, beginning to gain a bit of momentum and Rennie in the Hibs goal had to pull off some fine saves. The champions dropped down a gear at the start of the second half and paid the price when Ferries beat Rennie with a powerful shot. A few minutes later Bone conceded his second penalty of the game, a soft one by all accounts, but this time Ferries converted to level the scores. It is perhaps fitting that United's final goal was scored by Ferries who appears to have been the highest goalscorer in the history of the club. Research carried out by Graham McKenzie suggests Ferries scored at least 69 during his time with the Blues. Hibs reacted by upping the tempo but there was to be no further scoring.

Victoria United - Douglas, Kilgour, Craig, Robertson, McHardy, Murray, Knowles, Stephen, Lindsay, Ferries, G. Ritchie.

Hibernian - Rennie, Gray, Bone, Harrower, Wilson, Robertson, McCartney, Atherton, McGeachan, McMahon, Stewart.

Referee - Mr McLeod, Orion

Aberdeen 2, Orion 0
Provost Fleming Charity Shield Final, Pittodrie Park, 15th May 1903

This was to be the last match played by Aberdeen and Orion before the completion of the merger and it was perhaps fitting that a trophy should be at stake. The Provost Fleming Shield, which is still being played for today under the name of the Aberdeenshire Shield, was up for grabs and the Friday evening match attracted a *"fairly good attendance of spectators"* to Pittodrie. There was no special fanfare to mark the occasion. Indeed I could find no mention of the historic significance of this match at all in any contemporary reports. Aberdeen looked the brighter of the sides in the opening exchanges and there was little surprise when Charlie Mackie gave the Whites the lead after half an hour. The score remained unchanged by the interval and the quality of play was described as *"mediocre."* Aberdeen continued to dominate in the second half and eventually doubled their lead when McDonald pounced on some hesitancy shown by Orion's Willie Ritchie to bundle both the ball and the 'keeper into the net. Orion failed to threaten the Aberdeen goal and the home side ran out comfortable winners. It is interesting to note that even at this date, there was still some uncertainty over the proposed merger as Baillie Glass, in presenting the trophy to the winners, expressed a hope that *"should amalgamation take place,"* efforts should still be made by the local club to support charity.

Aberdeen - Bisset, Walker, Ross, Sangster, Thomson, Murphy, Gaitens, C. Mackie, McDonald, Buchan, Shiach

Orion - Ritchie, Willox, Grant, Fraser, Low, Bremner, Prophet, Thom, Lawrie, Henderson, Hogg.

Referee – Mr. P. Simpson, Aberdeen

Northern League 1902-1903

		P	W	D	L	F	A	Pts
1	Dundee A	24	17	4	3	58	27	38
2	Lochgelly United	24	12	8	4	52	30	32
3	Cowdenbeath	23	10	8	5	41	25	28
4	Orion	24	10	6	8	47	40	26
5	Arbroath	24	9	8	7	47	43	26
6	Dunfermline Athletic	23	8	6	9	32	33	22
7	St Johnstone	21	8	6	7	37	42	22
8	Victoria United	23	9	4	10	34	44	22
9	Montrose	23	9	3	11	38	41	21
10	Forfar Athletic	24	7	5	12	47	63	19
11	Dundee Wanderers	22	7	3	12	28	37	17
12	Aberdeen	23	4	7	12	24	42	15
13	Lochee United	24	4	6	14	32	52	14

Note – Many fixtures do not appear to have been completed.

Aberdeen – Northern League 1902-1903

	Date		Opposition	F	A	Venue
Northern League	16/08/1902	Aberdeen	Orion	1	2	Cattofield
Northern League	23/08/1902	Aberdeen	Dunfermline Athletic	1	0	Dunfermline
Northern League	30/08/1902	Aberdeen	St Johnstone	1	1	Pittodrie
Northern League	13/09/1902	Aberdeen	Forfar Athletic	2	1	Pittodrie
Northern League	20/09/1902	Aberdeen	Montrose	0	4	Montrose
Northern League	27/09/1902	Aberdeen	Dundee A	0	1	Dens Park, Dundee
Northern League	04/10/1902	Aberdeen	Arbroath	1	1	Pittodrie
Northern League	11/10/1902	Aberdeen	Victoria United	0	1	Central Park
Northern League	18/10/1902	Aberdeen	Dunfermline Athletic	0	1	Pittodrie
Northern League	25/10/1902	Aberdeen	Dundee A	1	3	Pittodrie
Northern League	01/11/1902	Aberdeen	Lochee United	1	4	Dundee
Northern League	08/11/1902	Aberdeen	Cowdenbeath	2	2	Pittodrie
Northern League	29/11/1902	Aberdeen	Cowdenbeath	0	1	Cowdenbeath
Northern League	13/12/1902	Aberdeen	Lochee United	1	0	Pittodrie
Northern League	27/12/1902	Aberdeen	Dundee Wanderers	0	1	Pittodrie

	Date		Opposition	F	A	Venue
Northern League	24/01/1903	Aberdeen	Lochgelly United	1	2	Pittodrie
Northern League	14/02/1903	Aberdeen	Forfar Athletic	2	2	Station Park,Forfar
Northern League	21/03/1903	Aberdeen	Orion	1	1	Pittodrie
Northern League	04/04/1903	Aberdeen	Arbroath	3	3	Gayfield Park
Northern League	11/04/1903	Aberdeen	St Johnstone	1	1	Perth
Northern League	25/04/1903	Aberdeen	Lochgelly United	0	5	Lochgelly, Reid's Park
Northern League	04/05/1903	Aberdeen	Montrose	2	4	Pittodrie
Northern League	11/05/1903	Aberdeen	Victoria United	3	1	Pittodrie

Note: Aberdeen defeated Dundee Wanderers 3-2 at Clepington Park on 15th November 1902. This was meant to be a Northern League match but the referee took ill before kick-off and the game had to be played as a friendly as a Wanderers official took over the officiating duties. The problems Wanderers were having in attracting fans were illustrated by the estimated attendance for this game being around the 30 mark. This game does not seem to have been replayed.

Aberdeen – Other Games 1902-1903

Competition	Date		Opposition	F	A	Venue
Scottish Qualifying Cup	06/09/1902	Aberdeen	Victoria United	1	4	Central Park
Friendly	15/11/1902	Aberdeen	Dundee Wanderers	3	2	Clepington Park, Dundee
Friendly	20/12/1902	Aberdeen	Aberdeen University	1	1	Pittodrie
Friendly	01/01/1903	Aberdeen	Broxburn	1	0	Pittodrie
Friendly	02/01/1903	Aberdeen	Orion	3	2	Cattofield
Friendly	03/01/1903	Aberdeen	Stenhousemuir	2	1	Pittodrie

Orion – Northern League 1902-1903

	Date		Opposition	F	A	Venue
Northern League	16/08/1902	Orion	Aberdeen	2	1	Cattofield
Northern League	23/08/1902	Orion	Lochgelly United	2	2	Cattofield
Northern League	30/08/1902	Orion	Forfar Athletic	0	0	Station Park,Forfar
Northern League	13/09/1902	Orion	Arbroath	1	1	Gayfield Park
Northern League	27/09/1902	Orion	Dunfermline Athletic	1	0	Cattofield
Northern League	04/10/1902	Orion	Dundee A	1	2	Cattofield

	Date		Opposition	F	A	Venue
Northern League	11/10/1902	Orion	Dundee A	0	2	Dens Park, Dundee
Northern League	25/10/1902	Orion	Montrose	4	0	Cattofield
Northern League	08/11/1902	Orion	Lochgelly United	0	4	Lochgelly
Northern League	15/11/1902	Orion	Victoria United	1	2	Central Park
Northern League	29/11/1902	Orion	Dundee Wanderers	2	1	Dundee
Northern League	06/12/1902	Orion	Montrose	0	1	Links Park, Montrose
Northern League	20/12/1902	Orion	St Johnstone	4	4	Perth
Northern League	03/01/1903	Orion	Dundee Wanderers	2	3	Cattofield
Northern League	14/02/1903	Orion	Arbroath	4	3	Cattofield
Northern League	28/02/1903	Orion	Lochee United	4	3	Cattofield
Northern League	07/03/1903	Orion	Lochee United	1	2	Dundee
Northern League	14/03/1903	Orion	Dunfermline Athletic	1	1	Dunfermline
Northern League	21/03/1903	Orion	Aberdeen	1	1	Pittodrie
Northern League	28/03/1903	Orion	Cowdenbeath	0	1	Cowdenbeath
Northern League	04/04/1903	Orion	Forfar Athletic	6	2	Cattofield
Northern League	11/04/1903	Orion	Cowdenbeath	3	1	Cattofield
Northern League	25/04/1903	Orion	Victoria United	2	1	Cattofield
Northern League	09/05/1903	Orion	St Johnstone	5	2	Cattofield

Orion – Other Games 1902-1903

Competition	Date		Opposition	F	A	Venue
Scottish Qualifying Cup	06/09/1902	Orion	Peterhead	7	1	Cattofield
Scottish Qualifying Cup	20/09/1902	Orion	Victoria United	4	0	Central Park
Friendly	22/09/1902	Orion	Dundee	0	4	Cattofield
Scottish Qualifying Cup	18/10/1902	Orion	Inverness Caledonian	1	2	Inverness
Friendly	13/12/1902	Orion	Kings Park	4	1	Cattofield
Friendly	02/01/1903	Orion	Aberdeen	2	3	Cattofield
Scottish Cup	24/01/1903	Orion	Nithsdale Wanderers	0	1	Sanquhar

Victoria United – Northern League 1902-1903

	Date		Opposition	F	A	Venue
Northern League	16/08/1902	Victoria United	Arbroath	4	2	Gayfield Park
Northern League	23/08/1902	Victoria United	Cowdenbeath	2	2	Pittodrie
Northern League	30/08/1902	Victoria United	Dundee Wanderers	2	0	Central Park
Northern League	13/09/1902	Victoria United	Dundee A	0	0	Central Park
Northern League	04/10/1902	Victoria United	Montrose	1	4	Links Park, Montrose
Northern League	11/10/1902	Victoria United	Aberdeen	1	0	Central Park
Northern League	18/10/1902	Victoria United	Lochgelly United	2	0	Central Park
Northern League	25/10/1902	Victoria United	Lochee United	2	1	St. Margaret's Park, Lochee
Northern League	08/11/1902	Victoria United	Dunfermline Athletic	2	1	Central Park
Northern League	15/11/1902	Victoria United	Orion	2	1	Central Park
Northern League	29/11/1902	Victoria United	Montrose	1	2	Central Park
Northern League	13/12/1902	Victoria United	Cowdenbeath	0	2	Cowdenbeath
Northern League	20/12/1902	Victoria United	Forfar Athletic	2	1	Central Park
Northern League	27/12/1902	Victoria United	St Johnstone	4	1	Central Park
Northern League	03/01/1903	Victoria United	Dundee A	0	6	Dens Park, Dundee
Northern League	10/01/1903	Victoria United	Lochee United	1	1	Central Park
Northern League	24/01/1903	Victoria United	Dunfermline Athletic	1	3	East End Park, Dunfermline
Northern League	14/02/1903	Victoria United	Lochgelly United	2	3	Lochgelly
Northern League	21/03/1903	Victoria United	Dundee Wanderers	0	3	Dundee
Northern League	18/04/1903	Victoria United	Forfar Athletic	1	4	Station Park,Forfar
Northern League	25/04/1903	Victoria United	Orion	1	2	Cattofield
Northern League	09/05/1903	Victoria United	Arbroath	2	2	Central Park
Northern League	11/05/1903	Victoria United	Aberdeen	1	3	Pittodrie

Victoria United – Other Games 1902-1903

Competition	Date		Opposition	F	A	Venue
Scottish Qualifying Cup	06/09/1902	Victoria United	Aberdeen	4	1	Central Park
Scottish Qualifying Cup	20/09/1902	Victoria United	Orion	0	4	Central Park

Competition	Date		Opposition	F	A	Venue
Friendly	28/02/1903	Victoria United	Mossend Swifts	11	2	Central Park
Friendly	04/04/1903	Victoria United	Junior Select	1	1	Central Park
Dewar Shield	11/04/1903	Victoria United	East Stirlingshire	2	0	Central Park
Dewar Shield Final	02/05/1903	Victoria United	Dundee A	1	2	Pittodrie
Friendly	13/05/1903	Victoria United	Hibernian	2	2	Central Park

Note: The game against the Aberdeen Junior Select was abandoned in the second half because of torrential rain and flooding.

Aberdeenshire Cup 1902-1903

	Date			F	A	Venue
Aberdeenshire Cup	22/11/1902	Victoria United	Peterhead	3	1	Central Park
Aberdeenshire Cup	31/01/1903	Aberdeen	Orion	0	0	Pittodrie
Aberdeenshire Cup	07/02/1903	Orion	Aberdeen	0	4	Cattofield
Final	07/03/1903	Victoria United	Aberdeen	2	2	Cattofield
Final Replay	14/03/1903	Victoria United	Aberdeen	4	1	Cattofield

Provost Fleming Shield 1902-1903

	Date			F	A	Venue
Fleming Shield	28/03/1903	Aberdeen	Peterhead	2	1	Pittodrie
Fleming Shield	29/04/1903	Victoria United	Orion	1	2	Pittodrie
Final	15/05/1903	Aberdeen	Orion	2	0	Pittodrie

Rhodesia Cup 1902-1903

	Date			F	A	Venue
Rhodesia Cup	01/11/1902	Orion	Victoria United	0	0	Cattofield
Rhodesia Cup	22/11/1902	Aberdeen	Orion	2	1	Pittodrie
Rhodesia Cup	06/12/1902	Aberdeen	Victoria United	2	2	Pittodrie
Rhodesia Cup	17/01/1903	Aberdeen	Victoria United	0	2	Pittodrie
Rhodesia Cup	21/02/1903	Victoria United	Orion	2	0	Central Park
Rhodesia Cup	18/04/1903	Orion	Aberdeen	1	3	Cattofield
Rhodesia Cup	07/05/1903	Victoria United	Aberdeen	2	2	Central Park

Note: The Aberdeen-Victoria United game on 6/12/1902 was stopped 15 minutes early because of darkness and replayed on 17/01/1903

Appendix 1 - **Where they played**

Aberdeen F.C.

Aberdeen Football Club, when formed in 1881, played practice games at the Links and at Hayton, Woodside, but the club soon reached agreement with Aberdeenshire Cricket Club to play at the Holburn Grounds located in the area now bounded by Irvine Place, Pitstruan Place, Broomhill Road and Allan Street. Aberdeen's first Scottish Cup tie, against Dundee Harp in October 1882, was played at Aberdeen Grammar School grounds, although the other home matches that season were played at Holburn. Only one home game was played in 1883-1884 and that was also at Holburn. In 1884-1885 and 1885-1886 Aberdeen played their home games at the Recreation Grounds, Inches. These grounds were located on low lying land next to the old line of the River Dee in what is now the Poynernook and lower Market Street area. This land was subsequently reclaimed and developed. In 1886-1887 games were played at the Recreation Grounds but the Holburn Grounds were also used. Aberdeen's opening game of

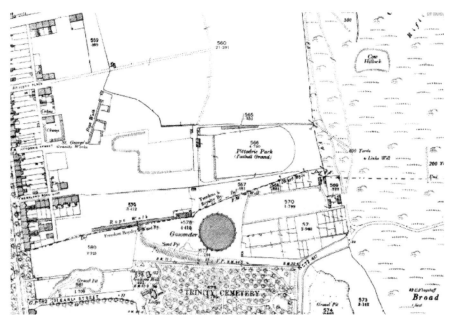

Pittodrie Park in 1901
Reproduced from the (1901) Ordnance Survey map

season 1887-1888, at the beginning of September, was played at Central Park, Kittybrewster (the new home of Orion) but from then until mid-February 1888 they again played at Holburn. At that point the Whites relocated to Chanonry, playing their first game at the Old Aberdeen venue on 25th February 1888. This was to be Aberdeen's home until the end of season 1897-1898 when the Chanonry ground was purchased by the University to be laid out as a botanical gardens. Aberdeen took up residence at Central Park for the 1898-1899 season, before moving to Pittodrie. The club's first game at Pittodrie was played in September 1899.

The Inches 1867. This area was later laid out for football and other sports prior to the land being fully reclaimed and developed for industrial purposes (now the Poynernook area). Reproduced from the (1867) Ordnance Survey map

Orion F.C.

Orion formed in October 1885 and played their first game, against Aberdeen, at the Recreation Grounds, Inches. They also played at Duthie Park and the Links during the rest of this season. At the start of season 1888-1889 they moved to an enclosed ground at Central Park, Kittybrewster where they stayed until the end of season 1893-1894 when they moved up the hill to a new ground leased from Aberdeen Town Council. This was to be known as Cattofield, but was initially on occasion referred to as Orion Park. The first game here was played in August 1894 against Dundee. Despite complaints from residents in the surrounding areas in the early years, Orion remained at Cattofield until the merger with Aberdeen and Victoria United in 1903.

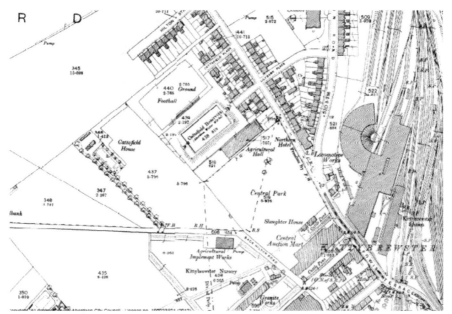

Orion's Cattofield ground is shown immediately north of Cattofield Reservoir. Cattofield Place now runs through the middle of the ground. Kittybrewster station, used by many visiting clubs, is shown in the south east corner of the map. Central Park is also shown. All three clubs, Orion, Aberdeen and Victoria United, played here at one time or another. Reproduced from the (1901) Ordnance Survey map

Victoria United F.C.

Victoria United formed in 1889 and the club was based at the Victoria Bridge Grounds in Torry. The Vics remained there until the end of season 1891-1892 when for some reason they relocated to a pitch between the railway line and the River Dee at Old Ford Road. This became known as the Wellington Bridge Grounds due to its proximity to that river crossing. United's first game at the new ground was on 22nd October 1892, against Brechin. United moved back to Victoria Bridge Grounds for one game, a Scottish Cup tie against Aberdeen in September 1893, but played the remainder of their home fixtures that season at Wellington Bridge. At the beginning of season 1894-1895, however, the Vics had moved back to their original home in Torry. In 1899-1900 the Vics were once again seeking to relocate and the club looked for a ground close to Holburn Street station, but this came to nothing. United played their final game at the Victoria Bridge Grounds in May 1900 when a defeat by Forfar Athletic cost them the

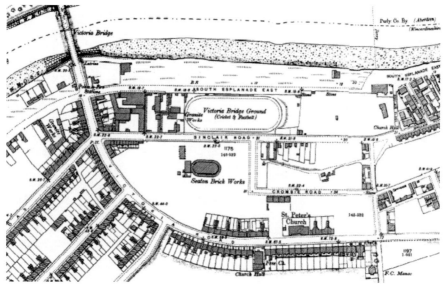

Victoria Bridge Grounds – original home of Victoria United
Reproduced from the (1901) Ordnance Survey map

Northern League title. The club was forced to look elsewhere for a ground, but, unable to find anything close to their spiritual home on the south side of the city, the Vics moved up to Central Park. Central Park wasn't available for the opening league match of the 1900-1901 season against Dundee A so that game was played at Orion's Cattofield Park. The Vics' first match as tenants of Central Park was against Aberdeen in the Scottish Qualifying Cup at the beginning of September. There they stayed until the 1903 merger.

Appendix 2 - **Titles and trophies**

Northern League positions

	Aberdeen	Orion	Victoria United	No of Teams in League	Champions
1891-1892	6	x	x	8	East End, Dundee
1892-1893	6	x	x	10	Arbroath
1893-1894	8	x	4	8	Arbroath*
1894-1895	x	x	x	x	+
1895-1896	4	7	x	8	Forfar Athletic
1896-1897	7	1	3	8	Orion
1897-1898	8	6	1	8	Victoria United
1898-1899	5	1	7	8	Orion
1899-1900	3	6	2	8	Dundee Wanderers
1900-1901	4	2	6	10	Dundee A
1901-1902	4	8	10	12	Raith Rovers
1902-1903	12	4	6th equal	13	Dundee A

*1893-1894 season ended in chaos with many fixtures not played. Arbroath were top but no flag awarded.

+ 1894-1895 – League competition not held.

X – Club not in the league

Northern League - Summary of achievements by Aberdeen clubs
Summary

Orion	2 titles	Once runners-up
Victoria United	1 title	Once runners-up
Aberdeen	No titles	Best position 4th

Aberdeenshire Cup
Aberdeenshire Cup - First held 1887-1888

Season	Winners	Runners-Up			Venue	
1887-1888	Aberdeen	Rangers, Aberdeen	7	1	Chanonry	
1888-1889	Aberdeen	Orion	4	3	Chanonry	
1889-1890	Aberdeen	Orion	8	3	Torry	After 2-2 draw
1890-1891	Orion	Caledonian	4	1	Torry	

Season	Winners	Runners-Up			Venue	
1891-1892	Victoria United	Aberdeen	2	0	Chanonry	
1892-1893	Victoria United	Orion	3	2	Chanonry	
1893-1894	Victoria United	Orion	6	3	Chanonry	
1894-1895	Orion	Aberdeen	5	0	Victoria Bridge Grounds	
1895-1896	Victoria United	Aberdeen	6	2	Cattofield	
1896-1897	Orion	Victoria United	5	2	Chanonry	After 2-2 draw
1897-1898	Aberdeen	Orion	3	2	Victoria Bridge Grounds	
1898-1899	Orion	Victoria United	5	1	Cattofield	After 0-0 draw
1899-1900	Victoria United	Peterhead	5	2	Pittodrie Park	
1900-1901	Orion	Victoria United	2	1	Pittodrie Park	
1901-1902	Aberdeen	Victoria United	1	0	Cattofield	
1902-1903	Victoria United	Aberdeen	4	1	Cattofield	After 2-2 draw

Total Wins

Victoria United	6
Aberdeen	5
Orion	5

The original trophy was presented to the Aberdeenshire Football Association by Maitland Moir in 1887. After Aberdeen won the competition for the first two years it was announced that the club would be allowed to keep the trophy and a new one would be commissioned. The Aberdeenshire Cup is still being competed for today. The first name on the current trophy is that of Orion for season 1890-1891 which suggests that Aberdeen kept the original trophy after wining it for three years. The whereabouts of the original trophy are unknown.

Charity Cup
Charity Cup First held 1888-1889

Season	Winners	Runners-Up			Venue
1888-1889	Orion	City Rangers	8	1	Chanonry
1889-1890	Orion	Aberdeen	2	1	Victoria Bridge Grounds
1890-1891	Victoria United	Orion	2	1	Victoria Bridge Grounds
					After 2-2 draw
1891-1892	Victoria United	Orion	3	0	Chanonry

Season	Winners	Runners-Up			Venue	
1892-1893	Aberdeen	Victoria United	3	0	Chanonry	Match abandoned
1893-1894	Orion	Victoria United	5	3	Chanonry	
1894-1895	Victoria United	Aberdeen	6	2	Cattofield	After 1-1 draw
1895-1896	Orion	Aberdeen	3	1	Victoria Bridge Grounds	
1896-1897	Victoria United	Aberdeen	2	1	Cattofield	
1897-1898	Orion	Victoria United	6	4	Chanonry	
1898-1899	Victoria United	Aberdeen	7	1	Cattofield	

Last played for in 1898-1899. Competition replaced by the Provost Fleming Charity Shield.

Lord Provost Fleming Shield
Lord Provost Fleming Shield (First awarded 1900-1901)

1900-1901	Victoria United	Orion	2	1	Cattofield	
1901-1902	Victoria United	Peterhead	2	0	Cattofield	
1902-1903	Aberdeen	Orion	2	0	Pittodrie	

Gershon Cup

Gershon Cup First held 1893-1894	Winners
1893-1894	Orion
1894-1895	Orion
1895-1896	Victoria United
1896-1897	Orion

This round robin competition ended in 1896-1897 but was replaced by the Rhodesia Cup which was played for on the same basis.

Rhodesia Cup

Rhodesia Cup	First held 1898-1899
1898-1899	Orion
1899-1900	Orion
1900-1901	Victoria United
1901-1902	Orion
1902-1903	Victoria United

Appendix 3 - **Main local cup competitions - winning team line-ups**

Aberdeenshire Cup

1887-1888　　　**Aberdeen**　　　Rangers, Aberdeen　　7　　1

D. Wood, Key, Lothian, Hinton, J. Thomson, Glennie, Haselwood, Lumsden, T. Ketchen, Ferry, Clark

1888-1889　　　**Aberdeen**　　　Orion　　　4　　3

D. Wood, Key, J.Wood, McCann, J. Thomson, Glennie, Smith, Mitchell, T. Ketchen, J.M.Key, Brown

1889-1890　　　**Aberdeen**　　　Orion　　　8　　3

D. Wood, J.Reith, A.Wood, T. Ketchen, A.D. Farnworth, J.Thomson, A. Whitehead, M.Campbell, W.A. Key, W.S. Brown, P. Wallace

1890-1891　　　**Orion**　　　Caledonian　　4　　1

Low, Edwards, Foote, Baird, MacKay, Gordon, Gloag, Leggatt, Andrews, Kelly, Whitehead

1891-1892　　　**Victoria United**　　Aberdeen　　2　　0

Cannon, Thomson, Ririe, Ross, Stewart, Duffus, Wallace, Sinclair, Binks, Simpson, Ferries

1892-1893　　　**Victoria United**　　Orion　　3　　2

Gray, Anderson, Ririe, Hickie, Stewart, Ross, Turner, Benzie, Sutherland, Annand, Ferries

1893-1894　　　**Victoria United**　　Orion　　6　　3

Cannon, Anderson, Ririe, Morrice, Stewart, Annand, Turner, Smith, Sutherland, Forsyth, Ferries

1894-1895　　　**Orion**　　　Aberdeen　　5　　0

Morrison, Mackay, Ross, Wright, Low, Currie, Gloag, Benzie, Thom, Leggatt, Stopani

1895-1896　　　**Victoria United**　　Aberdeen　　6　　2

Gillespie, Anderson, Ririe, Morrice, Gordon, Annand, MacConnochie, Forsyth, Caie, Burnett, Ritchie

1896-1897　　　**Orion**　　　Victoria United　　5　　2

McBean, Jas Low, Ross, Dawson, John Low, Currie, A.Macfarlane, M.Mcfarlane, Thom, Leggatt, Hogg

1897-1898　　　**Aberdeen**　　　Orion　　　3　　2

Ritchie, John Davidson, McConnochie, J. Mackie, Joe Davidson, Thomson, Livingstone, Gray, Jenkins, Clark, Shiach

1898-1899　　　**Orion**　　　Victoria United　　5　　1

Watson, Livingstone, Ross, Currie, Low, Wilson, McPherson, Grant, Barron, Kane, Hogg

1899-1900　　　**Victoria United**　　Peterhead　　5　　2

Findlay, Kilgour, Thain, Dundas, Stronach, Thomson, McHardy, R.Ritchie, Taylor, Watson, G.Ritchie

| 1900-1901 | Orion | Victoria United | 2 | 1 |

Ritchie, Thomson, Ross, Currie, Willox, Wilson, Prophet, Livingstone, Barron, Brebner, Ritchie

| 1901-1902 | Aberdeen | Victoria United | 1 | 0 |

Bisset, O'Brien, Dakers, Sangster, Thomson, Robertson, Brash, C.Mackie, H.Livingston, Davidson, McHardy

| 1902-1903 | Victoria United | Aberdeen | 4 | 1 |

R. Murray, Kilgour, Craig, R.Ritchie, Jenkyns, Robertson, Duncan, Steven, Lindsay, Ferries, G.Ritchie

Charity Cup

| 1888-1889 | Orion | City Rangers | 8 | 1 |

Diack, Fettes, Jarvis, Milne, Mackay, Ewan, Fyfe, Gloag, Borthwick, F.Whitehead, Irvine,

| 1889-1890 | Orion | Aberdeen | 2 | 1 |

Love, McBain, Jarvis, Ewen, Mackay, Baird, Fyfe, Gordon, Edwards, Jopp, Whitehead

| 1890-1891 | Victoria United | Orion | 2 | 1 |

Cannon, Simpson, Ririe, Ross, Stewart, Duffus, Turner, Sinclair, Watson, Wallace, Ferries

| 1891-1892 | Victoria United | Orion | 3 | 0 |

Cannon, Ririe, Thomson, Duffus, Stewart , Ross, Turner, Sinclair, Binks, Annand, Ferries

| 1892-1893 | Aberdeen | Victoria United | 3 | 0 |

Ramsay, Ketchen, Wood, Morren, Singleton, Cobban, Fred Whitehead, White, Toman, McArthur, Frank Whitehead

| 1893-1894 | Orion | Victoria United | 5 | 3 |

Edwards, Ross, Mackay, Wight, Low, Currie, Johnston, James, Gloag, Openshaw, Stopani

| 1894-1895 | Victoria United | Aberdeen | 6 | 2 |

Insch, Anderson, Burgess, Morrice, Ririe, Annand, G. Macfarlane, A.Macfarlane, Clark, Forsyth, Ritchie

| 1895-1896 | Orion | Aberdeen | 3 | 1 |

McBean, Mackay, Ross, Wight, Low, Currie, Stopani, Thom, Gloag, Leggatt, Hogg

| 1896-1897 | Victoria United | Aberdeen | 2 | 1 |

Findlay, McNeill, Allan, Morrice, Thomson, McPherson, Law, Burnett, Stopani, Ritchie

| 1897-1898 | Orion | Victoria United | 6 | 4 |

Watson, Ross, Stopani, Currie, Low, Wilson, Webster, Murphy, Hogg, Leggatt, Barron

| 1898-1899 | Victoria United | Aberdeen | 7 | 1 |

Findlay, Kilgour, Thain, Dundas, Fraser, Thomson, McHardyGardiner, Watson, Taylor, Ritchie

Fleming Shield

1900-1901   Victoria United   Orion   2   1

Murray, Kilgour, Craig, Drummond, Stronach, A.Murray, Knowles, Duncan, Walker, Burnett, Ritchie

1901-1902   Victoria United   Peterhead   2   0

McBean, C.Kilgour, Craig, Bremner, A.Murray, R.Ritchie, Knowles, Ferries, Thom, Duncan, G.Ritchie

1902-1903   Aberdeen   Orion   2   0

Bisset, Walker, Ross, Sangster, Thomson, Murphy, Gaitens, C.Mackie, McDonald, Buchan, Shiach

Appendix 4 - **Club colours**

Aberdeen

When the club was formed in 1881 the colours chosen by members were *"maroon jerseys and blue knickerbockers with stripe."* This appears to have remained the favoured choice of kit until around 1886-1887. The SFA Annuals for 1886-1887 (published in 1886) and 1887-1888 (published in 1887), list Aberdeen's registered colours as amber and black jerseys with white knickers. A report published in the Aberdeen Journal seems to back this up. It stated that in the Aberdeen v Clubs of Town Select match, played on 12th March 1887, Aberdeen turned out in amber and black while the Select wore white. And a photograph from around this time suggests the jerseys may have been hooped. By the following season, 1887-1888, however, Aberdeen had switched to white shirts and blue shorts. These are the colours worn in the first Aberdeenshire Cup Final against City Rangers (who played in *"black and gold"*). The white top would remain the club's colour until the merger with Orion and Victoria United in 1903. In some of these seasons the shorts were black rather than blue (e.g. 1891-1892, according to the S.F.A). When the new Aberdeen club was formed in 1903, the old Aberdeen strip was worn for the first season before a change was made to black and gold vertical stripes.

Orion

The Orion club was formed in autumn 1885 but the first reference I can find to the colour of their strip is in October 1887 when they were reported to be wearing amber jerseys in a match against Arbroath Nomads at Kittybrewster. In January 1888, for the New Year's Day game with Glasgow Thistle, Orion's jerseys are described as being 'bismarck', which is a brownish-gold colour. By September 1888 the Aberdeen Journal announced that Orion would be wearing their new "uniform" of red and white stripes against Lochee in the Scottish Cup. The stripes were more usually described as being maroon and were worn with black or blue shorts. This would appear to have been the club colours from then until the 1903 amalgamation although the stripes appear to have become thicker as the years went on.

Victoria United

Victoria United originally played in light blue shirts and dark blue *"knickers."* Later the club colours were simply referred to as *"dark blue."* Photographs from the late 1890's and early 1900's suggest white shorts. White jerseys were worn as a change strip in 1891-1892 and 1892-1893. A change of striped jerseys (colour not known) was worn for a home Northern League match against Lochee United on 29th April 1899 as the visitors also wore blue. Stripes were also worn against Fraserburgh Wanderers the following season. The first choice coloured shirts appear to have varied from dark blue to a lighter shade of blue during the history of the club. In 1902 red shirts were worn for a game against Dundee.

Aberdeenshire F.A. and local select teams

In December 1888 the Aberdeenshire Football Association decided that county teams would play in *"scarlet jerseys"* and this seems to have remained the first choice colours of the select team for a number of years. In November 1891 the Aberdeenshire select that played a Glasgow select, was referred to as *"the Reds."* In September 1895 it was reported that the Aberdeenshire team that played the North of Scotland at Inverness wore red shirts (North of Scotland played in white).

Other clubs

Black Diamonds

An Aberdeen Journal report in December 1888 refers to the Diamonds playing in yellow jerseys.

Bon Accord

The original Bon-Accord club, formed in 1884 according to S.F.A. records, played in *"black and white striped jersey and white knickers."* By 1891-1892 the SFA registered colours for Bon Accord were "dark blue".

Caledonian

The Holburn club's S.FA. registered colours in 1890-1891 were "blue and black vertical stripes."

Culter

Culter's S.F.A. registered colours in 1896-1897 were *"red shirts and black knickers."*

Peterhead

Peterhead's S.F.A. registered colours in 1896-1897 were *"blue and white jerseys with black knickers."*

Rovers

Aberdeen Rovers first appear as a registered S.F.A. club in 1884 with colours of *"blue jersey and white knickers."*

Appendix 5 - **Highest scores**

This section features all games involving the main Aberdeen clubs in which the winning margin has been 10 goals or more.

Aberdeen F.C.

Aberdeen were better at handing out big defeats than being on the receiving end of them. Of the 22 games featuring 10 goal winning margins in which Aberdeen were involved, the Whites lost just two : 13-1 to Queen's Park and 11-1 to Arbroath.

Competition	Date						Venue
Aberdeenshire Cup 2R	17/11/1888	Aberdeen	Rosebery	23	0		Chanonry
Friendly	14/09/1995	Aberdeen	Brechin	18	0		Chanonry
Friendly	09/03/1895	Aberdeen	Banchory	15	0		Burnett Park, Banchory
Friendly	25/02/1893	Aberdeen	Fraserburgh Thistle	14	0		Fraserburgh
Friendly	28/12/1895	Aberdeen	Fraserburgh	13	0		Chanonry
Friendly	12/09/1896	Aberdeen	Stonehaven	13	0		Stonehaven
Scottish Cup 4R	09/11/1889	Queen's Park	Aberdeen	13	1		Chanonry
Friendly	02/03/1889	Aberdeen	Rovers	14	2		Chanonry
Friendly	26/12/1885	Aberdeen	Gladstone	13	1		Recreation Grounds
Aberdeenshire Cup 1R	19/11/1892	Aberdeen	Peterhead	12	0		Peterhead
Friendly	27/11/1886	Aberdeen	Ellon Gordon	11	0		
Aberdeenshire Cup 1R	03/12/1887	Aberdeen	Albert	11	0		Holburn
Friendly	22/09/1888	Aberdeen	St Mirren,Aberdeen	11	0		Chanonry
Friendly	14/09/1889	Aberdeen	City Rangers	11	0		Chanonry
Friendly	30/03/1889	Aberdeen	Stonehaven Thistle	12	2		Stonehaven
Friendly	06/05/1889	Aberdeen	Elgin Rangers	11	1		Elgin
Scottish Cup	02/09/1893	Aberdeen	Fraserburgh Wanderers	11	1		Chanonry
Northern League	09/09/1893	Arbroath	Aberdeen	11	1		Gayfield
Aberdeenshire Cup	10/12/1898	Aberdeen	Fraserburgh Wanderers	11	1		Central Park

Competition	Date					Venue
Friendly	29/10/1887	Aberdeen	Britannia	10	0	Holburn
Friendly	29/09/1888	Aberdeen	Black Diamonds	10	0	Chanonry
Friendly	25/10/1890	Aberdeen	Thistle	10	0	Chanonry

Orion

Arbroath's famous 36-0 thrashing of Bon Accord in the 1885-1886 Scottish Cup wasn't the only time the Angus club inflicted pain on an Aberdeen side. The two heaviest defeats in Orion's history came at Gayfield on consecutive Scottish Cup visits.

Competition	Date					Venue
Scottish Cup 1R	11/09/1886	Arbroath	Orion	20	0	Gayfield
Scottish Cup 1R	03/09/1887	Arbroath	Orion	18	0	Gayfield
Aberdeenshire Cup SF	12/12/1896	Orion	Culter	18	0	Cattofield
Aberdeenshire Cup 1R	06/10/1888	Orion	Victoria	17	0	Central Park
Friendly	15/10/1887	Orion	Caledonian	16	1	Central Park
Friendly	12/11/1887	Orion	Britannia	14	0	Central Park
Aberdeenshire Cup	12/12/1891	Orion	Peterhead	15	2	Peterhead
Friendly	30/03/1889	Montrose	Orion	13	0	Links Park, Montrose
Friendly	20/08/1892	Orion	Ellon	13	0	Ellon
Aberdeenshire Cup1R	19/11/1892	Orion	Stonehaven	13	0	Central Park
Charity Cup	24/02/1894	Orion	Peterhead	11	0	Wellington Bridge Grounds
Charity Cup	27/03/1897	Orion	Culter	11	0	Culter
Friendly	17/09/1890	Orion	Hawthorn,Peterhead	12	2	Central park
Friendly	28/11/1891	Orion	Aberdeen Thistle	10	0	Central park
Friendly	11/02/1893	Orion	Glasgow Wanderers	10	0	Central park
Friendly	30/03/1895	Orion	Ellon	10	0	Ellon
Scottish Cup	27/01/1900	Kilmarnock	Orion	10	0	Kilmarnock

Victoria United

Arbroath again feature prominently by having inflicted Victoria United's heaviest defeat, a 14-3 thrashing in a Northern League match. Incredibly, Vics had led 3-1 at one point and it was 3-3 at halftime.

Competition	Date					Venue
Aberdeenshire Cup1R	19/10/1895	Victoria United	Turriff Our Boys	21	0	
Friendly	26/12/1891	Victoria United	Black Diamond	13	0	Victoria Bridge Grounds
Friendly	12/03/1892	Victoria United	Stonehaven	13	1	
Aberdeenshire Cup 1R	28/10/1893	Victoria United	Fraserburgh Wanderers	13	1	Fraserburgh
Friendly	11/04/1891	Victoria United	Thistle	12	0	Victoria Bridge Grounds
Northern League	13/01/1894	Arbroath	Victoria United	14	3	Gayfield Park, Arbroath
Friendly	10/09/1892	Victoria United	Stonehaven	13	2	Urie
Unemployed Benefit Match	16/02/1895	Victoria United	Aberdeen University	11	0	Victoria Bridge Grounds
Friendly	07/02/1891	Montrose	Victoria United	11	1	Links Park, Montrose
Friendly	16/08/1889	Celtic	Victoria United	10	0	Victoria Bridge Grounds
Friendly	22/03/1890	Arbroath	Victoria United	10	0	Gayfield Park, Arbroath
Friendly	12/11/1892	Victoria United	Our Boys Blairgwrie	10	0	Wellington Grounds
	16/03/1895	Montrose	Victoria United	10	0	Links Park, Montrose
Charity Cup	30/03/1895	Victoria United	County	10	0	Victoria Bridge Grounds